Benedek/Benoît-Rohmer/Karl/Nowak (Eds.)

European Yearbook on Human Rights 2010

BWV·BERLINER
WISSENSCHAFTS-VERLAG

intersentia

neuer
wissenschaftlicher
Verlag

European Yearbook on Human Rights 2010

edited

by

Wolfgang Benedek

Florence Benoît-Rohmer

Wolfram Karl

Manfred Nowak

Associate Editor:

Matthias C. Kettemann

European Academic Press

Antwerp · Berlin · Vienna · Graz 2010

Bibliographic information published by the Deutsche Nationalbibliothek

The Deutsche Nationalbibliothek lists this publication in the Deutsche Nationalbibliografie; detailed bibliographic data are available in the Internet at http://dnb.d-nb.de.

Publication in Belgium:
ISBN 978-94-000-0063-6
Intersentia N.V.
Groenstraat 31
B-2640 Mortsel (Antwerpen)
Phone: +32 3 680 15 50, Fax: +32 3 658 71 21

Publication in Germany:
ISBN 978-3-8305-1774-0
BWV Berliner Wissenschafts-Verlag
Markgrafenstraße 12-14
D-10969 Berlin
Phone: +49 30 84 17 70-0, Fax: +49 30 84 17 70-21

Publication in Austria:
ISBN 978-3-7083-0688-9
Neuer Wissenschaftlicher Verlag GmbH Nfg KG
Argentinierstraße 42/6, A-1040 Wien
Phone: +43 1 535 61 03-24, Fax: +43 1 535 61 03-25
E-mail: office@nwv.at

Geidorfgürtel 20, A-8010 Graz
E-mail: office@nwv.at

www.nwv.at

Print: Text-Print Nyomdaipari Kft., Györ

European Yearbook on Human Rights 2010

Editors:

Wolfgang Benedek — European Training and Research Centre for Human Rights and Democracy (ETC) University of Graz

Wolfram Karl — Austrian Institute for Human Rights (OIM) University of Salzburg

Florence Benoît-Rohmer — European Inter-University Centre for Human Rights and Democratisation (EIUC), Venice

Manfred Nowak — Ludwig Boltzmann Institute of Human Rights (BIM), University of Vienna

Associate Editor:

Matthias C. Kettemann — University of Graz

European Training and Research Centre for Human Rights and Democracy (ETC) Graz

Österreichisches Institut für Menschenrechte

Austrian Institute for Human Rights (OIM) Salzburg

European Inter-University Centre for Human Rights and Democratisation (EIUC) Venice

Ludwig Boltzmann Institute of Human Rights (BIM) Vienna

Editors' Preface

Dear readers,

the volume of human rights scholarship in Europe and its quality is constantly growing. This is partly due to the crucial role of human rights as a *leitmotif* and condition in the process of European integration, and partly to the human rights challenges that the new members of an enlarged Council of Europe and of the European Union face. The European Court of Human Rights in Strasbourg is overwhelmed by the growing number of cases; OSCE is confronted with new human rights challenges in Eastern Europe and the Caucasus; and the EU Fundamental Rights Agency (FRA), established in Vienna in 2007, is about to increase its capacities in order to better fulfil its mandate which, though broad, still does not cover a number of important human rights issues within the European Union.

2009 was a year rich in human rights developments in Europe and on the international plane. The political and legal developments make it difficult even for experts to keep up, such has their speed increased. In order to fully grasp the challenges ahead, it is important to identify and critically assess the past year's most important developments in the human rights realms in Europe and beyond.

To this end, we have brought together almost 30 human rights experts which map and analyze, in 24 contributions, the major human rights developments in Europe in 2009.

Obviously, the most important event has been the coming into force of the Lisbon Treaty which gave binding force to the Charter of Fundamental Rights of the European Union and, together with the Protocol No. 14 to the European Convention on Human Rights (which was ratified by Russia in January 2010) provides the legal basis for the accession of the EU to the Convention

The structure of the Yearbook follows the successful first edition of last year. After devoting the first section to four essential "Topics of the Year", the human rights developments in the European Union, the Council of Europe and OSCE are being introduced and discussed from a variety of perspectives before a review of developments in the civil society sector and cross-cutting issues complete the picture.

Among the topics of the year, we have the pleasure to welcome a contribution by the European Commissioner for Human Rights, Thomas Hammarberg, calling for more respect for the rights of migrants in Europe today. Manfred Nowak, UN Special Rapporteur on Torture, provides an overview of how human rights have developed in Europe since the end of the Cold War. Florence Benoît-Rohmer, Secretary General of the European Inter-University Centre (EIUC) in Venice, looks into the role of values and fundamental rights in the Treaty of Lisbon and Gerald Staberock from the International Commission of Jurists highlights the changes and continuing challenges with regard to counter-terrorism and human rights.

The section on the European Union is opened by an overview of the main developments in the human rights field by Wolfgang Benedek and a basic introduction into the European Agency for Fundamental Rights and its practice in 2009 by Hannes Tretter and Anna Müller-Funk. This part also contains the Yearbook's first contribution in French, namely on the protection of fundamental rights in the Lisbon Treaty by Jean Paul Jacqué. Michael Reiterer reviews the EU Foreign Policy after Lisbon and Markus Möstl analyzes whether human rights have been successfully mainstreamed into the EU Common Security and Defence Policy. A new ground-breaking move by the EU is its accession to the UN Convention on the Rights of Persons with Disabilities, described by Davide Zaru and Maria Zuber. The section's final contribution by Theodor Rathgeber deals with the activities of the UN Human Rights Council and the role of the European Union in it in 2009.

In the section on the Council of Europe, Philip Czech reviews major 2009 decisions regarding jurisdiction of the European Court of Human Rights. Brigitte Ohms describes the way towards Protocol No. 14 and acknowledges the important role Protocol No. 14bis played for its coming into force. The following article by Agnieszka Szklanna provides insights into the impact of pilot judgments of the European Court of Human Rights. Andrew Dremczewski and James Gaughan introduce the parliamentary dimension of implementing judgments of the Strasbourg Court. Two further articles, by Rory O'Connell and Joachim Renzikowski deal with the case-law of the European Court on human rights with regard to socio-economic rights of non-nationals and retro-active criminal liability. Additionally, the contribution by Franziska Klopfer gives an overview about the outstanding role of the Council of Europe with regard to dealing with the challenges of information society and freedom of expression and information online while Emma Lantscher describes the evolution and value of the thematic commentaries of the Advisory Committee of the Framework Convention for the Protection of National Minorities.

In the section on developments with regard to the OSCE, Jens-Hagen Eschenbächer and Bernhard Knoll follow up on the developments in the OSCE region with regard to human rights and security in 2009, while Christian Strohal promotes the need for a stronger peer engagement in the OSCE with regard to election monitoring. Finally, Ženet Mujić provides insights into the mandate and work of the OSCE Representative on Freedom of the Media.

The volume concludes with a section on civil society and cross-cutting issues, in which Sihem Bensedrine strongly criticizes the realpolitik of the European Union with regard to Tunisia from the point of view of a Tunisian NGO activist in the field of defending the freedom of the media, while Matthias C. Kettemann calls for a synthetic approach towards human rights and internet governance in Europe.

All in all, the Yearbook 2010 provides a unique overview of developments in the field of human rights in Europe containing both comparative studies and thematic investigations of particular issues. The volume thus provides a rich picture of the practice on human rights in Europe confirming this regions important and standard-setting role with regard to the promotion and protection of human rights in the world.

The editors would like to express their special thanks to the European Inter-University Centre (EIUC) in Venice for its financial contribution and to all members of the Scientific Advisory Board. The editorial board would also like to welcome Florence Benoît-Rohmer from the EIUC as replacement for Anja Mihr, who has moved to the Human Rights Centre of the University of Utrecht. The editors would like to renew, at this point, the invitation to human rights researchers and practitioners interested in offering articles on recent developments and future challenges regarding human rights in Europe.

Special thanks go to the European Yearbook of Human Rights' associate editor, Matthias C. Kettemann, who has shouldered most of the editorial work and thus made a major contribution to the high quality of this volume.

We would also like to thank Herbert Klein and Günter Milly from the Neuer Wissenschaftlicher Verlag, Vienna, for their support in publishing this book together with their partners in the framework of the European Academic Publishers (EAP).

Graz, Venice, Salzburg, Vienna (May 2010)

Wolfgang Benedek, Florence Benoît-Rohmer, Wolfram Karl, Manfred Nowak
(editors)

Table of Contents

Abbreviations

A	A-Series
AC(FC)	Advisory Committee under the Framework Convention for the Protection of National Minorities
ACP	African, Caribbean and Pacific States
AFET	Committee on Foreign Affairs Security, Defence and Human Rights
AFSJ	Area of Freedom, Security and Justice
AoC	Affirmation of Commitment
APT	Association for the Prevention of Torture
Art.	Article(s)
AU	African Union
BBC	British Broadcasting Corporation
B-H	Bosnia and Herzegovina
BOCOG	Beijing Organizing Committee for the Games of the XXIX Olympiad
CAHDI	Committee of Legal Advisers on Public International Law
CAT	UN Convention against Torture
CBSS	Country-Based Support Schemes
CCoBH	Constitutional Court of Bosnia and Herzegovina
CDDH	Steering Committee for Human Rights
CFI	Court of First Instance
CFSP	Common Foreign and Security Policy
CIS	Commonwealth of Independent States
CIVCOM	Committee for Civilian Aspects of Crisis Management
CMPD	Crisis Management and Planning Directorate
CNN	Cable News Network
CoE	Council of Europe
COHOM	Working Group of the Council of the European Union on Human Rights
CONOPS	Concept of Operation
COREU	Correspondance Européenne
COSI	Standing Committee on Internal Security
CPCC	Civilian Planning and Conduct Capability
CPT	Committee for the Prevention of Torture
CRT	Crisis Response Teams
CSDP	Common Security and Defence Policy
CTC	UN Counter-Terrorism Committee
CTED	Executive Directorate of the UN Counter-Terrorism Committee
DCI	Development Cooperation Instrument
DEVE	Committee on Development
DG	Directorate-General of the European Commission
DOC	Department of Commerce
DPA	Dayton Peace Agreement
DROI	Sub-Committee on Human Rights
EASO	European Asylum Support Office
ECC	Electoral Complaints Commission
ECCAR	European Coalition of Cities against Racism
ECHR	European Convention on Human Rights and Fundamental Freedoms

ECJ	European Court of Justice
ECommHR	European Commission of Human Rights
ECOSOC	Economic and Social Council
ECPT	European Convention on the Prevention of Torture
ECRI	European Commission against Racism and Intolerance
ECtHR	European Court of Human Rights
EDA	European Defence Agency
EDF	European Development Fund
EEAS	European External Action Service
EEG	Eastern Europe Group
EHRLR	European Human Rights Law Review
EIDHR	European Initiative for Democracy and Human Rights
EIUC	European Inter-University Centre for Human Rights and Democratization
ENP	European Neighbourhood Policy
EP	European Parliament
EPC	European Political Cooperation
ESDP	European Security and Defence Policy
ESS	European Security Strategy
EU	European Union
EU EOM	EU Election Observation Mission
EuGRZ	Europäische Grundrechtezeitschrift
EUMC	European Monitoring Centre on Racism and Xenophobia
EUMC	European Union Military Committee
EUMS	European Union Military Staff
EUOM	European Union Observation Mission
EuroDIG	European Dialogue on Internet Governance
EuroISPA	European Internet Services Providers Association
FCNM	Framework Convention for the Protection of National Minorities
FIDH	Fédération Internationale des Ligues des Droits de l'Homme
FLAG	Free Legal Assistance Group
FRA	Fundamental Rights Agency
FRALEX	Fundamental Rights Legal Experts
FRP	Fundamental Rights Platform
GA	General Assembly
GC	Grand Chamber
GRULAC	Group of Latin American and Caribbean Countries
GSP	Generalized System of Preferences
HRC	Human Rights Council
HRDs	Human Rights Defenders
HRIC	Human Rights in China
HRLR	Human Rights Law Review
HRW	Human Rights Watch
ICANN	Internet Corporation for Assigned Names and Numbers
ICC	International Criminal Court
ICCPR	International Covenant on Civil and Political Rights
ICESCR	International Covenant on Economic Social and Cultural Rights
ICLQ	International and Comparative Law Quarterly
ICRC	International Committee of the Red Cross
ICTs	Information and Communication Technologies
ICTY	International Criminal Tribunal for the former Yugoslavia
IEC	Independent Election Commission
IHL	International Humanitarian Law

INGO	International Non-Governmental Organization
INTA	Committee on International Trade
IOC	International Olympic Committee
ISFE	Interactive Software Federation in Europe
ISPs	Internet Service Providers
IT	Information Technologies
JNA	Yugoslav People's Army
JPCs	Joint Parliamentary Committees
LGBT	Lesbian, Gay, Bisexual, Transgender
LIBE	Committee on Civil Liberties, Justice and Internal Affairs
MC-NM	Committee of Experts on New Media
MC-S-CI	Ad hoc Advisory Group on Cross-border Internet
MC-S-PG	Advisory Group on Public Service Media Governance
MFA	Ministry of Foreign Affairs
MFN	Most-Favoured Nation Status
MoU/JPA	Memorandum of Understanding/Joint Project Agreement
NAM	Non Aligned Movement
NATO	North Atlantic Treaty Organization
NGO	Non-Governmental Organization
NILR	Netherlands International Law Review
NLOs	National Liaison Officers
NPMs	National Preventive Mechanisms
ODIHR	Office for Democratic Institutions and Human Rights
OHCHR	Office of the High Commissioner for Human Rights
OIC	Organization of the Islamic Conference
OJ	Official Journal
OPCAT	Optional Protocol to the UN Convention against Torture
OPLAN	Operation Plan
OPPD	Office of Promotion of Parliamentary Democracy
PACE	Parliamentary Assembly of the Council of Europe
para(s)	paragraph(s)
PC	OSCE Permanent Council
PIC	Peace Implementation Council
PJC	Police and Judicial Co-operation in Criminal Matters
PMG	Politico-Military Group
PMCs/PSCs	Private Military and Security Companies
PNR	Passenger Name Record
PPE	European People's Party
PSC	Political and Security Committee
RAXEN	Racism and Xenophobia Expert Network
REACT	Rapid Expert Assistance and Cooperation Teams
RED	Race Equality Directive
RJD	Reports of Judgments and Decisions
RTL	Re-education through Labour
SC	Security Council
SFRY	Socialist Federal Republic of Yugoslavia
SITCEN	Joint Situation Centre
SPT	Subcommittee on the Prevention of Torture
TEC	Treaty establishing the European Community
TEU	Treaty on European Union

TEU (Lisbon)	Treaty on European Union as amended by the Treaty of Lisbon
TFEU	Treaty on the Functioning of the European Union
TFUE	Traité sur le fonctionnement de l'Union européenne
TUE	Traité sur l'Union européenne
UDHR	Universal Declaration of Human Rights
UN	United Nations
UNCRPD	United Nations Convention on the Rights of Persons with Disabilities
UNDP	United Nations Development Programme
UNDPKO	UN Department of Peacekeeping Operations
UNMIK	UN Interim Administration Mission in Kosovo
UPM	Union pour la Méditerranée
UPR	Universal Periodic Review
v.	versus
WEOG	Western European and Others Group

I

Topics of the Year

Thomas HAMMARBERG[*]

Respecting the Rights of Migrants in Today's Europe: A Call for Action

Table of Contents

Keywords

Human rights, migrants, refugees, asylum seekers, non-refoulement, irregular migrants, detention, decriminalization of migration

A   Introduction

Protecting the human rights of migrants – immigrants, refugees and asylum seekers – in the 47 member States of the Council of Europe has been a key priority for the Commissioner for Human Rights ("the Commissioner") since the creation of this institution in 1999. The obvious reason is that migrants are one of the most vulnerable social groups in need of special protective measures by states.

---

[*]   This article is based on a publication currently being prepared by the Office of the Commissioner for Human Rights which will summarize the positions adopted by the Commissioner on a certain number of subjects concerning the protection and promotion of human rights, including the protection of the human rights of migrants. For more information on the mandate and the work of the Commissioner for Human Rights, please see www.commissioner.coe.int.

In the last few years, an increasing trend of xenophobic and anti-foreigner discourse has penetrated public discourse in large parts of Europe. Anti-migrant policies and approaches have been increasingly supported by mainstream political parties and politicians at all levels. The results are more restrictions for migrants entering Europe and a political approach almost exclusively centred on security aspects. In fact, European policies in this field are no longer in line with international human rights standards.

Without questioning the legitimate interest of states to manage immigration, the Commissioner has recommended steps to ensure that migrants do not suffer any violations of their rights and fundamental freedoms as protected by the European Convention on Human Rights (ECHR), the UN Refugee Convention and other relevant conventions in the field of human rights.

Within Europe there is clearly a need for further responsibility-sharing: every country should contribute in a spirit of solidarity. Collective and coordinated efforts are needed to create migration policies and practices which are firmly human rights-based. Currently, these are still very much repellent and reactive in nature. European countries need to develop comprehensive, long-term and sustainable national action plans in which host states, transit states and states of origin work together, having as their priority the effective protection of the human rights of people who feel obliged to migrate for a better life.

The Office of the Commissioner has covered a wide range of situations including asylum seekers; migrants in an irregular situation; minors in an irregular situation; trafficking; human rights of internally displaced persons (IDPs); stateless people; and Roma migration.

A large number of country-monitoring reports published following visits by the Commissioner to member states have been centred on the issue of migrants' human rights in the country in question. Viewpoints[1] published fortnightly have dealt several times with the subject of forced migration and statelessness. In 2009, a report[2] on Roma migration which was drafted in co-operation with the OSCE High Commissioner on National Minorities was published. In February 2010, an Issue Paper[3] on the human rights implications of the criminalization of migration in Europe was published.

This article examines two specific aspects covered by the Commissioner in his approach: the right to seek and to enjoy asylum in Europe (section B) and the rights of migrants in an irregular situation (section C). The purpose is to spell out which positions both the first Commissioner Alvaro Gil Robles and the present office-holder have taken – largely based on their country visits.

---

1   Office of the Commissioner for Human Rights, Viewpoints, "It is wrong to criminalize migration" (29 September 2008); "Children in migration should get better protection" (6 August 2007); "The new European migration policy should be based on human rights principles, not xenophobia" (17 December 2007) and "Migrants should not be denied their human rights" (30 May 2006).

2   Office of the Commissioner for Human Rights/High Commissioner on National Minorities, Study on "Recent Migration of Roma in Europe", 10 December 2008, available at: www.commissioner.coe.int.

3   Office of the Commissioner for Human Rights, Issue Paper on "Criminalisation of migration in Europe: Human Rights implications", Strasbourg, 4 February 2010, CommDH/IssuePaper(2010)1.

B   The Right to Seek and to Enjoy Asylum

The Commissioner has noticed alarming trends in the treatment of asylum seekers in all parts of Europe eroding the established principles of international law. In efforts to control migration flows, streamline asylum procedures and fight against abusive asylum requests, states are undermining the rights of genuine asylum seekers. Individuals seeking asylum are frequently detained and unable to access asylum procedures; these procedures often fall short of international standards for fairness; and, as a result, genuine asylum seekers are denied international protection. In some cases, individuals are also returned to countries where they risk torture, or inhuman or degrading treatment in violation of the principle of *non-refoulement*.

The right to apply for asylum in another country is a fundamental right recognized by international law. The "right to seek and to enjoy in other countries asylum from persecution" is a key provision in the Universal Declaration of Human Rights, which was adopted in 1948 by the General Assembly of the United Nations. Some of those who seek to enter Europe have indeed a well-founded fear of persecution as defined by the UN Refugee Convention and its Protocol. They are under threat because of their ethnicity, religion, nationality, political opinion or membership of a particular social group.

1   Ensuring Asylum Seekers' Effective Access to Asylum Procedures

The Commissioner's country reports detail a range of actions taken by states that have made it impossible for genuine refugees to apply for asylum.

States should ensure that all foreign nationals seeking asylum in their countries are in fact able to gain access to asylum procedures and benefit from a thorough, fair, individual examination of their claim. This includes individuals stopped at points of entry (air, land or sea borders) as well as those intercepted at sea, found stowed away on boats or stopped while disembarking from an airplane. Furthermore, extra-territorial controls must not be conducted to the detriment of rights guaranteed by the UN Refugee Convention.

On arrival, everyone whose right of entry is disputed must be given a hearing, where necessary with the help of an interpreter whose fees must be met by the country of arrival, in order to be able to lodge a request for asylum. This must entail the right to open a file after having being duly informed, in a language which the applicant understands, about the procedure to be followed. The practice of *refoulement* "at the arrival gate" is unacceptable.[4]

Furthermore, factors such as an individual's irregular entry to the country or lack of identity documents should affect neither their possibility of applying for asylum nor the consideration given to their claim. Likewise, failure to meet certain formal requirements, such as submitting an application in the national language, is an unacceptable reason for refusal to thoroughly examine an individual's asylum claim.

---

4   See Office of the Commissioner for Human Rights, Recommendation on "the rights of aliens wishing to enter a Council of Europe member State and the enforcement of expulsion orders", CommDH(2001)19, 19 September 2001.

European Union countries have drawn up lists of countries of origin which are considered safe. Applications from these countries are processed through simplified, speedy procedures or in some cases rejected outright. This is problematic; even in countries that are considered generally safe there may well be situations where not all individuals or groups of individuals are actually safe.

For instance, there might be instances of discrimination of such severity as to amount to inhuman or degrading treatment within the meaning of Article 3 of the European Convention on Human Rights, particularly towards members of minority groups or of the lesbian, gay, bisexual and transgender communities. Each application should be examined individually, taking into account the applicant's particular circumstances.[5]

2 Asylum Legislation in Line with International Standards

Countries should enact specific legislation on asylum in line with both the UN Refugee Convention's and the European Convention on Human Rights' requirements. The legal meaning of 'persecution' should encompass persecution by non-state agents in situations where the state concerned is incapable of offering protection to the person in danger. In addition, States should seek to extend the legal definition of persecution on account of membership of a particular social group, to cover persecution based on gender or sexual orientation.

3 Humanitarian Protection

European states have introduced temporary humanitarian protection for persons not qualifying for refugee status under the UN Refugee Convention, but whose forced return is nonetheless not possible because this would expose them to certain serious risks in their country of origin. Such protection may, for instance, cover individuals fleeing their countries because of civil wars. Such efforts are welcome, but we should be aware that this form of protection can not substitute the status provided by the UN Refugee Convention or other possible, durable forms of international protection.

4 Fair Procedures

All asylum procedures should meet international standards of fairness. Asylum seekers need to be given sufficient time to fill in forms, gather documents and prepare a coherent account of their reasons for seeking asylum. While procedures should not be delayed, time limits must not be so short as to jeopardize a foreign national's effective right to seek asylum or other fundamental human rights, in compliance with the principle of *non-refoulement*.

It is also essential that all asylum seekers be systematically given access to legal assistance from the outset of the application process. In addition to improving the legal protection of asylum seekers, such an arrangement would in some instances diminish the number of appeals to courts as it would mean that the initial interviews with the authorities and the subsequent applications would be

---

5   See Council of Europe, Committee of Ministers, Guidelines on human rights protection in the context of accelerated asylum procedures, 1 July 2009, Guideline II, para. 2.

better prepared. Asylum seekers should be able to benefit equally from this aid whether they are detained or not. Furthermore, lawyers dealing with immigration and asylum matters should be adequately qualified in this area, and where necessary, receive special training.

It is critical that interpretation services be available to asylum seekers whenever needed, including in order to assist them: in understanding documents handed to them or information provided to them; in submitting forms in a national language; during interviews and hearings.

It is also important that the personal testimony of asylum seekers is heard by those making decisions on admissibility in complex or contested cases and by those deciding on the merits of an asylum claim. Contradictions in statements by asylum seekers should not be considered of crucial importance when the merits of their applications are examined. Genuine victims of persecution are often in a vulnerable psychological state and have serious problems relating to people in positions of authority.

Procedures such as arrests at the arrival gate and questioning that can last seven or eight hours or even longer, do nothing to inspire trust. Rather, they elicit surprise, tension and fear. In such a climate, quite apart from the difficulties that may arise because of the lack of adequate assistance, it is hardly surprising that it is sometimes difficult to persuade applicants to co-operate. In any event, it seems unreasonable to expect their statements to be totally consistent and perfectly clear.

Decisions handed down on the merits of a case should be motivated, with a legal explanation provided.

When asylum seekers are minors, the best interests of the child should be taken into account in the asylum procedure.

Decisions so intimately affecting the enjoyment of fundamental human rights, and with potentially irreversible consequences, should be subject to appeal before a competent authority or body composed of members who are impartial and who enjoy safeguards of independence, preferably a court. This authority or body should be empowered to consider all aspects of each case as an arbiter and guarantor of respect for human rights.

Asylum seekers should benefit from sufficient time for preparing their appeal and have effective access to legal assistance and representation and interpretation services. Furthermore, where asylum seekers submit a credible claim that a removal order could lead to a real risk of persecution or the death penalty, torture or inhuman or degrading treatment or punishment, the appeal against the removal order should result in its suspension.

5   Non-Refoulement

When asylum applications are refused, states must nonetheless ensure that they do not violate the principle of *non-refoulement*, enshrined in Article 33 of the UN Refugee Convention, and the fundamental guarantees set out in Article 3 of the European Convention on Human Rights, which prohibit *in absolute terms* the forced return of a foreigner liable to be subjected to torture, inhuman or degrading treatment or punishment. The Commissioner has made clear in numerous reports that diplomatic assurances do not provide an adequate safeguard against such ill treatment.[6]

D   The Rights of Migrants in an Irregular Situation

Though, for obvious reasons, precise statistics are not available it is estimated that there are more than 5.5 million irregular migrants within the European Union and more still in other parts of Europe. In the Russian Federation it is estimated that there are no less than 8 million.

They arrive across the ocean in ramshackle and dangerous boats, many losing their lives along the way, with their anonymous bodies occasionally washing up on European shores. They arrive via land hidden in the back of smugglers' trucks, travelling thousands of miles in cramped and dangerous conditions. They find ways to cross land borders in secret, or avoid border controls with false documents. Some overstay their visas in European countries.

In whatever way they arrive, they join the ranks of Europe's *sans papiers*, with no rights in their countries of residence and vulnerable to many forms of exploitation and abuse. Many already owe large debts to smugglers or have become victims of traffickers before arriving in their destination countries. European countries tend to approach this population as a "security threat" – seeking to protect borders, criminalize migrants, lock them up in prison-like conditions, and expel them as quickly as possible, even to countries where they risk persecution and torture.

1   Intercepting Irregular Movement and Receiving Migrants

When intercepting irregular movement, or preventing irregular entry, states must respect the individual's right to leave his or her own country. Measures to control the entry of non-nationals and prevent irregular border crossing must be compatible with the prohibition on inhuman or degrading treatment and punishment, and with the right to life. Indeed, the European Court of Human Rights (ECtHR) found that an order to border guards to fire in order to protect borders "at all costs" was incompatible with the right to life.[7] Actions involving other forms of violence and abuse also violate basic human rights standards.

The reception procedures are paramount and need more resources, better trained border police and clear, human rights-based policies in order to function effectively and humanely. The challenge for national authorities, often with limited resources, is to protect the rights of migrants, and identify and protect asylum seekers in the course of operations to rescue, receive, and where appropriate return, those arriving by sea and land. Accommodation facilities, food and

---

6   Memorandum by the Commissioner of Human Rigths, following his visit to the United Kingdom on 5-8 February and 31 March-2 April 2008, CommDH(2008)23, Strasbourg, 18 September 2008; Memorandum by the CommHR following his visit to Italy on 19-20 June 2008, CommDH(2008)18, Strasbourg, 29 July 2008; Report by CommHR following his visit to Italy on 13-15 January 2009, CommDH(2009)16, Strasbourg, 16 April 2009.

7   ECtHR, Streletz, Kessler and Krenz v. Germany, judgment of 22 March 2001, application nos. 934044/96, 35532/98 and 44801/98.

living conditions provided to migrants must meet basic standards of decency.

Furthermore, given their particular needs and vulnerability, traumatized or injured migrants should be afforded basic humanitarian assistance, including medical and psychological care upon arrival. They also have the right to access health care in the event of illness and their children have the right to education without discrimination. Obstacles – such as making access contingent on a certain length of presence on national territory – should not be placed in the way of access to these rights.

2   Decriminalizing Migration

Despite a widespread trend to the contrary among states, international law has clearly established the principle that foreign nationals whose only offence is the violation of provisions relating to migration should not be treated by transit or host States as criminals or potential criminals.[8] Criminalizing foreigners is extremely harmful and leads to inextricable situations in which these persons, who are in no sense offenders, are treated as if they were guilty of a crime. Where countries have established criminal law provisions relating to foreigners' irregular entry and stay, the Commissioner has recommended decriminalizing of such offences.

The principle of not criminalizing irregular migrants should apply to all aspects of their treatment. In accordance with this approach, the derogatory term "illegal migrant" should not be used – it puts a criminal stamp on the individual.

3   Conditions of Detention

Although states are not prohibited from detaining irregular migrants to prevent unauthorized entry, or with a view to deportation or removal, a state's power to detain a migrant is limited, and it must protect the rights of those detained in full compliance with human rights law, notably with Articles 3 and 5 of the European Convention on Human Rights and the European Court of Human Rights' pertinent case law.[9] Irregular migrants who are detained for breaching provisions relating to migration are not criminals and should be held in appropriate conditions. Detention should be used only as a last resort, judicially authorized, and not for an excessive period of time.

As concerns pre-deportation detention, it should only be applied when it is thoroughly justified and when it is clear that the deportation can in fact take place in the immediate future. Authorities should keep the number of rejected asylum

---

8   See Article 17, paragraph 3, of the 1990 International Convention on the Protection of the Rights of all Migrant Workers and Members of their Families, which expressly holds that if migrants are detained for violating provisions relating to migration, they should be held separately from convicted persons or persons detained pending trial. See also Article 5 of the 2000 UN Protocol against the Smuggling of Migrants which expressly proscribes the criminal liability of migrants who have been the object of conduct relating to their being smuggled into a country; see also Issue Paper: Criminalisation of Migration in Europe: Human Rights Implications, published by the Commissioner's Office in February 2010, available at: www.commissioner.coe.int.

9   See e.g. ECtHR, Riad and Idiab v. Belgium, judgment of 24 January 2008, John v. Greece, judgment of 10 May 2007, S.D. v. Greece, judgment of 11 June 2009.

seekers and irregular migrants as well as the time they have to spend in detention to the strict minimum.

Detention must not be used with the intention of pressurizing an individual to co-operate with authorities to facilitate the deportation process. In situations where it is impossible to deport foreigners whose applications to stay have been finally rejected, the authorities should find alternative solutions to confinement in centres for indefinite periods.

4 Removal

Collective expulsion of foreign nationals is prohibited by international law, notably by Article 4 of Protocol No. 4 to the European Convention on Human Rights. In all cases, return should take place in safe and dignified conditions. Removal is strictly prohibited when it would constitute *refoulement* of a refugee to a situation of persecution, or of a refugee or migrant to a situation where there is a real risk of "irreparable harm" such as unlawful killing or torture, either in the first country or in any country of subsequent removal.

The Commissioner has made clear in numerous reports that diplomatic assurances do not provide an adequate safeguard against such ill treatment. The prohibition of *refoulement* also implies that states need to ensure that deportees are not asylum seekers; individuals must be given sufficient time to apply for asylum, taking into consideration that many arrive physically and mentally distressed after dangerous journeys. In human rights law, the prohibition applies irrespective of any security considerations in the host state. This principle must also be firmly respected when migrants are intercepted at sea or at points of entry to the country.

Individuals must be given the opportunity to challenge removal orders before a competent authority or body composed of members who are impartial and who enjoy safeguards of independence, preferably a court. Such appeals should have a suspensive effect when the returnee has an arguable claim that the removal order could lead to a real risk of the death penalty, torture or inhuman or degrading treatment or punishment.

Legal proceedings must fully respect procedural guarantees, particularly the right to legal assistance and representation and an interpreter. The grounds for the decision should be indicated along with the appeals that can be made. All cases of unlawful deportations or returns should be thoroughly investigated and the appropriate administrative and criminal sanctions imposed.

In this context, attention should be drawn to the importance of carefully respecting Protocol No. 4 to the ECHR and the *20 Guidelines on Forced Return*,[10] issued by the Council of Europe Committee of Ministers, which prohibit collective expulsion orders and require that each case be examined individually and that deportation orders also be individually adopted.

Where a forced return is unavoidable, it must be carried out with complete transparency in order to ensure that fundamental human rights are respected at all stages. There are clear limits to the means and degree of coercion which European States may use to enforce removal. The European Committee for the

---

10   Council of Europe, Committee of Ministers, 20 Guidelines on Forced Return, 5 May 2005, www.coe.int/t/cm.

Prevention of Torture (CPT) has set standards in this area. Any force used should be no more than is reasonably necessary. It would be entirely unacceptable for migrants to be physically assaulted as a form of persuasion to board a means of transport or as a punishment for not having done so. Any medication must only be given on the basis of a medical decision and in accordance with medical ethics.

The Committee recommends "an absolute ban on the use of means likely to obstruct the airways [nose and/or mouth] partially or wholly, which create a considerable risk to the lives of the persons concerned." Security considerations can never serve to justify escort staff wearing masks during deportation operations. The practice is highly undesirable since it could make it difficult to ascertain who is responsible in the event of allegations of ill-treatment.[11]

E   Conclusion

The alarming trends both in the treatment of asylum seekers all over Europe and in the criminalization of irregular entry and the presence of migrants as part of a so-called "migration management" must be questioned. These trends effectively erode the established principles of international law and humanitarianism.

States have a legitimate interest in controlling their borders. They have, in principle, the right to decide on the entry and stay of foreign nationals. However, state sovereignty is not absolute in this area. There are binding international agreements concerning the rights of individuals to seek asylum through fair, rights-based procedures.

The criminalization of irregular migrants is a disproportionate measure which exceeds a state's legitimate interest in controlling its borders. Criminalizing irregular migrants effectively puts them on a par with the smugglers or employers who in many cases have exploited them. Such policies cause further stigmatization, even though the majority of migrants contribute to the economic development of European states and enrich their societies.

These policies are not even effective since all they do is marginalize this part of the population even more, without attaining the aim of controlling borders. Irregular migrants will continue to enter Europe as long as they are in need of a job and/or personal safety and European states are in real need of labour. Thus, is the real solution not to build a strategy based on this reality and on the respect of the international standards safeguarding the human rights of those concerned?

---

11   European Committee for the Prevention of Torture, Foreign nationals detained under aliens legislation, 7th General Report, CPT/Inf(97) 10, para. 36; Deportation of foreign nationals by air, 13th General Report, CPT/Inf (2003) 35, paras. 36 and 38.

Manfred NOWAK

The Development of Human Rights in Europe after the End of the Cold War[*]

Table of Contents

Keywords

Human rights, Council of Europe, European Union, CSCE/OSCE, enlargement, integration, human rights monitoring, all-European system of human rights protection

A   Introduction: Poznan Conference on "Perspectives of an All-European System of Human Rights Protection"

In late 1988, Dzidek Kedzia, then Director of the Poznan Centre for Human Rights at the Polish Academy of Sciences, approached me in my function as Director of the Netherlands Institute of Human Rights at the University of Utrecht.

---

[*]   The article was originally published in Amir Eshel/Wolfgang Mueller/Roland Hsu/Arnold Suppan/Sean McIntyre (eds.), Austria and Central Europe Since 1989, Vienna 2010, and is included with the kind permissions of the original publisher.

He wished to initiate a common research project and to organize a high level conference in Poznan with the aim of investigating whether the Cold War and the emergence of two different and partly antagonistic concepts of human rights in Eastern and Western Europe had effectively destroyed the common philosophical and cultural roots of human rights in Europe dating back to the French Revolution. In fact, we assumed that the axiological foundations of the Western and Socialist concepts of human rights were common and compact enough to provide a basis on which a pan-European system for human rights protection could be built for both Western and Eastern Europe. Despite the opening up of the Soviet Union thanks to President Gorbachev's policies of "glasnost" and "perestroika", at that time our optimistic hypothesis was not shared by many in the international and European human rights community. On the contrary, most Western NGOs and academics seemed to be more concerned with the strengthening and development of human rights in Latin America, Africa and Asia than with the highly politicized East-West confrontation on human rights despite the depressing situation of human rights in Central and Eastern Europe.

While we were conducting initial research and preparing our conference with the active support and participation of the Council of Europe (Peter Leuprecht, then Director of Human Rights), the Ford Foundation and the European Cultural Foundation, the "velvet" human rights revolutions swept away repressive regimes in Central and Eastern Europe (e.g. in Czechoslovakia, East Germany and Romania) and led to the fall of the Iron Curtain. Earlier than we had expected and without much research conducted, our hypothesis turned out to be true, and the people of Central and Eastern Europe proved with their "revolution of the feet" that the classical European ideals (pluralist democracy, rule of law and human rights) hold true for all peoples in Europe.

When our International Conference on the "Perspectives of an All-European System of Human Rights Protection" was finally held in October 1990 under the auspices of Catherine Lalumière, Secretary General of the Council of Europe, we no longer discussed any axiological foundations and abstract possibilities, but the concrete perspectives of an all-European system of human rights protection and the respective roles of the Council of Europe (CoE), the Conference on Security and Cooperation in Europe (CSCE) and the European Communities. We called for better coordination and division of labour between these three organizations but saw no need for establishing a new institutional framework for a pan-European human rights mechanism.[1]

B   The CSCE as a Catalyst for the Velvet Revolutions

In retrospect, it became clear that the CSCE had played an important role as a catalyst for the fall of the Socialist regimes in Central and Eastern Europe.[2] The

---

1   See Zdzislaw Kedzia/Anna Korula/Manfred Nowak (eds.), Perspectives of an All-European System of Human Rights Protection – The Role of the Council of Europe, the CSCE, and the European Communities, Proceedings of the Poznan Conference, 1 (1991), Zdzislaw Kedzia/Peter Leuprecht/Manfred Nowak (eds.), All-European Human Rights Yearbook, Arlington 1991.

2   Cf., e.g., Arie Bloed (ed.), The Conference on Security and Cooperation in Europe, Analysis and Basic Documents 1972-1991, Dordrecht 1993; Arie Bloed/Pieter van

historic Helsinki Final Act of August 1975 had provided the foundation for a process of East-West negotiations, mutual political commitments and recommendations, addressed in the framework of the three "baskets" of the Helsinki process. Human rights were among the ten fundamental principles of the CSCE and also formed the core of the third (humanitarian) basket. Based on the commitments in this basket, human rights activists in virtually all Central and Eastern European countries began to establish "Helsinki Committees" and comparable non-governmental organizations (NGOs), such as the "Charta 77" in Czechoslovakia and "Solidarność" in Poland. They linked up with the "Helsinki Movement" and international human rights,[3] called for the observance of freedom of speech, religion, assembly and other CSCE-based human rights commitments and soon became the nucleus of a civil society that ultimately triggered the "velvet revolutions" of 1989.

The third Helsinki Follow-up Meeting, after Belgrade and Madrid, took place in Vienna between 1986 and 1989. Under the lead of President Mikhail Gorbachev, the Soviet Union, Poland and Hungary started a reform process which led to a much more open human rights dialogue. But the Socialist States were in fact split into three camps. The German Democratic Republic (GDR), Czechoslovakia and Bulgaria were still resistant to any structural reforms, and Ceauşescu's Romania had become an outcast that threatened to topple consensus in Vienna several times. Despite this rift in the Communist bloc, or perhaps because of it, diplomats in both the East and West succeeded in turning the Vienna Concluding Document of 15 January 1989 into a milestone of diplomacy which already harboured the seeds of future revolutions.

One of the outcomes of Vienna was an agreement to hold Human Dimension Conferences in Paris (1989), Copenhagen (1990) and Moscow (1991) at which concrete human rights violations could be addressed in a formalized inter-state complaints procedure, the so-called "Vienna Mechanism". In retrospect, the Copenhagen Human Dimension Document of 1990 with its comprehensive and forward-looking provisions and commitments to human rights and minority protection reflects the revolutionary mood of that time. The attempted coup against President Gorbachev at the time of the Moscow Human Dimension Conference in 1991 is no less significant.

Shortly before, Presidents Mikhail Gorbachev and François Mitterand started an initiative to build a "common European house". On 21 November 1990, the CSCE Heads of State and Government adopted the Charter of Paris for a New Europe, in which they solemnly declared the end of the Cold War and promised a "new era of democracy, peace and unity" in Europe based upon the three pillars of (Western) European values, namely pluralist democracy, the rule of law and human rights.

Dijk (eds.), The Human Dimension of the Helsinki Process – The Vienna Follow-up Meeting and its Aftermath, Dordrecht: 1991; Manfred Nowak, Introduction to the International Human Rights Regime, Dordrecht 2003, 215 et seq.

3   The different "Helsinki Committees" in Western, Central and Eastern Europe together formed the International Helsinki Federation with its seat in Vienna. "Helsinki Watch" was the first of a number of so-called "Watch Committees" that later joined to become the Human Rights Watch, today one of the world's biggest human rights organizations with its headquarters in New York.

C   From the CSCE to the Comprehensive Security Model of the OSCE

At the time when the CSCE Heads of State and Government solemnly proclaimed peace and unity, the nationalists in Yugoslavia, the Soviet Union and other parts of Central and Eastern Europe misused the ideological vacuum and widespread feeling of insecurity among many people after the collapse of the Socialist regimes by inciting to ethnic and religious hatred which led to the dissolution of multi-national states, violent minority conflicts, ethnic cleansing and the first genocide in Europe after the Nazi Holocaust half a century ago.

The CSCE reacted swiftly to these new challenges by reorienting itself from the roots and developing the concept of comprehensive security encompassing human rights, democracy and the rule of law. At the Helsinki Summit of 1992, the CSCE established the High Commissioner on National Minorities as an instrument of early warning and conflict prevention at the earliest possible stage. Although this instrument was founded too late to prevent ethnic cleansing in the former Yugoslavia and armed conflicts in the Caucasus region, the quiet diplomacy skills of Max van der Stoel were instrumental in preventing a variety of potentially dangerous minority conflicts in the Baltic States and other regions of Central and Eastern Europe from escalating into violence and armed conflicts.

At the Budapest Summit of 1994, the CSCE was transformed into the Organization for Security and Cooperation in Europe (OSCE) with permanent structures, including a Vienna-based Secretariat and Permanent Council meeting on a weekly basis. The Heads of State or Government decided to develop a common and comprehensive security model for Europe which resulted in the "Security Model for the 21st Century" adopted during the Lisbon Summit 1996 and the Istanbul "Charter for European Security" of 1999. While recognizing that "peace and security in our region are best guaranteed by the willingness and ability of each participating state to uphold democracy, the rule of law and respect for human rights", the Heads of State or Government confirmed in Istanbul that early warning mechanisms, rapid expert assistance and cooperation teams (REACT) and long-term field operations in post-conflict situations are at the heart of the comprehensive security model of the OSCE. In fact, OSCE field missions were instrumental for monitoring and building capacity in the field of human rights and democratization in the context of complex international peace building operations, above all in Croatia, Bosnia and Herzegovina and Kosovo. In addition, the Office of Democratic Institutions and Human Rights (ODIHR) in Warsaw organized election monitoring and assistance missions and similar activities in many OSCE and neighboring countries, including Afghanistan.

As an institution of East-West dialogue and détente, the CSCE encompassed all European countries plus the United States and Canada, i.e. NATO countries, Warsaw Pact countries and the so-called "neutral and non-aligned" countries, including Austria, Finland, Sweden, Switzerland and Yugoslavia. Only Albania, because of its isolated position and close relationship with China, was excluded from the Helsinki process originally encompassing 35 states. With the dissolution of the Soviet Union and Yugoslavia, membership increased to presently 56 states, i.e. all European states (with the exception of Kosovo so far), the five Central Asian states, Canada and the US. Because of its primary responsibility for systematic human rights violations in the Balkans, the membership of the Federal

Republic of Yugoslavia (Serbia and Montenegro) was suspended in 1992, and the country was only readmitted after the fall of the Milošević regime.

D   The Development of the Council of Europe (CoE)

The CoE is the oldest of the European organizations. It was founded by 11 states in 1949 as an organization of Western European liberal democracies based on the three pillars of (Western) European values. By adhering to these European values as admission criteria, the member States of the CoE distinguished themselves from both fascist states, such as Spain and Portugal until the end of the Franco and Salazar regimes, and from Communist states of Central and Eastern Europe. During the military dictatorship under Papadopoulos in the late 1960s, Greece was forced to leave the organization after gross and systematic human rights violations had been established by the European Commission of Human Rights. Greece was readmitted after its return to democracy in 1974. By the end of the Cold War, membership of the CoE had grown to 23 Western European states with Finland admitted in 1989.[4]

The promotion and protection of human rights always constituted the main activity of the CoE, with the European Convention on Human Rights (ECHR) as its flagship. The Convention is the first regional human rights treaty, adopted already in 1950. Together with various Additional Protocols (APs), it contains a broad range of civil and political rights. From the very beginning, the ECHR established a system of inter-state and individual complaints which became a model for later treaties in other regions and in the United Nations. Although this system was optional, most CoE member states gradually accepted the competence of the European Commission of Human Rights to examine individual complaints as well as the jurisdiction of the European Court of Human Rights, established in 1959. During the first 30 years of its existence, the Court and its jurisprudence gained solid authority and recognition among CoE member states due to its progressive and dynamic interpretation of human rights which at the same time recognized legitimate state interests in restricting human rights.[5] In 1989, the European Convention for the Prevention of Torture (ECPT) also entered into force and entrusted the Committee for the Prevention of Torture (CPT) with the task of carrying out preventive visits to all places of detention in CoE member states. The protection of economic, social and cultural rights was, however, less well developed: on the basis of the European Social Charter of 1961, states were comparatively free to select the rights they wished to comply with (system of "à la carte" ratification), victims had no right to individual complaints, and the monitoring of state compliance was in principle entrusted to inter-governmental bodies.[6]

---

4   Cf. Nowak (2003), 157 et seq.
5   For this doctrine of a "broad margin of appreciation" see Pieter van Dijk/Godefridus J. H. van Hoof, Theory and Practice of the European Convention on Human Rights, Antwerp/Oxford, 4th ed. 2006, 340; Jochen Frowein/Wolfgang Peukert, Europäische Menschenrechtskonvention: EMRK-Kommentar, Kehl/Strasbourg/Arlington, 3rd ed. 2009, 334 et seq.; Christoph Grabenwarter, Europäische Menschenrchtskonvention, Munich, 4th ed. 2009, 117 et seq.
6   Cf., e.g., Krzysztof Drzewicki/Catarina Krause/Allan Rosas (eds.), Social Rights as Human Rights – A European Challenge, Turku 1994.

With the end of the Cold War, the CoE reacted quickly and invited the transition countries of Central and Eastern Europe to join. Hungary was the first former Communist state, having joined in 1990, followed by Poland in 1991 and Bulgaria in 1992. Formally, admission of new member states, of course, depended on their compliance with the three pillars of the CoE. Various CoE bodies defined a variety of specific admission criteria for each candidate country, but in practice the organization and its member states adopted a policy of speedy admission and a very liberal interpretation of its own admission criteria. Typical examples of this policy were the admission of countries such as Albania, Croatia, the Ukraine and the Russian Federation in the years 1995 and 1996 as well as of Georgia, Armenia, Azerbaijan, Bosnia and Herzegovina, and Serbia and Montenegro between 1999 and 2003. This policy was and is based on the philosophy that the human rights performance of Central and Eastern European states can be better monitored and controlled after accession than before. The CoE clearly aimed at becoming an all-European organization, even at the expense of its comparatively high standards of human rights protection. This policy was, of course, not uncontroversial, but it contributed decisively to the process of European integration after the fall of the Iron Curtain. In fact, during the 20 years since 1989, the membership of the CoE more than doubled to 47 states. With the exception of Belarus and the Holy See, all European States, including the Russian Federation, Turkey and the Caucasus Republics are presently members of the CoE.

With admission to the CoE, new member states are required to ratify the ECHR with all Additional Protocols, as well as the ECPT. This has a number of important consequences for the protection of civil and political rights in Central and Eastern Europe: by having to ratify the 6th and 13th APs, all transition countries had to abolish the death penalty, and Europe (with the exception of Belarus) is today a death-penalty-free zone.[7] The CPT has access to all 47 member states of the CoE and can carry out unannounced visits to all places of detention, even in Chechnya and other North Caucasus Republics of the Russian Federation. Finally, some 800 million human beings in Europe, from Lisbon to Vladivostok, and from Reykjavik to Nicosia, have the right to lodge an individual human rights complaint directly with the European Court of Human Rights in Strasbourg.

The right of direct access to the Strasbourg Court is a fairly new achievement and reconfirmed the pioneering role of the CoE in the international protection of human rights. This fundamental reform of the "Strasbourg machinery" was also partly a result of the accession of new member states, which has led to a further increase in the number of individual complaints and long delays in the examination of these complaints. With the entry into force of the 11th AP in 1998, the members of the former European Commission and Court of Human Rights, which until then had been working on a voluntary and part-time basis, were replaced by full-time professional judges of a newly established single and permanent European Court of Human Rights. Furthermore, the optional clauses were deleted, which meant that individual and inter-state complaints before an independent court became compulsory for all CoE member states. Finally, the Committee of Ministers as the highest political body of the CoE was eliminated from the deci-

---

7   The last execution in Europe (with the exception of Belarus) took place in 1996 in the Russian Federation. Although the Russian Federation has not formally abolished capital punishment, it passed a moratorium on executions in the same year.

sion-making procedure and its role reduced to supervising the execution of the binding judgments of the Court at the national level.

The creation of the single European Court of Human Rights is undoubtedly the most important development of human rights protection in Europe since the end of the Cold War. But the CoE did much more in creating new mechanisms to respond to new human rights challenges. By having carried out an impressive number of regular and *ad hoc* visits to places of detention in all 47 member states of the CoE since 1990, the CPT has made a remarkable contribution to the prevention of torture and ill-treatment and to improving conditions of detention in Europe.[8] In addition, the Committee of Ministers decided in 1999 to create a CoE Commissioner for Human Rights as an independent non-judicial institution to promote and ensure human rights. The two Commissioners appointed so far, Alvaro Gil Robles from Spain and Thomas Hammarberg from Sweden, have carried out many missions to member states and contributed significantly to the strengthening of human rights in Europe. The European Charter for Regional or Minority Languages and the European Framework Convention for the Protection of National Minorities were adopted in 1992 and 1995, respectively, as attempts to combat increasing minority conflicts in Europe. Their domestic implementation is monitored by independent expert bodies.

Similarly, in 1993 the European Commission against Racism and Intolerance (ECRI) was established by the first Council of Europe Summit in Vienna in order to combat the growing phenomenon of racism and xenophobia in Europe. In 2005, the CoE Convention on Action against Trafficking in Human Beings was adopted, which puts more emphasis on the protection of victims of trafficking than the Optional Protocol to the UN (Palermo) Convention against Transnational Organized Crime of 2000. It requires the criminalization of trafficking and provides for a Group of Experts on action against trafficking in human beings (GRETA) as a monitoring mechanism. Even in the field of economic, social and cultural rights, some progress has been achieved. On the basis of an AP to the European Social Charter of 1995, a system of collective complaints to an independent expert body, the European Committee of Social Rights, has been introduced, and the entire system is in the process of being consolidated by the Revised European Social Charter of 1996 which entered into force in 1999.[9]

E   From the European Communities to the European Union

In the treaties establishing the three European Communities during the 1950s human rights were not explicitly mentioned.[10] The European Communities instead aimed at securing peace and security in Europe by means of economic

---

8   See Ursula Kriebaum, Folterprävention in Europa, Vienna 2000 and Malcolm D. Evans/Rod Morgan (eds.), Protecting Prisoners: The Standards of the European Committee for the Prevention of Torture, Oxford 1999.

9   See, e.g., David Harris and John Darcy, The European Social Charter, New York, 2nd ed. 2001; Andrzej Świątkowski, Charter of Social Rights of the Council of Europe, The Hague 2007.

10   See the Treaties of Paris of 1951 (European Steel and Coal Community) and of Rome 1957 (European Economic Community and Euratom). For the following, see Nowak (2003), 235 et seq.

integration and creating a Common Market. With the Maastricht Treaty of 1992/93, the European Union (EU) was created in addition to the European Community (EC). Its final objective is the creation of the "United States of Europe" by means of an enhanced economic and political integration process. Human rights constitute an important element of this European integration process. According to Article F(2) of the Maastricht EU Treaty, the Union shall respect fundamental rights, as guaranteed by the ECHR and the constitutional traditions common to the member states.

The end of the Cold War definitely accelerated and at the same time complicated the process of European integration. In addition to the traditional economic admission criteria, the EU adopted in 1993 in Copenhagen political criteria stipulating that candidate countries must have in place stable institutions guaranteeing democracy, rule of law, human rights and protection of minorities. With the Amsterdam amendment of 1997/99, these political admission criteria were integrated into the EU Treaty. According to Article 6, the EU is founded on the traditional (Western) European principles of liberty, democracy, respect for human rights and the rule of law. Only European states that respect these principles may apply to become a member of the EU in accordance with Article 49. In addition, Article 7 of the EU Treaty even provides for the possibility to suspend certain membership rights in the event of a serious and persistent breach of the principles laid down in Article 6. After the experiences with the "EU sanctions" against Austria in reaction to the inclusion of a far-right-wing party into the Austrian Government of 2000, the EU Treaty, as amended in Nice in December 2000, extended the possibility of suspending certain membership rights to situations that present a clear risk of a serious breach of fundamental rights.

Between 1989 and 2009, EU membership more than doubled from 12 to 27 member states. In 1995, three neutral states (Austria, Finland and Sweden) joined the Union, and in 2004 the most comprehensive enlargement round led to the admission of ten new states, including in addition to the Mediterranean islands of Cyprus and Malta eight Central and European transition States: the Czech Republic, Estonia, Hungary, Latvia, Lithuania, Poland, Slovakia and Slovenia. In 2007, Bulgaria and Romania followed. Croatia and Turkey presently have the status of candidate countries. Most of the remaining CoE states in the Balkan region and the former Soviet Union are eager to join the EU as quickly as possible. With the recent financial and economic crisis even Western European states that so far have refrained from joining the EU, such as Iceland, Liechtenstein, Norway and Switzerland, seem to be more interested in membership. In other words: the EU common market with open borders and the Euro as a common European currency constitutes a major incentive for all other European states, particularly in Central and Eastern Europe, to join the process of European economic and political integration. At the same time, European states, from the United Kingdom to Poland and Austria, are extremely eager to uphold their independence and sovereignty in a united Europe.

The gradual transition of the European Communities to the European Union necessarily leads to a greater emphasis on human rights, both in the EU's internal and external policies. While the EU has adopted human rights as one of its main objectives in its Common Foreign and Security Policy (CFSP) and in its bilateral and multilateral development policies and intends to become a major global player in international human rights fora, its internal human rights achievements are less impressive.

Nevertheless, the EU has taken various important steps to improve its internal human rights record and to react to the criticism of applying double standards. In 1997, the European Monitoring Centre on Racism and Xenophobia (EUMC) was established in Vienna in order to react to the increasing phenomenon of racism and xenophobia in Europe. In 2007, EUMC was transformed into the European Fundamental Rights Agency (FRA), but member states were extremely reluctant to grant the Agency any significant monitoring rights beyond racism and xeno- phobia. During the Nice Summit of December 2000, the EU adopted the Charter of Fundamental Rights as a modern, but non-binding bill of rights for the Euro- pean Union. All attempts to make the Charter binding by including it into the EU Treaty or a future "Constitution of Europe" have failed so far.[11] With the adoption of two important directives in 2000 aimed at combating racism in all fields as well as discrimination on various grounds in the field of employment and occupation, the EC, on the basis of Article 13 of the EC Treaty, has taken an important step to combat discrimination by non-state actors. Again, states are not particularly eager to fully implement these directives and the Community Action Programme to Combat Discrimination. Most disappointing are the efforts of the EU to adopt a policy of developing a common European asylum policy and of harmonizing European migration policies. Many European governments, including Austria, seem to be more interested in defending a "Fortress Europe" against immigration from third countries, including Eastern Europe, than to adopt a future-oriented asylum and migration policy that would also take into account demographic trends, openness towards a multi-cultural society in Europe and the need to accept immigration as a means to uphold our high economic and social standards.

With the recent establishment of military and police missions in the Balkans (Bosnia and Herzegovina, Macedonia and Kosovo), the EU is gradually taking over the responsibility from the United States, the United Nations, NATO and the OSCE for securing peace, security and human rights in the post-conflict societies of the former Yugoslavia. But the difficulties with peace-building in Bosnia and Herzegovina and in relation to the independence of Kosovo illustrate that there is still a long way to go until Brussels becomes the decisive pull factor for settling ethnic/religious conflicts and building a sustainable peace. The same holds true for the weak role of the EU in settling disputes in the Caucasus region.

To sum up, the EU was highly successful in facilitating the peaceful economic and political transformation of ten Central and Eastern European states, includ- ing three former (Baltic) Republics of the Soviet Union, from Communism to a market economy, based on the European values of liberty, human rights, plural- ist democracy and the rule of law. But the EU remains fairly weak in its efforts to solve ongoing ethnic, religious and minority conflicts in Europe outside its own borders. Apart from combating discrimination, racism and xenophobia, the inter- nal human rights policies of the EU are also far from encouraging. But the newly created Fundamental Rights Agency in Vienna has potential to change this situa- tion.

---

11   See Official Journal of the European Union, "Consolidated versions of the Treaty on European Union and the Treaty on the Functioning of the European Union", C 115, Vol. 51, 9 May 2008.

F   Major Human Rights Problems in Europe Since 1989

Although Europe is the region with the highest standards of human rights and the most advanced mechanisms for the international protection of human rights worldwide, the "old continent" struggles with a number of major human rights problems, many of which were created or at least aggravated by the end of the Cold War and the fall of the Iron Curtain twenty years ago. Nationalism, racism, xenophobia and minority conflicts led to an increase of hatred and violence in many countries of Western, Central and Eastern Europe. Some of the more dangerous situations in Central and Eastern Europe, such as the dissolution of the former Czechoslovakia, minority conflicts between Slovakia and Hungary, the secession of the Baltic Republics from the Soviet Union and the treatment of the Russian minority in these countries, could be solved by means of de-escalation and silent diplomacy facilitated by many actors, above all the EU, the CoE and the OSCE. Unfortunately, other ethnic, religious and minority conflicts, in particular those related to the dissolution of the former Soviet Union and Yugoslavia, led to armed conflicts in the Balkan and Caucasus regions, to systematic policies of "ethnic cleansing" and in Bosnia and Herzegovina even to the first genocide in Europe exactly 50 years after the Nazi Holocaust.

The European organizations, which were undergoing a rapid transformation process in reaction to the end of the Cold War, were unable and its member states also partly unwilling to prevent these gross and systematic human rights violations in Europe. It was only due to the political and military pressure by the United States, facilitated by NATO, that the Dayton Peace Agreement of 1995 put an end to the genocide against the Muslim population in Bosnia and Herzegovina, and that a further genocide could be prevented against the Albanian population of Kosovo in 1999. Similarly, the creation of the International Criminal Tribunal for the Former Yugoslavia (ICTY) in 1993 in The Hague was the result of a US initiative in the UN Security Council. Most of the political and military leaders responsible for war crimes, genocide and crimes against humanity in the former Yugoslavia have been brought to justice before the ICTY. This institution moreover facilitated the adoption of the Rome Statute for a permanent International Criminal Court in 1998.

When the "revolution of the feet" in 1989 brought about the fall of the Iron Curtain, Western European states and their citizens were eager to show their solidarity with the people of Central and Eastern Europe whose human rights, including freedom of movement and the right to leave one's own country had been violated for decades by repressive Communist regimes. But soon this solidarity gave way to a narrow-minded attitude of replacing the Iron Curtain by a new "Fortress Europe", stirred up by racist and xenophobic fears and policies of right-wing political parties all over Western Europe. Instead of building a common "European House", as promised in the Paris Charter for a New Europe of 1990, Western European states adopted increasingly restrictive asylum and migration policies directed primarily at immigrants from Central and Eastern Europe. While the people of this region enjoyed their newly achieved right to leave their own country, those who had been fighting for this right for decades were increasingly closing their borders and denying their European neighbours the right to enter their countries. This policy also contributed significantly to the emergence of an extremely lucrative transnational organized crime of human trafficking. While the

EU's "Schengen" and "Dublin" borders are gradually shifting towards the East, the problem of excluding third-country nationals from the "Fortress Europe" remains the same.

The extremely rapid transformation of Central and Eastern European states from Communism to pluralist democracy and a free-market economy, based on the global trend of neo-liberalism, led to a feeling of insecurity and an ideological vacuum among the population of these countries in transition. This contributed to nationalism and racism on the one hand, and to turbo-capitalism and organized crime on the other. While Russian "oligarchs", war lords in the Balkans and the Caucasus region or the leaders of human-trafficking gangs and other manifestations of transnational organized crime earned a fortune within a few years, a significant part of the population of the transition countries in Central and Eastern Europe were endangered by poverty and/or susceptible to nationalistic, racist and religious policies of the extreme right. As a result, gross and systematic human rights violations have been and are increasingly being committed in Europe by non-state actors, including rebel groups, war lords, terrorists, traffickers, mafia bosses and other representatives of transnational organized crime. In many countries, organized crime is closely connected to and intertwined with state structures and authorities.

The increase of terrorism and organized crime, before and after the terrorist attacks of 11 September 2001 in the United States, lead to severe restrictions of various human rights, such as personal liberty, dignity and integrity, freedom of expression and assembly, privacy and data protection, all in the context of counter-terrorism strategies. In addition to serious human rights violations committed by European states, such as Turkey and the Russian Federation, in fighting terrorist and insurgent movements on their own territory, many European governments actively cooperated with the Bush Administration's so called "global war on terror", which magnanimously undermined historical achievements in the struggle for the international rule of law and human rights. Typical examples of serious human rights violations, committed by the CIA and other US authorities with the active cooperation of European governments and intelligence agencies, are the creation of secret places of detention, a "spider web" of "extraordinary rendition" flights, practice of torture as a means of "enhanced interrogation", arbitrary and prolonged detention of terrorist suspects, inhuman conditions of detention, the secret surveillance of citizens and use of personal data.

The "implosion" of the Communist regimes in Europe and the end of the Cold War occurred at a time when the neo-liberal policies of Ronald Reagan and Margaret Thatcher had an enormous influence on the global economy and financial markets. After many years of over-regulation and repression by an almighty state apparatus, the people of Central and Eastern Europe were extremely attracted to policies of privatization, deregulation and the replacement of state functions by market forces. In reaction to the Socialist concept of comprehensive state obligations to fulfil economic, social and cultural rights at the expense of civil and political rights, the new governments in Central and Eastern Europe readily abandoned its responsibilities towards ensuring the rights to work, health, education, housing, social security and similar economic, social and cultural rights. While the people in the transition countries enjoyed the newly achieved rights to private property, freedom of movement, expression, religion, assembly, the right to vote and other civil and political rights, many individuals lost their jobs, access to adequate housing, education and health care. Despite rapid economic growth and accumulation of wealth by the new elites, poverty increased and vulnerable groups, such as Roma and other minorities, the elderly and immigrant communities suffered from the non-fulfilment of basic economic, social and cultural rights. Similar trends can also be observed in many Western European countries.

G   Did the Western and Socialist Concepts of Human Rights Merge into an All-European System of Human Rights Protection?

In principle, the former Socialist countries of Central and Eastern Europe were gradually transformed into "Western European" societies based on liberalism, market economy, pluralist democracy, rule of law and human rights. The Central and Eastern European transition countries were quickly admitted to the existing Western European regional organizations, such as the CoE and the EU, on the condition of complying with Western European human rights standards. They had to ratify the ECHR; abolish the death penalty; open up their prisons, police detention facilities and psychiatric hospitals to scrutiny by the CPT; provide ethnic, religious and linguistic minorities with a minimum of protection; develop effective national mechanisms for the protection of human rights and allow their citizens unrestricted access to the European Court of Human Rights. In other words: civil and political rights improved rapidly thanks to this speedy admission policy.

Despite a certain overlapping, there remains a basic division of labour in the protection of human rights between the EU, the CoE and the OSCE. The CoE is the main organization that develops regional human rights standards and monitoring mechanisms and that provides an individual remedy in case of violations of civil and political rights. The OSCE deals on a political level with structural patterns of human rights violations, in particular during and after conflict situations. Its major tool is to dispatch long term missions in the context of complex peace operations, specialized in promoting democracy and human rights. The EU is less concerned with protecting human rights within its member states but has a major input on the human rights situation in candidate countries by applying fairly strict political admission criteria. The traditional Western concept of human rights, namely the focus on civil and political rights as individual claims against undue state interference, is still dominating the all-European human rights discourse. The integration of Central and Eastern European countries into Western European organizations did, however, not lead to any increased interest in the promotion and protection of economic, social and cultural rights. On the contrary, the politicians of these countries were assuming a very critical attitude towards the so-called "second generation" of Socialist welfare rights. It seemed that the implosion of Communism and the transition of these societies into Western European liberal democracies also meant that economic, social and cultural rights would disappear from the agenda of European regional organizations.

In reality, one can however observe the opposite, namely a trend towards increased acceptance of economic, social and cultural rights. But this time the incentive did not come from Eastern Europe, but from the countries of the South, from the global academic community and the non-governmental human rights movement. Encouraged by the end of the Cold War and certain prospects for a new international order based on human rights, democracy and the rule of law, world leaders called for a second World Conference on Human Rights. It was originally planned to be held in Berlin as the new symbol of a united Europe, but the government of the recently united Germany eventually declined the offer of the United Nations for financial reasons. This provided the Austrian government with the unique chance to host this important World Conference in 1993 in Vienna. The human rights movement originally had high expectations that the Vienna Conference would provide an opportunity to overcome the ideological East-West conflict which had obstructed any significant progress in the international protection of human rights for some 40 years and to move from standard-setting to effective implementation of all human rights. But the preparations for the Vienna World Conference in the different world regions revealed that the East-West conflict was gradually being replaced by an equally ideological North-South conflict that in fact continues until today.

It was primarily Asian governments that put the universality of human rights in question, which promoted so-called "Asian values" versus Western liberalism and individualism, and which criticized the North for applying a neo-colonial attitude based on imposing Western human rights on the rest of the world. In addition, the systematic policy of "ethnic cleansing" and genocide against the Muslim population of Bosnia and Herzegovina, taking place only a few hundred kilometres from the venue of the World Conference, was a reason for Islamic states to criticize Europe for applying double standards. The conflict about the universality of human rights nearly led to the failure of the Vienna World Conference. It was only in the last minute that a compromise could be achieved. The South accepted the recognition of the universality of human rights in the Vienna Declaration and Programme of Action, but in turn the North had to accept the equality, indivisibility and interdependence of all human rights. Based on the compromise of Vienna and the insistence of the governments of the South, the main contribution of the Socialist concept of human rights to the international human rights discourse, namely the equal protection of economic, social and cultural rights, is gradually being accepted by the traditional Western European organizations. The CoE, by adopting an Additional Protocol to the European Social Charter in 1995, introduced a system of collective complaints against violations of economic, social and cultural rights before an independent European Committee of Social Rights. The adoption of the Revised European Social Charter in 1996 constituted another step in the direction of taking economic, social and cultural rights more seriously. Similarly, the EU accepted these rights when proclaiming the EU Charter of Fundamental Rights in 2000. Although Europe is still far from treating economic, social and cultural rights on an equal basis with civil and political rights, the "Socialist" rights have been gradually incorporated into the constitutions of many European states, and some of the traditional arguments against these rights, such as their alleged "non-justiciability" (that courts may not entertain and give effect to such rights), are slowly losing ground even in Austria and other traditional Western European countries. This trend is further underlined by the recent adoption of an Optional Protocol to the International Covenant on Economic, Social and Cultural Rights by the United Nations that provides for an individual complaints mechanism.

Closely related to the gradual recognition of economic, social and cultural rights is another development. The traditional Western concept of reducing human rights to individual claims against undue state interference is gradually being replaced by the recognition of the three aspects (three-fold) of state obligations to respect, fulfil and protect all human rights. The obligation to respect means the duty of states to refrain from unduly interfering with human rights and applies equally to the right to life, access to justice, education or health care. The same holds true for the obligation to fulfil these rights by means of positive legislative, administrative, judicial and other measures as well as to protect these rights against undue interference by private actors.

Although the Socialist concept of human rights was "submerged" into the Western concept of human rights after the end of the Cold War, we can nevertheless conclude that its main elements, such as the recognition of economic, social and cultural rights as well as the obligation of states to fulfil and protect human rights by means of positive measures, are today accepted in Europe thanks to certain global trends and compromises between the North and the South.

H How Did the European Organizations Deal with the Enlargement Process?

By opening themselves up to speedy admission of the transition countries, the CoE and EU provided to the people of Central and Eastern Europe a fairly well developed and sophisticated system for the protection of human rights. The process of admission to these two organizations on the basis of certain political admission criteria, including human rights, led to structural reforms and had a major impact on the enjoyment and protection of human rights in the candidate countries. After admission to the CoE, individual cases of human rights violations are successfully taken care of by the European Court of Human Rights and other monitoring bodies. The EU provides additional protection, particularly in the field of equality and non-discrimination.

On the other hand, none of the European organizations has so far developed appropriate mechanisms to prevent or remedy gross and systematic human rights violations. This was demonstrated before the end of the Cold War, notably in the cases of systematic human rights violations in Turkey and the Northern part of Cyprus after the Turkish occupation. But these situations dramatically increased since 1989, as can be illustrated by the most serious human rights violations in Bosnia and Herzegovina, Kosovo, the Russian Federation (e.g. Chechnya), Georgia (e.g. Abkhazia and South Ossetia), or Armenia (e.g. Nagorno Karabagh). In addition, widespread violations of human rights caused by human trafficking and other forms of transnational organized crime have increased after the end of the Cold War and have not been effectively addressed by any of the European organizations. The same holds true for poverty and poverty-related human rights violations.

In addition, the enlargement process also had a detrimental impact on the efficiency of European organizations and some of their monitoring mechanisms. Most importantly, the European Court of Human Rights is no longer able to deal with its caseload within a reasonable time, primarily because of the huge amount of individual applications against the Russian Federation and some other Eastern European states. To a certain extent, these problems could be solved by the entry into force of the 14th AP to the ECHR, but this remedy has been blocked for a considerable time by the non-ratification of the 14th AP by the Russian Federation. This obstruction and a similar attitude of the Russian Federation in the Committee of Ministers and other bodies make many people within the CoE wish the Russian Federation had never been admitted. But no Member State would have the courage to start an initiative towards its exclusion from the CoE.

After the speedy admission of twelve new member states, mostly from Central and Eastern Europe, in 2004 and 2007, the enlargement and institution-building process of the EU seems to be in a crisis as well. With 27 members, the structures and decision-making procedures of the Union simply have reached their limits and are in urgent need of reform. But many of the new and old member states continue to insist, for example, on keeping "their" Commissioner, "their" voting rights in the Council, on changing the EU Presidency every six months, and will not give up the claim that EU documents and speeches need to be translated into all languages spoken in the EU. Member states are so concerned about their sovereignty, e.g. in the context of asylum and migration policy, that they are very reluctant to delegate powers to "Brussels". The efforts of the EU to reform its internal structures by adopting a European Constitution with a binding EU Charter of Fundamental Rights or only the revised Lisbon Treaty have met with severe opposition by certain governments and by the people of France, the Netherlands and Ireland who voted in a referendum against these changes.[12] Without the necessary structural changes, a further enlargement of the EU seems, however, to be extremely difficult. In addition, candidate countries such as Turkey and Croatia face severe opposition by many of the current member states. The enthusiasm over European integration after the end of World War II and again after the end of the Cold War seems to have given way to a high degree of Euro-scepticism and a lack of vision by the present political leaders of Europe. One may hope that the current financial and economic crisis and the stabilizing factor of the EU and the Euro might lead again to more support for the EU. But it is also high time to re-think some of the policies of the last decades, such as the full endorsement of neo-liberal economic policies and a certain neglect of human rights, in particular economic, social and cultural rights.

Finally, it is fair to say that the comprehensive security model of the OSCE is in a deep crisis. There are many reasons for this, including the unilateral policies of the Bush Administration in the US and the re-emerging power of the Russian Federation. The recent conflict between the Russian Federation and Georgia concerning Abkhazia and South Ossetia is a striking example that the conflict prevention mechanisms of the OSCE are simply not working. Some of the OSCE participating States, including Turkmenistan, Uzbekistan and other Central Asian Republics, are accused of gross and systematic violation of human rights without the OSCE being able to take any meaningful action. Many unresolved territorial conflicts, such as in Armenia, Georgia and Moldova, have not been properly addressed by the OSCE. The question of the independence of Kosovo from Serbia seems to be dealt with primarily outside the OSCE rather than by its conflict resolution mechanisms.

---

12   The Lisbon Treaty finally entered into force on 1 December 2009.

I   Conclusions: Human Rights in Europe 20 Years after the End of the Cold War

Undoubtedly, a study on the improvement of human rights in Europe 20 years since the end of the cold war may pose enormous practical and policy issues. In this article, I assessed the early initiatives towards an all-European system of human rights protection; the birth and role of the CSEC; the consequences of the integration of many Central and East Europe countries on promotion of human rights in Europe; and the growing challenges of the OSCE. As such, I have considered all possible factors to address the following direct questions:

- Has the situation of human rights in Europe improved during the twenty years since the end of the Cold War?
- Have the human rights monitoring mechanisms of the European regional organizations been strengthened since then?
- Did the fall of the Iron Curtain and the re-unification of Central, Eastern and Western Europe have a positive effect on the promotion and protection of human rights?
- Have the antagonistic Western and Socialist concepts of human rights merged into a genuine synthesis of an all-European system of human rights protection?

Indeed, the re-unification of the Central, East, and Western Europe has enhanced the promotion and protection of human rights in Europe. Most of the former Socialist countries of Central and Eastern Europe have been successfully integrated into the traditional Western European human rights protection systems developed by the CoE and the EU. The level of human rights protection in many of these countries has reached that of the "old" member states in Western Europe.

The Western concept of human rights still dominates the all-European system of human rights protection, while the recognition of economic, social and cultural rights as well as of State obligations to respect, fulfil and protect all human rights is increasingly growing.

Some states and individuals have long questioned the responsiveness and efficiency of the existing European organizations to the demands of member states, and raised critical concerns relating to the protection of human rights in Europe. However, no significant steps have been taken in response to such critiques. Rather than creating a new all-European organization for the protection of human rights, this function was taken over by the CoE, the EU and the OSCE. While the CoE provides to some 800 million people living in its 47 member States the right to a remedy for violations of civil and political rights before an independent full-time European Court of Human Rights in Strasbourg, the OSCE is dealing more with gross and systematic violations of human rights during and after a conflict situation. The EU is primarily concerned with promoting human rights in its external relations. These three European organizations pursued and managed major developments and structural changes in order to meet the new challenges, such as enlarged membership, minority conflicts, racism, xenophobia, ethnic cleansing, armed conflicts and genocide. Nevertheless, none of these organizations developed efficient mechanisms to deal with gross and systematic human rights violations. As the United Nations human rights programme, the major European organizations responsible for the promotion and protection of human rights find themselves, 60 years after the Universal Declaration of Human Rights and 20 years after the fall of the Iron Curtain, in a veritable crisis. While the 1990s brought some important improvements, such as the International Criminal Court, the single European Court of Human Rights, the recognition of human rights, the rule of law and democratization as essential elements of peace operations and poverty reduction strategies, the last decade must unfortunately be considered as a lost decade for the advancement, implementation and enforcement of human rights. But with the Obama Administration in the US, the Lisbon Treaty in Europe and the Corfu process in the OSCE things might change again.

Florence BENOÎT-ROHMER

Completing the Transformation: Values and Fundamental Rights in the Treaty of Lisbon

Table of Contents

Keywords

EU, Treaty of Lisbon, human rights, values, ECHR, Charter of Fundamental Rights, opt out, accession

A   Introduction

The developments of the construction of Europe show a desire to deepen the values that the Union upholds and that inspire its actions. The Paris and Rome Treaties remained silent with regards to values and did not mention in their respective preambles the principles of peace and freedom, a lacuna that can be explained by their economic purpose. Nevertheless, with the Single European Act, member states declared themselves

> "determined to work together to promote democracy on the basis of the
> fundamental rights recognized in the constitutions and laws of the Member

States, in the Convention for the Protection of the Human Rights and Fundamental Freedoms and the European Social Charter, notably freedom, equality and social justice.[1]

The Treaty of Maastricht, passed after the reunification of Germany, puts the emphasis on the need for the Union to respect fundamental rights (former Article F (2), renumbered Article 6 (2)). It is only with the Amsterdam Treaty of 2 October 1997 that the Union clearly declared its will to build not only an economic Europe, but also a political Europe founded on fundamental values shared by all member states. A new paragraph was therefore added to Article F (renumbered 6(1)) of the TEU declaring "The Union is founded on the principles of liberty, democracy, respect for human rights and fundamental freedoms, and the rule of law, principles which are common to the Member States". The Lisbon Treaty completes this evolution. Under the influence of the Charter of Fundamental Rights, it turns the principles into values,[2] so as to prevent any confusion between the principles and the four freedoms recognized by the Treaty, but mostly to symbolically emphasize their significance. The addition of a specific article on the values that constitute the European identity and characterize the European society model is in itself an important step in the identification and enumeration of the founding values of the Union.

In each of these matters, the Lisbon Treaty takes up most of the innovations included in the text of the late Constitution for Europe. It can therefore be considered the outcome of a debate that took place during the Convention on the future of the European Union. The Convention had debated at length the matter of values, considering that it was fundamental to a European Union with a stronger political dimension.

Even though the Lisbon Treaty does not have a constitutional nature, it enshrines the most important developments the Constitution would have brought. Insofar as they pertain to human rights and values and their role in the post-Lisbon EU, they will be analyzed in the following. Section B will argue that the values have an unquestionable position in the Treaty and are expected to allow for the emergence, among Europeans, of a feeling of belonging, not to a traditional international organization but to a real community of values. Asserted in the Preamble, they are consecrated in Article 2 of the Treaty, second only to the provisions establishing the Union. They are also included in the Charter of Fundamental Rights, which is invested with the same values as the treaties (C). In addition, the Treaty foresees the accession to the European Convention on Human Rights (D). In this instance, a minimum set of values would be shared by the entire continent and would be reviewed, as a last resort, by the same court, the European Court of Human Rights. In section E, some conclusions will be offered.

---

1   Single European Act of 28 February 1986, OJ L 169 of 29 June 1987, preambular para. 3.
2   The Preamble of the Charter states that "the Union is founded on the indivisible, universal values of human dignity, freedom, equality and solidarity; it is based on the principles of democracy and the rule of law".

B   The Proclamation of Values on Which the Union is Founded

The Lisbon Treaty,[3] like the Constitution, emphasizes that the Union is based on a set of values shared by member states. These values constitute a common heritage they want to assert and promote. They are referred to in the Preamble of the Treaty on European Union (TEU) and laid down in Article 2. EU policy must embody them; the institutions must abide by them in their activities, and so do the member states when implementing EU law.

These values originate from the principles that structure the constitutions of the member states and that appeared, even before the Maastricht Treaty, in Community law as construed by the Court of Justice.

1   The Statement of Values

A paragraph with clear references to values, taken from the Preamble of the Treaty establishing a Constitution for Europe, has been added to the Preamble of the TEU. Under a compromise reached with difficulty during the Convention, it refers to "the cultural, religious and humanist inheritance of Europe, from which have developed the universal values of the inviolable and inalienable rights of the human person, freedom, democracy, equality and the rule of law". European Union member states also reiterate their attachment to the respect for human rights and fundamental freedoms, as well as to the fundamental social rights as defined in the European Social Charter and in the 1989 Community Charter of the Fundamental Social Rights of Workers.

As regards the "cultural, religious and humanist inheritance of Europe", churches in certain member states, including Poland, tried to have a reference to the "Christian values" that inspired European integration included in the Preamble, causing a number of controversies broadly discussed in the media. The status quo of a neutral formulation was not questioned during the drafting of the Lisbon Treaty.

Even though the Treaty does not contain any reference to Christianity or Judeo-Christian heritage, churches managed to include a specific article aiming at preserving their different legal statuses in Europe. Article 17 of the Treaty on the Functioning of the European Union (TFEU) repeats the wording of Declaration 11 to the Final Act of the Treaty of Amsterdam, under which "[t]he Union respects and does not prejudice the status under national law of churches and religious associations or communities in the Member States". The Treaty insists on the identity and specific contribution of churches and of philosophical and non-confessional organizations, as well as on the need to "maintain an open, transparent and regular dialogue with these churches and organisations".

The first sentence of Article 2 of the TEU includes a listing of the values of the Union. The wording is identical to that of Article I.2 of the Treaty establishing a Constitution for Europe. The debates on this article were particularly fierce during

---

3   References to articles in the "Lisbon Treaty" should be understood to denote the relevant articles in the consolidated versions of the Treaty on European Union (TEU) and the Treaty on the Functioning of the European Union (TFEU), OJ C115, 9 May 2008, and articles in the actual Treaty of Lisbon, OJ C306, 17 December 2007.

the drafting of this treaty, but it was agreed that the values that would be included needed to be specific and applicable in order to enlist the support of the European public opinion and allow for consequences in case of an infringement.

The inspiration for the list of the values in Article 2 can unquestionably be found in the principles enumerated in Article 6 (1) of the former TEU and in the values detailed by the Charter of Fundamental Rights. New values were nevertheless added, including the respect for human dignity, equality and the respect of the rights of persons belonging to national minorities. As a matter of fact, Article 2 TEU specifies that the Union is "founded on the values of respect for human dignity, freedom, democracy, equality, the rule of law and respect for human rights, including the rights of persons belonging to minorities".[4]

The respect for human dignity had to be included in the list of these values, if only to remind that today's Europe was built on the desire to prevent WWII crimes from re-occurring. Article 2 states, in line with the Universal Declaration of Human Rights, that the respect for human dignity is a fundamental value in Europe and that human dignity is the basis of all rights. Article 2 also echoes the Charter of Fundamental Rights, whose first title is dedicated to this value. Finally, another origin of the dignitarian approach can be found among the unchangeable sections of the German Basic Law.

Equality was included in the list of values by reason of the indivisible link between equality and freedom. The significance of this value had already been underlined by the Amsterdam Treaty, which had added an article to the Treaty establishing the European Community, giving the Council the ability, through a co-decision procedure with the European Parliament, to "take appropriate action to combat discrimination based on sex, racial or ethnic origin, religion or belief, disability, age or sexual orientation".

The insertion in the Constitution and in the Lisbon Treaty, of a reference to the rights of persons belonging to minorities was not disputed, even by France, which nevertheless does not recognize the existence of minorities on its territory. This can be explained by the fact that the chosen wording clearly indicates that persons are entitled to rights, not groups. The Treaty would therefore not compel member states to recognize the existence of minorities entitled to collective rights. However, it can be noted that the usual qualifier "national" was not added to the term "minorities". Does this imply that the Union follows the Council of Europe in protecting not only the so-called "historical" minorities but also the more recent economic minorities that arose with immigration?

The second sentence of Article 2 clarifies the values mentioned in the first sentence by referring to the specificities of the European model of society. After long discussions, a consensus was reached on including pluralism, non-discrimination, tolerance, justice, solidarity and equality between women and men. Some authors consider that these values are less precise than those in the first sentence, and that they will not allow for the imposition of sanctions in case

---

4   This article is the direct successor of Article 6 (1) TEU, which insists on the attachment of the Union to the principles and fundamental values shared by all member states, as they constitute the basis of the Union and its three pillars. Under Article 6 (1), "[t]he Union is founded on the principles of liberty, democracy, respect for human rights and fundamental freedoms, and the rule of law, principles which are common to the Member States".

of an infringement. They are nevertheless an exemplification of the values previously defined and can be used to interpret and clarify their concrete meaning.[5]

Compared to former Article 6 TEU, the references to solidarity and equality between women and men are new. Mentioning solidarity shows the Union's attachment to social rights and puts the emphasis on the development of a political and social Europe. If a European model exists, it notably differentiates itself from the American one by giving a greater importance to social matters, no matter how diverse the situation is, in this respect, in the different member states. This value and its different aspects are described in Title IV of the Charter of Fundamental Rights. Moreover, the Treaty reinforces the solidarity between member states when one of them is the target of a terrorist attack or the victim of a natural or man-made disaster. It also emphasises the need for solidarity in energy matters.

Under pressure from feminist organizations, the equality between women and men was finally inserted in the list of founding values of the Union, even though some considered that the principle of equality, mentioned in the first sentence of the article, already included equality between the sexes. Besides, it is part of the Union *acquis*. Equality between men and women is also guaranteed as an aim of the Union in Article 3 TEU. Further, Article 8 TFEU, stating that the Union shall aim to eliminate inequalities and promote equality between men and women, is contained in Title II TFEU as a provision having general application. Other provisions of the Treaty are also related to equality in the labour market or in terms of pay,[6] or to the protection of human beings against trafficking and sexual exploitation.[7] The Charter of Fundamental Rights reinforces the importance of this value by consecrating, in Article 23, the principle of equality between men and women in all areas.

Contrary to the Preamble of the Charter of Fundamental Rights, which refers to the universality of rights, the provisions of the Lisbon Treaty do not mention it. This is due to the fact that the members of the Convention considered it was necessary to define the values specific to the Union as elements of a European identity. Consequently they chose not to refer to the potential universality of these values, even when they thought it was the case. The inspiration for Article 2 can mainly be found in the Copenhagen Declaration on European Identity of 14 December 1973.[8]

Article 3 of the Treaty sets the Union's aims at the definition and implementation of its policies. It states that these policies shall serve the Union's values, peace and the well-being of its peoples. A list of other, more detailed and numerous aims is added. Many of them are illustrations of the values that inspire the Union's actions. In this context, the Union is under the general obligation to combat ex-

---

5   See François Xavier Priollaud/David Siritsky, Le Traité de Lisbonne, texte et commentaire, article par article, des nouveaux traités européens (TUE-TFUE), Paris 2008, 33.
6   Article 157 TFEU.
7   Articles 79 and 83 TEU.
8   Declaration on European Identity of 14 December 1973, adopted at the Copenhagen European Summit by the heads of state or government of the nine member states of the European Community, in: Bulletin of the European Communities, December 1973, no. 12, 118-122, http://www.ena.lu/declaration_european_identity_co penhagen_ 14_december_1973-02-6180.

clusion and discrimination. Under Article 3 (3), the Union "shall combat social exclusion and discrimination, and shall promote social justice and protection, equality between women and men, solidarity between generations and protection of the rights of the child." The promotion of scientific and technological advance, as well as the protection and improvement of the quality of the environment, the cultural and linguistic diversity and the protection and enhancement of Europe's cultural heritage also become aims of the Union.

In its relations with the rest of the world, the Union commits to promoting its values and interests. Article 3 (5) gathers the aims relating to the common foreign and security policy of the pre-Lisbon TEU and the provisions from the TEC relating to cooperation and development, including

"peace, security, the sustainable development of the Earth, solidarity and mutual respect among peoples, free and fair trade, eradication of poverty and the protection of human rights, in particular the rights of the child, [...] the development of international law[,]"

the latter referring to respect for the principles of the United Nations Charter. The Treaty includes, as a new objective, the protection of the rights of the child on the international scene.

2   Legal Significance of the Statement of Values

Like the Constitution, the Treaty gives more than a simple rhetorical significance to the list of values of the Union. It clearly states that the respect for and the commitment to promote the founding values of the Union constitute one of the requirements for the accession of new member states. The wording of Article 49 of the TEU, by which "[a]ny European State which respects the values referred to in Article 2 and is committed to promoting them may apply to become a member of the Union", leaves no doubt about it. The *acquis communautaire* is as a consequence reinforced considering that the Amsterdam Treaty had already imposed the respect by all candidate states of the principles in the former Article 6(1) of the TEU.

Moreover, the infringement of these values by a member state can lead to serious consequences for the state in question. The Treaty still includes the procedure created by the Amsterdam Treaty and under which a serious breach by a member state of the common values of the Union can lead to the suspension of certain rights deriving from the application of the Treaty to the member state in question, including its voting rights in the Council (Article 7 TEU).

C   The Binding Nature of the Charter of Fundamental Rights of the European Union

After the Treaty of Amsterdam, the European Union decided to get its own Charter of Fundamental Rights, as there was not enough political will to revise the treaties to allow for the accession of the Community/Union to the European Convention on Human Rights. The Charter, signed and proclaimed by the European Parliament, the Council and the Commission in Nice on 7 December 2000, manages to list in a single text the fundamental rights the Union already had to abide by and enumerates the rights upon their object, thus referring to the founding values of the European Union: dignity, freedoms, equality, solidarity, citizens' rights and justice. In the Preamble of the Charter, member states claim their resolution to "share a peaceful future based on common values". The Preamble follows:

"Conscious of its spiritual and moral heritage, the Union is founded on the indivisible, universal values of human dignity, freedom, equality and solidarity; it is based on the principles of democracy and the rule of law".

The Charter favours the construction of a European identity based on the preservation and development of a common heritage of principles and values in which European citizens should recognize themselves. In addition, it includes rights that are added to those already laid down in the European Convention on Human Rights, in particular social rights for workers, the protection of personal data, bioethics and the right to good administration.

Nevertheless, the Charter used to suffer from an innate weakness: being formally non-binding. As member states chose not to insert it in the Treaty of Nice, it only had the value of an interinstitutional agreement, even though the practice of the institutions would facilitate its integration into Community law[9] and the Advocate Generals of the European Court of Justice (ECJ) and the Court itself would increasingly refer to its provisions.[10]

1   Legal Value

The Constitution dealt with the matter of the legal value of the Charter by inserting it in its second part. The choice to "deconstitutionalize" and simplify the Treaty following the negative referenda in France and in the Netherlands means that the text of the Charter is not included in the Treaty of Lisbon. Article 6 simply refers to the Declaration of 7 December 2000, as adapted in Strasbourg on 12 December 2007. This reference shows the importance that the Union gives to the protection of the fundamental rights that found it. Under Article 6(1), the Charter has the same legal value as the treaties, and is therefore part of primary law. It would certainly have been wiser to take into account the symbolic meaning of including the Charter itself in the revised founding treaty of the Union, especially at a time when European citizens complain about the aridity of the text

---

9   Along with the Council and the Commission, the Parliament inserted in the reasons for the legislations, each time it appeared necessary, a reference to the pertinent provisions in the Charter. This practice led the Court of Justice to take into account the Charter when interpreting these texts. The Court made a first explicit reference to the Charter in a judgment on family reunification (ECJ, judgment of 27 June 2006, Case C-540/03, Parliament v. Council). More recently, the Court referred to the provisions of the Charter on the right to strike to clarify the links between this right and the freedom of establishment (ECJ, Grand Chamber, judgment of 11 December 2007, Case C-438/05, International Transport Workers' Federation & Finnish Seamen's Union v. Viking Line ABP & OÜ Viking Line Eesti; and ECJ, Grand Chamber, judgment of 18 December 2007, Case C-341/05, Laval un Partneri Ltd. See also ECJ, judgment of 3 April 2008, Case C-346/06, Dirk Rüffert v. Land Niedersachsen).

10   On the legal value of the Charter and the British and Polish opting out, see also the contribution of Jean Paul Jacqué, in this volume, at 123.

of the treaty, as they hardly understand it and many fail to perceive its purpose and what is at stake.

Article 6 still contains references to the European Convention on Human Rights and to the constitutional traditions common to the member states, as basis for fundamental rights, through general principles of law. The Charter is not considered the exclusive basis for fundamental rights. As a result, general principles of law remain a complementary basis, which could allow the Court to make adjustments to the protection of fundamental rights to take into account societal developments and even go beyond the language of the Charter.[11] The reference to general principles also reduces the impact of the British and Polish opting outs, which will be discussed further in the text. Thus, if a right cannot be implemented due to the opting out provision, the Court can still protect it through the general principles of law.

Compared to the first version of the Charter as proclaimed at Nice, the Convention had inserted a number of changes, especially in Title VII, in order to clarify the rules of interpretation of the rights guaranteed by the Charter when they arise from the constitutional traditions common to the member states, to refine the distinction between the rights and principles in the field of social rights, and to adequately take into account the national practices and legislations. That is why the representatives of the three institutions decided to proclaim once again, in the European Parliament, the Charter of Fundamental Rights of the European Union as amended by the Convention, in December 2007, the day before the Treaty amending the TEU and turning the Treaty establishing the European Community into the TFEU was signed in Lisbon.

Nevertheless, the binding value of the Charter was only acknowledged after certain guarantees were granted to the United Kingdom, which had feared that the Union would unduly infringe on state competences in fundamental rights matters. To facilitate its ratification by the British Parliament, the Lisbon Treaty, in Article 6 insists twice that the Charter cannot be used to create new EU competences. First, para. 2 indicates: "The provisions of the Charter shall not extend in any way the competences of the Union as defined in the Treaties". What is more, para. 3 explicitly states:

"The rights, freedoms and principles in the Charter shall be interpreted in accordance with the general provisions in Title VII of the Charter governing its interpretation and application and with due regard to the explanations referred to in the Charter, that set out the sources of those provisions."

In addition, Title VII of the Charter indicates in Article 51 (2) that it does not establish any new power for the Union, or modify the division of powers between the Union and member states, and the explanations give a restrictive interpretation of the Charter. As if this were not sufficient, the Declaration concerning the Charter of Fundamental Rights of the European Union at the end of the Treaty reminds that the Charter only confirms the fundamental rights guaranteed by the

---

11   See Frédéric Sudre, Commentaire de l'article I.9 du traité établissant une constitution pour l'Europe, in: Laurence Burgorgue-Larsen/Anne Levade/Fabrice Picod (eds.), Traité établissant une constitution pour l'Europe, Commentaire article par article, Brussels 2007, 143.

European Convention of Human Rights and as they result from the "constitutional traditions common to the member states" and indicates that

"The Charter does not extend the field of application of Union law beyond the powers of the Union or establish any new power or task for the Union, or modify powers and tasks as defined by the Treaties."

These clarifications could have satisfied the United Kingdom, but they were nonetheless considered to be insufficiently visible, and were therefore repeated in a protocol annexed to the Treaty. This protocol grants the United Kingdom and Poland an exemption from the application of the Charter of Fundamental Rights.

2   The British and Polish Opting Out Provisions

The redrafting of the text of the Constitution was the occasion for two states, Poland and the United Kingdom, to be granted an opting out provision from the application of the Charter of Fundamental Rights. Negotiations between member states showed that most of the states that had already ratified the Constitution did not want to back down from the innovations in the Constitution, even if that meant that certain states would be exempt from abiding by some common provisions. The states in question used these exemptions to enhance their chances to convince their public opinions into voting in favour of the ratification of the Treaty. The President of the Czech Republic also lobbied to be granted the same clause on the occasion of the ratification of the Treaty of Lisbon.[12]

In particular, the British government wanted to ensure that British social legislation would not be affected by the implementation of the Charter and that British citizens would remain subjected to British judges for the interpretation of this legislation. The United Kingdom, followed by Poland, thus made the insertion of a protocol on the Charter a *sine qua non* condition of their approval of the Treaty. Consequently, Protocol No. 30 was added to the Treaty in order to clarify the legal significance of the Charter for the British and Polish legal systems. It can be perceived as granting a wide system of exemptions to the two concerned states.

The British government mainly wanted to avoid a referendum on the ratification of the Treaty. Prime Minister Gordon Brown feared that a conflict with the Conservative Party on this matter would weaken his position, already shaky according to the polls, before the next general elections. For this reason, anything with a constitutional value had to be avoided; and the Charter appeared as such to the eyes of the British. In addition, British employers strongly resisted the social rights included in the Charter, and in particular the right to strike. The British government was as a result looking for exemption from some of these rights. The Polish had no particular reluctance about the social rights but rejected the application of the provisions of the Charter on private and family life, as these provisions were considered too liberal since they notably allow homosexual marriage. Such fear is odd considering that the relevant provisions of the Charter largely draw their inspiration from the European Convention on Human Rights to which Poland is a party and that the provisions refer to national laws on matters that appear outside the Convention.

---

12   Protocol 30 to the TEU only refers to the United Kingdom and Poland. The Treaty would have to be revised to insert such a clause, which presently seems unrealistic.

The Preamble to Protocol 30 first notes that the Charter only reaffirms rights, freedoms and principles without creating new ones. This observation deprives the Protocol of some of its relevance. As a matter of fact, what is the use of an opting out clause on a part of the *acquis* when the Preamble reaffirms the respect of Poland and the United Kingdom for this *acquis*? The system is composed of three provisions.[13] According to the first one, the Charter does not extend the ability of the Community judge and of national judges to give a ruling on the consistency of British and Polish legislation with the provisions of the Charter. Even if the extension is not permitted, there is no restriction to the current situation. As a result, the second provision states that the rights in Title IV of the Charter (Solidarity) are not justiciable, unless national law has provided for them. Finally, the reference in the Charter to national laws and practices shall only apply "to the extent that the rights or principles that it contains are recognised in the law or practices of Poland or of the United Kingdom".

Such an exemption can be perceived as shocking, and one can rightfully question the scope of this provision that allows the United Kingdom and Poland to exempt themselves from the application of the Charter. Considering that fundamental rights are part of the fundamental values of the Union and that candidate states have to respect them, it is hardly acceptable that member states would be exempt from them. The introduction of a double standard in terms of fundamental rights is therefore quite surprising.

In practice, the Court of Justice will have to interpret the scope of the Protocol. Since the Charter only applies to areas subject to EU law, the Protocol brings no changes when it comes to areas that are not within the field of competence of the Union. In such a case, the United Kingdom and Poland were and remain free to act as they wish, with respect for the European Convention on Human Rights and for other international instruments they are a party to.

Within the field of EU law, the Protocol leaves unchanged the obligation for the Union to respect the Charter. The judge will still have the opportunity to check the conformity of EU legislation with the Charter. The only uncertainty lies with the obligations of the United Kingdom and Poland when they act within the field of application of EU law. Will they then be subjected to the Charter? A negative answer would imply that EU law does not apply uniformly between member states since some of them would be subjected to obligations when some others are not. Under a consistent case-law of the Court of Justice, the obligation of member states to respect fundamental rights when they implement EU law results from the principle of sincere cooperation between member states and the Community. Does the Protocol put this principle into reconsideration?

---

13   Article 1 of Protocol 30 states, about Poland and the United Kingdom, that:

    "1. The Charter does not extend the ability of the Court of Justice of the European Union, or any court or tribunal of Poland or of the United Kingdom, to find that the laws, regulations or administrative provisions, practices or action of Poland or of the United Kingdom are inconsistent with the fundamental rights, freedoms and principles that it reaffirms.

    2. In particular, and for the avoidance of doubt, nothing in Title IV of the Charter creates justiciable rights applicable to Poland or the United Kingdom except in so far as Poland or the United Kingdom has provided for such rights in its national law."

In a report on the Lisbon Treaty, the House of Lords established that the Protocol does not lead to a different application of the Charter to Poland and the United Kingdom. After having analyzed the Charter and the Protocol at length, the House considers that the Charter only reaffirms pre-existing rights and that the Protocol only clarifies the interpretation and the scope of application of the Charter where the explanations had not eliminated all ambiguities, in particular regarding the social rights mentioned in Title IV.

> *"Indeed, given that, despite media reports, it is an interpretative Protocol rather than an opt-out, it is perhaps a matter of regret, and even a source of potential confusion, that it was not expressed to apply to all Member States."*[14]

The United Kingdom has now made this interpretation its official position and even disputes, with regards to its own situation, the use of the term "opting out".

D   Accession of the Union to the European Convention on Human Rights

The preparation work for the Constitutional treaty was the occasion of a debate on the accession of the European Union to the ECHR. For long, States failed to agree on this matter.[15] Certain states clearly opposed it and considered that such an accession would undermine the autonomy of the Community legal system and weaken the European Court of Justice in comparison to the European Court of Human Rights by creating a hierarchy between the Courts in favour of the one based in Strasbourg. Despite these considerations, also shared by the ECJ,[16] Article I-9 of the Constitution established that "The Union shall accede to the European Convention for the Protection of Human Rights and Fundamental Freedoms". The Lisbon Treaty also includes the principle of the accession, which reinforces the protection of fundamental rights.

In the meantime, the European Convention on Human Rights was amended to make such an accession possible. Certain provisions of the Convention had to be revised in order to allow an international organization to become party to the Convention. Protocol 14 will come into effect in June 2010 following its ratification by Russia in January 2010, and negotiations on a treaty on the accession of the Union to the European Convention on Human Rights can start.

---

14   UK House of Lords/European Union Committee, The Treaty of Lisbon: an Impact Assessment, 10th Report of Session 2007-2008, vol. 1, p. 102.
15   See, amongst others, Gérard Cohen-Jonathan, L'adhésion de la Communauté européenne à la Convention européenne des droits de l'homme, JTDE 17 (1995), 49; Florence Benoît-Rohmer, L'adhésion de l'Union à la Convention européenne des droits de l'homme, RUDH 12 (2000) 1-2, 57; Oliver de Schutter, L'adhésion de la communauté européenne à la CEDH comme élément du débat sur l'avenir de l'Union, in: Marianne Dony/Emmanuelle Bribosia (eds.), L'avenir du système juridictionnel de l'Union européenne, Brussels 2002, 247.
16   See also ECJ, Opinion 2/94, 28 March 1996 (Accession by the Community to the European Convention for the Protection of Human Rights and Fundamental Freedoms), where the Court decided that, as Community law then stood, the Community had no competence to accede to the Convention.

1   The Commitment to Accession

Article 6 (2) TEU as amended by the Lisbon Treaty contains an absolute obligation: "The Union shall accede to the European Convention for the Protection of Human Rights and Fundamental Freedoms". The belief that the accession of the Union to the European Convention on Human Rights is a great contribution to the creation of a coherent human rights protection system in Europe finally prevailed[17] and it is now agreed that the human rights protection systems need to be harmonized so as not to weaken the holistic protection in Europe and not to lower legal certainty. This kind of harmonization can only be done if the European Convention on Human Rights is the minimum standard common to European democracies. Any situation in which two human rights protection systems, that of the European Convention and that of the Union, are in competition must be avoided and it must be ensured that the European minimum standard of the ECHR is applied to any person under the Union's jurisdiction. In this context, and without reconsidering the value and scope of the Charter that can have its own effects, the accession of the Union to the EHCR will imply that the same minimum set of values will be shared by the entire continent and that the review will be carried out, as a last resort, by the same Court, the European Court of Human Rights. The accession would prove, on the political level, the existence of a continent-wide solidarity in the field of human rights.

In practical terms, the accession will simplify legal procedures. As a matter of fact, the current "route" of a possible victim is quite complicated since, after exhaustion of legal remedies at the national and Community levels, they must then bring a case before the Strasbourg Court, not against the perpetrator of the act concerned (the Union or the Community), but against a Council of Europe member state. The potential condemnation of the state is no guarantee of the remedy of the situation, since it depends on a third party to the case, the European Union. The saga of the right to vote at European elections of the inhabitants of Gibraltar gives a striking illustration of this situation. The lenient intervention of the European Court of Justice was necessary to find a solution that the European institutions had previously failed at reaching.[18] Moreover, since the *Bosphorus* judgment,[19] the future plaintiff has to subtly analyze the protection guaranteed by Community law in order to determine whether or not it is equivalent to that guaranteed by the Convention. Such variables may influence prospective applicants in their decision to refrain from submitting an application, which undermines access to justice. Furthermore, it is quite illogical to join a state as party to the

---

17   See, in particular: Hans Christian Krüger/Jörg Polakiewicz, Propositions pour la création d'un système cohérent de protection des droits de l'homme en Europe, RUDH 13 (2001) 1-4, 1; Report by the Steering Committee for Human Rights (CDDH), Study of Technical and Legal Issues of a Possible EC/EU Accession to the European Convention on Human Rights, DG II(2002)006 of 28 June 2002.

18   ECJ, Grand Chamber, 12 September 2006, Case C-145/04, Spain v. United Kingdom.

19   ECHR, Grand Chamber, 30 June 2005, application no. 45036/98, Bosphorus Hava Yolları Turizm ve Ticaret Anonim Şirketi v. Ireland. See Florence Benoit-Rohmer, À propos de l'arrêt Bosphorus Air Lines: l'adhésion contrainte de l'Union à la Convention, RTDH 2005, 267; Jean Paul Jacqué, L'arrêt Bosphorus, une jurisprudence "So lange II" de la Cour européenne des droits de l'homme?, RTDE 2005, 756.

action for an act it is not responsible for, when the one responsible for it, the Union, cannot be held liable. In this respect, the accession brings some simplification. Finally, it will give Article 1 of the Convention under which contracting stats "shall secure to everyone within their jurisdiction the rights and freedoms [guaranteed in the ECHR" a greater significance by certainly making it applicable to all acts within its scope.

Like the European Constitution, the Lisbon Treaty makes provision for the accession of the Union to the European Convention on Human Rights, but the provisions on the implementation of the accession have been changed. Article 218 TFEU specifies that the Council must reach a unanimous agreement on the accession to the Convention and that this agreement will enter into force after it has been ratified by the member states "in accordance with their respective constitutional requirements", and not by qualified majority. One should not attach too much importance to this modification since it was made to avoid any transfer of competence that would need in certain states, including Denmark, to be approved by referendum, and since it was not driven by any suspicion towards the Convention. In any case, since all member states are party to the Convention, their agreement will be necessary to have the agreement on the accession of the Union ratified by their respective national parliaments. As a consequence, the necessity of a unanimous agreement brings no fundamental change.

2 Terms of Accession

Since the accession in itself is no longer opposed, the terms of its implementation can be discussed. Protocol No 8 clarifies the framework of the accession negotiations. Under Article 1 of the Protocol, the agreement "shall make provision for preserving the specific characteristics of the Union and Union law". The Protocol also requires the implementation of "the mechanisms necessary to ensure that proceedings by non-Member States and individual applications are correctly addressed to Member States and/or the Union as appropriate". In addition, Article 2 specifies that the Union is free to choose which protocols to the European Convention on Human Rights it becomes a party to, but shall in this respect ensure that it does not "affect the situation of Member States".

a Obligation to Preserve the Specificity of the Union

This obligation bears important consequences for the implementation of the review by the Court and for the institutional details of the accession. Considering the sharing of powers between the Union and member states, it must be ensured that all proceedings are made against the entity truly responsible for the infringement. Regarding states, the decision is not easy in cases where Union law gives some discretion to them. In this case, it must be established if the infringement was occasioned by an act laying within these discretionary powers. It would be unacceptable to let the European Court of Human Rights establish this, as it would make it the judge of the division of powers between the Union and its member states. It is therefore necessary to create a system under which an individual can simultaneously start proceedings against the Union and a member state, leaving it to the Union to choose, possibly with the opinion of the Court of Justice of the European Union, who will be the defendant. A similar solution can already be found in Annex IX, Article 6 (2) of the UN Convention on the Law of the Sea.[20]

Another issue is the participation of the Union in the Strasbourg control machinery. Regarding the Court, the specificity would justify the need for a "judge of the Union". Nevertheless, it must be decided whether the person should participate with a right of discussion and vote on all cases or only when the Union is a party to the case. The adequate terms of participation of the Union to the work of the Committee of Ministers must also be found.

It has been suggested to allow the ECJ to refer a question to the European Court of Human Rights for a preliminary ruling. This would not take into account the specificity of the Union, which should, in its sphere of competence, be considered as any other party. Moreover, can one only imagine the length of the proceedings in a case referred to the Court of Justice for a preliminary ruling and in which the Court would itself refer the question to the European Court of Human Rights for a preliminary ruling? Four of five years could be necessary before the national court can decide on the substance of the case. Such a system could deter the claimants, leading to serious issues in terms of uniform application of Community law. The only reasonable solution, because it leaves the individual free to choose, is to allow individual applications after exhaustion of legal remedies at the national level.

b   Respect for the Powers of EU Institutions

This requirement of the Protocol on the accession of the Union to the ECHR aims at preserving the role played by the Court of Justice, which will remain the exclusive reviewer of the legality of Union acts. The Strasbourg judgements will remain declaratory and the institutions of the Union will draw the consequences of a possible sentence.

In addition, and as it vigorously reminded just recently, the Court of Justice of the Union has an exclusive competence to settle disputes between member states on the application of the Treaty. Therefore, these issues should be excluded on the occasion of the accession, to the benefit of the Court of Justice of the Union. This principle is laid out in Article 3 of the Protocol.[21]

c   Commitments Undertaken by Member States and by the Union

Article 2 of the Protocol on the accession of the Union to the ECHR is an attempt at settling the relations between the commitments of the Union and those of the

---

20   The provision lays down that
"Any State Party may request an international organization or its member States which are States Parties for information as to who has responsibility in respect of any specific matter. The organization and the member States concerned shall provide this information. Failure to provide this information within a reasonable time or the provision of contradictory information shall result in joint and several liability."

21   "Nothing in the agreement referred to in Article 1 shall affect Article 344 of the Treaty on the Functioning of the European Union." Under Article 344 TFEU, "member states undertake not to submit a dispute concerning the interpretation or application of the Treaties to any method of settlement other than those provided for therein".

member states, as regards to the Convention.[22] Each must keep control of their own commitments and be free to decide on their significance. The commitments undertaken by the Union shall not affect member states in their area of competence. In other terms, the participation of the Union in a protocol shall not create obligations in the area of competence of a member state that would have chosen not to ratify it, and vice versa.

E   Conclusion

The Lisbon Treaty completes an evolution that started with the first decisions of the Court of Justice on fundamental rights. It shows the transformation of a Community that was first mainly economic into a Union based on shared common values. These values were not absent in the 50s, but, after the failure of the European Political Community, it was politically incorrect to mention them.

Nevertheless, the Lisbon Treaty does more than just to reaffirm pre-existing principles. Through the Fundamental Rights Charter, which is incorporated by way of reference, it gives citizens a list of their rights and settles the issue of the conflicts between EU law and the European Convention on Human Rights, both in their material and procedural aspects. The position given to the Convention attests to the existence of a community that, beyond the 27, stretches to all the members of the Council of Europe. The Convention is the continental common base. In this respect, even though the authors of the Treaty of Lisbon denied for political reasons that they created a constitutional framework, they did constitutional work.

---

22   Article 2 of the Protocol provides:
"The agreement referred to in Article 1 shall ensure that accession of the Union shall not affect the competences of the Union or the powers of its institutions. It shall ensure that nothing therein affects the situation of Member States in relation to the European Convention, in particular in relation to the Protocols thereto, measures taken by Member States derogating from the European Convention in accordance with Article 15 thereof and reservations to the European Convention made by Member States in accordance with Article 57 thereof."

Gerald STABEROCK[*]

Time to Take Stock and Undo the Damage? Reflections on Counter-Terrorism and Human Rights

Table of Contents

Keywords

Human rights, counter-terrorism, accountability, extraordinary renditions, torture, complicity, targeted sanctions, intelligence services, criminal justice system

A   Assessing the Damage

Almost nine years after the terrorist acts of September 11, 2001, the international community has reached a critical turning point in its approach to countering terrorism. The taking of office of a new administration in the United States in early 2009 has raised expectations about a renewal of the U.S. commitment to international law. It raised hopes also globally for integrating human rights law into

---

[*]   The author is Director of the Global Security and Rule of Law Initiative at the International Commission of Jurists (ICJ). The views in this article, however, are expressed in the author's individual capacity and do not necessarily reflect the views of the ICJ or of its Eminent Jurists Panel on Terrorism, Counter-Terrorism and Human Rights.

counter-terrorism and of a review, including in Europe, of counter-terrorism laws and policies adopted since 9/11.

To be clear, terrorism is a real threat in many parts of the world, in particular in many non-Western states. Terrorism and counter-terrorism have a profound impact on societies and on the rule of law. There are no easy solutions. As the Council of Europe Commissioner for Human Rights, Thomas Hammarberg, made clear, however, the tragic mistake after 9/11 was not the determination to respond, but the choice of methods.[1]

No one should underestimate the extent to which core elements of human rights law have been questioned, such as the absolute prohibition of torture and cruel and inhuman or degrading treatment or punishment or the right to due process and fair trial. Indeed, for the first time since World War II, much of the debate focused not on strengthening but on lowering the protective reach of international law. The fact that such challenges have come from liberal democracies, including from European countries, has had knock-on effects in other parts of the world. Counter-terrorism laws have migrated to other jurisdictions, with few safeguards, and the capacities and competencies of security apparatus have been upgraded without ensuring necessary accountability mechanisms. Authoritarian regimes have claimed new legitimacy for repressive laws, such as administrative detention laws, or security and military courts with jurisdiction over civilians and a sub-standard of due process.[2]

If further proof was needed, the report of the Eminent Jurists Panel on Terrorism, Counter-Terrorism and Human Rights, entitled *'Assessing Damage, Urging Action'*, provides evidence as to the extent of the erosion of the human rights framework.[3] In what is arguably the most comprehensive study undertaken so far, an independent panel of jurists commissioned by the International Commission of Jurists (ICJ) examined the impact of counter-terrorism on human rights over a period of three years.[4] The panel conducted a series of sixteen public hearings, similar to parliamentary inquiries, covering more than thirty countries and held extensive consultations with governmental and security officials, the legal community, civil society, victims of terrorist violence and counter-terrorism.[5]

---

1   Thomas Hammarberg, Serious human rights violations in war on terror must be corrected and never repeated, International Rehabilitation Center for Torture Victims (IRCT) Newsletter 2 (March 2008) 2, at 2.
2   Cf. International Commission of Jurists, Eminent Jurist Panel on Terrorism, Counter-Terrorism and Human Rights, Assessing Damage, Urging Action, Geneva, February 2009, http://ejp.icj.org/IMG/EJP-Report.pdf, at 28, 108, 137 (hereinafter: "Assessing Damage (2009)").
3   Assessing Damage (2009), ibid.
4   The panel was chaired by Justice Arthur Chaskalson (South Africa), Mary Robinson (Ireland), Stefan Trechsel (Switzerland), Robert K. Goldman (United States), Georges Abi-Saab (Egypt), Hina Jilani (Pakistan), Vitit Muntharborn (Thailand) and Raul Zaffaroni (Argentina). For more information, see http://ejp.icj.org.
5   Hearings and sub-regional hearings were held in: Australia, Canada, Colombia, East Africa (Uganda, Kenya, Tanzania), the European Union, Israel and the Occupied Palestinian Territory, the Middle East (Egypt, Jordan, Syria and Yemen), North Africa (Algeria, Morocco and Tunisia), Pakistan, the Russian Federation, South Asia (Indonesia, Philippines, Thailand), the Southern cone of Latin America (Argentina, Brazil, Chile, Paraguay and Uruguay), the UK, including a hearing in Northern Ireland on lessons learnt from the past, and the United States of America.

Its report examines the consequences of pursuing counter-terrorism within an over-reaching war paradigm and calls for the repudiation of policies grounded therein. It emphasizes the need to place criminal justice systems at the heart of strategies to prevent and counter terrorism. In this regard it identifies a harmful accountability gap in countering terrorism that has arisen due to the growth of intelligence agency powers without the necessary safeguards and corresponding oversight. It examines critically the scope of intelligence-based 'preventive' counter-terrorism measures, including administrative detention, control orders, national security deportations and the placing of individuals on 'terrorism lists'. It warns of the displacement of ordinary justice systems, increasing secrecy preventing accountability, and the danger of 'temporary' measures becoming permanent features of law in many states. Having seen human rights violations committed with impunity and legal infrastructures being altered in its totality, the report calls for a stocktaking process at the universal, regional and national level to ensure compliance with international law.[6]

B   Taking Stock of Policy Changes in 2009

This article will seek to take stock of progress made in 2009 on critical issues identified by the study of the Eminent Jurists Panel. It will address the relationship of security and human rights (1), assess the integration of human rights into UN responses to terrorism (2), and look at the extent of legal policy change in the United States (3). In addition, it will reflect on systemic challenges, such as intelligence accountability (4) and the central role of a criminal justice approach in countering terrorism (5).

1   Human Rights and Security

Since 2001, there has been a stark refocus towards a state-centered notion of security. On a more positive note, human rights references are now typically added to counter-terrorism resolutions. However, this is rarely translated into the operative part of resolutions and often not reflected in its implementation.[7] It is fair to say that the security-dominated discourse over the last years has diminished consensus on concepts such as of 'comprehensive security' more seriously than such references may suggest.[8]

---

6   Assessing Damage (2009), at 164.
7   See, e.g., UN Security Council Resolution 1456 (2003) of 20 January 2003, UN Doc. S/RES/1456 (2003); UN Security Council Resolution 1624 (2005) of 14 September 2005, UN Doc. S/RES/1624 (2005). The Eminent Jurists Panel, therefore, speaks of human rights being treated as 'add on' to security, Assessing Damage (2009), at 13.
8   The concept of comprehensive security is recognized in particular in the context of the Organization for Security and Cooperation in Europe, in which security includes a human (rights) dimension as part of a positive notion of security, see OSCE Human Dimension Commitments – A Reference Guide, Warsaw 2001, at 2. See also the contributions by Bernhard Knoll/Jens-Hagen Eschenbächer and Christian Strohal, in this volume, at 287 and 297, respectively. The recent example of Sri Lanka may provide an additional challenge, as its military defeat of the LTTE at the expense of serious violations of human rights and humanitarian law, risks being an appealing example of a 'security first' approach for other countries.

The metaphor of a 'balance', too, can falsely present imperatives of security and human rights at opposing ends. Human rights law provides a framework created by states keenly aware of their security needs. It ensures that crisis responses are a continuation and not an abrogation of the rule of law. This is the *rationale* of the system of limitation clauses and – in case of truly exceptional circumstances when the "life of the nation is threatened" – of temporary derogations that are strictly necessary, proportionate and non-discriminatory.[9] As the Eminent Jurists Panel report shows this is not only theoretic. Lessons from past cycles of terrorism and counter-terrorism indicate that respect for human rights law ensures an accountable, viable response to terrorism and that their disregard and the constant lowering of accountability mechanisms has serious long-term consequences for societies.[10] Whatever the level of the threat may be today, a discourse of the exceptional and unprecedented carries inherent dangers for human rights as it all too easily results in equally exceptional and unprecedented responses.

Many of the measures taken today, such as the militarization of justice systems, holding persons without charge or trial, and criminalizing controversial speech, have been tried before. The ordinary justice system exposes conduct as murder and crime. It ensures that terrorists cannot hide behind ideology and present themselves as victims of the state. Relevant for Europe are in particular the experiences in Northern Ireland during the so-called 'Troubles'. Some 'security measures' used by British authorities, such as internment and the so-called 'five (interrogation) techniques' have been recognized as a failure also from a security perspective.[11] Lacking accountability and the arbitrary use of security measures alienated communities creating support to a group of initially marginal importance. Temporary measures also became permanent and over time changed or 'seeped' into legal and institutional cultures. In fact what was meant to be the cure became over time part of the problem. These experiences highlighted in the Eminent Jurists Study should serve as a point of caution also for current approaches to counter radicalization. Indeed, disregard of human rights and a perception of arbitrariness can be one of the most radicalizing factors. A sense of being targeted by counter-terrorism sits deeply within Muslim minority communities also in Europe. The majority population may feel that their 'walk of life' has not been changed as a result of counter-terrorism and that interferences into their liberty are to be accepted. The experience and perception, however, in minority communities tends often to be the opposite. Practices such as racial or ethnic profiling[12], arbitrary or disproportionate stop and searches[13], and the fact

9   Cf. UN Human Rights Committee, General Comment No. 29: States of Emergency (Article 4), UN Doc. CCPR/C/21/Rev.1/Add.11, 31 August 2001.
10   Assessing Damage (2009), at 26 et seq., with a detailed examination of lessons from the past. The panel held hearings on past experiences in Northern Ireland and the Southern cone of South America.
11   Committee on the Administration of Justice, 'The war on terror': lessons from Northern Ireland, Belfast, January 2008; Assessing Damage (2009), at 40 et seq.
12   Special Rapporteur on Human Rights and Counter-Terrorism, Report to the UN Human Rights Council, UN Doc. A/HRC/4/26, 29 January 2007, at 6 et seq.; András László Pap, Ethno-Racial Profiling in Law Enforcement: Concepts and Recommendations, in: Wolfgang Benedek/Wolfram Karl/Anja Mihr/Manfred Nowak (eds.), European Yearbook on Human Rights 2009, Vienna etc. 2009, 285-296.
13   See ECtHR, Judgment of 12 January 2010, Gillan and Quinton v. United Kingdom, Application No. 4158/05.

that a considerable part of Europe's counter-terrorism response was placed into immigration and alien law may have contributed to this perception.[14] It is therefore important from a human rights and security perspective alike to ensure that counter-terrorism strategies integrate – and are complemented by – clear anti-discrimination policies.

More generally, bringing human rights back into counter-terrorism requires an element of 'repair'. Re-affirmative statements by governmental or inter-governmental bodies, that there is no contradiction between security and human rights, and an unequivocal stand on norms, such as the absolute prohibition of torture, and cruel and inhuman or degrading treatment or punishment, help to reestablish consensus on the central importance of human rights.[15] It requires an approach that leaves no ambiguities about the commitment to uphold the universal prohibition of torture and cruel and inhuman or degrading treatment and the obligations flowing from it. It requires speaking out when torture is justified in the name of national security, including by potential allies. In this regard it is regrettable that some European countries have been part of moving the boundaries of the torture prohibition, as they relied on information obtained by torture from abroad or challenged the principle of *non-refoulement* that prevents the transfer of persons when there is a risk of torture or other serious human rights violations. Some of them have been at the forefront of reducing remedies in security deportations, some have argued for 'balancing' the interests of society and against the individual's risk of ill-treatment, or disregarded interim measures by international courts in a number of cases.[16] They advocate at the national and EU level for the use of diplomatic assurances to deport persons when there is real risk of torture or ill-treatment.

This is not to say that there are no genuine challenges for governments when they seek to deport persons on national security grounds but may have insufficient evidence or chose not to disclose intelligence in court. However, universal and regional human rights bodies have all challenged such assurances when there are real risks of torture or other serious human rights violations.[17] The

---

14   Asssessing Damage (2009), at 93 et seq.
15   See also Wilton Park, Conference Report, Terrorism, Security and Human Rights: Opportunities for Policy Change, Report, 2009, at 3, http://www.wiltonpark.org.uk/documents/conferences/WP992/pdfs/WP992.pdf.
16   Assessing Damage (2009), at 100 et seq. Instances of interim measures by the European Court of Human Right being ignored include a series of cases in Italy, see International Commission of Jurists, Submission to the Universal Periodic Review of Italy, 7th Session of the Working Group on the Universal Periodic Review, February 2010, at 2; ECtHR, Al-Sadoon v. United Kingdom, Judgment of 2 March 2010, Application No. 61498/08 which reaffirms the binding nature of interim measures and the principle of *non-refoulement* for extra-territorial transfers.
17   UN High Commissioner for Human Rights, Report on the protection of human rights and fundamental freedoms while countering terrorism, UN Doc. E/CN.4/2006/94, 16 February 2006, paras. 10 et seq. and 34; Report of the Special Rapporteur on torture, and other cruel and inhuman or degrading treatment or punishment, UN Doc. A/60/316, 15 August 2005, para. 51; EU Network of Independent Experts on Fundamental Rights, Opinion No. 3-2006, May 2006; Council of Europe Commissioner for Human Rights, Thomas Hammarberg, Viewpoint: 'The protection against torture must be strengthened', 18 February. See also for the ECtHR, Saadi v. Italy, Grand Chamber, Application No. 37201/06; Rybikin v. Russia, Application No. 8320/04; Ben Khamais v. Italy, Application 2947/06, para. 127; UN Committee against Torture,

Eminent Jurists Panel, with the benefit of examining states from which assurances are sought, concurred, noting that such assurances are problematic from a principled and practical perspective.[18]

Much would be gained by a proper identification of the 'problem'. The problem is not the legal norm that prevents the transfer of persons to torture but it is the systematic practices of torture in the receiving country. International law has instruments that allow much-needed lawful co-operation in counter-terrorism. But as with extradition and mutual legal assistance it is human rights violations and not human rights norms that are the impediments. A refocus on anti-torture policies could address systemic problems, such as the unfettered powers of the military or intelligence. Ironically, the role of these very same institutions has been reinforced by some of the international cooperation and technical assistance provided post 9/11.

2 An Integrated Approach

a Human Rights and the Security Council

Long-term responses to the threat of terrorism should include human rights at all levels, including within the counter-terrorism response of the Security Council. UN human rights experts, such as the Special Rapporteurs on Torture and on Human Rights and Counter-Terrorism and United Nations treaty bodies, have generally stood up to the challenge. Their impact, however, has suffered from a lack of decisive responses by the UN Human Rights Council, the UN's main political body on human rights,[19] and from a lack of integration in the Security Council's response, a driving force in the proliferation of counter-terrorism laws.[20]

The Counter-terrorism Committee (CTC) and its Executive Directorate (CTED) charged with monitoring the implementation of resolutions 1373 and 1624 have over time (very reluctantly) accepted human rights in their terms of references and reporting guidelines. A senior human rights officer was also appointed to the CTED. Recently, the Security Council started to refer also to the General Assembly's Global Counter-Terrorism Strategy, which establishes human rights as a crosscutting issue in all pillars of the UN strategy.[21]

For the first time, there now appears some openness towards a meaningful integration of human rights into the Security Council's work, reflected in pledges for closer cooperation between CTED and the UN High Commissioner for Hu-

Views of 20 May 2005, Agiza v. Sweden, Communication No. 233/2003, UN Doc. CAT/C/34/D/233/2003 (2005) and UN Human Rights Committee, View of 10 November 2006, Alzery v. Sweden, UN Doc. CCPR/C/88/D/1416/2005.
18   Assessing Damage (2009), at 105.
19   On the activities of the UN Human Rights Council in 2009, see the contribution of Theodor Rathgeber, in this volume, at 183.
20   Mainly as a result of UN Security Council Resolution 1373 (2001) of 28 September 2001, UN Doc S/RES/1373 (2001) and UN Security Council Resolution 1624 (2005).
21   UN Global Counter-Terrorism Strategy, General Assembly Resolution 62/272 of 15 September 2008. See also UN Security Council Resolution 1904 (2009) of 15 December 2009, UN Doc. S/RES/1904 (2009).

man Rights[22] and a rare civil society briefing, convened by Mexico, in which the International Commission of Jurists was asked to brief members of the Security Council on the lessons from its Eminent Jurists Panel and the integration of human rights into counter-terrorism.[23]

It will be of great importance to integrate human rights in country assessments, and to include human rights experts in any country visit to avoid that one side of the UN commands the very same laws criticized as incompatible with human rights law by the other. There is equal need for more transparency on the advice provided and some change of perspective: the absence of accountable rule of law compliant institutions impedes effective counter-terrorism often far more than the lack of legislation. Advocating for 'robust' laws without addressing judicial and legal accountability almost inevitably results in an environment prone to abuse. Experience advocates against a 'one-size fits all' approach and advice on legislation should be sensitive to the rule of law realities in the given country. These considerations are also relevant for other organizations that are providing support (or pressure) to the adoption of counter-terrorism legislation, be it bilaterally or through regional or universal assistance, such as the Prevention of Terrorism Branch at the UN Office for Drugs and Crime.

In practice clauses that require states to implement counter-terrorism measures with respect for human rights law, while being important, are alone insufficient to prevent states claiming legitimacy for laws that disrespect those. Some states, also in Europe, for example, went beyond the criminalization of incitement to terrorism required by Resolution 1624 (also beyond the scope of the Council of Europe Convention on the Prevention of Terrorism),[24] and have extended criminal law towards forms of indirect encouragement through glorification, broadly defined provisions of promoting terrorism, apologia and extremism.[25] These provisions have a stifling effect on freedom of expression and on civil society and the media.[26] Human rights bodies have, therefore, recommended that such laws maintain a clearer link between the statement made, the intent to incite and the risk created by such statement.[27] This benchmark should also guide the CTC and lawmakers in Europe to avoid overreaching legislation.

---

22   See the briefing of the UN High Commissioner for Human Rights to the Counter-Terrorism Committee of the Security Council, 29 October 2009, http://www.un.org/sc/ctc/pdf/HC_statement_to_CTC_29_Oct_09.pdf.

23   See International Commission of Jurists (ICJ), Press Release, 30 November 2009, http://www.icj.org.

24   UN Security Council Resolution 1624 (2005), para. 1; see also Article 5 of the Council of Europe Convention on the Prevention of Terrorism requiring the criminalization of public provocation to terrorism.

25   Assessing Damage (2009), at 127 et seq.

26   On the impact of such laws, see ibid.; and Council of Europe/David Banisair, Speaking of Terror, A survey of the effects of counter-terrorism legislation on freedom of the media in Europe, Strasbourg 2008.

27   Report of the Special Rapporteur on Human Rights and Counter-Terrorism, UN Doc. A/HRC/4/26/Add. 1, who suggested to develop jointly good practices for the CTC/CTED. See Assessing Damage (2009), at 132.

b   Reform of the Targeted Sanctions Scheme

The most prominent human rights issue in relation to the Security Council has for
long been the placing of individuals and entities on terrorism lists pursuant to UN
Security Council Resolution 1267.[28] It obliges states, inter alia, to freeze the
named individuals' (and organizations') assets and enforce travel bans.

The list predates 9/11 and refers to "Al Qaeda, Taliban and those associated
with" them but has been understood expansively in its immediate aftermath.[29]
The lack of due process for those listed, usually on the basis of secret intelligence, has put states into a difficult position to comply with their Chapter VII
obligation on the one hand and their international human rights obligations on the
other. A series of incremental reforms established basic administrative fairness,
such as the provision demanding a statement of reasons from the country proposing the addition of an individual to the list, of notification and the ability for
individuals to access a focal point to channel requests for de-listing to the Security Council, and in 2008 an internal review of names contained on the listed.[30]

These changes did not, however, address the heart of the problem, which is
the lack of an effective remedy and the lack of clear time-limits and measures to
ensure proportionality. Decisions of the European Court of Justice in 2008 and
2009 that held that – for the purposes of implementation of Security Council
Resolutions by the EU – full compliance with fundamental rights had to be ensured, increased the pressure for reforms at the UN level.[31] These decisions
overruled the Court of First Instance that had considered that targeted sanctions
could only be reviewed for violations of *ius cogens* rights, leaving those affected
practically without recourse.[32] The UN Human Rights Committee[33] and national
courts, such as in Canada, describing the Kafkaesque situation of those listed,
added significantly to this pressure.[34]

28   UN Security Council Resolution 1267 (1999) of 15 October 1999, UN Doc.
      S/RES/1267 (1999). For more information on the "1267 Committee", see http://www.
      un.org/sc/committees/1267/index.shtml.
29   Thomas Biersteker/Sue Eckert, Addressing Challenges to Targeted Sanctions: An
      Update of the "Watson Report", HEI Geneva/Watson Institute, Providence 2009.
30   See UN Security Council Resolution 1617 (2005), UN Doc. S/RES/1617 (2005); UN
      Security Council Resolution 1735 (2006), UN Doc. S/RES/1735 (2006); UN Security
      Council Resolution 1822 (2008), UN Doc. S/RES/1822 (2008). See George A. Lopez/
      David Cortright/Alistair Millar/Linda Gerber-Stellingwerf, Overdue Process: Protecting
      Human Rights while Sanctioning Alleged Terrorists, A report to Cordaid from the Fourth
      Freedom Forum and Kroc Institute for International Peace Studies at the University of
      Notre Dame, April 2009, http://www.fourthfreedom.org/pdf/Overdue_process.pdf.
31   Court of Justice of the European Communities, Judgment of 3 September 2008, Kadi
      and Al Barakat Foundation v. the Council of the European Union; Joint cases
      C-402/05 P and C-415/05. Court of First Instance of the European Communities,
      Judgment of 9 June 2009, Case T-318/01, Omar Mohammed Othman v. Council and
      Commission.
32   European Court of Justice, Court of First Instance, Judgment of 21 September 2005,
      Kadi and Yusuf v. The Council of the European Union, Cases T-315/01 and T-306/01.
33   UN Human Rights Committee, Views of 9 December 2008, Sayadi and Vinck v.
      Belgium, UN Doc. CCPR/C/94/D01472/2006, No. 1472/2006.
34   Federal Court of Canada, Abdelrazik v. Minister of Foreign Affairs, (2009) FC 580,
      4 June 2009, para. 51. The case concerned a Canadian citizen prevented from return-
      ing to Canada from its Embassy in Sudan as a result of the travel ban resulting from

Progress was finally made in 2009, as SC resolution 1904 creates the Office of the Ombudsperson to assist the Sanctions Committee of the Security Council in reviewing de-listing requests of individuals or entities.[35] The Ombudsperson is to be appointed by the Secretary General and described as an eminent person with expertise, inter alia, on human rights. This is significant as it establishes for the first time a mechanism that (at least indirectly) challenges decisions of the Security Council itself, and that, if successful, may over time become an important precedent.

The practical effect, however, remains to be seen. Much will depend on the ability of the appointee to conduct independent reviews and the extent of access to confidential information. The ability to make reasoned opinions and the degree to which those will be made public would be clear benchmarks. Delisting will remain difficult, as it still requires a decision by consensus and thus allows all Security Council members, and not only the Permanent members, to wield a veto power. Resolution 1904 (2009) avoids any language that suggests the Ombudsperson review might amount to a judicial control or be a quasi-judicial mechanism.[36] Despite its potential, it will thus be insufficient to ensure full compliance with the right to remedy under international law.

It is worth recalling, that other national and regional lists, based on resolution 1373 raise similar human rights concerns.[37] In a recent ruling by the UK Supreme Court, the lack of judicial control, including of the new Ombudsperson process, was specifically noted in orders quashing the domestic implementation of financial sanctions under both 1267 and 1373.[38] In September 2009, the European Court of First Instance, too, annulled the designation of a litigant under the EU's own lists because it was not grounded on a decision by a "competent authority".[39]

So far legal challenges against listings have succeeded on procedural grounds and focused on elements of due process. The next generation of cases is likely to challenge directly the quality of the evidence and question the proportionality of such measures. Being a "designated terrorist supporter" is an extremely grave interference with the right to private life and a person's reputation, but also their right to property and economic, social and cultural rights. Such designations do not only lead to a seizure of proceeds of potentially illicit gains – known from organized crime statutes – but also future gains with certain humanitarian exceptions. While nominally preventive such measures are tantamount to

---

his inclusion on the consolidated list (The judgment is available at http://v1.theglobeandmail.com/v5/content/features/PDFs/sudan.pdf).

35   Security Council Resolution 1904 (2009), of 17 December 2009, para. 20 et seq.

36   For details on the procedures see Security Council Resolution 1904 (2009), op. cit., Annex II.

37   Security Council Resolution 1373 (2001), op. cit., para. 1 (c), requires the freezing of funds and financial assests of person who commit, or attempt to commit, terrorist acts or participate in or facilitate the commission of terrorist acts, and has been used as legal basis for national terrorism lists.

38   HM Treasury v. Mahammed Jabar Ahmed, (2010) UKSC 2, per Lord Hope, para. 78, per Lord Phillips, para. 149.

39   Court of First Instance of the European Communities, judgment of 30 September 2009, Case T-341/07, Jose Maria Sisson v. Council of the European Union, in which the Court considered that a refugee board's decisions would not satisfy the requirements of a "competent national authority" under Article 2 (3) of Regulation No. 2580/2001 and Article 1 (4) of Common Position 2001/931.

punitive measures. The suggestion of a potentially indefinite designation of an individual (more so than organizations) as international supporter of terrorism (on the basis of mere intelligence) is irreconcilable with the rule of law and constitutes a disguised derogation of human rights law.

3   Continuity of, and Departures from, the 'War Paradigm'

a   Policy Change

The adoption of three executive decrees by President Obama on his first day in office and the unequivocal affirmation that there was no inherent contradiction in protecting security and upholding the rule of law were a recognition that the world's superpower had lost its moral (and legal) compass. These measures promised an end to torture, and cruel and inhuman or degrading treatment and committed the President to the closure of the US detention facility in Guantána-mo Bay within a year.[40] Trials by military commissions were suspended pending review on how to try terrorism suspects in the future and a task force was to study future detention policies. To the United States and the international community, the executive orders represented an element of 'catharsis' not to be underestimated.

The Eminent Jurists Panel in its analysis addressed the "war paradigm" – current during the Bush administration – as a legal construct that conflated acts of terrorism with war – a concept that it found not to have gained support globally – and as a national security doctrine akin to those of the military dictatorships of Latin America in the 1970s and 1980s.[41] Similar to the "war on terror" discourse the national security doctrine was based, philosophically, on an existential fight between evil and good, against an unusual irregular enemy, to be defeated by the military by whatever means necessary.[42] The new US administration has largely avoided the aggressive "war on terror" rhetoric though President Obama has said, for example, in his Inaugural Address, that "our nation is at war against a far-reaching network of violence and hatred", referring to Al Qaida. The administration, however, regularly underlines its commitment to the rule of law and has taken steps to end extra-legal policies, such as torture and 'extra-ordinary' renditions.[43] This indicates an important departure from the war paradigm as an aggressive national security doctrine.

b   Entrenchment of Legal Policies

The situation is very different when it comes to the continuation of legal policies. It appears that forms of renditions are to continue, and short-term detention by

---

40   The White House, Executive Order: Ensuring Lawful Interrogations, 22 January 2009, http://www.whitehouse.gov/the_press_office/EnsuringLawfulInterrogations.
41   Assessing Damage (2009), at 49-64.
42   Assessing Damage (2009), at 37-38, 65-66.
43   Statement to Employees by Director of the Central Intelligence Agency Leon E. Panetta on the CIA's Interrogation Policy and Contracts, 9 April 2009, https://www.cia.gov/news-information/press-releases-statements/directors-statement-interrogation-policy-contracts.html.

the CIA may still be possible.[44] Interrogations under the Army Field Manual retain techniques that raise concerns under the prohibition of cruel and inhuman or degrading treatment and laws, such as the Military Commissions Act, retain a narrow definition of torture, and cruel and inhuman or degrading treatment, and cut remedies regarding treatment and transfer of detainees.[45] By the end of 2009, the new US administration delayed the closure of the detention facility at Guantánamo Bay without a fixed date. It also suspended the return of detainees of Yemeni origin and continues to oppose resettlement of detainees into the United States even where they are cleared for release (in some cases for years) but cannot be returned to their home countries for fear of torture or persecution.[46]

More than the existence of a facility at Guantánamo Bay, it is the continuation of the legal regime associated with it that raises human rights concerns. The US administration has announced that it would continue to detain persons without charge or trial.[47] It is open whether this will be limited to detention at Guantánamo Bay and possibly other oversees locations or whether it will seek general legislation on administrative detention. While it established new procedures for those detained in Bagram airbase in Afghanistan, those processes provide less guarantees than to those held at Guantánamo Bay, and the administration seeks to prevent such detentions from judicial scrutiny. This is also problematic, as a good number of those detained were not arrested in connection with the actual armed conflict in Afghanistan.[48] It has also continued to litigate any case up to the highest instance – as a result of which – there has not been a single detainee to the authors' knowledge being freed on the basis of a final court order.[49]

---

44 See also regarding possible forms of transfer: Department of Justice, Press Release, Special Task Force on Interrogations and Transfer Policies, Recommendations to the President, 24 August 2009. Joint study on global practices in relation to secret detention in the context of countering terrorism of the Special Rapporteur on the promotion and protection of human rights and fundamental freedoms while countering terrorism, the Special Rapporteur on torture and other cruel, inhuman or degrading treatment or punishment, the Working Group on Arbitrary Detention and the Working Group on Enforced or Involuntary Disappearances, Advance unedited version, A/HRC/13/42, 26 January 2010, section 2 (g) (hereinafter: "Joint Study on Secret Detention" 2010).

45 Army Field Manual, Human Intelligence Collector Operation, FM2-22.3 (FF 34-52), September 2006, Appendix M, paras. M-1, M-30, containing inter alia regimes of isolation and sleep deprivations.

46 See the governments brief in Jamal Kiyemba, et al. v. Barack H. Obama, Supreme Court, No. 08-1234. Also Brief of Amici Curiae Amnesty International, International Commission of Jurists, Human Rights Watch in Support of Petitioners, http://www.icj.org/IMG/08-1234_Amicus_Brief.pdf.

47 Remark by President Obama at the National Archives, 21 May 2009.

48 The government appealed the ruling in Fadi Al-Maqaleh et al. v. Robert Gates of the US District Court for the District of Columbia that held that non-Afghan detainees held at Bagram could invoke habeas corpus in the US courts. These detainees had been captured outside of Afghanistan and thus could not legitimately be deprived of the right to habeas corpus review by moving them to the battlefield for the purposes of detention.

49 Court procedings have, however, been instrumental in bringing to light individual cases and the adminsitration has released or transfered individuals while cases were litigated, especially when superior courts decisions were imminent.

To the extent that a criminal justice approach is taken, the US administration has expressed a preference for civilian trials but decided to retain military commissions and Congress is, at the time of writing, threatening to introduce legislation preventing any trial of 'unprivileged belligerents' before ordinary federal courts.[50] While the Military Commissions Act was amended to improve some procedural rules, such as the exclusion of statements obtained through cruel, inhuman or degrading treatment,[51] other defects such as its limited independence and its applicability to civilians as understood in international law remain. The resurrection of military commissions is disappointing in light of their inability to proceed with cases over years and will inevitably fail to restore confidence into the fairness of trials, which would be so much needed in light of the legacy of abuse. Other difficulties may result from it, such as potential difficulties for European countries to provide mutual legal assistance.

Both the continuation of detention without charge and military commission trials, are not only incompatible with human rights law,[52] they are also grounded in an expansive interpretation of the new notion of an 'unprivileged enemy belligerent' which replaced the designation as 'enemy combatant'. It continues to include not only those who directly participate in hostilities but also any individual that purposefully and materially supported hostilities against the United States or its coalition partners – without clearly identifiable limit as to the location of the support provided.[53]

c   Unaddressed Impunity

One year after the taking of office of the new administration, impunity for serious human rights violations and crimes under international law, including torture and enforced disappearances, persists. International law entails, among other duties, the positive obligation to conduct independent investigations with the aim of bringing those responsible to justice, and to provide remedy and reparation to victims.

An investigation by a federal prosecutor has been initiated, but it is has been made clear that it will not result in prosecutions of those who acted within the legal advice provided in a series of infamous 'torture memos'.[54] A recent decision of the Department of Justice overruled earlier findings of its ethics committee that had recommended disciplinary actions against the legal architects of the interrogation policy.[55] These legal memoranda had argued for a definition of torture rendering it meaningless and authorized enhanced interrogation techniques that

---

50   Remark by President Obama at the National Archives, 21 May 2009.
51   House of Representatives, National Defense Authorization Act for Fiscal Year 2010, Report 11-228.
52   On military trials of civilians and the deficiencies of the military commissions system, see Assessing Damage (2009), at 60-61 and 136. On administrative detention outside a bona fide declared state of emergency, see ibid. at 119-20.
53   Statement by the Department of Justice, March 2009. See the 2009 Military Commissions Act, § 248a (6), which includes "anybody who has purposefully and materially supported hostilities against the United States or its coalition partners".
54   Statement of Attorney General Eric Holder regarding a Preliminary Review into the Interrogation of Certain Detainees, 24 August 2009, http://www.justice.gov/ag.
55   See US House of Representatives, Committee on the Judiciary, DOJ Report on Bush Administration Interrogation Memos and Related Documents http://judiciary.house.gov/issues/issues_OPRReport.html.

clearly included treatment that constitutes torture and cruel, inhuman or degrading treatment.[56] Rather than misguided legal advice they were part of a strategy that sought to immunize against possible future legal challenges.[57]

The absence of criminal accountability is matched with a lack of effective civil remedies and reparation for victims of serious human rights violations. Despite some policy revisions on the scope of the state secrets privilege that had prevented a number of legal challenges to succeed, none of the remedies have been successful so far, nor was there any reparation or public apologies in even well documented cases of abuse.[58] A closer analysis of the ongoing litigation is striking as it reveals limited if any evidence of a policy shift. The US administration continues to appeal progressive rulings that set limits to the scope of state secrets privileges and much like its predecessor it invokes national security and war powers prerogatives to prevent access to civil remedies.[59] Courts, too, so far have remained largely deferential to the executive in accepting assertions of special factors precluding remedies, including the protection of national security and foreign relations, in cases involving civil damages for torture and prolonged arbitrary detention.[60] This confirms a broader global experience that framing counter-terrorism as armed conflict or war regularly creates an environment in which courts tends to be more deferential to claims of the executive.

Addressing gross violations of human rights and crimes under international law may not be an easy task and the attention given to the United States should not prevent us from addressing other countries in which torture and enforced disappearances are committed with impunity. However, the US policy was unique, amongst others because of its planned nature and distorted legal justifi-

---

56 See in this regard, Sir Nigel Rodley, Absolute Means Absolute, in: Wolfgang Kaleck/ Michael Ratner/Tobias Singelnstein/Peter Weiss (eds.), Prosecuting International Human Rights Crimes (2007), at 185 et seq.; For a frightening example of a legal authorization of interrogation techniques that constitute torture and cruel or inhuman or degrading treatment as understood under universal human rights law, see Department of Justice, Office of Legal Counsel, Memorandum for John Rizzo, Acting General Counsel of the Central Intelligence Agency, Interrogations of al Qaeda Operative, 1 August 2002.

57 Philip Sands, Torture Team, Deception, Cruelty and the Compromise of Law, London 2009; Jane Mayer, The Dark Side: The Inside Story of How The War on Terror Turned into a War on American Ideals, New York 2008; Karen J. Greenberg/Joshua L. Dratel (eds.), The Torture Papers, Cambridge 2005.

58 On the State Secrets Doctrine, see White House, Executive Order, Classified National Security Information, 29 December 2009. On different impediments to accountability, see also Assessing Damage (2009), at 85 et seq.

59 For example, the administrations appealed the decision of Court of Appeals in Mohamed v. Jeppesen Dataplan, Inc., 579 F.3d 943 (9th Cir. 2009), in June 2009 requesting a rare en banc hearing to reconsider the Court of Appeals ruling that had limited the state secrets privilege to an evidentiary principle. The administration's brief does not in any way signify a change of legal position with regard to invoking state secrecy (The case concerns civil damages for complicity in extra-ordinary renditions). See also the recent amicus brief filed by the administration in Padilla et al. v. John Yoo, US Court of Appeals for the Ninth Circuit, No. 09-16478, arguing that special factors counsel against a civil remedy against John Yoo as the detention and treatment as enemy combatant implicates war powers and matters of national security.

60 See, for example Arar v. Ashcroft, 585 F.3d 559, 574-82 (2nd Cir. 2009); Rasul v. Myers, 563 F.3d 527, 532 n. 5 (D.C. Cir. 2009); Al-Zahrani v. Rumsfeld, 2010 WL 535136 at 9-10 (D.D.C. Feb. 16, 2010).

cation. The Bush administration's euphemistic argument of not endorsing torture while constructing a policy that formalizes nothing else but torture and/or other equally prohibited cruel, inhuman or degrading treatment or punishment and an acknowledged policy of secret detention, which included placing individuals outside the protection of the law – thus constituting the crime of enforced disappearances – is indeed of special character. The nature of these policies and their justification as legal requires them not only to be ended but even more so to be denounced and qualified in legal processes as criminal and as grave violation of the law to prevent a future return of such policies.

The US is facing a 'democratic' change in governance – different to overcoming dictatorships or legacies of apartheid – and has all the tools at its disposal to address criminal activity – including by government officials. If impunity continues as the administration moves out of the 'war paradigm' it does damage to yet another foundation of human rights law with consequences far beyond the US alone.

4   Ensuring Intelligence Accountability

One of the most difficult and systemic challenges for the protection of human rights to be addressed in counter-terrorism is intelligence accountability. There is clear evidence of a growing significance accorded to intelligence and intelligence cooperation, and of a paradigm shift away from a criminal justice model towards a preventive intelligence-driven response to terrorism.[61] It is manifested in increasing intelligence collection and sharing with limited thresholds, reduced (judicial) safeguards,[62] and the emergence, especially in Europe, of intelligence-based administrative measures with limited due process guarantees, such as deportations, forms of administrative controls or the freezing of funds.[63] In other states, security services have displaced the ordinary justice and law enforcement structures, often resulting in arbitrary detention, torture, cruel and inhuman or degrading treatment or enforced disappearances and manifestly unfair trials.[64] In countries with a weak rule of law tradition, the limited safeguards that may exist regularly fail when those security services are involved. Pressure by Western states to upgrade the security apparatus can also affect transition processes and result in anxieties about a return of powers that had been abused in the past.[65]

In other words, intelligence plays a crucial role in preventing terrorism, amongst others in analyzing and identifying threats, in leading law enforcement to prevent and prosecute terrorist acts. Intelligence cooperation is undoubtedly required to tackle transnational threats, which in turn requires trust and confidence between services. At the same time, intelligence service have to be accountable under human rights law and the legal framework governing their activities must contain effective controls and safeguards to prevent abuse.

---

61   Assessing Damage (2009), at 67 et seq.
62   See Special Rapporteur on Human Rights and Counter-Terrorism, Privacy report, UN Doc. A/HRC/13/37, 28 December 2009.
63   Assessing Damage (2009), at 91 et seq.
64   Assessing Damage (2009), at 73-90; Special Rapporteur on Human Rights and Counter-Terrorism, Intelligence Report, UN Doc. A/HRC/10/3; Joint Study on Secret Detention (2009).
65   See, for examples, Assessing Damage (2009), at 75, with references on intelligence reforms in Indonesia.

a   Addressing Complicity

Issues of intelligence accountability have been raised in Europe notably in regard to allegations of complicity with the US system of extraordinary renditions and secret detention. While public attention has dissipated, new details emerge about the extent of engagement of European states in such practices, such as revelations about secret detention facilities in Lithuania.[66] Allegations of complicity into torture and arbitrary detention also came to the fore in relation to other countries, such as a good number of cases in which UK officials are alleged to have been involved in abuse in Pakistan, raising calls for a broader inquiry into the nature of intelligence cooperation.[67] A global study on secret detention by four UN human rights experts released in December 2009 illustrates the global dimension of secret detention.[68] It confirms the need for independent investigations and a reform of the "enabling legal framework".[69]

Despite inquiries by the European Union and the Council of Europe and some national parliaments there have been only a handful of criminal investigations and only a few instances of institutional reforms.[70] Much of the response by governments tries to suggest that incidents of cooperation with abusive foreign services or with the US system of renditions were isolated. This appears doubtful taken that US extraordinary renditions and secret detention were based on a government policy and not on individual excesses of intelligence services. It also appears clear that intelligence contacts are usually more than singular events and usually based on continuous cooperation out of mutual interest.

The notion of complicity has many facets and is even more difficult to prove in an environment of secrecy maintained by two or more intelligence services.[71]

---

66   A recent parliamentary inquiry in Lithuania confirmed that secret detention facilities were provided to the US. A criminal investigation is now required to identify concrete cases of secret detention. Information also confirms that secret detention sides were located in Poland and a limited investigation is said to be underway.

67   See United Kingdom, Joint Committee on Human Rights, Allegations of UK Complicity in Torture, Twenty-third Report of Session, 2008-09, 21 July 2009.

68   Joint Study on Secret Detention (2009).

69   Ibid., at 162 et seq.; Assessing Damage (2009), at 74, 89, recommending that intelligence agencies should not have arrest and detention powers.

70   Council of Europe Parliamentary Assembly, Committee on Legal Affairs and Human Rights, Rapporteur Dick Marty, Alleged secret detentions and unlawful inter-state transfers involving Council of Europe member states (hereinafter: "2006 Marty Report"), Council of Europe Doc. 10957, 12 June 2006; Council of Europe Parliamentary Assembly, Committee on Legal Affairs and Human Rights, Rapporteur Dick Marty, Secret Detentions and illegal transfers of detainees involving Council of Europe member states: Second Report (hereinafter: "2007 Marty Report"), Council of Europe Doc. 11302 rev., 11 June 2007. See also, Report of the Temporary Committee on the alleged use of European countries by the CIA for the transportation and illegal detention of prisoners (2006/2200 (INI)), Rapporteur Claudio Fava, A6-9999/2007, European Parliament, Resolution on the alleged use of European countries by the CIA for the transportation and illegal detention of prisoners, P6 TA PROV (2007) 0032.

71   Complicity can be understood as a criminal law concept under domestic or international law, as contained for example in Article 4 of the Convention against Torture, or in the Rome Statute or the ICTY Statute. In addition, human rights treaties define when a state engages responsibility by participating in violations by agents of another state and general rules on state responsibility also help to identify when a state

Accountability for human rights violations is further complicated by the concept of 'plausible deniability' and the fact that intelligence is shared on the condition not to be exposed in legal processes. Where legal remedies are used, state secrets privileges and similar doctrines have frustrated the right to remedy and reparation. It is thus important that States establish an effective and clear regulatory framework and guidelines that prevent intelligence officers from taking part in operations that may establish the responsibility of the state for violation of human rights or incur individual criminal responsibility for aiding, assisting or being complicit in crimes under international law, such as torture.[72]

There are various forms in which a State may incur responsibility for participation or complicity in serious human rights violations. State responsibility, for example, can be triggered through interrogations or interviews of persons held by another state where the state knew or ought to have known that the person was facing a real risk of torture or other human rights violations.[73] States have also passed on information or sent questions to another state knowing or ought to have known that there were real risks that such information results in torture or cruel, inhuman or degrading treatment or arbitrary detention.[74] The receipt of information obtained by torture has been particularly problematic, as states claim that they are entitled to use such information for 'operational purposes'. A number of authoritative reports have suggested that especially when information exchange is continuous or solicited, it engages the responsibility of the state.[75] The principles of state responsibility also provide that a state may be responsible where information is shared in the knowledge, including arguably constructive knowledge ('ought to have known') that it has been obtained or is likely to result in torture or other serious human rights violations. The Eminent Jurists Panel report highlighted, that regular exchange of illicit information creates a market, in which the 'consumer' of such information 'encourages' such practices, or 'in the language of criminal law where States are aiding and abetting torture or other serious human rights violations of other states'.[76]

In terms of prosecutions, the only case that resulted in convictions so far is the Abu Omar case, in which CIA officials were convicted in 2009 in *absentia* for the kidnapping, of Omar, in the streets of Milan and his subsequent rendition to Egypt. The investigation revealed evidence – much of which is in the public domain – of involvement and knowledge of the Italian Military Intelligence Services. The case is an illustration of some of the challenges prosecutors may face when investigating crimes committed by the intelligence community. The Italian government decided to invoke extensive state secrecy claims leading to the acquittal of all Italian intelligence officers. In addition, instead of supporting the investigation of a serious crime extradition requests were not transmitted to the US without

---

is participating in a wrongful act of another state, including by aiding and abetting, and when recognizing as lawful a situation resulting from ius cogens violations (Articles 16, 40, 41 ILC Rules on State Responsibility).

72 See recommendation of the Eminent Jurists Panel in Assessing Damage (2009), at 90.
73 Special Rapporteur on Human Rights and Counter-Terrorism, Intelligence Report, 4 February 2009, UN Doc. A/HRC/10/3, para. 55 et seq.
74 Ibid.
75 Ibid.; Assessing Damage (2009), at 84 et seq.; United Kingdom, Joint Committee on Human Rights, Allegations of UK Complicity in Torture, Twenty-third Report of Session 2008-09, 21 July 2009.
76 Assessing Damage (2009), at 85.

any reasons given to the prosecution. In Germany, too, the investigation into the abduction of German citizen Khalid Al Masri in Macedonia and his subsequent extraordinary rendition to US detention in Afghanistan was hampered by the decision of the German authorities not to submit extradition requests to the United States.[77]

Similarly, secrecy and the interest in maintaining intelligence cooperation continue to be invoked to prevent accountability. In a series of cases in the United Kingdom, the authorities seek to prevent disclosure of UK involvement into torture and other serious abuse by claiming that such disclosure would threaten intelligence cooperation with the United States in the future.[78] The 'irony' of such claims appears to be, that both sides involved in alleged crimes under international law, such as torture, have an equal obligation to investigate wrongdoing and to provide effective remedies and eventually reparation.

The difficulties in ensuring accountability through the legal process reveals a need to ensure that state secrets and other national doctrines cannot be invoked in ways that prevent disclosure of crimes under international law and responsibility for serious human rights violations.[79] State secrecy provisions should be revised, taking into account states' positive obligation to investigate serious human rights violations and complicity in international crimes. This requires independent mechanism to scrutinize information that is claimed to be secret. Similarly, the reluctance to process extraditions requests in such cases, even in countries where this falls into the political prerogative, sits uneasily with states positive obligation to investigate and to provide remedies and reparation.

b   Standards for Intelligence Accountability

European countries have some of the most advanced intelligence oversight structures. Yet, none of these mechanisms appears to have rung the alarm bells over patterns of complicity in serious human rights violations in the name of counter-terrorism. It was left to individual journalists and a few principled prosecutors to do so. This factor alone should be sufficient reason to assess and review the adequacy of existing oversight arrangements.

Most of the existing oversight is the response to past abuse of intelligence powers. It often came about as a result of independent review commissions that inquired into violations of the law and made recommendations about needed institutional and legal changes. The Arar Inquiry in Canada, which assessed the role of Canadian officials in the rendition of its citizen to Syria, is one of the rare examples of such processes following recent revelations and should be an example to be followed in Europe.[80]

There is obviously no single model of oversight that secures human rights and respect for the rule of law. It is the combination of sufficiently resourced internal and external mechanisms, including parliamentary oversight, inspector

---

77   Spiegel, Germany Drops Pursuit of CIA Kidnappers, 24 September 2007. An appeal against this decision is pending.

78   R (Binyam Mohammed) v. Secretary of State for Foreign and Commonwealth Affairs [2009] EWHC 2973 (Admin); R (Binyam Mohammed) v. Secretary of State for Foreign and Commonwealth Affairs [2009] WEHC 2549 (Admin).

79   Assessing Damage (2009), at 90.

80   Canadian Commission of Inquiry into Actions of Canadian Officials relating to Maher Arar, 12 December 2006, www.ararcommission.ca.

generals or ombudsman offices, and judicial controls that can ensure account-ability.[81] What appears to be central, however, is that oversight mechanisms have a mandate that includes respect for human rights law and extends to inter-national cooperation. As there is increasing cooperation amongst intelligence agencies, it may also be worth exploring new ground in allowing for some ex-changes between oversight mechanisms of friendly countries.[82] Research also indicates the need that military intelligence is made subject to civilian oversight and that there are complaint procedures and protection for whistleblowers.[83]

There have been a number of calls for international guidelines to clarify legal standards applicable to the intelligence community and to define principles of effective oversight.[84] Some important ground was made in this direction in 2009 as the UN Human Rights Council requested a compilation of good practices on legal and institutional mechanism of intelligence accountability.[85] The study, which is expected in 2010, should provide further clarity and a nucleus for future principles on intelligence accountability, similar to those existing for other actors, such as law enforcement, prosecutors or prison officials, judges or lawyers.

5   Primacy of the Criminal Justice System

Acts of terrorism are criminal acts and the primacy of the criminal justice re-sponse is therefore vital for a viable counter-terrorism strategy.

States often resort, partially as a result of a perceived weakness, corruption and length of the ordinary justice system, to special state security and/or military courts. It would be important to strengthen regular justice systems and support a strong rule of law-compliant law enforcement and legal system instead.[86] In fact one of the consequences from the Eminent Jurists Study is that building justice systems should be a prime global objective of the international community.

In a similar vein, it is an increasing trend in Europe, to establish a variety of preventive or administrative legal responses to terrorism – parallel to criminal sanctions – that are based on secret intelligence information that the person concerned can hardly see or contest.[87] These may include preventive detention, control orders and national security deportation. There appears little progress in this area over 2009.

---

81   Assessing Damage (2009), at 90.
82   Special Rapporteur, Intelligence Report, 4 February 2009, UN Doc A/HRC/10/3, para. 50.
83   2007 Marty Report, paras. 126-127, 197-200. There have also been increasing reports of intelligence surveillance of journalists reporting alleged wrongdoing by se-cret services, see Council of Europe/David Banisair, Speaking of Terror (2008).
84   Council of Europe, Parliamentary Assembly, Committee of Ministers, Secret deten-tions and illegal transfers of detainees involving Council of Europe Member States: Second Report – Recommendation 1801 (2007), Reply from the Committee of Minis-ters, adopted on 16 January 2008, Doc. 11493, 19 January 2008; Special Rappor-teur on Human Rights and Counter-Terrorism, Intelligence Report, para. 78; Assess-ing Damage (2009), at 91.
85   UN Human Rights Council, Resolution 10/15 of 20 March 2009, para. 12.
86   Assessing Damage (2009), at 165.
87   Ibid., at 94 et seq.

Without going into details about problems associated with each of these measures,[88] what is striking is that they should not be viewed as being a more convenient alternative to criminal prosecutions. Many of these schemes severely impact the lives of individuals, often more than criminal sanctions.[89] The example of being placed on terrorist lists has been mentioned, but control orders as in the United Kingdom are of such severity that they appear to be a de facto emergency measure making a normal life impossible. National security-motivated removals to countries in which a person may never have lived or may risk ill-treatment or torture are further illustrations of this point.

Such measures are based on intelligence with limited due process guarantees, as highlighted in the report of the Eminent Jurists Panel. In 2009, both the European Court of Human Rights,[90] in relation to administrative detention in the UK, and the House of Lords,[91] in relation to UK control orders, have set standards on the due process to be met, and require at the least that the affected person has sufficient information about the allegations to allow a meaningful defense. Disclosure to a security cleared advocate alone who is not allowed to communicate with the subject of such orders was not considered to be sufficient protection in these cases. An additional typical challenge yet to be addressed in such cases is the duration of nominally 'preventive measures'. Arguably, over time intelligence needs to be turned into evidence if so-called preventive mechanisms are meant to be proportionate and avoid being a disguised derogation of human rights law outside a genuine state of emergency.

Finally, from a policy perspective, preventive measures not only impact the individual concerned. They are often perceived as being targeted at a particular community, risking alienation of communities.[92] Prevention needs to be understood holistically, including the protection of human rights and the prevention of alienation.

C   Conclusions

The year 2009 has seen important developments and the new US administration brought a much-needed change in atmosphere in the global debate on terrorism. The establishment of an Ombudsperson at the Security Council may not go all the way to secure full compliance with human rights law but has been more progress than expected even by most insiders.

This new environment has, however, not yet been translated globally into decisive legal reforms on the domestic level. In Europe, too, the realization that it has been part of a global erosion of human rights is often absent. In particular there appears little awareness that counter-terrorism laws may well have, unintended, long-term consequences. Some of those may only be fully grasped through a review of the implications of the measures adopted in their totality. It is

---

88   Ibid., at 118-122.
89   Ibid., at 92.
90   ECtHR (Grand Chamber), A. v. UK, judgment of 19 February 2009, Application No. 3455/05.
91   House of Lords, Secretary of State for the Home Department v. AF, (2009) UKHL 28 Judgment of 10 June 2009.
92   Assessing Damage (2009), at 91 et seq.

all too natural for any executive in times of crisis to opt in case of doubt for over-inclusion rather than the opposite. Internal and external processes that review the impact of laws are therefore logical to refine policies. Independent impact assessments including on the combined effect of laws are required to prevent the sliding expansion and seepage of special powers. The need for review to prevent the 'normalization of the exceptional' is indeed one of the most important conclusions of the global study of the Eminent Jurists Panel. The adoption of the Lisbon Treaty may provide new opportunities, including through the extension of community law to the area of justice and home affairs, and the broadened mandate of the Fundamental Rights Agency of the EU to conduct thorough studies on the impact of legislation.

The continuation of administrative detention and military commissions in the US is an example of an entrenchment of laws that in addition makes universal human rights advocacy more difficult vis-à-vis those states who have conveniently presented Western approaches as a recognition of their own long-standing security laws. It is also clear that changing the discourse in the US, in which senior former officials continue to publicly justify torture, will be a longer-term challenge. Progress made so far may not necessarily be irreversible.

This makes advocacy, and a clear and principled position of European partners, even more important. Europe can provide more help in the resettlement of detainees to make the closure of Guantánamo Bay possible.[93] However, it was never really the facility in Guantánamo Bay, but the legal regime of detention that was in need of abolition. Silence and complacency towards the continuation of laws and policies, such as military trials for civilians, potentially indefinite administrative detention and most of all impunity for torture and enforced disappearances, however, is not acceptable wherever these practices take place. Not challenging these practices also risks leaving the ground exclusively to those in the United States who aggressively advocate the return of the Bush era 'war on terror' policies.

The last eight years have challenged the foundations of international law. To some in Europe this may sound to be a too drastic conclusion. For someone who has accompanied the panel and listened to those directly affected in various parts of world it is far more than rhetoric. It has also undermined the legitimacy of and public support to counter-terrorism, which should not be in anybody's interest. In light of the experiences reflected in the Eminent Jurists Panel report key agendas for the international community should be the strengthening of justice systems and of accountability mechanisms in counter-terrorism.

Ultimately, if the international community was to accept impunity for well-documented human rights violations and crimes under international law committed in the name of national security it will create a dangerous 'crack' in international law. It would expose the international legal order to further accusations of selectiveness and double standards in which the mighty have a privilege to decide whether to comply with the law or not.

---

93   See also Joint Statement of the European Union and its Member States and the United States of America on the Closure of the Guantanamo Bay Detention Facility and Future Counterterrorism Cooperation, based on Shared Values, International Law, and Respect for the Rule of Law and Human Rights, Press Release, 2951st Council meeting, External Relations, 10939/09, 15 and 16 June 2009. Subsequently, a number of EU member states have accepted detainees on their jurisdiction.

II

European Union

Wolfgang BENEDEK

EU Action on Human and Fundamental Rights in 2009

Table of Contents

Keywords

asylum, business, democracy, European Court of Justice, European Union, Fundamental Rights Agency, ICC, Lisbon Treaty, minorities, migration, NGOs, parliament, persons with disabilities, Stockholm Programme, terrorism, trafficking, women

A   Introduction

2009 has been a breakthrough year for the foundations of the European Union's system of human and fundamental rights protection. The Treaty of Lisbon, which finally came into force on 1 December 2009, defines human rights as an essential part of the values of the EU (Article 2 Treaty on European Union (TEU) (Lisbon)), a commitment that is discussed in detail in the contributions of Benoît-Rohmer and Jacqué in this volume.[1] The principles of democracy, the rule of law, the univer-

---

1   See the contributions by Florence Benoît-Rohmer and Jean Paul Jacqué, in this volume, at 49 and 123, respectively.

sality and indivisibility of human rights and fundamental freedoms, the respect for human dignity and the principles of equality and solidarity highlighted in Article 21 TEU are guiding the policies of the European Union at the international level. Accordingly, Article 6 (1) TEU as amended by the Lisbon Treaty now refers to the obligatory Charter of Fundamental Rights and thus provides the EU with a modern set of largely justiciable rights, which can be applied together with the fundamental rights derived by the European Court of Justice from the common constitutional traditions of member states as general principles of the law of the European Union. Together with the commitment, in Article 6 TEU (Lisbon) to join the European Convention for the Protection of Human Rights and Fundamental Freedoms (ECHR), the EU has obtained a strong legal basis for its human rights policy, which now needs to be met by a similar strong political commitment to its implementation in practice. According to the 2009 Annual Report on EU Action in the Field of Human Rights and Democracy in the World "a commitment to human rights and democracy is at the heart of the EU".[2]

This contribution first gives an overview of the major events in the development of the EU human rights agenda since 1998 in order to provide the background for the events to be reported for 2009 (B.1.). It further introduces the internal and external dimension of the EU's human rights policies and instruments (B.2. and B.3.) before giving an overview of the work of EU bodies (C). Furthermore, major developments in the thematic work of the EU are reviewed (C and D). Finally, some conclusions are made with regard to the general developments in the EU policies on human rights in 2009 (E).

Given the wide scope and complexity of EU human rights action, this contribution provides only a general overview and aims to give the reader a framework within which to approach and assess the complexities of the topic. Some of the issues under review are dealt with in depth by other contributions to this volume's section on the EU. Where appropriate, reference will be made.

This contribution builds on the study "European Union Human Rights and CFSP Policy in 2008" which was published in the European Yearbook on Human Rights 2009[3] using an enlarged framework for introducing legislative action, policies and other activities on human and fundamental rights. In doing so it benefits from the fact that this volume contains a separate contribution on "Mainstreaming Human Rights in the Common Security and Defense Policy of the European Union".[4] As Michael Reiterer points out, human rights will play an even larger role in the European Foreign Policy after Lisbon.[5] Furthermore, the EU's human rights policy is constantly developing, as can be seen in its multilateral approaches pursued in the UN Human Rights Council[6] as well as in the EU's steps to become a formal party to multilateral conventions like the UN Convention

---

2   See Council of the European Union, Human Rights and Democracy in the World, Report on EU Action, July 2008 to December 2009 (in the following: "Annual Report 2009"). For the first time, this report is only available electronically on the website of the Council, at http://www.consilium.europa.eu/showPage.aspx?id=1689&lang=EN.

3   See Wolfgang S. Heinz/Josefine Liebl, European Union and Human Rights and CFSP-Policy in 2008, Wolfgang Benedek/Wolfram Karl/Anja Mihr/Manfred Nowak (eds.), European Yearbook on Human Rights 2009, Vienna 2009, 85-98 (in the following "EYHR 2009").

4   See the contribution by Markus Möstl, in this volume, at 153.

5   See the contribution by Michael Reiterer, in this volume, at 141.

6   See the contribution by Theodor Rathgeber, in this volume, at 183.

on the Rights of Persons with Disabilities.[7] Additionally, human rights policies play a major role in the bilateral and interregional relations of the European Union.[8]

B   Development of the EU Human Rights Agenda

1   Major Events since 1998

Since 1998 in particular, the European Union has established its human rights policy, inspired by a report of a panel of eminent persons[9] and based on the results of a major project of the Academy of European Law in Florence on a Human Rights Agenda for the European Union.[10] Since then, the call for an 'ever closer union' in need of a human rights policy[11] has been responded to by increasingly systematic action of the EU which has, step-by-step, built up the instruments for a systematic human rights policy, strongly encouraged by the European Parliament.[12] The report of eminent persons of 1998 contained a number of suggestions, like an Annual Report by the Council, a Human Rights Agency and a Commissioner for Human Rights – instruments that have gradually been implemented.

Since 1983, the European Parliament has been issuing a regular annual report on human rights in the world, which, since the 1990s has been complemented by a report on fundamental rights in the European Union. Additionally, since 1998/1999 the European Council publishes its own Annual Report on Human Rights that until 2009 covered the periods from July to June of the next year and was presented at the occasion of the Human Rights Day in December of the respective year, while from 2010 on it will cover the full calendar year.[13] In 2003, the European Council decided to establish a human rights agency, which was finally set up in 2007 as the "Fundamental Rights Agency", succeeding the European Monitoring Centre for Racism and Xenophobia established already in 1997.

The European Union has a number of additional instruments for the promotion of human rights, such as the European Instrument for Democracy and Human Rights (EIDHR)[14] that was established in 2006 replacing the previous European Initiative for Democracy and Human Rights of 1994 and that provides funding for human rights policies and actions, including the support of several master

---

7   See the contribution by Davide Zaru and Maria Zuber, in this volume, at 169.
8   See Council of the European Union, Human Rights and Democracy in the World, Report (forthcoming).
9   Antonio Cassese/Catherine Lalumière/Peter Leuprecht/Mary Robinson, Leading by Example: A Human Rights Agenda for the European Union for the Year 2000, Florence 1998.
10   See also Philip Alston, The EU and Human Rights, Oxford 1999.
11   See Philip Alston and J. H. H. Weiler, An "Ever Closer Union" in Need of a Human Rights Policy, European Journal of International Law, 9 (1998) 4, 658-723.
12   See Geoffrey Harris, The Role of the European Parliament in Human Rights Protection, in: Benedek et al. (eds.), EYHR 2009, 109-120.
13   Accordingly, the annual report on 2008-2009 covers the period 1 July 2008 to 31 December 2009, see also B.4.
14   See Veronique Arnault, Implementation of the European Instrument for Democracy and Human Rights (EIDHR), in: Benedek et al. (eds.), EYHR 2009, 99-108.

programmes on human rights and democratization worldwide. Human rights and democratization have systematically been integrated into political dialogues and cooperation policies of the EU.[15] In addition, a number of EU guidelines on human rights, and international humanitarian law, *inter alia* one on human rights dialogues, have been elaborated, partly on the insistence of the European Parliament. Furthermore, today, human rights clauses are inserted in all cooperation agreements of the European Union with non-EU countries; human rights have been mainstreamed in EU Crisis Management Operations and a personal representative of Javier Solana for human rights has been appointed who also heads the respective division in the European Commission. Since 2010, the European Commission for the first time has a Commissioner who besides justice and citizenship is also responsible for fundamental rights.[16]

Judicial cooperation and internal affairs, formerly part of the third pillar, have through the entry into force of the Lisbon Treaty been incorporated into the Treaty on the Functioning of the European Union (TFEU) in order to increase the effectivity of joined policies on and policing of border control, asylum and immigration under title V on the space of freedom, security and law. Under the Swedish Presidency the EU's approach was further substantialized through the Stockholm Programme[17] on an open and secure Europe serving and protecting the citizens of December 2009. The "depillarization" brought by the Lisbon Treaty creates new opportunities for extending the role of the European Court of Justice (ECJ) and of the FRA to this formerly purely intergovernmental policy field which is particularly sensitive with regard to human rights. All these developments and the policies and instruments established reflect that the European Union is increasingly contributing to a "European Approach" to human rights.[18]

2   Internal EU Policies and Instruments

The year 2009 had major significance for EU human rights policies and instruments in the internal dimension of the European Union, particularly in light of the replacement of the Hague Programme on Freedom, Security and Justice by the Stockholm Programme, a major policy effort of the Swedish Presidency. During its preparation various EU bodies, like the European Parliament and the Fundamental Rights Agency, played an important role. The Stockholm Programme, officially named the 3rd Multi-Annual Programme on an Area of Freedom, Secu-

---

15   See Communication from the Commission on "The European Union's Role in Promoting Human Rights and Democratisation in Third Countries", COM(2001) 252 final.
16   The Commissioner for Justice, Fundamental Rights and Citizenship is Viviane Reding, former Commissioner for Information Society and Media (2004-2010). See also the contribution of Jean Paul Jacqué, in this volume, at 123.
17   See Communication, An Area of Freedom, Security and Justice Serving the Citizen, COM (2009) 262 final of 10 June 2009, which provides the framework for that field for the period 2010 to 2014. See also European Parliament Resolution of 25 November 2009 on the Communication from the Commission to the European Parliament and the Council – An area of freedom, security and justice serving the citizen – Stockholm programme, P7_TA(2009)0090.
18   See Wolfgang Benedek, International Law of Human Rights: The European Approach, in: Hans-Peter Neuhold (ed.), European and US Approaches to International Law, Favorita Papers, Vienna 2006, 25-38.

rity and Justice (AFSJ), was adopted by the European Council of 10-11 December 2009 and covers the years till 2014.[19] There is still a need of clarification regarding the role of FRA in its implementation due to the abovementioned 'depillarization' of the EU. The overdue revision of the FRA's mandate is expected to take this into account. Already, FRA has been invited to advise other EU bodies in this respect. Although it remains open how the new commissioner and vice-president of the European Commission responsible for justice, fundamental rights and citizenship, Viviane Reding, will approach her function towards building a European area of fundamental rights, it is clear that the further harmonization of European policies in the field of asylum and migration towards a Common European Asylum System will raise major fundamental rights issues.

Within its activities towards a global approach to *migration* adopted by the European Council in 2005, the European Union has undertaken several initiatives like mobility partnerships with countries of origin like Moldova and Cap Verde as well as Georgia. With regard to Africa an EU-Africa Partnership on Migration and Employment has been supported, while the project 'Building migration Partnerships' has been started together with Eastern European countries in 2009.[20] Additionally, a structured dialogue on migration was launched in June 2009 with Latin American countries. In October 2008, the European Council adopted the "European Pact on Immigration and Asylum".[21] In September 2009, the Commission published the Communication on Policy Coherence for Development including a section on coherence of migration policy with development policy.[22]

After the Commission had presented the first set of legislative proposals in the field of *asylum* in December 2008, namely amending the directive on reception conditions for asylum seekers, of the Dublin Regulation and the Eurodac regulation, it also put forward, in October 2009, proposals for the amendment of the qualification directive and the asylum procedures directive to improve the coherence of EU instruments in that field.[23] In December 2009 agreement was reached on the establishment of a European Asylum Support Office (EASO), which will be the EU's Operational Agency to coordinate cooperation on asylum between member states and to assist member states to implement a more con-

---

19 See General Secretariat of the European Council, Conclusions of the European Council of 10-11 December 2009, EUCO 6/09 of 11 December 2009.

20 EU, First Action Plan (2008-2010), For the Implementation of the EU-Africa Strategic Partnership http://www.africa-eu-partnership.org/pdf/eas2007_action_plan_2008_2010_en.pdf#page=42, and Building Migration Partnerships: Joint declaration from the Ministerial Conference held in Prague on 27-28 April 2009, http://www.mvcr.cz/mvcren/article/building-migration-partnership-joint-declaration.aspx.

21 European Pact on Immigration and Asylum, No. 13340/08, ASIM 72, adopted by Council of the European Union on 15-16 October 2008.

22 Communication from the Commission, Policy Coherence for Development - Establishing the policy framework for a whole–of–the-Union approach, EU Doc. COM(2009) 458 final, 15 September 2009.

23 Proposal for a Directive of the European Parliament and of the Council on Minimum Standards on Procedures in Member States for Granting and Withdrawing International Protection, EU-Doc. 14959/09, 23 October 2009 and Proposal for a Directive of the European Parliament and of the Council on Minimum Standards for the Qualification and Status of Third Country Nationals or Stateless Persons as Beneficiaries of International Protection and the Content of the Protection Granted, EU-Doc.14863/1/09, 23 October 2009.

sistent and fair asylum policy. The objective is to complete the Common European Asylum System by 2012. Non-EU countries are receiving financial assistance through the thematic programme on migration and asylum 2007-2013.[24]

Another area of concern in 2009 was *trafficking in human beings*. In March 2009, the Commission proposed a new framework decision on fighting trafficking in human beings and the protection of their victims.[25] The EU Policy Framework on trafficking dating back to October 2005 claims to pursue a multidisciplinary as well as a human rights-based approach combining law enforcement, prevention and victims' support.

With regard to the external dimension of human trafficking, the Council in December 2009 adopted an "action-oriented paper" on strengthening the EU external dimension on action against trafficking in human beings with a set of recommendations for the Commission.[26] The fight against trafficking is also a priority in the geographic and thematic cooperation of the European Union with non-EU countries through instruments like mainstreaming in country strategy papers and funding from several budget lines with a particular focus on combating child trafficking.

The European Union also undertook efforts to strengthen respect for diversity and non-discrimination, racism and xenophobia, both inside and in cooperation with international procedures like the UN Special Rapporteur on contemporary forms of racism, xenophobia and related intolerance. With regard to the rights of persons belonging to *minorities*, the European Union continued its focus on the *Roma* Community as the largest ethnic minority of the European Union. In 2009, the European Platform for Roma Inclusion was established in which key stakeholders develop strategies on the effective inclusion of Roma in Europe. The first meeting of the platform took place in April 2009 in Prague and adopted ten common basic principles for effective policies for Roma inclusion, while the second platform meeting in Brussels in September 2009 was devoted to the issue of education of Roma.

With regard to the fight against *terrorism* one emphasis of the EU was put on combating radicalization and recruitment, two issues on which the Council has adopted a strategy and an action plan. They include measures against violent radicalization through the Internet, training of imams and capacity building of local police. A European Network of Experts on Radicalization was established by the European Commission as a platform for studies and discussions. There are numerous other activities concerning the implementation of the EU counter-terrorism strategy, which however, do not usually address the fundamental rights dimension.[27]

---

24   See EU, Europaid, http://ec.europa.eu/europaid/how/finance/dci/migration_en.htm.
25   See Council Framework Decision on preventing and combating trafficking in human beings, and protecting victims, repealing Framework Decision 2002/629/JHA, COM(2009) 136 final, 25 March 2009.
26   See Action-Oriented Paper on Strengthening the EU External Dimension on Action against Trafficking in Human Beings: Towards Global EU Action against Trafficking in Human Beings, http://www.se2009eu/en/the_presidency/about_the_eu/justice and_home_affairs.
27   See EU-Council Secretariat, Factsheet, The European Union and the Fight against Terrorism, 2 October 2009, www.consilium.europa.eu.

As a result of the entry into force of the Lisbon Treaty, the Justice and Home Affairs Council has established a new Standing Committee on Internal Security (COSI) in order to strengthen operational cooperation in that field. COSI will cooperate with agencies like EUROJUST, EUROPOL and FRONTEX and has been tasked to deal with immigration, frontiers and asylum. It remains open how fundamental rights aspects will be taken into account in its work. However, with the abolition of the pillar structure, measures by the EU and national governments in the field of justice and home affairs will now become subject to judicial review of the European Court of Justice and, in the future, also the European Court of Human Rights, which presents a major progress with regard to fundamental rights concerns.[28]

The Stockholm Programme contains several parts dealing with human rights, in particular part 2 on "Promoting Citizens' Rights: A Europe of Rights", which sets out an agenda of activities of the EU institutions in that field. In particular, the European Council

"invites the EU institutions and the member states to ensure that legal initiatives are and remain consistent with fundamental rights throughout the legislative process by way of strengthening the application of the methodology for a systematic and rigorous monitoring of compliance with the convention and the rights set out in the Charter of Fundamental Rights."

Violations of fundamental rights can be subject of *petitions* of European citizens to the European Ombudsman or petitions committee, which is dealing with breaches by member states.

The Council also "invites the EU institutions to make full use of the expertise of the European Union Agency for Fundamental Rights [...] and to use it for the communication to citizens of human rights issues affecting them in their everyday life".[29] Other chapters concern the full exercise of the right to free movement, living together in an area that respects diversity and protects those most vulnerable to racism and xenophobia, the rights of the child, vulnerable groups, victims of crime, including terrorism, the rights of the individual in criminal proceedings and the protecting citizens rights in the information society as well as participation in the democratic life of the Union. A variety of measures is envisaged in the fields indicated. This part concludes with the entitlement of Union citizens to protection in non-member states, meaning diplomatic and consular protection. The results show that the FRA has been able to make a difference when advising the Council on the Stockholm Programme although not all concerns raised in its pertinent thematic contribution have been taken into account.[30]

---

28 See also under C.4. The European Court of Justice.
29 See The Stockholm Programme, Council of the European Union, 2 December 2009, www.se2009.eu/polopoly_fs/1.26419!menu/standard/file/Klar_Stockholmsprogram.pdf.
30 See Fundamental Rights Agency, The Stockholm Programme: A Chance to Put Fundamental Rights Protection Right in the Centre of the European Agenda, http://fra.europa.eu/fraWebsite/attachments/FRA-comments-on-Stockholm-Programme.pdf.

3   External EU Policies and Instruments

The external policies and instruments of the European Union are part of the Common Foreign and Security Policy (CFSP) and the Common Security and Defence Policy (CSDP). In this volume a separate contribution can be found on the latter.[31] With regard to the instruments of the CFSP, human rights dialogues play a major role. There are various forms of human rights dialogues that are difficult to systematize, including "structured" human rights dialogues, dialogues in sub-committees under Association, Partnership and Cooperation Agreements, local dialogues and consultations on human rights issues. For example, human rights dialogues have taken place in May and November 2009 with China, with the African Union in November 2009 and with the Russian Federation in May 2009, while additional human rights 'consultations' are reported to have taken place between the EU and Russia in November. Further human rights dialogues have been conducted with Armenia, Uzbekistan, Turkmenistan, Kirgizstan, Georgia and Belarus, while 'local dialogues' are reported for Chile and Columbia, Indonesia.[32]

The human rights dialogues with China[33] are preceded by an academic dialogue which since 2009 is coordinated by the Irish Centre for Human Rights in Galway representing a large consortium of academic institutions in the European Union. This should give the dialogue more substance and continuity as well as a broader basis. Topics discussed in 2009 ranged from freedom of expression and the situation of human rights defenders to the death penalty, torture and ratification of the International Covenant on Civil and Political Rights by China to the independence of the judiciary and the situation in Tibet and Xinjiang.

Major instruments of external EU human rights policy are the *EU Guidelines on human rights and international humanitarian law* which have been partly revised and reissued in 2008 and 2009. There are eight guidelines, which also form part of a recent publication.[34] The eight guidelines deal with the death penalty (1998, updated 2008), torture and other cruel, inhuman or degrading treatment or punishment (2001, updated 2008), human rights dialogues with third countries (2001, updated 2009), children and armed conflict (2003, updated 2008), human rights defenders (2004, updated 2008), promotion and protection of the rights of the child (2007), violence against women and girls and combating all forms of discrimination against them (2008), and promoting compliance with international humanitarian law (2005). With regard to the guidelines relevant for mainstreaming human rights and gender into the European Security and Defence Policy, the Council published a compilation of relevant documents in 2008.[35] In addition to the guidelines, this compendium provides interesting ex-

---

31   See the contribution by Markus Möstl, in this volume, at 153.
32   See Council of the European Union, Human Rights and Democracy in the World, Report on EU Action, July 2008-December 2009, Brussels 2010.
33   See also Katrin Kinzelbach, The EU Human Rights Dialogues with China and the 2008 Olympic Games, in: Benedek/Karl/Mihr/Nowak (eds.) EYHR 2009, 37-60.
34   See Council of the European Union, EU Guidelines, Human Rights and International Humanitarian Law, European Communities, March 2009.
35   Council of the European Union, Mainstreaming Human Rights and Gender into European Security and Defence Policy, Compilation of Relevant Documents, Brussels 2008.

amples of the implementation of the guidelines and other human rights concerns of the EU, including a checklist on gender mainstreaming and on children affected by armed conflict, generic standards of behaviour for ESDP operations and language used in the planning and strategic documents of the European Crises Management Operations and job descriptions for human rights advisors.

Important information is gathered in form of *'human rights fact sheets'* to be produced by all heads of mission of the European Union on a regular basis. In this way the European Union gains first hand information on the situation of human rights in all countries where it is represented. Consequently, it is also the role of the European Union delegations to make formal demarches, to inquire into human rights situations and to serve as links to local NGOs.

4   Reporting on EU Policies on Human Rights

The most systematic report on EU action in the field of human rights is the annual report issued by the European Council since 1999, while the reports of the European Parliament on human rights in the world and on fundamental rights within the EU have changing emphases. Since the annual and special reports of the independent experts have been discontinued and because FRA is only issuing thematic reports, the reports of the Council and the Parliament are the only regular reports informing about the human rights policies of the EU in a comprehensive way. In particular, the annual report of the Council can be considered as the main authoritative source of information in this respect. However, important changes in the conception of these reports can be observed and will be analyzed subsequently.

The report by the European Council, issued under the responsibility of the respective presidency has experienced several changes of format. Whereas from the 1st report issued in 2000 to the 6th report in 2005 the focus was on both human rights within the European Union and actions of the EU on human rights in international affairs, the 7th report produced under the British chairmanship integrated the actions having an internal as well as an external dimension into the thematic part, while limiting the section on developments within the EU to the Fundamental Rights Agency, the personal representative of the Secretary General/ High Representative for human rights and the activities of the European Parliament. Since the Annual Report 2005 an additional focus has been put on the effectiveness of EU external action and since the Annual Report 2007 on the situation of human rights in individual countries, which aligns the EU Annual Report with the annual report of the US State Department on Human Rights Practices in Countries worldwide,[36] a significant drift away from the original conception.

In 2004, the Parliament's Annual Report on Human Rights in the World and the EU's Policy on the Matter was renamed Report on the Annual Report on Human Rights in the World and the EU's Policy on the Matter,[37] meaning that since that time the European Parliament based its report explicitly on a review of

---

36   See U. S. Department of State, 2009 Country Reports on Human Rights Practices, 11 March 2010.

37   See Annual Report on Human Rights in the World in 2003 and the EU's policy on the matter (2003/2005 (INI)) of 13 April 2004; A 5 – 0270/2004 and Annual Report on Human Rights in the World 2005 (2004/2151 (INI)) of 5 April 2005, A 6 – 0086/2005.

the Annual Report of the Council. Keeping with this practice, the Parliament's Committee on Foreign Affairs prepared the Report on the Annual Report on Human Rights in the World 2008 and the European Union's Policy on the Matter; it was adopted by the European Parliament in May 2009.[38]

Even though the Council's Annual Reports regularly emphasize the importance of dealing with human rights within the EU for reasons of its credibility as a global human rights actor, as does for example the 9th EU Annual Report on Human Rights 2007,[39] ever since the 10th Annual Report of 2008 the section on developments within the EU was abandoned while only the part on the actions of the European Parliament was maintained. Nothing can be found anymore on the activities of FRA or developments related to it, maybe because FRA is an independent agency. The report now starts off out with the EU instruments and initiatives in non-EU countries. This means that the annual report has turned out to be a report on EU action on human rights in the world and, indeed, the draft report for 2009 is entitled "Human Rights and Democracy in the World". Although information can still be found on developments within the EU in the thematic section, for example under the topics of asylum, migration, refugees and displaced persons, the internal dimension of human rights protection within the EU is given no visibility anymore, which may damage the credibility of the European Union human rights policy.

This problem is increased by the fact that the European Parliament changed its reporting format on fundamental rights in the European Union. While its report on 1998-1999 was entitled "Annual Report on Respect for Human Rights in the European Union"[40] and the following reports until 2001 were called "Report on Fundamental Rights in the EU"[41] and "Report on Human Rights Situation in the European Union"[42] and issued annually the most recent report on the situation of Fundamental Rights in the European Union, covers a period of four years (!), i.e. 2004-2008,[43] which shows the difficulties to develop a common position on the state of fundamental rights in the EU. Indeed, the EP in the introduction to the report "deplores the fact that the Member States continue to refuse EU scrutiny of their own human rights policies and practices."[44]

The elaboration of the Charter for Fundamental Rights of the European Union in 2000 provided the framework for the annual reports on the situation of fundamental rights within the European Union by the EU Network of Independent Experts on Fundamental Rights. This Network was set up by the European

38   See Report on the Annual Report on Human Rights in the World 2008 and the European Union's policy on the matter of 14 April 2009, Rapporteur: Raimon Obiols i Germà, A6-0264/2009 and the resolution of the EP of 7 May 2009, which comments on the Annual Report of the Council, 2008/2336 (INI), P6_TA(2009)0385 of 7 May 2009.
39   See EU Annual Report on Human Rights 2007, 7.
40   See Annual Report on Respect for Human Rights in the European Union (1998-1999), 29 February 2000 (1999-2000 (INI)), A 5 – 0050/2000.
41   See Report on the situation as regards fundamental rights in the European Union (2000) (2000/2231 (INI)).
42   See Report on Human Rights Situation in the EU (2001) (2001-2014 (INI)), A 5 – 0451/2002.
43   See Report on the Situation of Fundamental Human Rights in the EU 2004-2008 (2007/2145(INI)), Rapporteur: Giusto Catania, A6-0479/2008, 14 January 2009.
44   Ibid., para. 3.

Commission at the request of the European Parliament in 2002 and produced annual reports on all EU member states and a synthesis report with conclusions and recommendations[45] from 2002 till 2005 when its work was discontinued in view of the establishment of the Fundamental Rights Agency. In 2007, the FRA took up its activities which mainly encompass the collection of data and the production of reports in major fields of human rights policy according to the Programme of Action of the Agency.[46] Accordingly, FRA was not continuing with the practice of launching annual reports on fundamental rights in the EU. The scrutiny of the internal dimension has been rolled further back, mainly because of competence and sovereignty concerns and has been given a new format through the activities of FRA. Consequently, there is a certain imbalance between the external and the internal dimension of the human rights policies of the EU, which in the past was addressed by the European Parliament's Annual Report on fundamental rights. However, it can be hoped that the European Charter on Fundamental Rights as a binding instrument and the future accession of the EU to the European Convention on Human Rights will give a new impetus to efforts of mainstreaming human rights in the internal action of the European Union.

C   Human Rights and the Work of EU Bodies

1   The European Parliament

The European Parliament (EP) has always been a driving force for granting human rights a high standing in the EU. Its particular methodology and instruments have already been outlined in a previous contribution.[47] Its Committee on Foreign Affairs (AFET) and its Sub-Committee on Human Rights (DROI)[48] are mainly responsible for the external dimension of human rights in the EU, while its Committee on Civil Liberties, Justice and Internal Affairs (LIBE) mainly engages with the internal dimension. Both committees are responsible for preparing annual reports, which have been analyzed under B.4. However, besides this regular activity, they also publish *specific reports*, like the Report on Gender Mainstreaming in EU External Relations and Peace-building/Nation-building, adopted on 3 April 2009[49] and the report of the Committee on Development (DEVE) on the proposal for a regulation of the EP and the Council for amending the Regulations of 2006 on financing development cooperation and on promoting democracy and human rights worldwide of 1 December 2009.[50]

---

45   See, for example, Report on the Situation of Fundamental Rights in the European Union and its Member States 2005, http://ec.europa.eu/justice_home/cfr_edf/doc/report_eu_2005_en.pdf.

46   See Hannes Tretter and Anna Müller-Funk, in this volume, at 109.

47   See Geoffrey Harris, The Role of the European Parliament in Human Rights Protection, in: Benedek et al. (eds.), EYHR 2009, 109-119.

48   Since the 7th legislature (2009-2014) the Chair of the Subcommittee on Human Rights is Heidi Hautala, who replaced Hélène Flautre in July 2009.

49   European Parliament, Report on Gender Mainstreaming in EU External Relations and Peace-building/Nationbuilding, (2008/2198(INI)), 3 April 2009.

50   Report on the proposal for a regulation of the European Parliament and of the Council amending Regulation (EC) No 1905/2006 establishing a financing instrument for

An important instrument for the enforcement of human rights is the *human rights and democracy clause*, inserted since 1992 in more than 50 international agreements due to the insistence of the EP. It allows the EU to react to breaches of human rights and democratic principles. Measures taken can even include the suspension of agreements[51] in case the contracting country violates the human rights clause inserted in the agreement with the EU.[52]

The EP also actively takes part in the supervision of the EIDHR and follows closely the human rights dialogues organized as well as the work of the UN Human Rights Council, on which it also prepared a report.[53]

Additionally, the European Parliament frequently commissions *external studies* to analyze certain fields or issues of human rights to adapt its policies and activities. In 2009, the studies "Freedom of Religion or Belief and the Freedom of Expression", "Business and Human Rights in EU External Relations – Making the EU a Leader at Home and Internationally", "Nonviolent Civic Action in Support of Human Rights and Democracy", "Human Rights Mainstreaming in the European Unions External Relations" and "An Update on the Implementation of EU Guidelines on Torture and Other Cruel, Inhuman or Degrading Treatment and Punnishment" were published.[54]

In 2009, the European Parliament has passed a number of *resolutions* dealing with issues of human rights in the context of certain country situations or individuals, ranging from the resolution of 15 January 2009 on Iran: The Case of Shirin Ebadi[55] to the Resolution of 17 December 2009 on Azerbaijan: Freedom of Expression[56] or the Resolution on the same day on Uganda: Anti-Homosexual Draft Legislation.[57] Altogether 38 resolutions with a human rights dimension were passed in 2009.

In December 2009, the 21st *Sakharov Prize* for Freedom of Thought was awarded to the Russian Human Rights NGO "Memorial" and its main representatives on behalf of all other human rights defenders in Russia. The prize is endowed with a grant of € 50.000.

---

development cooperation and Regulation (EC) No 1889/2006 on establishing a financing instrument for the promotion of democracy and human rights worldwide.

51   Council of Europe, Press Release: Signing of the Partnership and Cooperation Agreement (PCA) at the Ministerial Troika Meeting opens new era for Indonesia-EU Relations, http://www.consilium.europa.eu/uedocs/cms_data/docs/pressdata/en/er/11114.pdf.

52   See, generally Lorand Bartels, Human Rights Conditionality in the EU's International Agreements, Oxford 2005.

53   The Development of the Human Rights Council including the role of the EU, Rapporteur Laima Liuicija Andrikienè, P6-TA(2009) 0021 of 14 January 2009.

54   Some of the reports are available on Parliament and Council websites. Unfortunately, the full text of most studies is not available. In some cases, however, studies have been published by the authors. See, e.g., Horst Fischer/Sébastien Lorion/ Georg Ulrich, Beyond Activism. The Impact of the Resolutions and Other Activities of the European Parliament in the Field of Human Rights Outside the European Union, EIUC Occasional Papers, Venice 2007.

55   See European Parliament Resolution of 15 January 2009 on Iran: The Case of Shirin Ebadi.

56   European Parliament resolution of 17 December 2009 on Azerbaijan: Freedom of Expression.

57   See European Parliament resolution of 17 December 2009 on Uganda: Anti-homosexual Draft Legislation.

The EP has undertaken numerous interventions in cases of individual and collective violations of human rights, a list of which is attached to its annual report on human rights. In 2009, it organized *hearings, conferences and workshops* on, inter alia, extrajudicial, summary or arbitrary executions, using the example of the Philippines, on the EU's role in combating human rights violations by private military and security companies (PMCs/PSCs), the human rights dimension of the Union for the Mediterranean, business and human rights, and human rights in Iran, Russia and Sri Lanka.

The activities of the EP in the field of human rights can be best followed through the annual report on human rights of the Council, where a specific section is devoted to the actions of the EP on human rights.[58] Furthermore, the EP has a very transparent policy of issuing press documents on most activities.[59]

Mainstreaming human rights continues to be a major concern and a task force of different services has been established to strengthen the *coherence* of the EU policies in human rights issues.[60] With regard to *democracy*, the Office of Promotion of Parliamentary Democracy (OPPD) established in 2008 continued its activities in several countries. The EP adopted a resolution on democracy-building,[61] and was engaged in several parliamentary dialogues with other regions and was also involved in election observation in several countries.[62]

2 The Council of the European Union

The Council of the EU as a body in which EU governments coordinate their policies does not inform in detail on its work regarding human rights. The Working Group on Human Rights (COHOM), created in 1987, meets on a monthly basis to discuss all matters related to human rights in the external relations of the European Union. It is composed of human rights experts from member states, who are in practice the heads of the human rights divisions in the respective ministries for foreign affairs. The agenda of its monthly meetings is partly shaped by the respective presidency and also the access to information on the work of this body largely depends on the information policy of the presidency.

In order to strengthen the cohesion of the services of the European Union in this respect, the former High Representative of the European Union for the Common Foreign and Security Policy and Secretary General of the Council of the European Union, Javier Solana, appointed a personal representative, Dr. Riina Ruth Kijonka, for human rights with regard to the common foreign and security policy in 2005. In 2007, Dr. Riina Ruth Kijonka was reappointed to this function in which she continued to serve during 2009.

For the strengthening of human rights and gender perspectives in the Common Security and Defence Policy (CSDP) a first meeting of gender advisors and focal points took place in Brussels in November 2009. Another important topic is

---

58 For a list of all EU Annual Human Rights Reports see http://www.consilium.europa.eu/showPage.aspx?id=970&lang=En.
59 For a list of press releases, see http://www.europarl.europa.eu/news/archive/search/topicSearch.do.
60 See Annual Report 2009 (forthcoming).
61 European Parliament Resolution of 22 October 2009 on democracy building in the EU's external relations, P7_TA(2009)0056 of 22 October 2009.
62 Annual Report 2009 (forthcoming).

the rationalization of the *human rights guidelines* in order to make them more operational. In March 2009, for example, an expert meeting on the implementation of the Guidelines on International Humanitarian Law (IHL) took place in Prague. Emphasis was put on increasing synergies between IHL and the relevant human rights guidelines.

Another concern of the Council was the relationship of *business and human rights*. A Council conference on "Protect, Respect, Remedy – Corporate Social Responsibility" took place in Brussels in November 2009.

The work of the Council and COHOM, in particular in 2009, focussed on several important issues which will be examined subsequently. Additionally, a variety of activities in the context of human rights dialogues as well as on thematic and country-situations took place which cannot be dealt with in detail in this contribution. Task force meetings took place on human rights defenders and a focal point facilitating better coordination of activities has been established on this issue as well. Another task force deals with children's rights and children in armed conflict.

The Council also entered new grounds with its decision concerning the accession of the European Union to the UN Convention on the Rights of Persons with Disabilities.[63]

Special attention was devoted to the role of the EU as an agent for human rights protection within the *United Nations*. A pertinent study on European power at the UN with a particular focus on the field of human rights found a decline in European influence and made several proposals on how to 'turn the tide'.[64] Interestingly this decline occurred despite the fact that, as announced by the Office of the UN High Commissioner for Human Rights (OHCHR), the voluntary contributions from EU member states in 2008 accounted for almost two thirds of all contributions. The European Union is also the major driving force behind numerous human rights initiatives in the UN General Assembly in New York and the Human Rights Council in Geneva.[65]

The Initiative on Democracy Support, a sensitive issue, was let by the Task Force on "Democracy building in EU external relations" and resulted in an EU Agenda for Action which was adopted by the Council in its conclusions of 16-17 November 2009.[66] With regard to the necessity of more visibility of the external human rights efforts of the European Union, the Council Secretariat and the services of the Commission produced a set of recommendations on how to increase the public profile of the EU as a major supporter of human rights initiatives, including mundane steps, such as revising the relevant websites.[67]

---

63   See David Zaru and Maria Zuber, in this volume, at 169.
64   See Richard Gowan and Franziska Brantner, A Global Force for Human Rights? An Audit of European Power at the UN, European Council on Foreign Relations, September 2008.
65   See the Annual Report 2009, Section 5.1 and 5.2 and Theodor Rathgeber, in this volume, at 183.
66   See Council of the European Union, Council Conclusions on Democracy Support in the EU's External Relations, External Relations Council Meeting of 17 November, 2009, http://www.epd.eu/uploads/4190067facf6ad89e7b0f113f3d21052.pdf.
67   See the EU portal on Activities of the European Union in human rights: http://europa.eu/pol/rights/index_en.htm; and on Promotion of Human Rights and Democratisation in the EU's External Relations, http://ec.europa.eu/external_relations/human_rights/index_en.htm.

In its annual Conclusions on Human Rights and Democratisation in Third Countries, the European Council emphasized that its continued commitment to human rights remained a priority of the Common Foreign and Security Policy. In this context, the Council underlines "the importance of integrating human rights aspects into all policy areas of the European Union, including all relevant geographical and thematic policies", i.e. mainstreaming human rights into all policies of the European Union.[68]

With regard to fundamental rights inside the European Union, the Ad Hoc Working Party on Fundamental Rights and Citizenship of the Council has to be mentioned, which is one among presently 29 working parties, groups or informal bodies working on, inter alia, immigration, asylum, migration, visa, terrorism, criminal law, organized crime, civil protection and Schengen within the framework of the Working Party Justice and Home Affairs. Little information is published on the activities of this working party except that it deals with matters of the Fundamental Rights Agency, the Daphne Programme on combating violence and preventing drug abuse and the Fundamental Rights and Citizenship Programme 2007-2013. This raises the question, how the human rights aspects are taken into account in the work of the various bodies in the context of justice and home affairs? The Ad Hoc Working Party on Fundamental Rights and Citizenship is obviously only covering part of the issues at stake. Another question is whether there should be a closer cooperation between the Ad Hoc Working Party on Fundamental Rights and Citizenship and COHOM, as has been recommended by the European Parliament in its Report on Fundamental Rights in the European Union 2004-2008.[69] The same report also calls for a twin-track analysis of the situation of human rights in the world and in each member states in order to emphasize the equal commitment of the Union to protecting human rights both inside and outside its borders and to avoid accusations of double standards.[70]

3   The European Commission

The European Commission has the main operational responsibility for respecting, protecting and fulfilling human rights in the European Union. Its services play an important role in managing human rights activities on a daily basis. The changes in the Commission as a result of the Treaty of Lisbon, in particular the appointment of a new Commissioner, whose portfolio explicitly includes fundamental rights, might result in changes in its services. In any case, the creation of a Commissioner on Human Rights as a long standing recommendation of the European Parliament and the fact that the portfolio of Commissioner Viviane Reding also includes justice and citizenship besides fundamental rights create new opportunities for a more coherent human rights policy of the European Union. Quite obviously, the mandate for fundamental rights can not mean that other commissioners, including the commissioner responsible for external relations

---

68   See Council of the European Union, Council conclusions on Human Rights and Democratization in third countries, Foreign Affairs Council meeting of 8 December 2009, http://www.consilium.europa.eu/ueDocs/cms_Data/docs/pressData/EN/foraff/111819.pdf.

69   See the Report of the European Parliament on the situation of fundamental rights in the European Union 2004-2008, (2007/2145(INI)), 5 December 2008, para. 17.

70   Ibid., para. 15.

and Vice-President of the Commission, Caterine Ashton, should not feel responsible to protect human rights. Rather as already pointed out previously, human rights are a cross-cutting issue and need to be mainstreamed in all activities of the European Union. However, it remains to be seen how the commitment to mainstreaming will be realized in the future and how the interplay between the different commissioners will work out.

The new system for Generalized Preferences (GSP) of 2008 foresees the possibility of gaining additional trade benefits, the so-called *GSP plus* if a country can demonstrate that it has ratified and effectively implemented 27 international conventions in the field of human and labour rights, sustainable development and good governance. Together with 14 other developing countries, for example, Sri Lanka benefited from this possibility. In December 2009, the Commission proposed the withdrawal of the GSP plus benefits from Sri Lanka, because the results of an investigation undertaken between October 2008 and October 2009, based on reports and statements by UN Special Rapporteurs and other UN bodies, showed that there were significant shortcomings in the implementation of three major UN human rights conventions, namely the International Covenant on Civil and Political Rights, the Convention against Torture and the Convention on the Rights of the Child. These findings led to a decision by the Council of the European Union of January 2010 to withdraw the GSP plus benefits from Sri Lanka.[71] This decision is remarkable both with regard to the fact that the European Union has made use of its power of withdrawal, but also because of the process leading to this decision, which consisted of an intensive inquiry of the situation regarding the implementation of major human rights conventions by the country concerned.

Of particular importance are the external cooperation programmes of the European Commission funded mainly by the European Instrument for Democracy and Human Rights (EIDHR) which covers the period 2007 to 2013.[72] As the previous yearbook contains an extensive article on the implementation of EDIHR[73] only a short update will be given here. EIDHR finances mainly projects of local and international civil society organisations. Only 10 % of the contributions go to international inter-governmental bodies. It is therefore the main instrument for working with civil society, in particular in difficult environments, when human rights are violated. Accordingly, emphasis is put on the support of human rights defenders and victims of human rights violations. For this purpose, the EIDHR has to be highly flexible. For some countries country-based support schemes are in place while at the country level support may be given for promoting governance and political participation and combating domestic violence, racism, xenophobia and discrimination. On the global level, the focus lies on the support of concerns connected with the EU Human Rights Guidelines, like the

71 See Council of the European Union, Implementing Regulation of the Council Temporarily withdrawing the special incentive arrangement for sustainable development and good governance provided for under regulation (EC) No. 732/2008 with respect to the Democratic Socialist Republic of Sri Lanka of 25 January 2010; see also the Press Release of the European Commission, Directorate-General for Trade of 15 February 2010.
72 See Regulation EC No. 1889/2006.
73 See Veronique Arnault, Implementation of the European Instrument for Democracy and Human Rights (EIDHR), in: Benedek/Karl/Mihr/Nowak (eds.), EYHR 2009, 99-107.

fight against torture, the death penalty, human rights defenders, women and children. The EIDHR also funds EU election observation missions.

One example for country-based support is the assistance to the NGO 'Memorial', to a human rights centre working for human rights defenders, for institutional capacity-building, the support to the International Criminal Court and to human rights education. With regard to the latter, the EIDHR supports regional master programmes on human rights and democracy, i.e. at the University of Pretoria for Africa, Sarajevo for South-East Europe, Sydney for Asia/Pacific and Buenos Aires for Latin America, while the main programme is based in Venice.[74]

Besides the external dimension of the work of the Commission, it should be emphasized that important aspects of human and fundamental rights are addressed in its work on the social dimension of the European Union, i.e. social inclusion, poverty, social cohesion, non-discrimination etc.[75] Again, these aspects would justify a separate contribution and can only be highlighted in this context.

4   Court of Justice of the European Union

The European Court of Justice (ECJ) has always had an important role in the field of fundamental rights in the European Union basing himself on common principles indentified in national legal systems of member states and of the European Convention on Human Rights.[76]

However, with the entry into force of the Treaty of Lisbon on 1 December 2009, a new area for its competence and activities has been opened. With the Treaty of Lisbon, legislation in the field of justice and home affairs, i.e. with regard to police and criminal law, will also take the form of regulations and directives and will come consequently under the jurisdiction of the ECJ. Though the third pillar is history, a distinction has to be drawn between measures adopted since the entry into force of the Lisbon Treaty and third pillar measures adopted before. For the latter a Transitional Protocol provides for a five year period during which the old rules on jurisdiction continue to be applied except for those cases, where a new act is adopted or a previous one is amended. The same can be expected to apply for treaties preceding the Treaty of Lisbon. Additionally, it is of great importance that future acts on justice and home affairs matters will be adopted by a qualified majority of the Council with the European Parliament having full co-decision rights.

The ECJ is now able to use the European Charter on Fundamental Rights as a legal basis. With regard to the European Convention on Human Rights, a Pro-

---

74   See also the first programme starting in 1997 was the European Master Programme on Human Rights and Democratization organized in Venice, which today is facilitated by the European Inter-University Center (EIUC) based at the Monastery San Nicolò on the Lido in Venice. See EIUC, E.MA after Ten Years, Celebrating a Unique European Cooperation, EIUC Occasional Papers, Venice 2008. However, this core programme has a different funding base. See also under C.3.; see also www.emahumanrights.org.

75   See, for example, the topics reported in the Social Europe e-newsletter of the directorate of Employment, Social Affairs and Equal Opportunities of the European Commission, http://ec.europe.eu/social.

76   See Paul Craig and Gráinne de Búrca, EU Law, Text, Cases, and Materials, 4th ed., Oxford 2008, 381 et seq.

tocol on accession needs to be negotiated and to come into force, which can well take more than two years.

With regard to decisions of the ECJ on fundamental rights in 2009, one case, *Jasna Detiček v. Maurizio Sgueglia* concerned the issue of the power of a member state to grant custody to one parent, if the Court of another member state has already granted custody to the other parent. In its judgement the court noted that

> *"one of the fundamental rights of the child is the right, set out in the Charter of Fundamental Rights of the European Union, to maintain a personal relationship and direct contact, on a regular basis, with both parents, and respect for that right is undeniably in the best interests of any child."*

It also observed that the wrongful removal of a child by unilateral decision of one parent will deprive the child of the direct contact with the other parent and that the

> *"balance and reasonable assessment of all interests involved must be based on objective considerations relating to the actual person of the child and his or her social environment, must in principle be carried out in proceedings before the Court which has jurisdiction as to the substance of the case."*[77]

With regard to EU fundamental rights and counter-terrorist blacklisting, the joint decisions of the Court of First Instance of September 2009 in *El Morabit v. Council of Ministers* has further developed European case law.[78]

The ECJ ruling in the data retention case *Ireland v. Council and Commission* of February 2009 should also be mentioned in this context. Ireland argued that Directive 2006/24/EC on the retention of data of 15 March 2006 (the Data Retention Directive) requiring member states to ensure that communication providers must retain, for a period between 6 months and 2 years, necessary data specified in the Directive, was adopted on a wrong legal basis, namely Article 95 EC, and consequently had to be annulled. However, the Court did not follow the argumentation of Ireland that Directive 2006/24/EC should have been adopted under the third pillar rather than under Article 95 EC with regard to the functioning of the internal market. The court stated that

> *"[i]t is apparent that the differences between the various national rules adopted on the retention of data relating to electronic communications were liable to have a direct impact on the functioning of the internal market and that it was foreseeable that that impact would become more serious with the passage of time. Such a situation justified the Community legislature in pursuing the objective of safeguarding the proper functioning of the internal market through the adoption of harmonised rules."*

Consequently, the Court dismissed the action of Ireland.[79]

---

77 See EJC, Case C-403/09 PPU, Jasna Detiček v. Maurizio Sgueglia, 23 December 2009.

78 See CFI, T-37/07 and T-323/07, El Morabit v. Council of Ministers, 2 September 2009.

79 See ECJ, Case C-301/06, Ireland v. Parliament and Council, 10 February 2009.

5 The Fundamental Rights Agency

With regard to the activities of the Fundamental Rights Agency, reference can be made to the contribution by Tretter and Müller-Funk in this volume[80] which provides a basic introduction into the activities of this agency, based in Vienna, which has been able within a relatively short time to take a central role regarding the provision of data, studies and materials on a range of fundamental rights issues in the European Union. With regard to 2009 the best source on its activities is its Annual Report and its Activity Report corresponding to its multi-annual framework.[81]

6 Cooperation with NGOs

When preparing its policies, the EU is also consulting with non-governmental organizations (NGOs) on human rights issues.[82] Since 1999, the respective presidency of the Council of the 2nd half of the year organizes an annual EU-NGO Forum on Human Rights with the purpose of providing opportunities for civil society from the global South to meet and exchange views with EU representatives and human rights experts. The Forum adopts conclusions and recommendations, which are presented at the COHOM, the Working Party on Human Rights. The 11th meeting of the Forum took place in Stockholm in July 2009 with a focus on children and the prohibition of all forms of corporal punishment, encompassing workshops on the implementation of legal networks, the implementation and mainstreaming of the EU guidelines on children and on children in conflict and crises situations.[83] The next EU-NGO Forum on Human Rights is to take place in Brussels in July 2010.

As a facilitator for these exchanges, the Human Rights and Democracy Network of Civil Society Organisations is active in Brussels.

D Thematic Issues

Within the context of human rights protection, the European Union has identified 21 thematic issues, which are given closer attention in its Annual Reports. These are:

- death penalty,
- torture and other cruel, inhuman and degrading treatment or punishment,
- rights of the child,
- children and armed conflict,
- human rights defenders,
- human rights of women, women, peace and security,

---

80 See Hannes Tretter and Anna Müller-Funk, in this volume, at 109.
81 See Fundamental Rights Agency, Annual Report 2009, http://fra.europa.eu/fraWebsite/attachments/FRA-AnnualReport09_en.pdf, and Activity Report 2009, http://fra. europa.eu/fraWebsite/attachments/FRA-ActivityReport09_en.pdf.
82 See, for an NGO perspective: Nicolas Jonathan Beger and James Higgins, Working for Human Rights in Brussels: Amnesty International's EU Office, in: Benedek et al. (eds.), EHYR 2009, 277-283.
83 11th Annual EU-NGO Forum on Human Rights, Focus on Children, Stockholm, 6-7 July 2009, http://www.humanrightsngoforum.eu.

- the ICC and the fight against impunity,
- human rights and terrorism,
- freedom of expression including new media, freedom of thought, conscience and religion,
- human rights and business,
- democracy support, election support,
- economic, social and cultural rights,
- asylum, migration, refugees and displaced persons, trafficking in human beings,
- racism,
- xenophobia,
- non-discrimination,
- respect for diversity; and
- rights of persons belonging to minorities, rights of persons with disabilities and indigenous issues.

A distinction is made between the first seven issues, which correspond to pertinent EU guidelines and the other 14. Obviously, there is no space to go into any detail on those issues, which have evolved historically and are dealt with in the Annual Report of the Council on less than 50 pages.[84] A new focus on country and regional issues, which has more than 80 pages, is one major reason for this finding.[85]

Only few major activities in 2009 in the field of thematic issues can be highlighted: The 20th anniversary of the adoption of the Convention on the Rights of the Child was commemorated with several activities, including making this issue the main topic of the 11th EU-NGO Human Rights Forum. The guideline on Human Rights Defenders and several other guidelines were revised and reissued by end of 2008. The 30th anniversary of the Convention on the Elimination of all Forms of Discrimination against Women (CEDAW) does not seem to have been specifically celebrated, but a number of activities are reported in that field like the process of developing an accountability mechanism and a set of indicators on the EU's policy on women, peace and security, launched by the pertinent ad hoc EU Task Force.

With regard to the International Criminal Court and the fight against impunity, the support of the EU for the ICC expressed itself also in an ICC-related clause, which is new since the revised Cotonou Agreement of 2005 and which in 2009 was included in the Trade Development and Cooperation Agreement with South Africa and the Partnership and Cooperation Agreement with Indonesia. According to the ICC clause, the parties agreed to share experience in the adoption of legal adjustment required to allow for the ratification and implementation of the Rome Statute of the ICC and to fight against international crime in accordance with international law, giving due regard to the Rome Statute. The revised Cotonou Agreement of 2005 also contains the obligation that "the party shall seek to take steps towards ratifying and implementing the Rome Statute and related instruments".[86]

---

84 See Annual Report 2009, section 4.
85 Compare the Annual Report 2008, which had about 70 pages on thematic issues and about the same space for country-focused issues, EU Annual Report on Human Rights 2008.
86 See Art. 11 para. 6 of the revised Contonou Agreement of 2005.

Already in 2002, the European Network of Contact Points for Genocide, Crimes against Humanity and War Crimes (The Genocide Network) was formed, which, in December 2009, met to consider its role under the new Eurojust Decision of December 2008.[87] Regarding the fight against impunity, the European Union and the African Union set up an expert group to clarify their approach to the limits of the principle of universal jurisdiction. The group handed in its report in April 2009.

Under the thematic area democracy and elections observation, we can note that seven missions took place during 2007: Afghanistan, Bolivia, Ecuador, Guinea-Bissau, Lebanon, Malawi and Mozambique.

The Stockholm Programme adopted in December 2009 has already been dealt with as have been other activities in the field of migration like the mobility partnership signed by the EU in November 2009 with Georgia and the amendments to certain directives in the field of asylum law.

With regard to trafficking in human beings, the Council of the EU adopted in December 2009 an "Action-Oriented Paper on Strengthening the EU External Dimension on Action against Trafficking in Human Beings: Towards Global EU Action against Trafficking in Human Beings". Closer cooperation between the EU and the United Nations in the struggle against all forms of discrimination expressed itself in an expert seminar and in the focus of the Human Rights Day 2009: the call to "embrace diversity - end discrimination".

Some other thematic issues have already been dealt with earlier in this contribution. As the example shows, there is a variety of ways and means of action of the European Union in order to advance the Human Rights Agenda in the 21 fields indicated and beyond. The closer look which the EU is taking on country situations can also be seen as an effort to strengthen the implementation of its external human rights policies on the ground.

Within the thematic issues there are efforts of cohesion visible insofar as topics are considered both in their external dimension of human rights and the internal dimension of fundamental rights. This is particularly visible with regard to issues like asylum, migration, refugees and displaced persons or racism, xenophobia, non-discrimination and respect for diversity, as it lies in the nature of these topics. However, the focus usually lies on the external dimension. For example, the section on persons with disabilities starts with a discussion of the UN framework and then provides information on the accession of the EU to the UN Convention on the Rights of Persons with Disabilities and on the inclusion of persons with disabilities in EU development cooperation. With regard to the European Disability Action Plan 2008-2009, the Council only mentions that the EU has committed itself to continue to address the human rights of disabled persons in the external relations policies and programmes of the EU.[88]

---

87   See Council Decision 2009/426/JHA of 16 December on the strengthening of Eurojust and amending Decision 2002/187/JHA, setting up Eurojust with a view to reinforcing the fight against serious crime.

88   Compare Section 4.20 of the Annual Report 2009.

E   Conclusions

2009 has been an important year for the fundamental rights framework and the pertinent policies of the European Union, because of the entry into force of the Lisbon Treaty and the Fundamental Rights Charter. The implications of this step, and the developments regarding the accession of the EU to the ECHR, will make 2010 and activities another crucial year for the future development of EU policies on fundamental rights. A central challenge, which will become even more important in the future, is the issue of the cohesion of EU human and fundamental rights policies, i.e. whether the EU will strive to give equal attention to the external dimension of human rights promoted in the world and the internal dimension of the protection of fundamental rights within the European Union. The reluctance of national governments to share their competences in this field is increasingly questioned by the now binding Charter on Fundamental Rights and the work of the Fundamental Rights Agency. However, with regard to the fundamental rights dimension of the European Area of Freedom, Security and Justice and the many bodies active in that field there is still a need for stronger mechanisms and procedures assuring coherence. Also, the visibility of the policies and activities in the field of fundamental human rights appears much lower than in the field of human rights in external affairs as can be seen best from the Annual Report by the Council. This may raise problems of double standards and credibility among partners of the EU. That this is highly problematic can be seen at the example of Human Rights Council, where the EU has substantial problems to convince other regions to share its concerns. The stronger focus on country and regional situations compared to thematic issues in the Annual Report 2009 contributes to this concern.

On the positive side the work of the Fundamental Rights Agency, which is gradually building up its capacities contributes to the credibility of the EU with regard to fundamental rights. In order to increase its potential impact, the FRA should be given a mandate for overseeing fundamental rights aspects of judicial and internal affairs, which would be logical after the depillarization brought by the Lisbon Treaty.

It remains to be seen whether the creation of a portfolio for fundamental rights with one commissioner will create new opportunities of a strengthened and more visible policy in this field.

Finally, the policies of the European Union with regard to human rights and fundamental rights have become so complex that it is difficult to be well informed about the major developments. Hopefully, this and the other contributions in this section will be useful for a better understanding of the still emerging human rights system of the European Union.

Hannes TRETTER and Anna MÜLLER-FUNK

The European Agency for Fundamental Rights in 2009: Opportunities, Responsibilities and Prospects

Table of Contents

Keywords

Human rights, fundamental rights, European Union, European Union Agency for Fundamental Rights (FRA), Treaty of Lisbon, Charter of Fundamental Rights

A   The Legal Framework of the European Union Agency for Fundamental Rights

The European Union Agency for Fundamental Rights (in the following: "Agency") was established through Council Regulation (EC) No 168/2007 of 15 February 2007 (in the following: the "Regulation") and opened its doors on 1 March 2007 in Vienna as the successor organization of the European Monitoring Centre on Racism and Xenophobia (EUMC). The establishment of the Agency was a long overdue step towards a stronger commitment to and coherence of EU policy with regard to human and fundamental rights, as was stipulated already in 1998 in the *Human Rights Agenda for the European Union for the Year 2000*. The authors of that document demanded the establishment of an EU Fundamental Rights Agency to strengthen the human rights coherence within the EU and among its member states.[1] This postulation tied in with what had already been laid out in

---

1   Antonio Cassese/Catherine Lalumière/Peter Leuprecht/Mary Robinson, Leading by

the EU's founding documents, in particular the Treaty of Maastricht 1992, wherein the EU explicitly commits itself to the protection of fundamental rights, as well as the Treaty of Amsterdam of 1997, which defines "the principles of liberty, democracy, respect for human rights and fundamental freedoms, and the rule of law"[2] as core principles of the EU.

In December 2000, shortly after these explicit commitments of the EU to fundamental rights, the Charter of Fundamental Rights of the European Union saw the light of day.[3] Along with the European Convention on Human Rights (ECHR) and the Regulation, it forms the main legal and conceptual framework behind the mandate of the Agency. For nearly a decade the Charter had merely moral and political authority and was used by the European Court of Justice in its judgments, but was not formally legally binding. However, on 1 December 2009 the Treaty of Lisbon entered into force, which elevated the Charter to the level of primary EU law. Article 6, para. 1, of the EU Treaty now provides that "[t]he Union recognizes the rights, freedoms and principles set out in the Charter of Fundamental Rights of the European Union of 7 December 2000, as adapted at Strasbourg, on 12 December 2007, which shall have the same legal value as the Treaties."

The Lisbon Treaty – which amends the Treaty on the European Union and the Treaty of the European Community (which mutated to the Treaty on the Functioning of the European Union) – also has an another important impact on the Agency's legal framework: Since the Lisbon Treaty leads to the "de-pillarization" as well as the "juridification" of the Union's policies, the thematic areas which the Agency can deal with are no longer limited to the former first pillar (Community law), but now include the former third pillar (Police and Judicial Co-operation in Criminal Matters). Consequently, wherever the Regulation is using the terms "European Community" or "Community law" these have to be read as having been replaced by "Union" and "Union law", respectively. The effects of this "de-pillarization" on the Agency and its mandate will be discussed in the following section of this paper.

This expansion of the Agency's mandate, the inclusion of the Charter into the EU Treaty and the establishment of the Agency, in conjunction with the recent appointment of Vivianne Reding from Luxemburg as the Commissioner for Justice, Fundamental Rights and Citizenship suggest that the EU is determined to strengthen and expand the role of fundamental and human rights in its policy and institutions. The purpose of this paper is to explore the role the Agency plays in this endeavour. We will thus start by discussing the mandate of the Agency in the light of the entering into force of the Lisbon Treaty (B). Thereafter, we will outline the tasks of the Agency that result from its mandate (C). After having examined the Agency's tasks we will provide an overview of its activities (D). In order to demonstrate how the Agency fulfils its tasks and how its activities are

---

Example – A Human Rights Agenda for the European Union for the Year 2000, Florence 1998.

2 Article 6, para. 1, Treaty of Amsterdam amending the Treaty on European Union, the treaties establishing the European Communities and Related Acts, available at http://eur-lex.europa.eu/en/treaties/dat/11997D/htm/11997D.html#0001010001.

3 Charter of Fundamental Rights of the European Union, Official Journal of the European Communities, C 364/1, 18 December 2000, available at http://www.europarl.europa.eu/charter/pdf/text_en.pdf.

structured we will then address the organisational structure and functioning of the Agency, as well as outlining the cooperation of the Agency with both, member states and civil society (E and F). We will conclude this article by providing a critical assessment of the perspectives of the Agency (G).

B   The Mandate of the Agency

The Agency is neither a prosecuting nor a monitoring body, nor a tribunal that handles individual or inter-state complaints. Rather, Article 2 of the Regulation commits it to being primarily a research and advisory body that shall "provide the relevant institutions, bodies, offices and agencies of the Union as well as its member states when implementing Union's law with assistance and expertise relating to fundamental rights in order to support them when they take measures or formulate courses of action within their respective spheres of competence to fully respect fundamental rights."[4] Thus, the field of activity of the Agency is predominantly confined to the application and interpretation of Union's law by its institutions and member states.

However, as laid down in its Regulation, conclusions, opinions and reports of the Agency may concern proposals from the Commission under Article 293 (former Article 250) of the EU Treaty or positions taken by the institutions (the European Parliament, the Council or the Commission) in the course of legislative procedures only where a request by the respective institution has been made.[5] This significantly limits the Agency's ability to continuously and preventively assess the conformity of legal instruments of the EU with fundamental rights, in a systematic manner and thus, limits the Agency's potential contribution to a greater coherence of the EU legal system in light of fundamental rights. However, the EU Commissioner for Justice, Fundamental Rights and Citizenship can encourage the Commission to seek the Agency's expert opinion, whenever a planned legal instrument of the EU raises questions or concerns with regards to fundamental and human rights. In addition, there are plans of the Commission to asses the mandate of the Agency, also with regards to its ability to provide expert opinion on EU legal policy proactively.

Until the Lisbon Treaty entered into force, the competence of the Agency was generally limited to the EU's 'internal affairs.' Therefore fundamental and human rights matters in the former third pillar of the EU, concerning Police and Judicial Co-operation in Criminal Matters (PJC) were not within the Agency's mandate. However, a declaration by the Council of the European Union of 12 February 2007, according to which the EU "institutions may, within the framework of the legislative process [...], benefit, as appropriate and on a voluntary basis, from such expertise also within the areas of police and judicial cooperation in criminal matters," lays out the possibility to consult the Agency in PJC matters and thus, to extend the Agency's mandate to the (former) third pillar.[6] Now, the question of the Agency's responsibility in PJC matters has been somewhat clarified by the

---

4   Article 2 of the Regulation.
5   Article 4, para. 2, together with para. 1 lit. d of the Regulation.
6   Declaration by the Council on the Consultation of the Agency within the Areas of Police and Judicial Cooperation in Criminal Matters of 12 February 2007, Council Document 6166/07.

Lisbon Treaty, since it led to the aforementioned "de-pillarization" of the structure of the EU.

Still, it is not within the Agency's regular mandate to be involved in sanction proceedings against member states as laid down in Article 7 of the new consolidated EU Treaty whenever there is a clear risk of a serious violation of the values referred to in Article 2 of the new Treaty by a member state. Yet, according to a further declaration of the Council of the European Union from 12 February 2007, the Council has the possibility to avail itself of the Agency's expertise in such cases.[7]

Furthermore, the competence of the Agency is generally limited to 'internal affairs of the EU'[8] even though Article 21 of the consolidated new EU Treaty stipulates that

"the Union's action on the international scene shall be guided by the principles which have inspired its own creation, development and enlargement, and which it seeks to advance in the wider world: democracy, the rule of law, the universality and indivisibility of human rights and fundamental freedoms, respect for human dignity, the principles of equality and solidarity, and respect for the principles of the United Nations Charter and international law".

Nevertheless, the Common Foreign and Security Policy (CFSP) of the Union lies still – despite the "de-pillarization" – clearly outside of the Agency's mandate.[9] Though, the Agency may give certain support to candidate countries that have concluded a Stabilization and Association Agreement with the European Union providing for a participation in the Agency's work, if the relevant Association Council chooses to do so.[10]

C   The Tasks of the Agency

Aside from defining the Agency's mandate, the Regulation also lays down its tasks, which can be subsumed broadly under the following three functions: the collection, analysis and dissemination of data; the provision of expert opinion;

---

7   Declaration by the Council on Proceedings under Article 7 of the Treaty on European Union of 12 February 2007, Council Document 6166/07.

8   See Article 3, para. 3, of the Regulation: "The Agency shall deal with fundamental rights issues in the European Union and in its Member States when implementing Community [since 1 December 2009: Union] law."

9   Only in a case, where a legal action of the Union is within the frame of CFSP (e.g.: trade or financial agreements, bi- or multilateral anti-terror measures, etc.) and has – intentionally or non-intentionally – an effect on the EU's internal legal order, the question arises whether this issue falls within the mandate of the Agency.

10   See Article 28 of the Regulation:
     "The Agency should be open to the participation of candidate countries. Furthermore, the countries with which a Stabilisation and Association agreement has been concluded should be allowed to participate in the Agency, since this will enable the Union to support their efforts towards European integration by facilitating a gradual alignment of their legislation with Community law as well as the transfer of know-how and good practice, particularly in those areas of the acquis that will serve as a central reference point for the reform process in the Western Balkans."

and the promotion of fundamental rights, i.e. the development of an appropriate communication strategy.[11]

The primary function of the Agency is the first function cited, namely the "provision of comparable and reliable information and data at a European level in order to assist the Union institutions and the Member States in respecting fundamental rights."[12] In addition, the Agency should "develop methods and standards to improve the comparability, objectivity and reliability of data at the European level, in cooperation with the Commission and the Member States."[13]

For this purpose the Agency uses both, current research results and information that has been provided by member states, Community institutions, EU bodies, research centres, national bodies, non-governmental organizations, third countries, international organizations and, last but not least, by the relevant bodies of the Council of Europe. In addition, the Agency commissions some of the necessary research to academic institutions and experts.

Furthermore, the Agency itself, within the framework of its work priorities and annual work programs, undertakes its own scientific research and develops preparatory and feasibility studies. On its own initiative or upon request by the European Parliament, the Council or the European Commission, the Agency compiles and publishes conclusions or expert opinions on specific topics and concerns related to the implementation of EU law for EU institutions, as well as the member states. The thematic areas, in which the Agency conducts its research, are determined by a Multi-annual Framework for the Agency (2007-2012),[14] which has been implemented by the Council on the basis of the Regulation. In addition to the thematic area that the Agency has to cover constantly, namely (1) "racism, xenophobia and related intolerance", it also has to concern itself, according to the Multi-annual Framework, with (2) "discrimination based on sex, race or ethnic origin, religion or belief, disability, age or sexual orientation and against persons belonging to minorities and any combination of these grounds (multiple discrimination)". The Agency can also work on (3) "compensation of victims", (4) "the rights of the child, including the protection of children", (5) "asylum, immigration and integration of migrants", (6) "visa and border control", (7) "participation of the EU citizens in the Union's democratic functioning", (8) "information society and, in particular, respect for private life and protection of personal data", as well as (9) "access to efficient and independent justice".[15]

What is noteworthy about this enumeration is the fact that prior to the Treaty of Lisbon not all of the listed thematic areas lay completely within the former first pillar of the EU. Yet, according to the Regulation, it was also clear that the Agency could only exercise its functions within the jurisdiction of EC law. Nevertheless, a meaningful study of any of these thematic areas was and still is only

---

11   Gabriel N. Toggenburg, The Role of the New EU Fundamental Rights Agency: Debating the "Sex of Angels" or Improving Europe's Human Rights Performance?, European Law Review, 2008/3, 392.
12   Article 4, para. 1, of the Regulation.
13   Article 4, para. 1 (b), of the Regulation.
14   Council of the European Union Council Decision (2008/203/EC) of 28 February 2008 implementing Regulation (EC) No 168/2007 as regards the adoption of a Multi-annual Framework for the European Union Agency for Fundamental Rights for 2007-2012.
15   Ibid., Article 2 (a)-(i).

possible with a comprehensive and overarching research approach, in order to produce professional and substantiated analysis. It would be meaningless and irresponsible to deal with topics like "information society", "asylum" or "access to efficient and independent justice" solely from a (former) first pillar perspective, without taking into account the (former) third one, namely Police and Judicial Co-operation in Criminal Matters. However, since the Lisbon Treaty entered into force, it is clear – as already mentioned – that the Agency's mandate has been extended to the matters of the former third pillar, too.

In order to respond flexibly to current fundamental rights challenges, the Agency can also, upon the request of the European Parliament, the Council of the European Union or the European Commission, engage in topics beyond the Multi-annual Framework, provided that the Agency's financial and human resources suffice.[16]

On the basis of its Multi-annual Framework, the Agency defines its annual work programmes that must accommodate its mission and conform to the strategic objectives of the Agency.[17] These objectives ensure that the Agency can cope with present and future challenges in the field of fundamental rights in a comprehensive manner. This approach is in particular reflected by multi-focus projects such as a current research project that is concerned with questions of access to justice in the context of data retention and data protection.

D   Recent, Current and Forthcoming Activities

Both, the aforementioned thematic areas and the strategic objectives are reflected by various projects that the Agency has completed in 2008 and 2009 as well as those it currently conducts.[18]

In the Agency's field of activity "discrimination based on sex, race or ethnic origin, religion or belief, disability, age or sexual orientation and against persons belonging to minorities and any combination of these grounds (multiple discrimination)", the Agency compiled and published the second part of a comprehensive report about homophobia in Europe.[19] In addition, the Agency prepared two detailed studies about the situation of European Roma citizens.[20] Moreover, the

---

16   See ibid., preambular para. 8. An example for such an undertaking by the Agency is a monitoring system, which assesses the impact of the global financial crisis on fundamental rights in Europe.

17   The FRA Mission and Strategic Objectives 2007-2012 have been approved by the Management Board of the Agency on 28 May 2009.
      http://fra.europa.eu/fraWebsite/attachments/FRA-mission-strategic-objectives_en.pdf

18   In the following, only a selection of projects is provided; for more information please visit http://fra.europa.eu/fraWebsite/products/products_en.htm.

19   FRA report, "Homophobia and Discrimination on Grounds of Sexual Orientation and Gender Identity in the EU Member States: Part II - The Social Situation", 31 March 2009, http://fra.europa.eu/fraWebsite/products/publications_reports/pub_cr_homophobia_p2_0309_en.htm.

20   FRA report, "The situation of Roma EU citizens moving to and settling in other Member States", http://fra.europa.eu/fraWebsite/attachments/Roma_Movement_Comparative-final_en.pdf, and FRA, "Housing conditions of Roma and Travellers in the European Union - Comparative report": http://fra.europa.eu/fraWebsite/attachments/ROMA-Housing-Comparative-Report_en.pdf).

Agency is currently working on a study that is concerned with the representation of migrants and minorities in the media, which will be published in 2010. Further projects are dealing with discrimination include: discrimination and victimization of migrants and other minorities in Europe, the impact of the EU Racial Equality Directive 2000/43/EC and diversity management.

In the thematic area "racism, xenophobia and related intolerance", the Agency issued, on the occasion of the UEFA European Football Championship a report about racism and sports,[21] along with a comprehensive study that dealt with the impact of racism and social marginalization using the example of the Muslim youth in Europe.

In its Annual Work Program 2009, the Agency particularly focused on "the rights of the child, including the protection of children", which is reflected by the research projects the Agency undertook 2009. In this context, the Agency developed indicators for the implementation, protection, respect and promotion of the rights of the child. Based on these, the Agency conducted a comparative study about the current situation of children's rights in the EU, including an assessment of legal instruments available in different member states.[22] Related to this study, the Agency is currently investigating the situation of unaccompanied minors seeking asylum in the EU, the results of which will be published in 2010. In addition the Agency recently published a handbook on strategies and perspectives on combating child trafficking in the EU.[23]

In the thematic area "participation of the EU citizens in the Union's democratic functioning," the Agency currently works on a detailed report about national human rights institutions and NGOs in the EU and their role in the formulation and implementation of human rights policy, which will be published in the first half of 2010.

With regards to the thematic area "asylum, immigration and integration of migrants" the Agency is currently compiling a study that compares legal practices of law enforcement and police detention in the different member states with regards to the return procedures of irregular immigrants.[24]

Regarding the issue "information society and, in particular, respect for private life and protection of personal data," the Agency is, after a thorough assessment of the legal instruments and institutions concerned with data protection in the EU, working on the publication of a handbook, which critically deals with "ethnic profiling" and presents "best practise" examples.

Finally, the Agency created the internal reporting system RADAR, which provides an extensive understanding of the impact of the global economic crisis on racism and xenophobia and acts as an early-warning system, using information and data provided by RAXEN (Racism and Xenophobia Expert Network) and

---

21 FRA report, "Racism and Ethnic Discrimination in Sport", http://fra.europa.eu/fraWebsite/research/research_projects/proj_racisminsport_en.htm.
22 FRA report, "Developing indicators for the protection, respect and promotion of the rights of the child in the European Union", http://fra.europa.eu/fraWebsite/attachments/RightsofChild_summary-report_en.pdf.
23 "Child Trafficking in the EU – Challenges, perspectives and good practices": http://fra.europa.eu/fraWebsite/attachments/Pub_Child_Trafficking_09_en.pdf.
24 "Rights of irregular immigrants in return procedures": http://fra.europa.eu/fraWebsite/research/research_projects/proj_migrantsreturnprocedures_en.htm.

FRALEX (Fundamental Rights Agency Legal Experts Group), as well as other EU agencies, international organizations, member states, the media and academia.

Additionally, the Agency formulates and provides "conclusions and opinions on specific thematic areas" for the EU and its member states. This is, however, strictly limited by the Regulation to matters that do not concern legislative matters.[25] Expert opinions on the latter can only be formulated and published by the Agency upon the request of the respective institution. This limitation does not only severely restrict the Agency's ability to play a part in the improvement the coherence of EU legal policy with fundamental rights, but also fails to fulfil the UN's Paris Principles, which set out minimum standards for national human rights institutions: "national institution[s] shall freely consider any questions falling within [their] competence [...] without referral to a higher authority."[26] Since the Commission considered the Paris Principles to be "a source of inspiration when establishing the Agency"[27] in the public consultation document concerning the establishment of the Agency, it is to be hoped that the joined efforts of the new Commissioner for Justice, Fundamental Rights and Citizenship, the European Parliament and the Director of the Agency with support of the Agency's Management Board will aid that the Agency's mandate has not only been inspired by, but its implementation is actually compliant with the Paris Principles, especially in light of the planned re-assessment of the mandate by the Council as proposed in the Declaration of the Council of the European Union from 12 February 2007.

However, the Stockholm Programme of the Council[28] at least invites the EU institutions

> "to make full use of the expertise of the Agency and to consult, where appropriate, with the Agency, in line with its mandate, on the development of policies and legislation with implications for fundamental rights, and to use it for the communication to citizens of human rights issues affecting them in their everyday life".

Unfortunately, a proposal of the Swedish EU Presidency in the second half of 2009, which foresaw an obligatory involvement of the Agency in all legal plans and drafts of the Union in order to secure conformity with fundamental rights standards was rejected.

Last but not least, the Agency is responsible for the promotion of, and the raising of awareness with regard to, fundamental rights issues in the EU and its member states to foster a "fundamental rights culture".[29] This is not only crucial with regards to policymakers but of particular importance with regards to those protected by fundamental and human rights provisions. A recent MIDIS study on discrimination showed that a vast majority of the population with a migration or

---

25   Article 4, para. 2, of the Regulation.
26   Article 3 (a) of the Paris Principles.
27   European Commission, Fundamental Rights Agency public consultation document COM(2004) 693 final, at 4.
28   Council of the European Union, The Stockholm Programme – An open and secure Europe serving and protecting the citizens, 23 November 2009, 16484/09, JAI 866, http://www.se2009.eu/polopoly_fs/1.19577!menu/standard/file/Draft_Stockholm_ Programme_16_October_2009.pdf.
29   European Commission, Compliance with the Charter of Fundamental Rights in Commission legislative, COM(2005) 172 final, at 3.

an ethnic minority background is not aware of the legal means available to them in the case of discrimination.[30] This demonstrates that legal instruments alone do not suffice in the comprehensive protection of human rights, but that these instruments have to be complemented with strong awareness raising measures, which the Agency has the competence to coordinate.

E   The Organizational Structure of the Agency

The organizational structure of the Agency is characterized by the extensive inclusion of and cooperation with relevant external actors and therefore comprises the following bodies: the Management Board, the Executive Board, the Scientific Committee, and the Director of the Agency.

The Management Board assembles one independent expert from each member state, who have been nominated by their respective government. The candidates have to demonstrate comprehensive knowledge of fundamental rights and extensive management experience, as well as considerable responsibility in either an independent national human rights institution or another public or private human rights institution. In addition, two representatives of the European Commission and one representative of the Council of Europe are members to the Management Board of the Agency, too. Since the beginning of 2010 the Management Board also includes representatives of the OSCE and the UN. The appointment of the members of the Management Board is limited to five years and is non-renewable. The Management Board elects two of its members as its Chairperson and Vice-Chairperson. The Board defines the Agency's priorities, establishes its budget and monitors the Agency's operations. The key responsibilities of the Board are the following: the appointment and (if necessary) the dismissal of the Agency's director, the adoption of the annual work programme and the respective annual draft and final budgets (including the financial rules applicable to the Agency), as well as the adoption of the Agency's annual reports.[31].

The Management Board is assisted in its tasks by the Executive Board, which comprises the Chairperson, and the Vice-Chairperson of the Management Board as well as two of its members and one representative of the European Commission and the Council.[32] The Executive Board's responsibility is, in addition to providing support to the Management Board, to assist and advise the Agency's director.

---

30   EU Agency for Fundamental Rights, EU-MIDIS, European Union Minorities Survey, Data in Focus Report, The Roma, 2009, http://fra.europa.eu.
31   Article 12, para. 6, of the Regulation.
32   On 15 December 2009, the Management Board of the Agency elected Ilze Brands-Kehris (Director of the Latvian Centre for Human Rights and Ethnic Studies) as its new Chairperson; Hannes Tretter (Director of the Ludwig Boltzmann Institute of Human Rights in Vienna) was reappointed as Vice-Chairperson; and Marie Staunton (CEO of the childrens' charity "Plan UK") and Linos-Alexandre Sicilianos (Law Professor at the University of Athens) have been elected as additional members; Aurel Ciobanu-Dordea and Emmanuel Crabit are the representatives of the European Commission and Guy de Vel (former Director of the Legal Department of the Council of Europe) represents the Council of Europe.

The Scientific Committee[33] consists of eleven independent experts, who are highly qualified in the field of fundamental rights and appointed by the Management Board in a transparent call for applications and selection procedure after having consulted the LIBE Committee of the European Parliament (Committee on Civil Liberties, Justice and Home Affairs).[34] The selection process also takes into account an even geographical representation of members of the Scientific Committee. The Committee's responsibility is to guarantee the scientific quality of the Agency's work and thus, is involved in the preparation of all documents that are published by the Agency, at the earliest possible stage.

The Director heads the Agency and manages its operations. He is appointed on the basis of personal merits, experience in the field of fundamental rights, as well as administrative and management skills for a period of five years which can be prolonged by three years. Due to the political dimension of the position, the European Commission, the European Parliament, the Council, as well as the Management Board of the Agency are involved in the selection process. On 7 March 2008, the Management Board appointed Morten Kjærum from Denmark as first Director of the Agency.[35]

In addition, the Agency cooperates, on the various levels of its organizational structures closely with a number of international institutions as well as member state bodies.

F   Partners and Cooperation of the Agency

A crucial aspect of the success of the Agency's work will be its choice of partners and the way in which it cooperates with them. Here a distinction has to be made between firstly the cooperation with European institutions and organizations, secondly the cooperation with independent expert groups that provide commissioned work and thirdly the cooperation with the European civil society.

Beside the cooperation with institutional partners, the cooperation and dialogue with the European civil society is of utmost importance. The Agency fosters it with a specifically developed communication strategy that on the one hand should raise the public awareness of fundamental and human rights issues and on the other hand is supposed to improve the cooperation of the Agency with key actors relevant to fundamental and human rights in Europe.

To engage in the latter, the Agency in 2008 created a cooperation network, the "Fundamental Rights Platform", which comprises representatives of non-governmental organizations dealing with fundamental and human rights, relevant advocacy groups and trade unions, appropriate social and professional organizations, churches, religious, philosophical and non-confessional organizations, universities as well as research institutions from all member states. The Funda-

---

33   The Scientific Committee's Chairperson is Stefano Rodota, its Vice-Chairperson Florence Benoît-Rohmer.

34   For More information about the LIBE Committee, see http://www.europarl.europa.eu/committees/libe_home_en.htm.

35   Morten Kjærum is a human rights expert with an NGO background, who for many years headed the Danish Institute for Human Rights. His appointment as Director of the Agency was generally appreciated since he has a long-standing human rights experience.

mental Rights Platform is involved in the formulation of the Agency's annual working programmes by providing comments and suggestion. The platform moreover provides feedback and suggests follow-up on the annual reports of the Agency. In addition, the members of the platform are responsible for communicating the outcomes and recommendations of conferences, seminars and meetings relevant to the work of the Agency. So far two meetings of the Agency and the Fundamental Rights Platform have taken place and the second call for participation in the platform just closed. [36]

Like its predecessor organization, the EUMC, the Agency cooperates closely with national experts from academia as well as practise, who mainly provide country-specific and/or thematic information and analytic capacities. Due to the significantly bigger budget of the Agency compared to that of the EUMC – which is linked to the correspondingly greater sphere of responsibility of the Agency – the Agency has considerably better financial and human resources and, thus, the ability to carry out necessary scientific work in-house. This is, for two reasons, of great importance: On the one hand the Agency needs its own scientific capacity to review and assess country specific reports and or thematic studies provided by external expert groups. On the other hand the Agency can now prepare integrated analysis and conclusions itself, and is not, like the EUMC, be entirely dependent on outside assistance. Nevertheless, the cooperation of the Agency with national experts is essential, since these have the necessary contacts and specialized knowledge regarding the national legal system and practice in their respective country, which is necessary for a profound collection of data and any scientific analysis. Currently, there are two groups of such national experts cooperating with the Agency: Firstly, RAXEN, which comprises organizations – so-called national focal points – who provide background material on racism, xenophobia and related intolerance, as well as national policies and initiatives promoting equality and diversity. Secondly, FRALEX that consists of legal experts, who report on legal aspects of fundamental rights issues at national and comparative level. Currently, it is planned to merge both expert groups in order to improve the scientific outcome by an intensified inter-disciplinary approach.

In particular regarding the data collection, the Agency cooperates closely with the Council of Europe, as laid down in the Regulation.[37] This dispels criticism that was voiced prior to the establishment of the Agency: Namely, that the Council of Europe (CoE) and its bodies would influence the work of the Agency, which would consequently result in a doubling of already existing structures. However, the recent years have shown that the opposite is the case, namely that the activities of the Agency complement those of the Council of Europe and its bodies: The Council of Europe (to whom all member states of the EU belong) is furthering the integration of the EU indirectly; it develops and improves common legal, in particular fundamental rights standards by creating specialized human rights conventions (inter alia on data protection and on the rights of persons belonging to national minorities). The European Court of Human Rights (ECtHR) on the other hand, provides jurisprudence in the field of human rights, while the Human Rights Commissioner of the CoE monitors the human rights situation in the CoE

---

36 For more information on the work of the Fundamental Rights Platform, please visit http://fra.europa.eu.

37 Cf. Articles 6-10 of the Regulation.

member states. The Agency's responsibility in turn encompasses to provide the necessary data, information and scientific assistance to ensure the conformity of EU law with fundamental rights, as well as to support member states in its implementation process.

Thereby, the Agency can on the one hand ease the burden of the busy ECtHR, especially in light of the reform process of the European Convention on Human Rights which will lead to the EU joining the Convention, and can on the other hand contribute to the legal harmonization of EU policy with regards to fundamental rights. The interplay of these organizations is working well and allows the European human and fundamental rights protection to function more efficiently. These benefits have meanwhile been commonly recognized and have led to the conclusion, on 18 June 2008, of an agreement between the EU and the Council of Europe, laying down the principles regulating the cooperation between the Agency and the Council of Europe.[38] This agreement states that both, the Agency's Director and the Secretariat of the Council of Europe, have a contact point in the respective organization for ensuring inter-institutional cooperation. According to the Regulation the Council of Europe seconds an independent expert to the Management Board of the Agency and has the right to choose additional representatives, as observing members of the Management Board (without the right to vote) to attend the meetings of the board. In return, representatives of the Agency can be invited to meetings of relevant consortia and agencies of the Council of Europe, when the Agency expresses its interest to attend such meetings.

Since the appointment of Morten Kjærum as the Director of the Agency, the Agency has significantly improved its contacts with the human rights bodies of the United Nations, in particular with the High Commissioner for Human Rights and the Organization for Security and Cooperation in Europe, particularly with the Office for Democratic Institutions and Human Rights in Warsaw and the High Commissioner on National Minorities in The Hague.

Finally, the appointment of so-called "national liaison officers" (NLOs) in each of the member states has significantly improved the possibilities of a closer and more efficient cooperation with the governments of the member states. The NLOs are the Agency's main contact point in the relevant member state and thus, improve the communication of the Agency with governments. They can comment on the draft of the Agency's annual work programmes and are provided with all studies and reports published by the Agency, and thereby facilitate the dissemination of the Agency's work.

G Perspectives and the Outlook of the Agency

As has been argued above, the Agency already plays a central role in improving the conformity of EU law with fundamental rights, as well as ensuring a better coherence of EU legal policy with regards to fundamental rights, by advising and supporting the relevant EU bodies. Additionally, the Agency already provides support and assistance to member states with regard to the implementation of

---

38   Agreement between the European Community and the Council of Europe on cooperation between the European Union Agency for Fundamental Rights and the Council of Europe, 18 June 2008, www.coe.int/t/der/docs/EUFRACoEAgreement_en.pdf.

the relevant policy and has developed strategies to improve the awareness of fundamental rights issues across the EU and its member states.

We need an Agency, which sharpens the fundamental rights profile of the EU and its member states, ideally by way of guaranteeing a "human rights based approach" of all EU politics. For this purpose – beside the expansion of the Agency's mandate to act more proactively and to be constantly involved in the EU law-making process – an outside perspective is of utmost importance, which the Agency, due to its cooperation with civil society, has. It is thus important to further develop and strengthen the Agency's relationship and communication with actors in the field of (European) fundamental rights. The launch of the Fundamental Rights Platform was therefore an important step in the right direction.

However, the Agency's mandate is unfavourably restricted in a certain way, as it has no authority to formulate and publish expert opinions on EU draft legislative matters on its own initiative, thus without a specific request by Parliament, Council, and Commission. It is to be hoped that a possible revision of the Regulation in conjunction with the Charter and the Stockholm Programme of the Council will lead to a broader involvement of the Agency in this respect.

There is some hope in this regard: The Agency's homophobia studies have been conducted upon request of the European Parliament, the Agency's expert opinion concerning the proposed Council Framework Decision on the Use of Passenger Name Record Data for Law Enforcement Purposes was requested by the French Presidency of the EU in the second half of 2008, further studies, e.g. the development of indicators for the protection of children's rights have been carried out upon request of the European Commission.

An important milestone in the history of the Agency is the fact that the Charter of Fundamental Rights is now legally binding, which significantly strengthens the legal and conceptual framework of the Agency. Since the Charter constitutes the legal document that represents what Article 2 of the EU Treaty considers the founding values of the Union, namely the "respect for human dignity, freedom, democracy, equality, the rule of law and respect for human rights, including the rights of persons belonging to minorities" it is also to be hoped that the Agency will play in future an active and clearly defined role in the sanction mechanism according to Article 7 of the Treaty, once the announced review of its mandate that was originally scheduled for December 2009 in the Declaration by the Council on the Review of the Remit of the Agency under Title VI of the Treaty on European Union[39] has taken place.

---

39   Declaration by the Council on the Review of the Remit of the Agency under Title VI of the Treaty on European Union of 12 February 2007, Council Document 6166/07.

Jean Paul JACQUÉ

Les droits fondamentaux dans le Traité de Lisbonne[*]

Table de matières

Mots-clés

Droits fondamentaux, Traité de Lisbonne, Charte des droits fondamentaux, compétence de l'Union, principes généraux du droit, Convention européenne des droits de l'homme, mécanisme de contrôle

A   Introduction

Les principaux progrès apportés par le traité de Lisbonne en matière de droits fondamentaux résident dans l'incorporation indirecte de la Charte des droits fondamentaux dans les traités et dans l'insertion d'une clause permettant, et

---

[*]   Ce texte est une version remaniée, mise à jour et complétée de la contribution de l'auteur aux mélanges en l'honneur du Professeur Jean Charpentier (Paris, 2009).

imposant, l'adhésion de l'Union à la Convention européenne des droits de l'homme. Il s'agit de l'aboutissement d'un processus entamé depuis de longues années. Dans le passé, l'effort du juge s'était essentiellement porté sur l'affirmation de ces droits dans le cadre de la Communauté à la suite des réactions des juridictions constitutionnelles nationales qui s'étaient notamment traduites dans l'arrêt *Solange I* de la Cour constitutionnelle allemande. En réponse à cette jurisprudence, assortie d'une menace indirecte sur la primauté, la Cour a répondu en assurant la protection des droits fondamentaux par le canal des principes généraux du droit ce qui a permis l'établissement, de manière toute casuistique, d'un catalogue jurisprudentiel des droits fondamentaux. Cette construction prétorienne a conduit à la reprise de la jurisprudence de la Cour dans l'article 6 du traité sur l'Union européenne.

L'article 6 du traité sur l'Union européenne (TUE) tel qu'il avait été introduit par le traité de Maastricht définissait le cadre dans lequel devait opérer le juge communautaire. Les droits fondamentaux protégés au sein de l'Union trouvent leur origine tant dans la Convention européenne des droits de l'homme que dans les traditions constitutionnelles communes aux Etats membres. La réception de ces droits dans l'ordre juridique communautaire s'effectue par le canal des principes généraux du droit. La Cour a cependant puisé à d'autres sources d'inspiration et fait appel à des conventions internationales auxquelles les Etats membres étaient parties, notamment en ce qui concerne les droits sociaux qui ne sont pas garantis par la Convention européenne des droits de l'homme. La Cour a ainsi donné une valeur particulière à la Charte sociale européenne conclue dans le cadre du Conseil de l'Europe[1] et à laquelle l'article 136 du traité CE fait référence.

La Charte des droits fondamentaux ne faisait partie du cadre de référence mis en place par l'article 6 TUE et sa prise en considération par le juge communautaire est le résultat d'un lent processus. Il est vrai que les auteurs du traité de Nice n'avaient pas souhaité incorporer la Charte dans le droit primaire et s'étaient contentés de donner à celle-ci la forme et la valeur d'un accord interinstitutionnel. Dans un premier temps, l'importance de la Charte s'est trouvée reflétée dans les conclusions des avocats généraux,[2] puis dans la jurisprudence du Tribunal de Première instance qui prenait la Charte en considération en raison du fait laquelle confirmait les traditions constitutionnelles des Etats membres[3]. Pour sa part, la Cour a d'abord fait usage de la Charte sans le dire lorsqu'elle a consacré le principe général de la dignité de la personne humaine.[4] Dans un second temps, dans une affaire relative au regroupement familial, la Charte a

---

1   Voir pour une jurisprudence récente les arrêts Viking du 11 décembre 2007 (point 43) et Laval du 18 décembre 2007, affaire C-341/05 (point 90), non encore publiés au recueil.

2   Il en concluait qu'il est « impossible d'ignorer les énonciations pertinentes de la charte ni surtout son évidente vocation à servir, lorsque es dispositions le permettent de paramètre de référence substantiel ... », Conclusions du 8 février 2001, BECTU, affaire C-173/99, rec. I-4851.

3   Arrêt du 30 janvier 2002, max.mobil c. Commission, affaire T-54/49, rec. II-313.

4   Arrêt du 9 octobre 2001, Pays-Bas c. Conseil, affaire C-377/99, rec. I-7079. En effet, l'arrêt reconnaît le principe sans indiquer aucune source. Or la Charte des droits fondamentaux est le principal texte qui fasse référence au principe de la dignité de la personne humaine dans l'Union.

servi d'instrument d'interprétation d'un texte communautaire parce qu'il en était fait mention dans la motivation du texte[5]. Enfin, après la signature du traité « constitutionnel »[6], toute réserve à l'égard de la Charte a disparu. Ainsi, pas après pas, la Charte a fait son chemin dans le système communautaire de droits fondamentaux. Sur un plan théorique, l'entrée en vigueur du traité de Lisbonne devrait modifier fondamentalement la situation puisque la Charte fera désormais partie du droit primaire. Mais, compte tenu du maintien des dispositions de l'actuel article 6, les principes généraux du droit conserveront une place. Ils perdent cependant leur exclusivité dans la mesure où la Charte constitue le principal instrument de protection.

Quant à l'adhésion de l'Union à la Convention européenne des droits de l'homme, elle est également le fruit d'une longue réflexion. Dès le 4 avril 1979, la Commission avait entamé les travaux sur une possible adhésion par la publication d'un mémorandum. Le 19 novembre 1990, la Commission rendait public une communication sur le même sujet et le Conseil entreprenait des travaux qu'il estimait ne pouvoir conclure sans solliciter l'avis de la Cour de justice laquelle subordonnait toute adhésion à une éventuelle révision des traités. Des propositions d'adhésion furent formulées lors des révisions successives des traités, mais sans succès. Il faudra attendre la Convention pour voir enfin la proposition tenue. Présente dans la constitution, sa place fut maintenue dans le traité de Lisbonne à l'article 6 TUE, accompagnée d'un protocole qui en fixe le cadre.

Dans ce contexte, il convient de s'interroger sur les normes désormais applicables dans le domaine des droits fondamentaux et d'en établir, le cas échéant, la hiérarchie, oui d'envisager les modalités qui devraient gouverner l'adhésion de l'union à la convention européenne des droits de l'homme.

B   Le nouveau cadre normatif de référence

Si la Charte devient l'instrument principal, elle n'est pas l'instrument exclusif puisque la référence aux principes généraux du droit subsiste à l'article 6.

1   La Charte au rang de source de droit primaire pour la protection des droits fondamentaux

A la différence de la constitution, le traité de Lisbonne n'incorpore pas la Charte des droits fondamentaux, mais donne à celle-ci la même valeur que les traités. La version de la Charte à laquelle il est fait référence n'est pas la version originale qui avait été signée par les institutions à Nice le 7 décembre 2000, mais la version révisée à l'occasion de son incorporation dans la constitution et qui a été signée par les institutions le 12 décembre 2007.[7] Tout comme la constitution, le

---

5   Arrêt du 27 juin 2006, Parlement c. Conseil, affaire C-540/03, rec. I-5769.

6   Voir les arrêts Viking et Laval (2007) précités. Coïncidence ou volonté de n'utiliser la Charte qu'après que celle-ci ait été approuvée non seulement par les institutions dans un accord interinstitutionnel, mais également par les Etats membres à travers la signature du traité établissant une constitution pour l'Europe.

7   En effet sur un plan technique, comme le traité de Lisbonne ne pouvait faire référence à la constitution et que le texte incorporé dans la constitution différait de celui de la charte initiale, il était nécessaire d'établir un nouveau texte authentique de la charte.

traité précise que l'interprétation de la Charte doit prendre en considération[8] les explications qui avaient été rédigées lors de l'élaboration de celle-ci.[9] L'intégration de la Charte dans le droit primaire n'est pas allée de soi. Dès la convention, les représentants britanniques avaient soulevé un certain nombre de question auxquelles il avait fallu apporter des réponses dans le texte même de la Charte. Mais cela n'a pas suffi puisque, bien qu'ayant signé le traité établissant une constitution sur l'Europe le gouvernement britannique est revenu sur la question lors de la négociation du traité de Lisbonne et a obtenu un protocole spécifique.

a   Le lien éventuel entre droits fondamentaux et compétences de l'Union

Le traité de Lisbonne prend soin de couper tout lien entre la Charte et les compétences de l'Union puisqu'il précise que les dispositions de la Charte ne peuvent étendre en aucune matière les compétences de celle-ci. Cette disposition porte témoignage d'une incompréhension qui s'est manifestée dès les premiers moments de la rédaction de la Charte et qui est loin d'avoir disparu aujourd'hui. Bien des membres de la Convention considéraient en effet qu'il devait exister une correspondance absolue entre droits fondamentaux et compétences communautaires. Selon eux, il ne pouvait pas d'une part être fait mention de certains droits dès lors que l'Union ne possédait pas de compétences dans un domaine qui touchait au champ d'application présumé de ces droits. D'autre part, toute mention d'un droit dans la Charte risquait à leurs yeux de donner naissance à une compétence de l'Union en rapport avec ce droit. En d'autres termes, le simple fait de mentionner dans la Charte la liberté d'expression pouvait selon eux donner compétence à la Communauté pour adopter des mesures en la matière. Plus clairement encore, l'interdiction de la peine de mort ne pouvait figurer dans la Charte puisque l'Union ne pouvait prononcer une telle peine.

Cette vision repose sur une méconnaissance complète tant des règles communautaires que des droits fondamentaux. S'agissant de ces derniers, leur caractère horizontal est admis depuis longtemps. Chacun sait que la législation en matière religieuse, domaine dans lequel l'Union n'a pas de compétence, n'est pas seule à pouvoir porter atteinte à la liberté religieuse, mais qu'une législation fiscale ou sanitaire pourrait indirectement engendrer une violation de cette liberté.[10] Si l'Union doit respecter les droits fondamentaux, ce n'est pas en raison d'une compétence particulière pour légiférer, mais parce que cette obligation de respect s'impose à elle de manière horizontale dans l'ensemble de ses activités. L'Union ne peut dans l'exercice de ses compétences porter atteinte aux droits fondamentaux qu'elle garantit, la même règle s'appliquant d'ailleurs aux Etats membres lorsqu'ils agissent dans le champ d'application du droit communau-

---

8   Outre les dispositions du titre VII de celle-ci.

9   Étrange destin que celui de ces explications qui ont été rédigées par le secrétariat de la Convention chargée de l'élaboration de la Charte, n'ont fait l'objet d'un très rapide coup d'œil des membres du présidium de la Convention par une procédure écrite, puis se voient transformées en élément d'interprétation authentique du document auquel elles sont rattachées.

10   Sur ce point, voir notre contribution aux mélanges Cohen-Jonathan, Droits fondamentaux et compétences internes de la Communauté, volume I, Bruxelles 2004.

taire. En résumé, l'obligation de respecter un droit fondamental ne donne pas naissance à une compétence de l'Union, elle impose seulement à l'Union de veiller à ce que, dans l'exercice de ses compétences propres, il ne soit pas porté atteinte à ce droit. Les droits fondamentaux constituent une limite générale à l'action de l'Union.

Cependant, les méfiances politiques à l'égard du risque d'une extension des compétences ont été telles que la clause relative à la sauvegarde des compétences communautaires n'a pas seulement été introduite dans la Charte, mais qu'elle figure à deux reprises à l'article 6 du traité de Lisbonne, sans tenir compte d'une déclaration tchèque dans le même sens. Les récents arrêts *Laval* et *Viking* de la Cour de Justice devraient cependant rassurer les esprits. Ces affaires mettaient en cause les rapports entre libre prestation de services, liberté d'établissement et droit de grève. Or, l'article 137 CE exclut expressément le droit de grève des compétences communautaires. Cela n'implique pas que la Cour de justice puisse faire abstraction de ce droit. Comme la Cour le rappelle dans ces affaires :

> *« s'il est vrai que, dans des domaines que ne relèvent pas de la compétence de la Communauté, les Etats membres restent, en principe, libres de fixer les conditions d'existence des droits en cause et les modalités d'exercice de ces droits, il n'en demeure pas moins que, dans l'exercice de cette compétence, lesdits Etats sont néanmoins tenus de respecter le droit communautaire [...]. Par conséquent, la circonstance que l'article 137 CE ne s'applique ni au droit de grève ni au droit de lock-out n'est pas de nature à soustraire une action collective telle que celle en cause au principal à l'application de l'article 43 CE. »* [11]

Certes, il s'agissait moins en l'espèce, de protéger un droit fondamental que d'établir dans quelle mesure un droit fondamental pouvait limiter une des libertés établies par le traité. Mais les arrêts de la Cour rompent sans ambiguïté le lien que l'on pourrait établir entre droit et compétence. Cette rupture n'est pas nouvelle. Elle était déjà manifeste lorsque, dans l'arrêt *Grant*, la Cour constatait que « si le respect des droits fondamentaux [...] constitue une condition de la légalité des actes communautaires, ces droits ne peuvent en eux-mêmes avoir pour effet d'élargir le champ d'application des dispositions du traité au delà des compétences de la Communauté ». [12]

Par contre, l'existence d'un droit reconnu au niveau de l'Union n'autorise pas la Cour à appliquer celui-ci hors du champ d'application du droit de l'Union. [13] Ainsi la Cour a refusé d'appliquer le principe de non-discrimination à une situation interne belge discriminant entre wallons et flamands alors qu'elle déclarait cette même législation flamande contraire au droit communautaire dès lors qu'elle s'appliquait aux travailleurs communautaires ayant exercé leurs droits à la libre circulation. [14]

---

11   Arrêt Laval précité, points 87 et 88.
12   Arrêt du 17 février 1998, affaire C-249/96, rec. I-621, point 45.
13   Arrêt du 29 mai 1997, Kremzow, affaire C-299/95, rec. I-2629.
14   Arrêt du 1 avril 2008, Gouvernement de la Communauté française et Gouvernement wallon, affaire C-212/06, non encore publiée au recueil.

b   Le statut distinct des droits et des principes

La Charte telle qu'elle a été modifiée par la Convention chargée de son élaobration tente de clarifier la distinction entre les droits et les principes. Lors de la rédaction de la Charte, certains membres de la Convention estimaient que ne pouvaient figurer dans celle-ci que des droits directement justiciables ce qui avait pour conséquence d'exclure un certain nombre de droits sociaux.[15] Un compromis fut trouvé au prix d'une distinction entre droits et principes. Durant la seconde Convention chargée de rédiger la constitution, les représentants britanniques ont fortement insisté pour clarifier cette distinction ce qui fut fait dans la nouvelle rédaction de l'article 52 de la Charte. Tandis que les droits peuvent être invoqués devant la Cour à l'encontre d'une mesure communautaire ou d'une mesure nationale d'application, la violation d'un principe ne peut être sanctionnée par un juge qu'à l'encontre d'une mesure qui le met en œuvre. Un particulier ne pourrait donc se prévaloir directement d'un principe puisque celui-ci ne créerait pas de droit subjectif à son profit.

Si l'on met de côté la question de l'identification des principes contenus dans la Charte,[16] le problème essentiel est celui de la justiciabilité de ceux-ci. Formellement, l'invocabilité d'un principe est subordonnée à l'existence d'une mesure de mise en œuvre adoptée par l'Union ou un Etat membre. Tout dépendra donc de la signification que l'on accorde à cette notion de mise en œuvre. Cette dernière n'intervient-elle que dans les seuls cas où l'objet d'un acte est explicitement de fixer les conditions d'application du principe ? Une telle vision ne paraît-elle pas trop restrictive ? S'il est vrai qu'un particulier ne peut invoquer un principe à l'encontre d'une mesure individuelle le concernant, ce principe permet-il pas de demander au juge d'apprécier la conformité d'une quelconque législation dont l'effet serait de remettre en cause ledit principe ? Ainsi, l'article 25 de la Charte reconnaît le droit des personnes âgées de participer à la vie sociale et culturelle. Ne pourrait-on invoquer une violation de l'article 25 à l'encontre d'une mesure de l'Union prise en matière d'emploi ou de libre prestation de services qui aurait pour conséquence d'exclure les personnes âgées ? En effet les principes fixent des objectifs à l'action de l'Union et celle-ci ne peut les méconnaître dans son œuvre législative. Bien entendu, seule l'adoption de mesures positives créera des droits subjectifs dont la violation pourra être sanctionnée par le juge. Certes l'abstention du législateur ne constituera pas une violation de la Charte, mais rien n'interdit qu'une mesure de portée générale de l'Union qui irait à l'encontre du principe subisse la censure du juge. L'avenir dira si la Cour est disposée à adopter cette interprétation qui semble d'ailleurs résulter des explications jointes à la Charte.

c   Le protocole relatif à la Pologne et au Royaume-Uni

Les réticences britanniques à l'égard de la Charte sont anciennes, mais, comme on l'a vu, elles avaient pu être surmontées lors de l'élaboration de la constitution par une distinction plus claire entre droits et principes et par une déclaration,

---

15   Mais pas tous les droits sociaux puisque certains comme les droits syndicaux, ou la protection contre le licenciement abusif sont incontestablement justiciables.

16   Les explications sous l'article 52 incluent une courte liste de principes dont il est précisé qu'elle n'est pas exhaustive.

d'ailleurs superfétatoire puisque le texte de la Charte l'indiquait déjà, selon laquelle celle-ci n'accroissait pas les compétences de l'Union. Pour aller dans le sens britannique, la présidence allemande avait retiré la charte des traités modifiés et l'avait incorporée par une simple référence à l'article 6 TUE en ajoutant que la Charte n'étendait pas les compétences de l'Union. Ceci n'était pas suffisant et le gouvernement britannique proposait au Conseil européen un protocole relatif au Royaume-Uni soigneusement rédigé dont l'objet essentiel était de soustraire à la compétence de la Cour de justice et des tribunaux britanniques le contrôle de la conformité des « lois, règlement, dispositions et pratiques ou action administrative du Royaume-Uni » avec les droits garantis par la Charte. Au dernier moment, la Pologne s'est jointe au Royaume-Uni. Sa préoccupation ne portait pas sur les droits sociaux puisqu'elle a éprouvé le besoin de rappeler dans une déclaration son attachement à ces droits, mais concernait la vie privée et familiale ainsi que le mariage. Sa crainte était notamment de se trouver contrainte de reconnaître les unions homosexuelles et d'assouplir sa législation sur l'interruption volontaire de grossesse. À vrai dire, on voit mal comment le protocole pouvait répondre aux préoccupations polonaises puisque celles-ci portent sur des aspects du droit de la famille qui sont déjà largement couvertes par la Convention européenne des droits de l'homme à laquelle la Pologne est partie.

La demande britannique a été entendue par les Etats membres et un protocole n° 30 sur l'application de la Charte des droits fondamentaux de l'Union européenne à la Pologne et au Royaume-Uni a été annexé au Traité de Lisbonne. Dans ces conditions, quelle est la situation de la Pologne et du Royaume-Uni par rapport à la Charte ?

La réponse dépend bien entendu d'une lecture très attentive du texte d'un protocole que la Cour sera sans doute appelée à interpréter. Tout d'abord, le préambule du protocole souligne que la Charte « réaffirme les droits, les libertés et les principes reconnus dans l'Union et les rend plus visibles, sans toutefois créer de nouveaux droits ou principes ». La formule n'est pas nouvelle puisqu'elle figure dans le préambule de la Charte. Le protocole rappelle ensuite les obligations qui incombent au Royaume-Uni et à la Pologne en vertu des traités et du droit de l'Union. Selon l'article premier, la Charte

> « n'étend la faculté de la Cour de justice de l'Union européenne, ou de toute juridiction de la Pologne ou du Royaume-Uni d'estimer que les lois, règlements, pratiques ou actions administratives de la Pologne ou du Royaume-Uni sont incompatibles avec les droits, les libertés et les principes fondamentaux qu'elle réaffirme. »

La lecture qui paraît découler de ces dispositions combinées entre elles est que puisque la Charte ne crée pas de droits nouveaux,[17] les deux Etats sont déjà liés par le contenu de la cette dernière au titre de l'acquis du droit de l'Union, y compris par le truchement des principes généraux du droit. Le protocole n'implique par les deux Etats puissent se soustraire à l'application de la Charte lorsqu'ils agissent dans le champ du droit de l'Union. En ce qui concerne

---

17   La question de savoir si la Charte crée ou non de nouveaux droits peut être discutée, mais ici l'important est qu'aux yeux du Royaume-Uni et de la Pologne, la Charte ne crée pas de nouveaux droits. Par cette reconnaissance dans le cadre du droit primaire, les deux Etats renoncent à contester l'application à leur encontre d'un des droits contenu dans la Charte au motif qu'il irait au delà du droit existant.

le contrôle juridictionnel, le protocole prévoit certes que la Charte n'en étend pas le champ du contrôle juridictionnel, mais elle ne le restreint pas non plus. Il en résulte que le contrôle de la Cour et des juridictions nationales continuera à s'exercer de la même manière qu'auparavant. Il n'y rien de nouveau dans cette affirmation puisque la volonté des auteurs de la Charte n'a jamais été de modifier le système de contrôle juridictionnel. Celui-ci se poursuivra dans le cadre classique du contrôle de légalité ou de l'interprétation du droit de l'Union effectué par la Cour. S'agissant des normes de référence, puisque la Charte reconnaît simplement des droits existants, ces droits pourront être pris en compte sans restriction par la Cour lorsqu'elle évaluera la conformité des normes nationales polonaises ou britanniques par rapport au traité.

Dans ces conditions, l'article 1 du protocole qui précise que la faculté du juge d'apprécier la compatibilité des mesures nationales par rapports aux droits, libertés et principes fondamentaux réaffirmés par la Charte ne limite en rien le contrôle exercé classiquement par le juge. Tout au plus peut-il interdire au juge d'utiliser la Charte pour juger des mesures nationales qui ne tombent pas dans le champ d'application du droit de l'Union. Mais cette « incorporation » de la Charte, pour employer une expression nord-américaine,[18] n'est pas envisagée par le Traité de Lisbonne et est exclue par la jurisprudence actuelle de la Cour. Mais on peut voir peut-être dans cet article premier le souci d'éviter toute évolution jurisprudentielle vers une éventuelle « incorporation ».

Le paragraphe 2 de l'article premier du Protocole précise que le titre IV, consacré aux droits sociaux, ne crée pas de droits justiciables dans les deux Etats sauf s'ils ont prévus de tels droits dans leur législation nationale. Cette précision modifie-t-elle la situation ? Il serait possible de retenir une interprétation stricte du protocole et de soutenir qu'en aucun cas la Cour de justice ne pourrait, dans une affaire concernant le Royaume-Uni ou la Pologne, appliquer un droit mentionné au titre IV si ce droit n'est pas reconnu par la législation nationale des pays concernés. Mais ce n'est pas semble-t-il ce qu'ont voulu exprimer les auteurs du protocole. Leur inquiétude est que les principes consacrés par la Charte puissent être directement invoqués devant une juridiction à l'égal de dispositions donnant naissance à des droits subjectifs. Dans ce contexte, le paragraphe 2 du protocole pris dans son sens littéral signifie-il autre chose que les droits ou principes visés au titre IV de la Charte ne peuvent être justiciables que lorsqu'ils sont été concrétisés par la législation de l'Union ou des législations nationales ? Or la Charte fait généralement suivre l'énoncé des droits sociaux d'une référence aux règles établies par le droit de l'Union et les législations ou pratiques nationales. Lorsque la Charte omet cette référence, c'est parce de telles règles existent déjà en droit communautaire comme en attestent les explications. En outre lorsqu'un droit est consacré dans l'ordre juridique de l'Union, les Etats membres sont tenus le respecter lors de la mise en œuvre de ce droit sans quoi l'application uniforme du droit serait mise en cause. Cette obligation

---

18 Selon la doctrine de l'incorporation, la Cour suprême des Etats-Unis peut apprécier la conformité des lois des Etats à certains amendements qui constituent le Bill of Rights par le biais du quatorzième amendement à la Constitution alors qu'à l'origine il avait été considéré que le Bill of Rights n'était opposable qu'à la législation fédérale. Cette question de l'incorporation a été très présente dans les débats de la convention chargée d'élaborer la Charte et le souci d'éviter celle-ci a conduit à la rédaction de l'article 51 de la Charte.

ne découle d'ailleurs pas de la Charte, mais du droit de l'Union et la jurisprudence est claire sur ce point. Dès lors, l'Etat doit respecter les droits fondamentaux établis par la législation de l'Union quelque soit l'état de sa législation interne. Par contre, dans les domaine dépourvus de tout lien avec le droit de l'Union, il reste libre. Ainsi l'obligation de respecter les droits fondamentaux de l'Union ne trouverait pas son origine dans la Charte qui ne ferait d'ailleurs, selon le protocole, que réaffirmer des droits existants, mais elle trouverait sa source dans l'obligation de respecter le droit de l'Union, obligation à laquelle le préambule du protocole fait référence.

Dans ce contexte la portée du protocole n'est pas d'exempter le Royaume-Uni et la Pologne du respect du contenu matériel de la Charte puisque qu'ils admettent que celui-ci fait d'ores et déjà partie du droit de l'Union que ce soit sur la base des principes généraux du droit ou de la législation existante. En outre, s'agissant des droits dont la justiciabilité est subordonnée à l'adoption de mesures de mise en œuvre, les deux Etats concernés admettent qu'ils seront bien entendu liés en vertu du principe de primauté par les mesures de mise en œuvre adoptées par l'Union. En l'absence de mesures de mise en œuvre, ils conserveraient leur pleine liberté. La seule obligation qui pourrait découler de ces droits ou principes non encore mis en œuvre pèserait non sur les Etats membres mais sur les institutions de l'Union. En effet, ces dernières ne peuvent porter atteinte dans la législation de l'Union aux principes contenus dans la Charte. Ainsi un règlement ou une directive adopté dans un domaine quelconque ne pourrait porter atteinte au niveau de protection sociale ou de protection de la santé existant dans l'Union, pas plus d'ailleurs qu'il ne pourrait être invoqué à l'encontre des règles nationales établies pour mettre en œuvre les droits et principes du titre IV.[19] La Charte impose dans ce domaine le respect d'une situation de standstill. Dans ce contexte, le protocole n'est guère utile puisqu'il vise à remédier à une situation que la Charte a naturellement exclue.

D'ailleurs, selon le gouvernement britannique lui-même, le protocole ne doit pas être interprété comme un opt out de la Charte, mais comme une simple mise en évidence de règles qui figurent déjà dans la Charte elle-même. Selon les déclarations du ministère des affaires étrangères devant le European Union Committee de la House of Lords, « The UK Protocol does not constitue an « opt out ». It puts beyond legal doubts the legal position that nothing in the Charter creates any new rights, or extends the ability of any court to strike down UK law ».[20] Le protocole constitue en quelque sorte une répétition des articles horizontaux relatifs à l'application et à l'interprétation de la Charte. Comme l'a constaté l'European Union Committee de la House of Lords,

« The protocol should not lead to a different application of the Charter in United Kingdom and Poland when compared with the rest of the Member States. But to the extent that the Explanations leave some ambiguity as to the scope and interpretation of the Charter rights, and as to the justiciabil-

---

19   Ce que fait naturellement le législateur communautaire lorsqu'il adopte une législation. Ainsi le règlement précise bien que les règles qu'ils pose pour éviter les entraves à la libre circulation ne remettent pas en cause le droit de grève.

20   UK House of Lords/European Union Committee, The Treaty of Lisbon : an impact assessment, 10th Report of Session 2007-2008, vol. I, p. 102.

ity of the Title IV rights especially, the Protocol provides helpful interpretation ».[21]

Mais, d'un autre côté, le protocole constitue un avertissement adressé au juge britannique contre toute tentative d'utilisation du titre IV dans des situations purement internes, notamment en ce qui concerne l'article 28 de la Charte sur le droit à la négociation et à l'action collective qui serait de nature à remettre en cause les spécificités britanniques en ce domaine.

2   Les autres sources de droits fondamentaux

Le rang de droit primaire accordé à la Charte aurait logiquement pu entraîner la disparition des références contenues dans l'article 6 TUE tant aux principes généraux du droit et aux traditions constitutionnelles communes qu'à la Convention européenne des droits de l'homme. Il n'en a rien été. D'ailleurs, la suppression de la référence aux principes généraux du droit eut été de toute manière inopérante puisque le recours à ceux-ci n'a jamais été fondé sur une autorisation expresse accordée par les traités. Cependant la multiplicité des sources de droits fondamentaux conduit inévitablement à s'interroger sur la manière dont celles-ci seront amenées à jouer.

a   Les principes généraux du droit, une source secondaire?

Compte tenu de la très large coïncidence qui existe actuellement entre le contenu de la Charte et les droits fondamentaux protégés au titre de principes généraux du droit, le maintien des dispositions de l'article 6 TUE ne devrait pas à court terme jouer un rôle essentiel. Cependant, la jurisprudence la Cour fondée sur les principes généraux du droit pourrait servir dans certains cas de guide à l'interprétation de certaines dispositions de la Charte. Ainsi l'article 51 de la Charte précise que celle-ci s'applique aux Etats membres « uniquement lorsqu'ils mettent en œuvre le droit de l'Union ». Les explications qui, selon l'article 6, paragraphe 1, doivent être dûment prises en considération pour l'interprétation et l'application de la Charte ne sont pas d'une clarté absolue sur ce point. Tout en rappelant que selon la jurisprudence l'obligation de respecter les droits fondamentaux s'impose aux Etats membres lorsqu'ils agissent dans le cadre du droit de l'Union, elles font référence à l'arrêt *Wachhauf*[22] qui ne vise que le cas de la mise en œuvre de ce droit. Dans cette hypothèse, quid des mesures nationales qui dérogent au droit de l'Union ? La Cour pourrait utiliser sa jurisprudence sur la portée des principes généraux pour clarifier la situation et conforter la thèse de l'application de la Charte aux Etats membres dans le cadre du droit communautaire. Il ne s'aglt que d'un exemple du jeu possible entre Charte et principes généraux et d'autres cas pourraient être évoqués, par exemple en ce qui concerne le droit de propriété ou le principe *non bis in idem*.

Mais, au-delà de cet usage interprétatif des principes généraux, ces derniers constituent une voie ouverte à la reconnaissance par la Cour de nouveaux droits. Selon l'article 6, paragraphe 3, du traité sur l'Union européenne qui repro-

---

21   Ibid., p. 106.
22   Arrêt du 13 juillet 1989, affaire 5/88, rec. 2609

duit le texte antérieur du TUE, le sources des principes généraux sont la Convention européenne des droits de l'homme et les traditions constitutionnelles communes aux Etats membres. Le rôle de la Convention sera évoqué plus loin. S'agissant des traditions constitutionnelles communes, celles-ci ne sont pas figées et tant le texte des constitutions que la jurisprudence des cours constitutionnelles nationales peuvent dégager de nouveaux droits, voire donner une extension nouvelle à des droits existants. Dans ce cas, le vecteur des principes généraux permettra d'incorporer ces innovations dans le droit de l'Union.

b   La Convention européenne des droits de l'homme, un statut en évolution

La Convention fait l'objet de nombreuses références dans le traité de Lisbonne. Tout d'abord, elle demeure l'une des sources de principes généraux du droit. Ensuite, la Charte lui fait tenir la place d'un standard minimum en dessous duquel la protection des droits fondamentaux dans l'Union ne saurait aller (article 53). Mais la Charte a voulu aller plus loin et imposer la cohérence entre la Charte et la Convention afin d'assurer une interprétation identique à des droits similaires. D'où l'article 52, paragraphe 3, de la Charte qui impose qu'en présence de droits identiques, il leur soit accordé le même sens et la même portée que dans la Convention avec la réserve que la protection offerte par l'Union puisse être plus étendue. L'identification de ces droits n'est pas aisée. Il existe des droits qui sont totalement identiques, des droits qui ont un sens plus large que ceux garantis par la Convention et enfin des droits qui, bien qu'identiques, ont un champ d'application plus large comme la règle *non bis in idem* ou le droit des syndicats à l'action collective. L'enjeu du débat est important puisqu'il conditionne la reprise ou non de la jurisprudence de Strasbourg par la Cour de Luxembourg. Il ne porte pas simplement d'ailleurs sur la définition des droits, mais également sur le régime des limitations puisque le régime prévu par l'article 52, paragraphe 1, n'est pas identique à celui de la Convention. En effet, en cas d'identité entre les droits, le régime de limitation prévu par la Convention s'appliquera. Dans les autres cas, le régime applicable sera celui de l'article 52 pour autant qu'il ne conduise pas à une protection inférieure à celle prévue par la Convention.

La rédaction de l'article 52 a fait, au sein de la Convention, l'objet de larges débats opposant les partisans de l'autonomie du droit communautaire aux défenseurs d'une application intégrale de la Convention européenne des droits de l'homme. Les premiers soutenaient que la formule du standard minimum accordé à la Convention par l'article 53 était suffisante tandis que les seconds plaidaient pour l'existence d'une système unique de protection au niveau européen afin d'éviter que le juge national se trouve dans l'obligation d'appliquer simultanément des normes différentes à un même droit. Un accord n'a pu être trouvé qu'au dernier moment. Mais, la question sera en grande partie réglée par l'adhésion de l'Union à la Convention prévue à l'article 6, paragraphe 2, du traité sur l'Union européenne. Dans ce cas, le statut de standard minimum de la Convention sera confirmé sous le contrôle de la Cour de Strasbourg. La Convention retrouvera le rôle subsidiaire que lui reconnaît la jurisprudence de Strasbourg. De la même manière, la mention de la Convention comme source des principes généraux du droit perdra de son intérêt puisque le juge de Luxembourg devra appliquer directement la Convention. Les problèmes soulevés par l'article 52, paragraphe 3, subsisteront-ils ? On pourrait en douter. Dans la mesure où le droit de l'Union ne va pas plus loin que la Convention, le juge appliquera naturellement cette dernière qui liera l'Union. Dans le cas contraire, il appliquera le droit de l'Union en prenant garde de ne pas violer la Convention. L'article 52 a été rédigé alors que la perspective de l'adhésion était encore fermée. Il perdra de son intérêt lorsque celle-ci sera réalisée.

Ainsi, après l'entrée en vigueur du traité de Lisbonne, l'Union devra vraisemblablement vivre avec un système écrit de protection des droits fondamentaux. Cette circonstance ne devrait pas à court terme soulever de grandes difficultés quant au contenu des droits déjà reconnus par la Cour. Par contre, l'apport de la jurisprudence sera important pour clarifier des questions comme celles du champ d'application, du régime applicable aux principes par rapport aux droits, de la portée du protocole *d'opting out* britannique et polonais ou des rapports avec la Convention européenne des droits de l'homme notamment en ce qui concerne le régime des limitations.

C   L'adhésion à la Convention européenne des droits de l'homme

La question de l'adhésion fait partie de la mise en œuvre du traité de Lisbonne. En effet, l'article 6 ne se limite pas à constituer une base juridique en vue de l'adhésion, mais en employant l'impératif, il impose sans doute possible à l'Union d'adhérer à la Convention. Un manquement à cette obligation justifierait une action en carence devant la Cour de justice puisque le texte français du traité sur l'Union européenne indique que « [l]'Union *adhère* » à la CEDH.

Sur le plan procédural, l'accord d'adhésion doit recueillir l'unanimité des membres du Conseil et l'approbation du Parlement européen. La constitution prévoyait la majorité qualifiée, mais l'unanimité lui a été substituée à la demande danoise. Ceci ne modifie guère la situation puisque de toute façon l'accord d'adhésion devra être ratifié par toutes les parties à la CEDH lesquelles incluent tous les membres de l'Union. De la même manière, l'exigence de ratification de la décision d'adhésion rencontre la nécessité pour les parties contractantes à la Convention de ratifier le protocole d'adhésion.

Ceci ne signifie pas pour autant que le processus sera aisé, car il implique que tous les membres de l'Union puissent se mettre d'accord dans un premier temps sur un mandat de négociation. Le risque existe de voir à cette occasion ressurgir toutes les réserves exprimées au fil du temps à l'encontre de l'adhésion. Même si le protocole relatif à l'adhésion fournit un certain encadrement, il laisse ouverte un grand nombre de questions sur lesquelles il n'est pas aisé de trouver un accord. Elles sont liées à la spécificité de l'Union ainsi qu'à la participation de celle-ci aux instances de Strasbourg. Certes le protocole 14 à la CEDH qui entrera en vigueur le 1er juin 2010 , règle au moins l'une d'entre elles puisqu'il contient un article 17 qui amende la Convention en prévoyant l'adhésion de l'Union. La question de principe est donc réglée, mais il reste d'importantes questions à trancher.

L'adhésion étendra le champ du contrôle juridictionnel des droits fondamentaux. En effet, l'article 275 du traité sur le fonctionnement de l'Union européenne (TFUE) exclut expressément du contrôle exercé par la Cour de justice les activités de l'Union au titre de la politique étrangère et de sécurité commune à l'exception des mesures restrictives prises à l'égard des particuliers. Mais la convention européenne des droits de l'homme s'applique à toutes les questions qui relèvent de la juridiction des parties contractantes. Il en résulte que la Cour de Strasbourg pourrait être amenée à connaître d'actes effectués dans le cadre d'interventions de l'Union européenne à l'extérieur.

1 Quel corpus de règles retenir pour l'adhésion ?

Si le traité prévoit l'adhésion de l'Union à la convention, rien n'est dit en ce qui concerne les protocoles. Diverses solutions sont envisageables. Il serait possible de ne faire adhérer l'Union qu'aux protocoles déjà ratifiés par tous les Etats membres. Cependant rien n'impose ce parallélisme. Les protocoles auxquels participera l'Union ne s'imposeront qu'à celle-ci et non aux Etats membres lesquels ne seront touchés que dans la mesure où ils mettent en œuvre le droit communautaire. En outre, dans certains cas, cela impliquerait une régression dans la protection qui sera offerte. Ainsi, par exemple, le droit de l'Union coïncide déjà avec les obligations qui résultent du protocole n° 12 relatif à la non-discrimination. Il n'existe donc aucune raison pour exclure ce protocole même s'il n'est pas ratifié par tous les Etats membres. Il en va de même des protocoles relatifs à la peine de mort. Celle-ci est déjà prohibée par la charte.

On pourrait suggérer de ne retenir que les protocoles qui correspondent à certaines compétences de l'Union. Mais ce serait tomber dans la confusion déjà exposée plus haut entre la compétence pour agir et l'obligation de respecter les droits fondamentaux. Ce n'est pas parce que l'Union n'aurait pas compétence pour statuer sur la peine de mort qu'elle ne pourrait porter atteinte au droit à la vie sous cet aspect particulier. Que l'on songe par exemple à la conclusion d'un accord d'extradition avec un Etat membre qui pratique la peine de mort. Si une disposition interdisant l'extradition au cas où la peine de mort serait prononcée n'y était introduite, l'Union pourrait porter atteinte au droit à la vie. La sagesse impose donc de choisir une vision large quant aux protocoles et, pour le moins, d'adhérer à tous les protocoles qui se réfèrent à des droits garantis par la charte.

2 La prise en compte des spécificités de l'Union

Deux éléments présentent une importance particulière : la préservation de la répartition des compétences entre l'Union et les Etats membres et la protection de la place et du rôle de la Cour de justice dans l'ordre communautaire.

Sur le premier point, il s'agit d'éviter, en cas de recours individuel, qu'à travers le choix du défendeur la Cour de Strasbourg puisse être amenée à se prononcer sur la répartition des compétences entre l'Union et ses Etats membres. En effet, cette question ne peut être laissée à la Cour de Strasbourg puisqu'elle relève de choix effectués par les auteurs des traités et qu'elle ne relève pas de la compétence de la Cour européenne des droits de l'homme.

En effet, il ne pas aisé pour un requérant individuel de déterminer lequel de l'Union ou de l'Etat membre est responsable d'une violation de ses droits, notamment lorsque le droit de l'Union laisse une certaine marge d'appréciation aux Etats. Dans ce cas, il faut décider si la violation est intervenue ou non dans le cadre de cette marge. Or laisser ce choix à la Cour EDH reviendrait à la laisser juge de la répartition des compétences entre l'Union et ses Etats membres ce qui n'est pas acceptable. Il convient donc de mettre en place un système qui permette à l'individu d'attaquer simultanément l'Union et un Etat membre en laissant à l'Union elle-même le soin de désigner, au besoin avec le concours de la Cour de justice de l'Union, qui sera défendeur. Une solution de ce type figure déjà à l'annexe IX, article 6, de la Convention sur le droit de la Mer à laquelle l'Union est partie.

Plus importante sans doute est la préservation de l'exclusivité du pouvoir d'interprétation du droit de l'Union par la Cour de justice. Cette exigence a été rappelée avec vigueur par la Cour de justice dans son avis sur l'Espace économique européen.[23] Or, selon certains, il ne serait pas exclu que la Cour de Strasbourg soit amenée à interpréter une disposition du droit de l'Union afin de déterminer la conformité de celle-ci avec la Convention. Ces Etats suggèrent d'insérer dans l'accord une disposition interdisant une telle pratique à la Cour de Strasbourg. Ils insistent également pour ne permettre la saisine de la Cour que par un système de renvoi préjudiciel par la Cour de justice lequel aurait pour effet de réserver à cette dernière le pouvoir d'interprétation. Une telle solution n'est pas indispensable dans la mesure où l'épuisement des voies de recours internes couvre également le renvoi préjudiciel à Luxembourg par les juridictions nationales. De la sorte, dans tous les cas, la Cour de Strasbourg ne pourrait être saisie qu'après que la Cour de justice se soit prononcée. Mais, au fond, cette crainte est largement surestimée. En effet, la Cour européenne des droits de l'homme refuse de se substituer aux autorités nationales lorsqu'il s'agit d'interpréter tant le droit national qu'un traité (en l'espèce les traités de l'Union). Comme elle le rappelait récemment dans une décision d'irrecevabilité :

> « *The Court reiterates that it is primarily for the national authorities, notably the courts, to interpret and apply domestic law. More specifically, it is not for the Court to rule on the validity of national laws in the hierarchy of domestic legislation (see also* Kruslin v. France, *24 April 1990, § 29,Series A no. 176-A). This also applies where international treaties are concerned; it is for the implementing party to interpret the treaty, and in this respect it is not the Court's task to substitute its own judgment for that of the domestic authorities, even less to settle a dispute between the parties to the treaty as to its correct interpretation (see* Slivenko v. Latvia [GC], *no. 48321/99, § 105, ECHR 2003-X)».*[24]

---

23   Avis 1/91 du 14 décembre 1991, rec. I-6079:
      « *Il s'ensuit que la compétence attribuée à la Cour EEE en vertu des articles 2, sous c), 96, paragraphe 1, sous a), et 117, paragraphe 1, de l'accord, est susceptible de porter atteinte à l'ordre des compétences défini par les traités et, partant, à l'autonomie du système juridique communautaire dont la Cour de justice assure le respect, en vertu de l'article 164 du traité CEE. Cette compétence exclusive de la Cour de justice est confirmée par l'article 219 du traité CEE selon lequel les États membres s'engagent à ne pas soumettre un différend relatif à l'interprétation ou à l'application de ce traité à un mode de règlement autre que ceux prévus par celui-ci. L'article 87 du traité CECA comporte une disposition dans le même sens. L'attribution de cette compétence à la Cour EEE est, dès lors, incompatible avec le droit communautaire.* »
24   Cour EDH, 20 janvier 2009, Bosphorus Airlines c. Irlande.

Cette obligation est rappelée dans les conclusions de la réunion de 2010 à Interlaken.[25] Enfin, il convient de rappeler qu'à la différence de la Cour de justice, la Cour de Strasbourg n'a pas le pouvoir d'annuler un acte de l'Union. Elle se limite à déclarer l'incompatibilité de celui avec la Convention dans un jugement déclaratoire laissant le soin à l'Union d'en tirer les conséquences. L'appréciation des conséquences de l'arrêt relève donc de la compétence de l'Union ce qui permet à celle-ci de conserver la pleine maîtrise du droit de l'Union à condition qu'il soit conforme à la Convention.

Certains estiment également que le contrôle du droit primaire par Strasbourg devrait être exclu. On voit là un mauvais souvenir de l'affaire *Matthews*.[26] Il s'agirait de revenir sur la jurisprudence selon laquelle les Etats membres sont responsables des violations de la Convention par le droit primaire. A vrai dire, il sera difficile de retenir une telle position qui constitue un recours en arrière par rapport à la situation existante et qui n'est pas spécifique à l'Union puisque la Cour de Strasbourg applique le principe du contrôle à toutes les organisations internationales.[27]

D'autres soutiennent encore que la solution retenue dans l'arrêt *Bosphorus*, c'est-à-dire un contrôle du droit de l'Union uniquement en cas d'insuffisance manifeste de la protection, devrait être maintenue.[28] En fait, après l'adhésion la situation sera différente. Il ne s'agira plus d'un recours contre un acte d'un Etat membre qui met en œuvre un acte de l'Union ne laissant aucune marge d'appréciation, mais d'un recours relatif à l'incompatibilité d'un acte de l'Union avec la Convention. Dans ces conditions, il n'existe guère de raison pour que l'Union soit traitée différemment des autres parties contractantes. On arguera que l'Union a bénéficié dans l'arrêt *Bosphorus* d'une présomption de protection équivalente à celle offerte par la Convention. Mais on voit mal pourquoi cette situation spécifique devrait persister. Les Etats parties à la Convention pourraient d'ailleurs également revendiquer une telle protection. Dans la mesure où le contrôle exercé sur ces derniers est complet, il n'existe aucune raison de soumettre l'Union à un régime de protection allégé. L'argument selon lequel l'Union n'est pas un Etat n'a guère de valeur dans la mesure où l'effet de ses actes est comparable à celui d'une législation nationale.

3   La participation de l'Union au mécanisme de contrôle

S'agissant de la Cour, la spécificité paraît imposer la présence d'un « juge de l'Union ». Il paraît naturel que l'Union réclame que ce juge bénéficie du même statut que les autres membres de la Cour. En cas de difficultés, une solution de repli pourrait être que ce juge ne participe avec voix délibérative qu'aux affaires qui mettent en cause le droit de l'Union et qu'il dispose d'une voix consultative dans les autres cas. . Quelle que soit la solution retenue, on pourrait faire valoir qu'elle peut conduire à la présence de deux juges de la même nationalité dans

---

25   « [E]viter de réexaminer des questions de fait ou du droit interne qui ont été examinées et décidées par les autorités nationales, en accord avec sa jurisprudence selon laquelle elle n'est pas un tribunal de quatrième instance. »

26   Cour EDH, GC, 18 février 1999, Matthews c. Royaume Uni.

27   Voir Florence Benoît-Rohmer, Les enfants de Bosphorus, RTDH 2010, p.18.

28   Cour EDH, GC, 30 juin 2005, Bosphorus Airlines c. Irlande.

une même affaire. Outre le fait qu'il existe de solutions pour éviter cette situation tant au stade de la recevabilité qu'à celui du fond, il convient de rappeler que le principe d'indépendance des juges constitue une garantie. En outre, la composition de la Cour avec un juge par Etat membre, si elle est maintenue dans l'avenir, est justifiée par l'exigence d'une représentation de toutes les cultures juridiques nationales. Il serait donc surprenant que la culture juridique de l'Union avec ses spécificités soit exclue de la Cour. Faut-il organiser une participation de l'Union à la désignation des juges en adjoignant par exemple des membres du Parlement européen à l'Assemblée parlementaire du Conseil de l'Europe lorsqu'elle statue sur la désignation des membres de la Cour. Le sujet est ouvert à la discussion, mais on pourrait à tout le moins admettre que le Parlement et le Conseil puissent être amenés à se prononcer sur la liste de trois juges soumise par l'Union au Conseil de l'Europe. Quant au Comité des ministres, la participation de l'Union aux travaux relatifs à la CEDH devra être assurée sous une forme adéquate. L'Union pourrait par exemple être représentée par la Commission avec éventuellement un statut consultatif ce qui est déjà le cas en application de l'accord quadripartite conclu avec le Conseil de l'Europe.

4   Le mode de contrôle

Il existe deux modes de saisine de la Cour de justice : la requête étatique ou la requête individuelle. S'agissant de la requête étatique, il semble difficile d'ouvrir celle-ci aux Etats membres sans porter atteinte au monopole de juridiction de la Cour de Luxembourg. Par contre, dans la mesure où l'Union souhaite obtenir un statut normal de partie contractante, il paraît difficile d'écarter l'éventualité de requêtes en provenance d'Etats tiers. On voit mal d'ailleurs ceux-ci accepter une adhésion de l'Union qui ne comporterait pas cet élément. S'agissant des requêtes individuelles, on a parfois suggéré que la Cour EDH soit seulement saisie par la Cour de l'Union de demandes préjudicielles. Une telle formule ne paraît pas respecter la spécificité de l'Union qui, dans le domaine de ses compétences, doit être considérée comme une partie comme une autre. D'ailleurs, peut-on imaginer la durée d'un litige dans lequel la Cour de l'Union elle-même saisie par voie préjudicielle saisirait à son tour d'une question préjudicielle la Cour EDH. Quatre ou cinq ans pourraient s'écouler avant que le tribunal national ne rende sa décision au fond. Une telle solution pourrait dissuader les requérants, ce qui poserait de sérieux problèmes en matière d'application uniforme du droit communautaire. Certes une telle solution aurait l'avantage de préserver l'exclusivité du pouvoir d'interprétation de la Cour, mais il n'est pas impossible qu'une juridiction nationale statue en dernier ressort sans utiliser la voie communautaire du renvoi préjudiciel. Faut-il dans ce cas prévoir que la Cour de Strasbourg rejette le recours pour non épuisement des voies de recours interne ou renvoie l'affaire à la Cour de justice avant de trancher au fond ?

    La voie la plus raisonnable semble être celle de la requête individuelle après épuisement des recours internes. Elle laisse le particulier libre de décider après la procédure à Luxembourg s'il souhaite prolonger le contentieux en allant à Strasbourg ou s'il accepte l'arrêt de la Cour de justice. Bien entendu, la règle de l'épuisement des voies de recours interne s'imposera. Ceci signifie que dans une affaire jugée devant le juge national, la demande préjudicielle constitue une voie de recours interne et la requête doit être déclaré irrecevable si le particulier n'a aps formé une telle demande. Bien entendu, si cette demande a été formée et que le juge national n'y a pas donné suite, la requête sera recevable.

En tout état de cause, l'adhésion ne pourra produire pleinement ses effets que si la Cour EDH parvient à accélérer son processus de décision. L'entrée en vigueur annoncée du protocole 14 est donc, à tous points de vue, un préalable indispensable et la réforme du système devra être poursuivi de manière diligente.

D Conclusion

En matière de droits fondamentaux, le traité de Lisbonne est le produit d'une longue évolution qui repose à la fois sur la volonté des maîtres des traités et sur l'œuvre de la Cour de justice. En ce domaine plus qu'en d'autres, le dialogue du juge et du constituant a été fructueux même si de longues années ont été né- cessaires pour que celui-ci porte pleinement ses fruits. Cependant, compte tenu des implications sur les ordres juridiques nationaux, la maturation de la réflexion des Etats membres a été très lente. La situation actuelle est le produit d'une série de tentatives infructueuses qui firent progressivement naître la conviction qu'une action est indispensable. Certes les changements intervenus laissent subsister des incertitudes. L'articulation du système devra être clarifiée. certains s'en étonneront et en feront reproche au constituant, mais toute révision de la charte constitutionnelle de l'Union, pour reprendre l'expression consacrée par la Cour, repose sur de nécessaires compromis entre des aspirations et des crain- tes divergentes. La caractéristique du compromis est de laisser subsister des zones d'ombres que la pratique et le juge se chargent au fil du temps de dissi- per. En outre, il est rare qu'un constituant puisse envisager toutes les consé- quences d'un texte fait pour produire des effets durant des décennies et qui devra s'adapter à des circonstances aujourd'hui imprévisibles. Or, plus particu- lièrement dans le domaine des droits fondamentaux, l'interprétation d'un texte ne peut rester invariable, mais est appelée à tenir compte de l'évolution des socié- tés et de la vision des valeurs qui la sous-tend. Il n'en demeure pas moins que, dans le traité de Lisbonne, le constituant a tenté de clarifier la question des sour- ces et dressé un catalogue de droits.

Michael REITERER

Human Rights as Part of the EU Foreign Policy After Lisbon: In Defence of Western Values and Influence?

Table of Contents

Keywords

European Union, EU foreign policy, European diplomacy, Treaty of Lisbon, European Security Strategy, coherence, normative power, soft power, Western values

A   Introduction

According to Karen Smith

"[t]he EU shares the 'principled belief' that human rights are a legitimate aim of foreign policy, but it has been divided over 'causal beliefs', or what sorts of policies promote human rights most effectively, and over whether human rights should be prioritized in particular cases."[1]

Karen Smith traces the origins of human rights promotion back to the European Political Cooperation (EPC), "one of the first topics on EPC's agenda", and puts it firmly in the context of the EU's Security Strategy:

"violations of human rights threaten security and stability within countries and between them. But it also reflects the belief, shared by the member

---

1   Karen E. Smith, European Union Foreign Policy in a Changing World, London 2008, 2nd ed., 111.

141

*states and the EU institutions, that human rights must be promoted inter-
nationally, for their own sake. The EU insists on the universality of human
rights, and rejects claims that promoting human rights is unwarranted interference in the domestic affairs of other states. However, considerations
of human rights are often 'trumped' by other objectives and interests."*[2]

Nevertheless, as Veronique Arnault underlines:

*"For the EU, support for human rights is not only a question of defending
principles and values. The EU believes that peaceful and stable societies
can only be created if human rights are respected, that States which respect human rights are more reliable international partners, and that socio-
economic development and democratisation processes are founded on
respect for human rights."*[3]

The High Representative of the European Union for Foreign Affairs and Security Policy, Catherine Ashton, confirmed already in her opening remarks at the
hearing of the European Parliament that human rights were one of her priorities.
"I intend to develop", she said, "on-going work on some thematic issues: non-
proliferation, counter-terrorism, human rights, energy and climate change. These
are not "stand alone issues" but part of our broader agenda."[4]

These three quotes show that academics, practitioners and politicians concur
in asserting that human rights are in the centre of European foreign policy. This
paper will explore whether this rhetoric has a chance of becoming reality under
the new Treaty of Lisbon (section B). However, in analyzing the new legal
framework not only the potential will become clear, but also new developments
will be identified, including the accession of the EU to the European Convention
of Human Rights.[5] Then the impact of this development on the EU's normative
power will be analyzed (C). Normative power and coherence in policies together
contribute in turning the EU into a role model that makes use of its 'soft power'.
In implementing the European Security Strategy, European diplomacy attempts
to project this attitude internationally (E and F). Special attention is devoted to
fighting terrorism because of its double edged nature: terrorism results in the
violation of human rights, but fighting terrorism also bears the risk of violating
human rights (G).

In my conclusions (H), I will argue that the Treaty of Lisbon is a further stepping
stone in establishing human rights as a constitutive element of the EU foreign
policy although implemented with varying degrees of consistency and rigour.

---

2   Ibid., 112.
3   Veronique Arnault, Implementation of the European Instrument for Democracy and
      Human Rights (EIDHR), in: Wolfgang Benedek/Wolfram Karl/Anja Mihr/Manfred No-
      wak (eds.), European Yearbook on Human Rights 2009, Vienna etc. 2009, 99-100.
4   Catherine Ashton, Opening remarks, European Parliament Hearing, Brussels, January
      11, 2010 at http://ec.europa.eu/commission_barroso/ashton/docs/ashton_ speech_
      hearing-ep.pdf.
5   See the contribution of Jean Paul Jacqué, in this volume, at 123.

B   The Lisbon Treaty: Framework for a Value-Based Foreign Policy

This connection between human rights and foreign policy is also reflected in the Treaty on European Union as amended by the Treaty of Lisbon.[6] Article 21 (1) of the Treaty on European Union now clearly provides that promoting human rights is one key element of its foreign policy:

> *The Union's action on the international scene shall be guided by the principles which have inspired its own creation, development and enlargement, and which it seeks to advance in the wider world: democracy, the rule of law, the universality and indivisibility of human rights and fundamental freedoms, respect for human dignity, the principles of equality and solidarity, and respect for the principles of the United Nations Charter and international law.*

However, "[t]he goal is not just to further human rights and democracy outside the EU's borders, but also to shape a distinct international identity for the EU as a values-driven normative power."[7] As Heinz/Liebl have pointed out this poses the challenge of preserving credibility in tackling "the discrepancy between the standards [the EU] applies internally and externally."[8] This discrepancy is also due to the fact that the EU is a relative latecomer compared to the Council of Europe, the architect of the European human rights system with the European Convention of Human Rights (1950) and its Protocols, and the European Court of Human Rights in Strasbourg. At the time Europe had taken the lead in protecting human rights because of the catastrophic experience in denying human rights which culminated in World War II. The EU proclaimed the non-binding Charter of Human Rights and Fundamental Freedoms only at the Nice European Council in 2000 which finally led to its inclusion into the Treaty of Lisbon that in turn foresees the EU's accession to the European Convention of Human Rights.

Credibility and engagement became increasingly important as the role of 'the West', i.e. of Europe and the US, as the human rights standard-setter is under siege: As a consequence of the 2008 and 2009 financial and economic crisis, we observe a certain shift of power from West to East which is not limited to economic power and political influence, but has also repercussions on the competition of ideas and values.

The West has striven to have its values accepted as universal, the Universal Declaration of Human Rights being the prime example. After the discussion on 'Asian values' has largely abated,[9] new important players have started to attack the universality of Western values. Dominique Moisi puts it like this:

---

6   See the consolidated versions of the Treaty on European Union and the Treaty on the functioning of the European Union, OJ C115, 9 May 2008.
7   Stephan Keukeleire/Jennifer MacNaughtan, The Foreign Policy of the European Union, London 2008, 223.
8   Wolfgang S. Heinz/Josephine Liebl, European Union Human Rights and CFSP Policy in 2008, in: Benedek et al. (eds.), European Yearboook (2009), 96.
9   See, for example, Andrew Clapham, Human Rights, Oxford 2007, 66-67:
     "A [...] strand of opposition sees Western human rights foreign policy as disguised hegemonic ambitions and rejects human rights as incompatible with so-called 'Asian values'. Part of the Asian values reaction is a simple rejection of Western interfer-

"For the first time in recent memory, the future of the planet will no longer be determined only by decisions taken by the democratic West. We may soon discover whether centralised, nondemocratic regimes such as China's may actually be better equipped to respond to economic crises than democratic countries such as the United States [and the EU]."[10]

Among the recent concrete examples is the sentencing in China to eleven years in prison despite international protests of one of the main opposition figures, Liu Xiaobo, for having criticized the Communist Party[11] or the struggle of Google with the Chinese authorities about censorship of the internet. Thereby the Party showed its determination to keep economic and political freedom apart. Furthermore, executing for the first time after decades a foreigner, the British national Akmal Shaikh, although mentally disturbed, for drug offences sent another message: China can risk the deterioration of diplomatic relations with the UK and it is not willing to accept Western standards or values, like the request for abolition of capital punishment where China is (sadly) leading the world.

C   Normative Power and Coherence

Thus, if the EU aims to preserve or even to extend its "normative power",[12] it will have to pay, according to Manners, much greater attention to "shape conceptions of 'normal' in international relations."[13] Manners argues that the EU's normative power is diffused through contagion, informational and procedural diffusion, transference, overt diffusion and influenced by the cultural filter. In applying these factors to one of the norms the EU seeks to europeanize (i.e. to redefine international norms in its own image), namely the abolition of the death penalty,[14] – he comes to the conclusion that the EU diffused its abolitionist policy "through procedural membership conditions, informational common strategies, and the overt role of EU delegations".[15] In pursuing this goal the EU is willing to impinge on state sovereignty, to intervene in support of individuals, to act despite the obvious absence of any material gain and to risk straining its relations not only with countries like China, Iran, Iraq, but also allies like the US and Japan. The

---

ence in the political affairs of certain countries in the Far East. But another part comes from a sense that the Western notion of human rights has paid too little attention to the correlative responsibilities which ought to accompany the exercise of human rights."

10   Dominique Moisi, The Geopolitics of Emotion, Doubleday 2009, xi-xii.

11   The High Representative of the European Union for Foreign Affairs and Security Policy, Catherine Ashton, expressed "deep regret" about the upholding of the ruling and called for the immediate release of Mr. Liu Xiaobo 12 February 2010; see http://www.consilium.europa.eu/uedocs/cms_data/docs/pressdata/EN/foraff/112890.pdf.

12   Charlotte Bretherton/Johan Vogler, The European Union as Global Actor, London 2006, 2nd ed., 42.

13   Ian Manners, Normative Power Europe: A Contradiction in Terms?, JCMS 40 (2002) 2, 239.

14   On EU policies regarding the death penalty, see William A. Schabas, The European Union and the Death Penalty, in: Benedek et al. (eds.), European Yearbook (2009), 133-145.

15   Manners, Normative Power Europe (2002), 252.

latter is an argument against accusing the EU of "cultural imperialism in disguise".[16]

Based on comparative case studies on death penalty and minority protection respectively, Lerch/Schwellnus conclude that the normative power of the EU succeeded in the first case as "the EU relied predominantly on universal rights-based arguments complemented in a careful and coherent way by value- and utility-based arguments when addressing different audiences."[17] Most importantly, coherence was achieved as the external promotion could rely on a well established internal norm: all member states had abolished capital punishment which therefore also became a prerequisite for joining the Union.

This value consensus was lacking internally in the case of minority protection, but not with regard to supporting the prosecution of international crimes. In addition to having campaigned strongly for the ratification of the Rome Statute of the International Criminal Court the EU has credibility in exhorting the extradition of suspected war criminals from the Balkans to the International Criminal Tribunal for the former Yugoslavia in The Hague in exchange for opening accession talks with interested countries, such as Serbia.

Finding the right policy mix of the instruments at the disposal of the EU, ranging from persuasion, education, human rights dialogues and consultations to the exercise of economic and diplomatic power through conditionality is the challenge, posed more clearly by the Treaty of Lisbon where 'coherence' is a key concept to shape a more unified EU foreign policy. Guidelines, albeit non-binding, on thematic human rights issues[18] serve as an important tool to achieve this goal.[19] The European Instrument for Democracy and Human Rights (EIDHR) aims "to support civil society organizations in helping them to become an effective force for political reform and protection of human rights in third countries."[20]

Furthermore, the above mentioned introduction of the Charter of Fundamental Rights into European primary law not only strengthens the protection of human rights within the EU-system but also answers to the concerns of European citizens. In addition to human rights protection in relation to nation states they also want to feel protected within the EU and vis-à-vis the institutions of the Union. At the same time this legal approach demonstrates to the partners of the EU worldwide that in legally implementing a comprehensive human rights protection system the EU may firstly, legitimately counter claims that it has not done its "homework" and secondly, make use of its normative power to defend the universality of human rights in rebuking claims that certain rights and values are not or no longer universal, a phenomenon epitomized by the Asian values discussion.[21]

---

16   Ibid., 253.
17   Marika Lerch/Guido Schwellnus, Normative by nature? The role of coherence in justifying the EU's external human rights policy, Journal of European Public Policy (2006) 13.2, 317.
18   Including on death penalty, torture and other cruel, inhuman or degrading treatment or punishment, human rights dialogues, children and armed conflicts, human rights defenders, rights of the child, violence against women and girls and combating all forms of discrimination against them, and promoting compliance with international humanitarian law.
19   Arnault, Implementation (2009), 100.
20   Ibid., 101. The annual budget for the period 2007-2013 is about € 150 million.
21   See Kishore Mahbubani, The New Asian Hemisphere – The irresistible shift of global power to the East. Public Affairs, New York 2008.

D   The EU as a Role Model

In taking up this challenge, the European Union could profit from its very nature and its special status as an international actor, which confer on it a particular way of participating in international politics. A Common – albeit not single – Foreign and Security Policy (CFSP), the European Security and Defence Policy (ESDP), a Common Trade Policy, the European Neighbourhood Policy (ENP), to name just a few, have become trademarks as well as expressions of the particular status of the Union. One of the major goals of the Treaty of Lisbon is to strengthen the external representation of the Union in order to equip it with the institutions needed and the procedures required, thus coordination should lead to consistency. As Article 26 (2) of the TEU lays down, "[t]he Council and the High Representative of the Union for Foreign Affairs and Security Policy shall ensure the unity, consistency and effectiveness of action by the Union."[22] Two new institutions, a prolonged Presidency of the European Council and the High Representative for Foreign and Security Policy, acting at the same time as Vice-President of the European Commission, as well as the President of the Commission should assure international visibility.

All these elements contribute to establishing the Union as a role model internationally, a role which has developed over decades.[23] Europe has come a long way during the last fifty plus years in building up a foreign policy capacity: From external aspects of the common agricultural and trade policies, to a world wide development policy based on economic cooperation, the EU was almost involuntarily driven to add a political dimension to its external relations.

The fall of the Berlin Wall and the Iron Curtain in 1989 was accompanied by the popularization of the "peace dividend". However, while war and genocide in former Yugoslavia characterized the 90s, the new century saw 9/11 followed by the second Iraq war. Although the success of the EU is built on its *soft power* and the civil instruments at its disposal, the EU had to learn that foreign and security policy is a necessary supplement for an effective international player.

Nevertheless, the EU's diplomacy is still different from the kind of diplomacy pursued by nation states: The CFSP is based on the historic experience of Europe to solve conflicts by non-military means. This has led to the creation of the EU, so far the most successful experiment in peace-making and peace-maintaining, secured by an elaborate institutional framework based on enforceable law. In the areas of community competence, e.g. outside the area of CFSP, the "community method", a balanced procedural and negotiating technique based on law provides the backbone for the success of the Union. It turned the Union into a global player more because of its civil than its military means and might.

The EU developed from a "civilian power by default" into a "civilian power by its own choosing".[24] This allows the Union to play a specific role in international politics whether foreign policy- or security-related. The Union has not only become a model for the organization and institutionalization of peaceful relations. It

---

22   Article 26 (2) TEU; see also Article 32 TEU.
23   Michael Reiterer, EU Foreign Policy: From Cooperation to Diplomacy, EU Studies in Japan 28 (2008), 27-44.
24   Stelios Stavradis, Why the militarising of the European Union is strengthening the concept of a civilian power Europe, EUI Working Papers 2001, http://www.iue.it/RSCAS/WP-Texts/01_17.pdf.

also turned into an actor aiming at the peaceful non-violent solution of global conflicts and tensions. It is therefore particularly well equipped to take on and deal with new, non-traditional security challenges.

Developing alternative strategies such as favouring arms control and disarmament, insisting on negotiating attempts between Syria and Iran, an even-handed approach to the Middle East, the fight against the root causes of terrorism (like exclusion, poverty, and dominance) rather than the symptoms, avoiding in this context the securitization, e.g. through the prioritization of security as part of the 'War on terror'[25], the commitment to the Kyoto Agreement and an effective post-Kyoto regime to be developed on the basis of the Copenhagen Accord[26] to fight climate change effectively, putting the interests of the individual human being more into the centre of politics than the interests of states (fight against death penalty; promoting human security) – all these policies exemplify the self-understanding of the European Union as a soft power. The use of political and diplomatic means to solve problems through legal means and procedures constitute the credentials of a modern civilian power.

E   European Diplomacy

The EU's High Representative strives to meet the challenge to formulate a coherent foreign policy, using a policy mix commensurate with a unique institution like the European Union. Combining the tools formerly available to the High Representative and the Commissioner for External Relations will allow to bundle efforts and to develop promises to be a European diplomacy:

Diplomacy[27] is not just another word for foreign policy; rather diplomacy is the technique providing the means to translate the goals of a foreign policy into action. Thus, European diplomacy will translate the goals of the CFSP and the ESDP into action, steered by the High Representative who will be supported by the European Union's delegations worldwide. While this diplomacy will bear some features of traditional diplomacy it will be mainly shaped by the ideas and means inherent in the above mentioned soft power concept and will thus be cooperative in nature.

The specificity of European diplomacy, different from the diplomacy of a hegemonic power, derives from the fact that it has a legal basis, is based on values and has primarily political means at its disposal. Contrary to a nation state, the Union pursues a policy of effective multilateralism. It places particular emphasis on the implementation and development of international law and the strengthening of the UN Charter, both at the regional and the global level.[28] Shared values need translation into shared interests,[29] in cooperation with part-

---

25   Alvaro de Vasconcelos, The European Security Strategy 2003-2008: Building on Common Interests. IISS, Paris, Report 2009, 5, 20, http://www.iss.europa.eu/uploads/media/ISS_Report_05.pdf.

26   The Copenhagen Accord, Decision CP15, 18 December 2009, http://unfccc.int/files/meetings/cop_15/application/pdf/cop15_cph_auv.pdf.

27   Brian Hocking, Diplomacy, in: Walter Carlsnaes/Helene Sjursen/Brian White (eds.) Contemporary European Foreign Policy, London 2004, 91-109.

28   Reiterer, EU Foreign Policy (2008), 3.

29   Antonio Missiroli, Revisiting the European Security Strategy – Beyond 2008, EPC Policy Brief, April 2008.

ners being guided by the same ones which could lead to real strategic partnerships. Effective multilateralism and the use of civil instruments are not slogans, they are the concepts and means at the EU's disposal.

European diplomacy will also exclude some features specific to nation states such as a standing army. It will consciously renounce other features like military intervention to realise national goals, while adding others like fostering human rights including campaigning against death penalty world wide or favouring inter-regionalism as a new diplomatic tool.[30] Its successful campaign to get the International Criminal Court off the ground is a good example. However, overcoming internal discrepancies, diverging interests and "profound philosophical and tactical differences"[31] will remain the main challenge for an EU with now 27 member states.

F   The European Security Strategy

Motivated by the lack of consensus within the EU on the Iraq War and aiming at providing a framework for defining common actions, The European Security Strategy (ESS) of 2003, titled "A Safer Europe in a Better World"[32] and its further development to include climate change as evidenced by the joint analysis of the High Representative and the European Commission ("Climate Change and International Security"[33]) as well as lessons learnt from its implementation[34] are designed to guide member states as well as the High Representative in meeting the challenge of pursuing a more coherent European foreign policy. Thus, in addition to the threats identified in the ESS, terrorism, proliferation of Weapons of Mass Destruction (WMD), organized crime, regional conflicts and state failure, climate change and energy security[35] were added.

This illustrates that today's threats and root causes of conflicts are not solely of a military nature, an insight easily overlooked by some in the aftermath of 9/11. Understood correctly, this terrorist attack clearly shows how important it is to adopt the mentioned soft power strategy in the context of a world fragmented by different interpretations of what security policy[36] means and implies.

---

30   Michael Reiterer, Interregionalism as a New Diplomatic Tool: The EU and East Asia, 11 EFA Rev. (2006), 223-244.
31   Trevor Salmon, The European Security and Defence Policy: Built on Rocks or Sand?, 10 EFA Rev. (2005), 371.
32   Council of the European Union, European Security Strategy (EES) of 2003, "A Safer Europe in a Better World", http://www.consilium.europa.eu/uedocs/cmsUp-load/ 78367.pdf.
33   Council of the European Union, Climate Change and International Security, http://www.consilium.europa.eu/ueDocs/cms_Data/docs/pressData/en/reports/99387.pdf.
34   Council of the European Union, Report on the Implementation of the European Security Strategy: Providing Security in a Changing World, 11 December 2008, Doc. S407/08, http://www.consilium.europa.eu/ueDocs/cms_Data/docs/pressdata/EN/reports/104630.pdf, 4.
35   Declaration of the European Commission upon the signing of the Nabucco Intergovernmental Agreement (2009), http://ec.europa.eu/deutschland/pdf/declaration_by_ the_european_commission_130709.pdf; Press statement: http://europa.eu/rapid/ pressReleasesActiondo?reference=IP/09/1114&format=HTML&aged=0&language= EN&guiLanguage=en.
36   Ulrich Schneckener, Die Zivilmacht Europa und die prä-westfälische Herausforderung, Zentrum für Konfliktsforschung der Philipps-Universität Marburg, 2005 http://web.uni-marburg.de/konfliktforschung/pdf/schneckener.pdf.

Europe will mainly tackle these threats through CFSP and ESDP, the collaboration in the fields of Justice, Freedom and Security, focusing on the stabilization of the adjacent area (Balkans, South-Eastern Europe, Mediterranean and Middle East) by way of an integrated energy and climate change policy adopted in December 2008 and by way of multilateral collaboration.

In doing so, the EU has to act in an increasingly multipolar world – it is the enlarged G20, no longer the G7 or G8 which has to find solutions to the ongoing financial and economic crisis. In the context of the WTO it is no longer the old quartet of the EU, US, Canada and Japan, like during the Uruguay Round, which steers the process but rather the EU, US, Brazil and India as the new quartet: a significant change. Although often challenged "'effectiveness' and 'multilateralism' appear mutually incompatible".[37] Multilateralism, a core concept of the ESS, has regained acceptance as the guiding principle in international politics as evidenced by the new approach to international politics by the Obama Administration or by the rise of the G20.

The EU approach to international politics, what has been termed, as mentioned above, "soft" or "smart"[38] or "transformative" power has become attractive. It has turned the EU into a role model, in Africa for the African Union and in Asia, where ASEAN gave itself recently a Charter,[39] clearly inspired by the EU.

G   Fighting Terrorism

Terrorism is in itself a threat to human rights but also counter-measures risk infringing human rights thereby creating a negative spiral of human rights violations. Terrorism seeks to undermine the openness and tolerance of societies. It threatens lives and poses a growing strategic threat to the whole of Europe. Terrorist movements are well-equipped, connected by electronic networks throughout the world, often linked to organized crime and willing to use unlimited violence to cause massive casualties. Terrorism arises out of complex causes such as the pressures of modernization, cultural, social and political crises and the alienation of young people living in foreign societies.

Europe is both a target and a base for such terrorism, as the murderous acts of London and Madrid in 2004 have shown. Logistical bases for Al Qaeda cells have been uncovered in the UK, Italy, Germany, Spain and Belgium. Concerted European action is therefore indispensable. Since 9/11 and even more after the mentioned terrorist attacks, Europe has intensified its fight against terrorism[40] by adopting The Hague Programme[41] in 2004 and a new Strategy for the external

---

37   Missirolli, Revisiting the European Security Strategy (2008), 26.
38   Joseph S. Nye, Get Smart – Combining Hard and Soft Power, Foreign Affairs, 88 (2009) 4, 160-163.
39   Charter of the Association of South-East Asian Nations, 20 November 2007, http://www.aseansec.org/21069.pdf.
40   See Council of the European Union (2008), supra note 34.
41   The Union's attention must focus on different aspects of prevention, preparedness and response: Council of the European Union, The Hague Programme: Ten priorities for the next five years, A partnership for European renewal: A Union against terrorism: Working toward a global response, http://ec.europa.eu/justice_home/news/information_dossiers/the_hague_priorities/doc/02_terrorism_en.pdf.

Dimension of Justice and Home Affairs in 2005.[42] The EU Counter-Terrorism Strategy of 2005[43] operationalized some aspects of the 2003 ESS with "almost 200 counter-terrorism measures, grouped around the four key concepts *'Prevent, Protect, Pursue, Respond'*".[44]

Like most of the EU foreign policy initiatives this one is also value driven. It highlights the respect for human rights and international law. Member states are mainly responsible for combating terrorism on their own. This is true particularly as they remain reluctant to share intelligence gathered by their respective security and secret services. Still, in 2004, by setting up the first Counter-Terrorism Co-ordinator[45] the EU made a step forward at the European level. All those instruments facilitate investigation across borders, allow for the co-ordination of prosecution efforts and of law enforcement in general.

Protecting societies against terrorism has become an important function of EU member states. International collaboration is indispensable since terrorist networks operate on a global scale and do not stop at international boundaries. The Global Initiative to Combat Nuclear Terrorism,[46] created in 2006 and spearheaded by the US and Russia, has gained within a short time wide acceptance. It now counts 76 partners, among them at present 24 EU member states while the EU as such holds an official observer status.

The ESS identified terrorism as one of the key threats for Europe. Thus, in recognition of the transnational character of terrorism the Treaty on the Functioning of the European Union of Lisbon now contains a "solidarity clause"[47] stipulating that the Union and its member states shall act jointly in a spirit of solidarity if a member state is the target of a terrorist attack or the victim of a natural or manmade disaster. Special reference is made to the "protection of democratic institutions and the civilian populations" certainly an issue intimately connected to the protection of human rights.

---

42 Council of the European Union, EU Strategy, External Dimension, http://www.consilium.europa.eu/showPage.aspx?id=1412&lang=EN.
43 Council of the European Union, EU Counter-Terrorism Strategy, http://register.consilium.eu.int/pdf/en/05/st14/st14469-re04.en05.pdf.
44 Victor Mauer, The European Union and Counter-Terrorism, in: Anne Deighton/Victor Mauer (eds.), Securing Europe?, Zürcher Beiträge zur Sicherheitspolitik (2006) 77, 94.
45 Gijs de Vries was the first Coordinator, followed, in 2007, by Gilles de Kerchove. He coordinates the work of the Council of the EU in the field of counter-terrorism, maintains an overview of all the instruments at the Union's disposal, closely monitor the implementation of the EU counter-terrorism strategy, and ensures that the Union plays an active role in the fight against terrorism.
46 US Department of State, Global Initiative to Combat Nuclear Terrorism, http://www.state.gov/t/isn/c18406.htm.
47 Article 222 (1) (a) provides:
"The Union and its Member States shall act jointly in a spirit of solidarity if a Member State is the object of a terrorist attack or the victim of a natural or man-made disaster. The Union shall mobilise all the instruments at its disposal, including the military resources made available by the Member States, to: (a) prevent the terrorist threat in the territory of the Member States; protect democratic institutions and the civilian population from any terrorist attack; assist a Member State in its territory, at the request of its political authorities, in the event of a terrorist attack; [...]."

H   Conclusions

Based on this analysis of the various elements discussed I would follow the main arguments of Howorth[48], namely that the strategic orientation of the Union builds on cooperative, multidimensional security taking into account "not only political and diplomatic disputes but also [...] such factors as economic development, trade disputes, and human rights abuses" linking security to the interlinked global public goods, thus following a comprehensive approach to security. This places the individual much more in the centre of the policy than the power oriented approach of realists – the term 'power' does not even appear in the ESS. Human security[49] could therefore be a concept complementing the ESS. While the importance of socio-economic factors has often been underestimated, attention nowadays paid to failed states, poverty, effects of climate change and violations of human rights show that a re-orientation towards taking soft security factors and new security threats including threats against human security more into account is underway.

Soft power combined with a focus on human security and the emphasis on the concept of responsibility to protect in promoting global governance to implement common values of human rights and the rule of law, social awareness based on the European social model and pursuing 'unity in diversity' are efficient poles of attraction. They render EU foreign policy actions more credible and assign the EU a specific niche in international politics in acting together with its member states or in complementing their actions.

In making the respect for human rights a precondition for accession to the EU, the Union has contributed to enlarging the realm of respect for human rights in Europe through exercising its soft power which grows in strength the more interested a country is in either joining or cooperating closely with the EU.

In taking up the challenge to pursue a value driven or at least value inspired foreign policy, the EU will have to use all the diplomatic means at its disposal to fend off attacks on universal values, the subordination of human rights under economic success and to resist the temptation to counterbalance the redistribution of economic and political power towards new actors like the BRIC (Brazil, Russia, India, China) through abandoning the innovative approach to foreign policy in favour of the traditional realist approach.

Conflict prevention is the more important task than conflict management or peacemaking, although the latter may be necessary to allow peacekeeping.

ESDP translates these values into action – more than twenty missions during the first ten years prove that actions are taken and not only papers written.

Coherence, or the lack thereof, remain the determining factors: coherence between actions of the EU, its member states or other international organizations like the UN, NATO but also NGOs working in the field. Coherence is also needed in developing policies with neighbouring countries, before they reach the status of candidate countries or alternative political arrangements are sought with them in order to bind important economic and political partners to the Union. The political manoeuvring which was necessary to finally integrate the Union for the

---

48   Jolyon Howorth, Security and Defence Policy in the European Union, London 2007, 200-201.
49   See ibid., and in particular the reference to Mary Kaldor's approach towards and work on human security, at p. 201.

Mediterranean[50] into the mainstream of EU politics and its institutions proves this proposition.

Because of its unique structure, the EU, although not yet a post-national institution, offers the coordination and combination of policy instruments which are required in a globalized environment where compartmentalisation, nationalisation of politics and single-handed actions are less and less effective.

Therefore and taking into account that, according to the European Security Strategy, "none of the new threats is purely militarily; nor can any be tackled by purely military means",[51] a policy mix and a mix of instruments is required for finding solutions which offer the EU the chance to become an effective player despite its weakness in military matters. Concentrating its efforts on providing human security allows the EU not only to fill a niche but is the policy in line with its basic design as a value driven polity.

Economic and financial expertise in crisis management on the European level and world-wide in the context of the G20 and the IMF contributed to avoid a systemic crisis and kept the financial architecture in Europe intact. The built-in stabilisers of the European economic model cushioned some of the negative aspects especially for the European citizens. Know-how acquired in developing the single market and the use of the Euro as a new stabilizer[52] is part of the Union's soft power and contributes directly to human security in avoiding to some extent big losses of personal savings, retirement and pension assets, home equity or the work place. To regain trust, credibility and influence lost, for the EU and the US, these qualities will be required to defend Western values and influence.

Meeting the requirements for a coherent human rights policy is especially demanding as the yardstick is coherence between internal and external policies as well as the consistency of executing the policy. If economic, political or geopolitical considerations override otherwise sacrosanct principles, the credibility gap becomes evident. This in turn feeds back negatively into internal and external constituencies thereby lessening the overall policy performance. Thus following consistently a human rights policy, making use of all instruments at the disposal of the Union and its member states is one of the important elements of EU foreign policy which also contributes to shaping the international identity of the Union as an international actor.

---

50   Michael Reiterer, From the (French) Mediterranean Union to the (European) Barcelona Process: The "Union for the Mediterranean" as Part of the European Neighbourhood Policy, 14 EFA Rev. (2009), 313-336.
51   European Security Strategy, at 7.
52   The Greek debt crisis of 2010 which threatened to derail the Euro provoked a strong showing of European solidarity and may result in a deepening of economic and financial governance thereby reinforcing the stability function of the European currency.

Markus MÖSTL

Mainstreaming Human Rights in the Common Security and Defence Policy: Reality or Catchphrase?

Table of Contents

Keywords

Human rights, mainstreaming, European Union, Common Security and Defence Policy, European Security and Defence Policy, crisis management, human security

A   Introduction

With the entry into force of the Treaty of Lisbon the European Security and Defence Policy (ESDP) was renamed Common Security and Defence Policy (CSDP).[1] Beyond this renaming, the tasks for which the member states of the European Union (EU) may use the CSDP have also been updated in the amended European treaty framework and now include "joint disarmament operations, humanitarian and rescue tasks, military advice and assistance tasks, conflict prevention and peace-keeping tasks, tasks of combat forces in crisis management, including peace-making and post-conflict stabilisation" (Article 43

---

1   This chapter will use the term CSDP only, unless older documents, statements or quotes explicitly refer to the ESDP.

Treaty on European Union (TEU)). The new catalogue of activities thus revises the Petersberg tasks enumerated in Article 17 of the Nice Treaty, but in fact the types of crisis management operations now foreseen in Article 43 TEU are not really new ones, as the Article now merely describes the activities undertaken by member states in practice already in the framework of the EU crisis management under the CSDP. In fact, the CSDP practice has always been "one step ahead" of the treaty in force.[2] Certainly, it has to be acknowledged that without this resolute practice the CSDP would not have achieved such an impressive record of international engagements. As of January 2010, the member states had launched no less than 22 operations on three continents.[3]

From a human rights perspective such a progressive and practice-oriented approach to crisis management also has risks and downsides. Potential shortcomings in the planning of possibly swift reactions, operational necessities, as well as interest driven agendas of member states might quickly result in peace operations in which human rights are unduly neglected. Therefore, and in order to shape crisis management operations in a beneficial manner, human rights should obtain an appropriate, central and institutionalized role in the CSDP. In fact, the existing legal framework and practice of the CSDP were already conducive to attributing due attention to human rights in EU crisis management operations. Most prominently, the EU member states started a process of mainstreaming human rights into the CSDP.[4]

In light of these developments, this chapter sets out to analyze where these mainstreaming activities have led and evaluates the current role of human rights in EU crisis management. Thus, after short introductory clarifications on the notion of mainstreaming human rights (section B), this contribution describes the legal and political basis of mainstreaming human rights in the CSDP (B.1.), illustrates the specifics of the EU approach to mainstreaming (B.2.) and assesses the role of human rights in the CSDP from an institutional, conceptual and operational perspective (B.3.). Finally, some conclusions on the current state of human rights in the CSDP will be offered jointly with recommendations for the enhanced inclusion of human rights in EU crisis management (C).[5]

---

2   E.g., the Lisbon Treaty for the first time refers to the European Defence Agency (EDA), which had already been set up by the EU member states in 2004 through Council Joint Action 2004/551/CFSP of 12 July 2004 on the establishment of the European Defence Agency, OJ L 245, 17.

3   For an overview of CSDP missions, see the official CSDP website at http://consilium.europa.eu/showPage.aspx?id=268&lang=en. See also CSDP, Mission Analysis Partnership, http://www.csdpmap.eu/index.html.

4   For detailed analysis of mainstreaming human security in United Nations Peace operations and EU crisis management operations, see Wolfgang Benedek/Matthias C. Kettemann/Markus Möstl (eds.), Mainstreaming Human Security in Peace Operations and Crisis Management. Problems, Policies, Potential, London/New York, forthcoming 2010.

5   This contribution was written in the framework of a project funded by the Jubiläumsfonds of the Oesterreichische Nationalbank (project number 12862). Parts of this contribution build on the author's contribution to the study "Human Rights mainstreaming in EU's external relations" by the European Inter-University Centre for Human Rights and Democratisation for the European Parliament. A summary of this study is available on the EIUC website at http://www.eiuc.org/index.php?option=com_content&task=view&id=314&Itemid=12.

B Mainstreaming Human Rights in Crisis Management Operations

On the international level, mainstreaming human rights has been a topic for the United Nations (UN) for more than a decade and has yielded varying results.[6] The different approaches taken by UN bodies show that although the concept of mainstreaming is not a new one, we still have to acknowledge that there is no universally agreed definition of mainstreaming human rights the member states of the EU could build on. Mainstreaming is still a process that has to be defined on a case to case basis. In order to provide an analytical framework for this chapter, mainstreaming human rights is here defined as a strategic process of deliberately incorporating human rights considerations into the bureaucratic procedures, programmes and policies of an international actor.[7] For the CSDP, mainstreaming human rights would thus describe the process of incorporating human rights into the CSDP institutions, the preparatory phase of an operation, and the activities and policies of an operation in the field as well as into the follow-up process after the end of an operation.

1 The Legal and Political Basis for Mainstreaming Human Rights in the CSDP

The importance and necessity of incorporating human rights into the CSDP has been acknowledged by the EU member states in different legal and political documents. The TEU provides the legal basis for mainstreaming human rights in the areas of the Common Foreign and Security Policy (CFSP) and the CSDP. According to Article 2 TEU human rights are one of the values the EU is founded on, and Article 3.5 TEU makes clear that the Union shall contribute to the protection of human rights also in its relations with the wider world. Article 21 TEU lists the objectives of the EU's external action and enumerates, among others, the consolidation and support of democracy, the rule of law, human rights and the principles of international law. Although these goals are defined in a very general manner, the member states of the EU and, more specifically, the European Council is obliged to take them into account when formulating the principles and general guidelines for the security and defence policy according to Article 26 TEU.

The importance of promoting human rights in the external relations of the EU was reinforced by the 2003 European Security Strategy[8] (ESS). The ESS identifies the protection of human rights as one of the best means of strengthening the international order. But obviously the ESS does not aspire to provide a stringent guidance for how to mainstream human rights into the bureaucratic procedures, programs and policies of the CSDP. Yet, this strategy document repeats and underlines the political willingness to include human rights considerations in

---

6   For the results of these efforts, see Gerd Oberleitner, A decade of mainstreaming human rights in the UN: achievements, failures, challenges, Netherlands Quarterly of Human Rights, 26 (2008) 3, 359-390.
7   Cf. ibid., 363.
8   European Council, A Secure Europe in a Better World: The European Security Strategy, Brussels, 12 December 2003, http://www.consilium.europa.eu/uedocs/cmsUpload/78367.pdf.

policies of the CFSP. Given the intergovernmental approach that still governs the CFSP and the CSDP after the entry into force of the Treaty of Lisbon, such political commitments remain of particular high importance.

The follow-up document to the ESS, the Report on the Implementation of the ESS, expressly reiterates the importance of mainstreaming human rights issues in all activities of the CSDP, including in CSDP operations.[9] It is worth mentioning here that the Implementation Report argues that this should be achieved through a people-based approach coherent with the concept of human security.[10] In a similar vein, the European Parliament recalled the importance of human rights mainstreaming for the CSDP in a resolution on the implementation of the ESS and CSDP under the heading of "Human security and the security dimension of development policy".[11]

Thus, it can be ascertained that there is a legal obligation for EU member states to use the instruments of the CSDP in a way that is conducive to increasing human rights protection in third countries and that these obligations are accompanied by ample political commitments.

2 The EU Approach to Mainstreaming Human Rights in the CSDP

The process of explicitly mainstreaming human rights into the CFSP and the CSDP started in 2006, when the Political and Security Committee (PSC) endorsed a paper on mainstreaming human rights.[12] In this paper, the Working Party on Human Rights (COHOM) gave initial recommendations on how to mainstream human rights across the CFSP and other EU policies "in order to archieve a more informed, credible, coherent, consistent and effective EU human rights policy".[13] The paper clarified that in doing so the EU does not have to start from scratch, as existing EU tools for raising human rights issues with third countries, such as

---

9　Report on the Implementation of the European Security Strategy - Providing Security in a Changing World, submitted to the European Council of 11-12 December 2008, Doc. S407/08, Brussels, 11 December 2008, http://www.consilium.europa.eu/ueDocs/ cms_Data/docs/pressData/en/esdp/104631.pdf, 10.

10　This explicit reference to the concept of human security demonstrates its increasing relevance in EU crisis management, not least because human rights are the core value of human security. On the concept of human security in the CSDP see, e.g., Markus Möstl, The European Way of Promoting Human Security in Crisis Management Operations: a Critical Stocktaking, in: Benedek/Kettemann/Möstl (eds.), Mainstreaming Human Security (forthcoming 2010). For the Human Security Study Group the primacy of human rights constitutes the first principle of a human security approach to EU crisis management. See Human Security Study Group, A European Way of Security: The Madrid Report of the Human Security Study Group comprising a Proposal and Background Report, Madrid, 8 November 2007, http://www.lse.ac.uk/ Depts/global/PDFs/Madrid%20Report%20Final%20for%20distribution.pdf.

11　European Parliament resolution of 5 June 2008 on the implementation of the European Security Strategy and ESDP (2008/2003(INI)), OJ C 285E, para. 20.

12　Council of the European Union, Mainstreaming human rights across CFSP and other EU policies, Doc. 10076/06, Brussels, 7 June 2006, http://register.consilium.europa.eu/ pdf/en/06/st10/st10076.en06.pdf.

13　Ibid., 2.

the human rights guidelines,[14] political dialogues, co-operation agreements, and multilateral fora should serve as a framework for an enhanced protection and promotion of human rights in third countries. For the operational branch of the CFSP, the COHOM suggested that the

> *"[...] protection of human rights should be systematically addressed in all phases of ESDP operations, both during the planning and implementation phase, including by measures ensuring that the necessary human rights expertise is available to operations at headquarter level and in the theatre; [as well as for the] training of staff; and by including human rights reporting in the operational duties of ESDP missions."*[15]

Shortly after this initial framework document was agreed upon, a number of more concrete proposals followed specifically for the CSDP mainstreaming policy. These suggestions comprised the proposals to develop a list of relevant human rights documents and to organize workshops in order to assist planners of CSDP operations in human rights issues. It was also proposed to develop a template for key human rights elements that could be included in CSDP planning documents. Further, the elaboration of a field manual on human rights and standardized training guidelines for CSDP personnel projected. Additionally, the idea was ventilated to include human rights aspects in all CSDP exercises.[16] Human rights advisors and focal points were suggested to be integrated in preparatory fact finding missions and later to be appointed in missions to assist the Operation Commander or the Head of Mission as a general rule for all CSDP operations. Further measures, such as generic job descriptions, appropriate reporting procedures on human rights aspects as well as the inclusion of experiences gained in the field of human rights in the lessons learned, were also recommended in order to complement the concrete framework for mainstreaming human rights in the CSDP.[17]

These suggestions were highly supported by both, the Committee for Civilian Aspects of Crisis Management (CIVCOM)[18] and the European Union Military Committee (EUMC).[19] CIVCOM stated that "human rights mainstreaming should

---

14 The guidelines on human rights now comprise a set of eight guidelines, which are of relevance for the CSDP: guidelines on the death penalty, on the EU policy towards third countries on torture and other cruel, inhuman or degrading treatment or punishment, on the human rights dialogues with third countries, on children in armed conflict, on human rights defenders, guidelines for the promotion and protection of the rights of the child, on violence against women and girls and combating all forms of discrimination against them, and guidelines on International Humanitarian Law. See http://consilium.europa.eu/showPage.aspx?id=1681&lang=de.

15 Council of the European Union, Mainstreaming Human Rights Across CFSP and Other EU Policies, Doc. 10076/06, Brussels, 7 June 2006, 2, http://register.consilium.europa.eu/pdf/en/06/st10/st10076.en06.pdf.

16 Council of the European Union, Mainstreaming of Human Rights into ESDP, Doc. 11936/4/06 REV 4, Brussels, 14 September 2006, http://register.consilium.europa.eu/pdf/en/07/st11/st11359-ex01.en07.pdf.

17 Ibid.

18 Committee for Civilian Aspects of Crisis Management, CIVCOM Advice on Mainstreaming of Human Rights into ESDP, Doc. 12986/06, Brussels, 19 September 2006, http://register.consilium.europa.eu/pdf/en/06/st12/st12986.en06.pdf.

19 European Union Military Committee, Military Advice on Mainstreaming of Human

be viewed as an integral part of the strategic objectives of ESDP missions",[20] and in the view of the EUMC the proposed measures to mainstream human rights would in particular add "legitimacy and credibility in the field, but also in the view of a more general public".[21]

Thus, the overall concept for mainstreaming human rights as well as the desired outcomes of mainstreaming human rights in the CSDP were made quite clear in policy documents and were appreciated by key advisory organs. The proposed measures, if implemented, would provide a sound framework in which norms, standards and principles of the international human rights system could be integrated into the bureaucratic procedures, programmes and policies of the CSDP and would be suitable to bring about a reorientation of existing CSDP policies towards human rights.

3 The Current Role of Human Rights in the CSDP

Since adopting a strategy for mainstreaming human rights is not an end in itself, important questions need to be addressed at this point: What results did this mainstreaming strategy yield? What role do human rights have for the CSDP and to what extent did the implementation of the mainstreaming strategy go beyond the rhetorical use of human rights language? The approach taken here to analyze these questions is to take a critical look at (a) human rights at the institutional level, by enquiring after the actors dealing with human rights in the CSDP, at (b) the civilian and military capabilities available for the CSDP, as well as existing EU human rights concepts for crisis management operations including human rights concepts available for the operation planning procedure, and finally (c) to look at the role of human rights in the mandates of operations and the work of specific human rights components in the field and in follow-up processes. Each of these aspects will be reviewed in the following.

a The Institutional Level: Actors Dealing with Human Rights in the CSDP

Mainstreaming human rights, as understood in this chapter, implies that human rights are perceived as a crosscutting issue that has to be put on the agenda of all relevant actors in the CSDP. Since mainstreaming human rights should result in a work ethics of all staff involved that is conducive to the promotion of human rights, human rights might also have to be taken into consideration by actors which are not explicitly mandated to deal with human rights issues – usually a difficult endeavour within the distribution of competences and institutional confines of the EU.

Nevertheless, such a comprehensive approach certainly entails the risk that well-intentioned efforts to include human rights in all actors' agendas could lead

---

Rights into ESDP, Doc. 13059/06, Brussels, 21 September 2006, http://register.consilium.europa.eu/pdf/en/06/st13/st13059.en06.pdf.

20   Committee for Civilian Aspects of Crisis Management, CIVCOM Advice on Mainstreaming of Human Rights into ESDP, Doc. 12986/06, Brussels, 19 September 2006, http://register.consilium.europa.eu/pdf/en/06/st12/st12986.en06.pdf.

21   Ibid., 2.

to a diffusion of human rights activities throughout all branches of the EU crisis management structures, leading to an insufficient focus of activities for specialized human right organs and ultimately to an unclear distribution of tasks. In the worst case, mainstreaming could become flattened to a catchword without practical results for potential beneficiaries, namely people caught up in crisis or conflict situations. Thus, in order to prevent the negative results of mainstreaming, one important question has to be addressed: Who are the relevant actors with the primary responsibility to address human rights in the CSDP and what is the proper balance between these dedicated human rights units and mainstreaming human rights across all actors involved?

From a conceptual point of view, the ideal answer to the second part of this question can only be a dual approach, meaning that dedicated institutional structures are created that help other branches of the CSDP to develop and reinforce their ability to advance human rights in and through their own work. This way the process of mainstreaming could best help providing the persons involved with proper human rights expertise for planning, implementing, monitoring and evaluating programs and simultaneously help creating a culture and a work ethics around and for human rights among all CSDP staff involved. This is a tall order, but any attempts to mainstream human rights cannot strive for less ambitious goals, if the CSDP truly aims to operate in a way which fosters international human rights law, as the member states' legal and political commitments imply.

In fact, numerous institutions deal with the CSDP in Brussels, which leads to a complex interrelationship of institutional actors, in which some deal more intensely with human rights than others. Riina Kionka, the former Personal Representative for Human Rights in the Area of CFSP,[22] is entrusted with the overall responsibility for driving forward the policy of mainstreaming human rights in the CFSP as she had the explicit mandate to mainstream human rights into all aspects of the EU's policy. She made continued efforts to bring human rights issues to the attention of the main political decision-making body in crisis management, the PSC, in order to raise human rights mainstreaming at a higher political level.[23] According to Riina Kionka, mainstreaming human rights into CSDP operations and missions means that "every operation should seek to promote the EU's core themes in this sector, as defined in various instruments".[24] Being also Head of the Human Rights Unit in Directorate-General E - External and Political-Military Affairs, Mrs. Kionka is furthermore responsible for human rights in crisis management within the Council Secretariat, and therefore

---

22   As of February 2010, Riina Kionka still maintains the post as "Former Personal Representative of the Secretary General/High Representative for Human Rights" with the same responsibilities as before. Initial policy proposals by Catherine Ashton, new High Representative of the Union for Foreign Affairs and Security Policy, indicate, however, that the post of a Personal Representative of the High Representative for Human Rights will not be kept in future. Author's interview with EU official, 4 February 2010.

23   Council of the European Union, EU Annual Report on Human Rights 2008, Brussels, Doc. 14146/2/08, 27 November 2008 REV 2, 21, http://www.consilium.europa.eu/uedocs/cmsUpload/st14146-re02.en08.pdf.

24   Riina Kionka, Mainstreaming human rights and gender into ESDP, in: ESDP Newsletter, European Security and Defence Policy 7 (2009).

is also responsible for administering efforts to include human rights in crisis management on the practical working level.

While the overarching responsibility for human rights in EU crisis management rests with the Human Rights Unit, various experts dealing with human rights in the General Secretariat of the Council are involved in the planning, review and follow-up to operations.[25] Especially the former Directorates-General 8 and 9 deserve mentioning here. These Directorates-General have recently been merged and now form the joint civilian and military Crisis Management and Planning Directorate (CMPD),[26] in which one person is currently working full time on human rights.[27] The CMPD also includes staff from the European Union Military Staff (EUMS) and is mainly responsible for the strategic planning of civilian and military CSDP Missions.

The EUMS has established an active point of contact for human rights, and the cooperation between CMPD and EUMS seems to be working well.[28] Being the main civilian advisory body, the CIVCOM gives essential advice on civilian matters in meetings of the PSC.[29] Human rights topics may thus be integrated into the draft documents and agenda meetings by these two bodies, when appropriate. Moreover, the delegations of the member states may push for human rights by putting a specific human rights theme on the agenda in the EUMC, CIVCOM, the Politico-Military Group (PMG) or the PSC. The activities and priorities of a Presidency actively promoting human rights issues certainly also have an impact on these bodies' decisions. This raises the question of what will happen in future, when representatives of the new High Representative of the Union for Foreign Affairs and Security Policy will chair the meetings.[30] Without the initiative of dedicated Presidencies some momentum to push for human rights topics could thus be lost. But even without having the Presidency, member states may influence the human rights agenda in crisis management. Austria, for example, currently drives forward the agenda on the protection of civilians with a working document, which could result in the adoption of a new concept for the protection of civilians, or at least in a revision of the current concept.[31]

Further actors involved in EU crisis management are tasked to deal with human rights at least on an irregular basis. The Civilian Planning and Conduct Capability (CPCC), being responsible for operational planning, appointed focal points for human rights and gender.[32] The legal service in the Council Secretariat

---

25 Hadewych Hazelzet, Human Rights Aspects of EU Crisis Management Operation: From Nuisance to Necessity, International Peacekeeping 13 (2006) 4, 567.
26 Author's interview with EU official, 4 February 2010.
27 Author's interview with EU official, 2 February 2010.
28 This point of contact mainly deals with gender issues. Author's interview with EU official, 4 February 2010.
29 Representatives of the Commission regularly participate at PSC meetings. For an example of the cooperation between Council and Commission see Joint Document by the Council and the Commission, Comprehensive approach to the EU implementation of the United Nations Security Council Resolutions 1325 and 1820 on women, peace and security, Doc. 15671/1/08REV 1, Brussels, 1 December 2008.
30 As of February 2010, representatives of the Spanish Presidency still chair the Council working group meetings.
31 Author's interview with EU Official, 4 February 2010. For the concept on the protection of civilians, see below at B.3.b.
32 Author's interview with EU official, 2 February 2010.

includes staff with special expertise in international humanitarian law and makes available its special expertise in the meetings of various working groups, such as the PMG or the CIVCOM. Building on confidential documents and human rights fact sheets compiled locally by EU Heads of Missions and member states, the Joint Situation Centre (SITCEN) collects files on almost every country of the world and includes this knowledge in its briefings for Council working groups where appropriate.[33]

Although COHOM's purview extends to human rights aspects of all external relations of the EU, this organ is not actively involved in the preparation and planning of specific crisis management operations per se; the working group has rather developed basic framework documents and statements on human rights mainstreaming in the CSDP and is usually also informed about human rights mainstreaming in crisis management by other Council working groups.

As can be seen, a considerable number of actors within the General Secretariat of the Council deals – at least occasionally – with human rights issues for the EU crisis management. Only few organs are explicitly tasked to deal with human rights issues on a daily basis, and some actors in practice deal with human rights "when appropriate". Thus, there are clear signs that there are not only a few dedicated human rights units dealing with human rights, but rather a considerable number of actors that may have human rights on their agenda, if the situation so demands. This might certainly be a step forward to find the proper balance between specialized human rights organs, namely the Human Rights Unit in the Council Secretariat, and mainstreaming human rights across the activities of all other relevant actors. Nevertheless, it cannot be ascertained that a work ethics around and for human rights has so far been developed on a broad basis by all actors involved.

b   The Preparatory Phase of Operations: Human Rights Concepts and Capabilities

Several human rights concepts have been developed specifically for the area of EU crisis management, which now serve as instructions for the relevant actors involved in CSDP, ranging from mission planners to civilian and military operation staff.[34] These concepts comprise guidelines, standards and checklists and cover a broad range of human rights issues relevant for crisis management operations. More specifically, concepts have been adopted on gender issues, children in armed conflict, international humanitarian law, the behavior of mission personnel and the role of civil society. Furthermore, a working document on the protection of civilians and a draft document on transitional justice have been elaborated.[35] These concepts, together with some limited examples of how the

---

33   Ibid.
34   Key human rights issues, such as combating torture, supporting human rights defenders, working towards the abolition of the death penalty will not be described here since they are only indirectly related to crisis management.
35   These two documents were never decided upon on ministerial level and are considered as works in progress. Author's interview with EU Official, 2 February 2010. On transitional justice it should be noted that the Council adopted an agreement with the International Criminal Court, containing an obligation of cooperation and assistance with a focus on exchanging information and documents of mutual interest. See

relevant documents have been integrated into the planning and lessons learned documents, have been compiled, during the Presidencies of Germany, Portugal and Slovenia, in a handbook on mainstreaming human rights and gender in the CSDP.[36] This handbook aims to set more general standards in the field of human rights in CSDP operations and – at least in theory – serves as an over-arching definition of human rights concepts relevant for operation planners, trainers and mission personnel. This stocktaking of human rights documents can be regarded as one result of the EU's efforts to mainstreaming human rights and obviously also aims at raising public awareness to the topic of human rights in the CSDP.

The existing EU concepts for ensuring and promoting human rights in crisis management are highly relevant for the civilian and military capabilities of CSDP operations. Since the year 2000, EU member states have developed four priority areas for civilian crisis management: police, strengthening the rule of law, strengthening civilian administration and civil protection. Additional support capabilities have been committed by member states in areas such as human rights, political affairs, gender, and security sector reform and should support integrated civilian crisis management missions.[37] With the Crisis Response Teams (CRTs) another instrument was added to the toolbox of civilian crisis management that could be of particular value for promoting human rights.[38]

Mainstreaming human rights has thus not resulted in the creation of a separate human rights instrument for civilian crisis management, but the tasks performed by the staff of the four priority areas of civilian crisis management as well as the CRTs are obviously intricately related to human rights issues. However, much remains to be done to improve the human rights expertise in the existing civilian capabilities. In this vein, the Civilian Headline Goal, to be achieved by the end of 2010 and aiming at improving the existing civilian capabilities, regards the further mainstreaming of human rights and gender as an important concern for immediate action.[39]

Human rights mainstreaming is of particular importance for all military components of CSDP operations. Since multinational troops might be deployed in

---

Agreement between the International Criminal Court and the European Union on co-operation and assistance, OJ L 115/50, 28 April 2006.

36 General Secretariat of the Council, Mainstreaming Human Rights and Gender into European Security and Defence Policy – Compilation of relevant documents, Brussels, 2008, http://www.consilium.europa.eu/ueDocs/cms_Data/docs/hr/new144. pdf. In the foreword to this publication, Javier Solana explains that the lessons learned in previous operations showed that including human rights and gender approaches in all ESDP operations makes them more effective, ibid., 5.

37 Ministerial Declaration at the Civilian Capabilities Commitment Conference, Brussels, 22 November 2004, http://bit.ly/950WrC, para. 4.

38 CRTs are small teams of pre-identified and trained experts, which may also include human rights experts, deployable on short notice. See Council of the European Union, CRT Generic Terms of Reference, Doc. 15406/05 (2005), 5 December 2005. For an insider's view on the potential of human rights promotion by CRTs, see Irene Kaufmann, The Civilian Response Team of the European Union: a European Contribution to Operationalizing Human Security in International Crisis Management?, in: Benedek/ Kettemann/Möstl (eds.), Mainstreaming Human Security (forthcoming 2010).

39 Council of the European Union, Civilian Headline Goal 2010, approved by the ministerial Civilian Capabilities Improvement Conference and noted by the General Affairs and External Relations Council on 19 November 2007, Doc. 14823/07.

complex situations that might raise intricate human rights questions,[40] the proper training of the military staff is key for the promotion of human rights through the CSDP. As for now, the member states are primarily responsible for training of CSDP personnel and it remains up to each member state to include human rights in these trainings. There are certainly good examples by national training institutions, such as those of Sweden, Austria, or Germany, which regularly offer human rights courses.[41] Although member states with a good record in providing human rights training open their trainings for the participation of other nations, it is virtually impossible for them to train the huge number of soldiers that might be deployed by all member states.[42] Thus, as long as there are no standard training guidelines and human rights modules for general CSDP courses on human rights as well as for the induction training for CSDP personnel by all member states, there cannot be a real common understanding of and attitude towards human rights among the military operation staff.[43]

Pocket cards are another means to raise human rights awareness among mission staff. So far, such guidance documents have been issued by the Heads of Mission for some specific missions. The pocket card for EUFOR Congo, for example, includes the following prescriptions on human rights:

"(1) Transfer of detained persons is allowed only to authorities who are specifically designated by EUFOR RD Congo.
(2) Report all observations regarding violations of Human Rights via your chain of command.
(3) Document all observations regarding violations of Human Rights.
(4) Protection of civilians under imminent threat of physical violence in the areas of your deployment is part of your mandate.
(5) Take care of particularly vulnerable groups (i. e. women, children)
(6) You are personally responsible for respecting and promoting Human Rights."[44]

Although these guidelines obviously have to remain limited in their content, they still constitute promising examples. Regrettably, it has to be noted though that pocket cards are not provided for a mission as a general rule or in a generic manner; the Heads of Mission rather decide on its content on a case to case basis.

---

40   See for examples Hazelzet, Human Rights Aspects (2006), 564.

41   Author's interview with EU official 2 February 2010.

42   The training activities by the European Security and Defense College (ESDC) are inapt in this respect, since the ESDC courses are mainly attended by diplomats and high ranking officials, but not by soldiers who have to deal with situations with human rights implications on the ground.

43   So far the Council welcomed an initiative to "improv[e] the coherence and quality of pre-deployment and training in general for staff deployed in ESDP missions […] inter alia through developing elements for the training curriculum on the implementation of UNSCR 1325 and 1820 for ESDP missions and operations". See Council Conclusions on ESDP, 2974th EXTERNAL RELATIONS Council meeting, Brussels, 17 November 2009.

44   Further guidance is given in this pocket card with regard to gender issues and child soldiers. Council of the European Union, Mainstreaming Human Rights and Gender into European Security and Defence Policy – Compilation of relevant documents, Doc. 11359/07 EXT 1, Brussels, 9 October 2007, 15.

Unfortunately, no pocket cards have been developed for civilian missions so far.[45]

It should be noted that human rights are taken into consideration in multinational civil and military exercises conducted by the EU member states on a yearly basis. Yet, nobody is deployed in the hypothetical countries of these exercises and the mere inclusion of rhetorical references to human rights aspects are not conducive to a joint understanding of human rights that could help improving the knowledge of how to use and implement existing human rights concepts.[46]

c   Human Rights in the Field: Human Rights Mandates and Components

Assessing the actual results of mainstreaming human rights in CSDP operations in the field is a challenging task, not only because there is no single set of appropriate tools to evaluate the mainstreaming of human rights, but also because many relevant documents, such as the concept of operations (CONOPS), the operation plan (OPLAN), the rules of engagement and internal reports by EU organs as well as relevant statistics are only partly accessible or not available to the public at all. What practitioners report is certainly promising,[47] but at the same time it is hardly enough to comprehensively assess the actual impact of mainstreaming efforts in the field. Accepting these limitations, some operational results will nevertheless be reviewed in the following with a focus on the human rights mandates and components of the EU crisis management operations.

The COHOM proposed that mandates for CSDP operations should include human rights provisions where applicable.[48] Yet in practice most mandates of CSDP operations do not explicitly refer to the promotion or protection of human rights as an aim or objective of the mission. So far, only eight out of 22 Joint Actions by the Council of the European Union establishing CSDP operations made an explicit reference to human rights. For example, the Joint Action establishing the rule of law mission in Kosovo clearly states that "EULEX KOSOVO shall: [...] (i) ensure that all its activities respect international standards concerning human rights and gender mainstreaming".[49] The Aceh Monitoring Mission (AMM) was tasked to "[...] monitor the human rights situation and provide assis-

---

45   Author's interview with EU official 2 February 2010.

46   Author's interview with EU official 4 February 2010.

47   Hazelzet reports that special annexes on human rights exists for some OPLANs (Kosovo and Georgia, 2008) that could be used as model for the future. See Hadewych Hazelzet, Six Years of Mainstreaming Human Rights into ESDP: a Success Story?, in: Benedek/Kettemann/Möstl (eds.), Mainstreaming Human Security (forthcoming 2010). See also the report by Monica Larsson, gender advisor in EUFOR Tchad/RCA: Monica Larsson, Implementing the directives to work with gender issues in the field – examples from EUFOR Tchad/RCA, in: Wolfgang Benedek/ Matthias C. Kettemann/Markus Möstl, 2nd Graz Workshop on the Future of Security, Workshop Report, June 2009, http://www.uni-graz.at/vrewww/english/research/ Workshop_II_Report.pdf.

48   Council of the European Union, Mainstreaming human rights across CFSP and other EU policies, Doc. 10076/06, Brussels, 7 June 2006, Annex II, 9.

49   Council Joint Action 2008/124/CFSP of 4 February 2008 on the European Union Rule of Law Mission in Kosovo, EULEX KOSOVO, http://www.eulex-kosovo.eu/ home/docs/JointActionEULEX_EN.pdf.

tance in this field in the context of the tasks set out in points [...]".[50] The police mission in the Democratic Republic of Congo takes "[...] care to promote policies compatible with human rights and international humanitarian law, democratic standards and the principles of good governance, transparency and respect for the rule of law".[51]

But of course many CSDP operations implicitly address human rights issues without referring to human rights in the mandate or the mission statement. The mandate of operation EUFOR Chad/RCA, for example, does not refer to human rights explicitly, but the support to humanitarian actions was the main aim of the mission as was the protection of civilians in danger, particularly refugees and displaced persons.[52] The same holds true for the military operation in Bosnia and Herzegovina (EUFOR-Althea) that contributes to the stabilization process of the country and thus has strong implications for the promotion of human rights.[53] The EU support to the African Union Mission in Darfur (AMIS) contributed to the protection of the civilian population and to the efforts aimed at improving the security level and the humanitarian situation in Darfur, but human rights are not mentioned in the mission mandate.[54] Thus, there seems to be a reluctance to include human rights in the mandates of operations. Apparently human rights are easily outweighed for other mission objectives and are therefore not included in the mandates in order to avoid mission creep.

The planners of EU crisis management operations have developed different human rights components to address human rights concerns in response to different challenges in CSDP operations. Various types of human rights instruments, such as monitors, focal points and points of contact, have already been incorporated in various CSDP operations. Human rights monitors played a central role in the Aceh Monitoring Mission, as the monitoring of human rights was a primary task of this operation. In this operation, which is often referred to as best practice of monitoring human rights in EU crisis management,[55] no less than 40 human

---

50   Council Joint Action 2005/643/CFSP of 9 September 2005 on the European Union Monitoring Mission in Aceh (Indonesia) (Aceh Monitoring Mission — AMM), http://consilium.europa.eu/showPage.aspx?id=1078&lang=en.

51   Council Joint Action 2007/405/CFSP of 12 June 2007 on the European Union police mission undertaken in the framework of reform of the security sector (SSR) and its interface with the system of justice in the Democratic Republic of the Congo (EUPOL RD Congo), http://eur-lex.europa.eu/LexUriServ/LexUriServ.do?uri=OJ:L:2007:151: 0046:0051:EN:PDF.

52   Council Joint Action 2007/677/CFSP of 15 October 2007 on the European Union military operation in the Republic of Chad and in the Central African Republic (in accordance with the mandate set out in UN Security Council Resolution 1778 (2007), http://eur-lex.europa.eu/LexUriServ/LexUriServ.do?uri=OJ:L:2007:323:0057: 0058:EN:PDF.

53   Council Joint Action 2004/570/CFSP of 12 July 2004 on the European Union military operation in Bosnia and Herzegovina, http://eur-lex.europa.eu/pri/en/oj/dat/2004/ l_252/l_25220040728en00100014.pdf.

54   Council Joint Action 2005/557/CFSP of 18 July 2005 on the European Union civilian-military supporting action to the African Union mission in the Darfur region of Sudan, http://eur-lex.europa.eu/LexUriServ/LexUriServ.do?uri=OJ:L:2005:188:0046:0051:EN:PDF.

55   Jeannette Böhme, Human Rights and Gender Components of UN and EU Operations: Putting Human Rights and Gender Mandates into Practice, Study for the German Institute for Human Rights, Berlin 2008, 20 et seq.

rights monitors were deployed.[56] The military operation EUFOR RD Congo included a human rights focal point,[57] as does the civilian operation EUPOL COPPS, in which human rights experts are part of the operation to provide advice to the mission on all human rights issues and policies in the region.[58] Similarly, a human rights point of contact has been established for EUJUST LEX.[59] EULEX Kosovo even has a whole human rights unit, although it has to be noted that this unit is not as close to the Head of Mission as it could be.[60] As EUFOR RD Congo for the first time included a full time gender advisor, it should be mentioned here that gender issues increasingly become an essential component of CSDP operations.[61] Unfortunately, it often remains difficult for an outsider to understand what concrete tasks are allocated to these human rights components and therefore it is also hard to assess to what extent they are qualified and trained to do their job. Specific job offer descriptions, although only available in limited number, offer some insights, but do not suffice for a comprehensive assessment.[62] However, more transparency in this regard would also ensure better accountability.

---

56   Hazelzet, Human Rights Aspects (2006), 571.
57   Jana Arloth/Frauke Seidensticker, The ESDP Crisis Management Operations of the European Union and Human Rights, Study for the German Institute for Human Rights, Berlin 2007, 38.
58   Cf. EUPOL COPPS information booklet, available at http://www.consilium.europa.eu/uedocs/cmsUpload/EUPOL%20COPPS%20booklet.pdf, 3.
59   Arloth/Seidensticker, ESDP Crisis Management (2007), 48.
60   Author's interview with EU Official, 4 February 2010.
61   Arloth/Seidensticker, ESDP Crisis Management (2007), 38. For the work of a gender advisor, see Larsson in Benedek/Kettemann/Möstl, 2nd Graz Workshop on the Future of Security (2008).
62   Generic job descriptions for human rights experts would allow for a more detailed assessment of the tasks designated for human rights experts. Yet in practice such generic documents are not available and indeed would not make much sense, since the activities of human rights experts heavily depend on the character and size of a mission. The respective job offer description for the European Union Monitoring Mission (EUMM) in Georgia sets out the main tasks for a human rights field office coordinator. These are:
       "To coordinate all human rights activities carried out at the field office level in accordance with the policy guidelines on Human Rights applicable in the Mission in close coordination with the political adviser for human rights; provide guidelines to Field Offices on how to follow cases of alleged human rights violations and give advice on appropriate follow-up actions; assist Field Offices monitors on the use of overt tactics, handling information of human rights violations and guide that appropriate actions are taken; assist in the establishing of working relationships with relevant local and international organizations operating in the AOR of their respective Field Offices, to facilitate the mutual exchange of information, thus allowing effective co-ordination and cooperation between the actors; provide guidelines and templates to Field Offices to produce periodic reports concerning information on human rights violations, and initiate appropriate analyses and action; identify specific training needs and organize training sessions, when deemed appropriate; prepare periodically special reports on Human Rights issues, and carry out any other Human Rights related activity as requested by HoOPS."
       Council of the European Union, European Union Monitoring Mission (EUMM) in Georgia, job description, http://www.consilium.europa.eu/uedocs/cmsUpload/Annex1-JobDescriptions.pdf, 14.

Human rights are also on the agenda of follow-up processes of operations. Hazelzet reports that there are lessons learned reports for AMM, EUMM Georgia, and EU SSR Guinea Bissau.[63] These very specific lessons learned documents are presented to member states in the PSC and kept available for further operations planning. The lessons learned are currently not yet streamlined or complied in a uniform manner, but improvements are apparently on the way. A database or at least a living document containing the reports from all practitioners' lessons is currently being planned, which would make it easier to draw on existing knowledge for the planning of new activities.[64]

C   Conclusions

This overview of EU human rights mainstreaming in CSDP has shown that human rights are still at the fringe of CSDP and the commitment to mainstreaming has not yet succeeded in systematically bringing human rights to the centre of institutions, debates and policies of the CSDP. Based on political and legal commitments, the adoption of an explicit human rights mainstreaming strategy in 2006 did not come out of the blue and therefore the member states could already build on institutions and procedures conducive to the promotion of human rights. This also implies that not all achievements with regard to human rights in the CSDP can be attributed to this mainstreaming strategy. Indeed, it remains questionable to what extent this strategy has influenced the programs, activities and decision-making procedures of the CSDP. Certainly, it can be concluded that the process of mainstreaming was helpful to summarize the existing knowledge, e.g. in the handbook on mainstreaming human rights. However, the decision to mainstream human rights did not pave the way for new concepts how to promote human rights through the CSDP. But in fact, no new concepts for protecting and promoting human rights in EU crisis management might be needed. The main challenge of mainstreaming human rights in the CSDP lies in the forceful practical implementation of existing tools.[65] Therefore, the adoption of a concrete timeframe to review the implementation of existing human rights concepts would constitute a useful tool. An over-arching timeframe would help to evaluate existing implementation actions and would also offer the possibility to draw conclusions regarding the effectiveness of each and every existing concept.

Mainstreaming human rights in the CSDP still appears to be the work of some dedicated actors, rather than an overarching process vigorously followed by all actors involved. Up to now it is up to a few committed personalities in specialized human rights units and dedicated staff in the field to make human rights a reality in the CSDP. If more actors involved in the preparation, conduct and follow-up of an operation would have a clearer understanding of the benefits of human rights, an increased focus on human rights and a stronger insistence on following human rights standards would presumably result.

Put more practically: Only if human rights are mentioned in the first draft documents for every operation, then it is likely that human rights will be included

---

63   See Hazelzet, Six Years of Mainstreaming (forthcoming 2010).
64   Author's interview with EU official, 4 February 2010.
65   For a quantitative measurement of the progress in mainstreaming human rights and gender into ESDP, see Hazelzet, Six Years of Mainstreaming (forthcoming 2010).

in the final version and thus, for example, in the OPLAN and the mandate of an operation. Therefore, further efforts should be made by specialized human rights units to ensure that each actor involved in the CSDP is better able to perform its role in promoting human rights.

The broad range of different human rights components available for CSDP operations and the relevance of human rights in the follow-up processes of an operation underline the growing importance of integrating strong human rights elements into CSDP operations. The explicit inclusion of tailored human rights mandates would, without doubt, make the overall legal commitment of the EU to promote human rights through crisis management operations more evident and would also counter the argument that human rights are in practice easily outweighed by other mission objectives. But this is certainly a tall order and since not all operations include human rights components yet, the general inclusion of human rights components in all CSDP operations would constitute a more realistic first step forward and would represent one of the most visible results of mainstreaming human rights in the CSDP. Such a more structured approach to human rights in the operational practice of the CSDP would also have strong implications for the overall perception of an operation by the local population. Yet the operational staff needs to be further sensibilized for the intrinsic and extrinsic benefits of running a human rights-based and -oriented mission. The top of the chain of command could be sensibilized for the overall benefits of human rights by placing human rights units and components closer to the Heads of Mission or Operation Commanders. A standard field manual on human rights drawing on existing manuals by other relevant actors, such as the UN, which has been planned as a part of the mainstreaming strategy, could help improving the sensitization for human rights among the civilian and military staff involved.

Mainstreaming human rights in the CSDP would be a timely and appropriate way to promote human security through EU crisis management operations. Yet, mainstreaming human rights in this policy area is still an unfinished task. Considerable discrepancies continue to exist between the member states' rhetoric and the operational practice of EU crisis management operations. The member states' openly declared commitment to promote human rights in the CSDP certainly raises expectations by people caught up in crisis situations. If the EU fails to meet these expectations in its operational practice, the local population – whose human rights missions set out to secure – might be disappointed. This might lead to reduced levels of local support and thus diminish the likelihood of the overall success of an operation. Mainstreaming human rights in the CSDP still runs the risk of becoming reduced to an attractive catchphrase. It is up to all personalities, institutions and organs involved to counter this risk and make human rights a reality in EU crisis management operations.

Davide ZARU and Maria ZUBER[*]

The EU as a Party of the Convention on the Rights of Persons with Disabilities: Implications for the Coherence of Internal and External EU Human Rights Policies

Table of Contents

Keywords

UN Convention on the Rights of Persons with Disabilities, human rights policy, third countries, fundamental rights, international responsibility of international organizations, implied competences, coherence, duty of cooperation

A   Introduction

In this contribution, we are going to briefly present and discuss the participation of the European Union (EU)[1] in the UN Convention on the Rights of Persons with

---

[*]   The views expressed in this contribution are exclusively personal and do not bind the European Union. The authors wish to thank Frank Hoffmeister of the European Commission's Legal Service for helpful comments on the draft.

[1]   As of 1 December 2009, due to the entry into force of the Treaty of Lisbon, the European Union replaced and succeeded the European Community pursuant to Article 1, Treaty on European Union, OJ C115, 9 May 2008, 16. However, in the present contribution, the appropriate references to the "European Community" will be kept when

Disabilities (hereinafter: UNCRPD). We intend to look at the conclusion by the EU for the first time ever of a core human rights convention from a procedural standpoint. Therefore, references to the substantive rights granted by the UNCRPD and to their implementation in the EU legal order will be only limited.[2] The conclusion of the UNCRPD by the EU contributes to further coordination between the regional and the universal systems for the protection of human rights as well as filling the potential responsibility gap for conduct falling under the competence of the EU. Most likely, the implementation of the UNCRPD within the EU will have broader implications, and not least a pedagogical impact vis-à-vis all EU institutions for instance in relation to the obligations deriving from an international human rights treaty or on the modalities of the (quasi-)judicial dialogue between EU institutions and UN human rights treaty bodies.[3]

Given the limited space of this contribution and the fact that the decision allowing the EU to accede to the Optional Protocol to the UNCRPD is still under negotiation, we intend to focus on the following dimensions: questions of EU competences in relation to human rights (B); division of competences between the EU and its member states and some related questions of international responsibility (C and D, respectively); and questions related to the impact for the EU's internal and external policies for the protection and promotion of human rights (E and F, respectively).[4]

Overall, the objective of this contribution is to verify, from both a normative and an institutional perspective, how the conclusion by the EU of the UNCRPD will influence the interrelationship between internal and external EU human rights policies. The final conclusions (G) will sketch a number of possible implications of the conclusion by the EU of the UNCRPD for the reshaping of the EU human rights policy in the EU's 'post-Lisbon' architecture, in particular with reference to the establishment of the High Representative for the Foreign and Security Policy/ Vice-President of the Commission, the creation of the European External Action Service (EEAS) and the establishment of the mandate of an EU Commissioner for Justice, Fundamental Rights and Citizenship. Some of the solutions identified in the case of the UNCRPD will no doubt be relevant for the negotiations on the

---

referring to events, policies or competences relating to the period preceding 1 December 2009. We will refer to the "European Union" when writing about events, policies or competences relating to the period that follows 1 December 2009 but also in all general remarks.

2 See, for additional references, inter alia, Mahmoud Zani, La Convention de l'ONU relative aux droits des personnes handicapées", Revue de droit international et droit comparé 85 (2008) 4, 551 et seq. For the European perspective, see, among others, Anna Lawson, The UN Convention on the Rights of Persons with Disabilities and European Disability Law: a Catalyst for Cohesion?, in: Oddný Mjöll Arnardóttir/Gerard Quinn (eds.), The UN Convention on the Rights of Persons with Disabilities: European and Scandinavian Perspectives, The Hague 2009; Gerard Quinn, Disability Discrimination Law in the European Union, in: Helen Meenan (ed.), Equality Law in an Enlarged European Union: Understanding the Article 13 Directives, Cambridge 2007.

3 For instance, in its consolidated jurisprudence, the European Court of Justice (ECJ) limited itself to arguing that "international treaties for the protection of human rights on which the member states have collaborated or of which they are signatories can supply guidelines which could be followed within the framework of Community law." See ECJ, Case 4/73, Nold v. Commission, judgment of 14 May 1974, [1974] ECR-491, at 13.

4 Because of the limited space, the use of footnotes and references to doctrine will be kept to a minimum to ensure a high level of readability.

accession by the EU to the European Convention for the Protection of Human Rights and Fundamental Freedoms (ECHR) of the Council of Europe.[5]

B   UNCRPD: The First Core Human Rights Convention the EU Joins

The UNCRPD is the first core UN human rights treaty that foresees the possibility of participation of regional integration organizations. The text of the UNCRPD, notably Article 44, clarifies that "regional integration organization" shall mean an organization constituted by sovereign states of a given region, to which its member states have transferred competences in respect of matters governed by the Convention. Such organizations shall declare, in their instruments of formal confirmation or accession, the extent of their competence with respect to matters governed by the Convention. Subsequently, they shall inform the depositary of any substantial modification in the extent of their competence.

It is in light of these provisions of the UNCRPD that one has to interpret the adoption on 26 November 2009 by the Council of the European Union (hereinafter: 'the Council') of the Decision concerning the conclusion by the European Community (EC) of the UNCRPD.[6]

It is worth recalling that, still in March 1996, responding to a request from the Council, the (then) 'European' Court of Justice expressed a clear opinion that as Community law then stood, the Community had no competence to accede to the ECHR. The Court's main argument was based on the fact that no Treaty provision conferred at that time on the Community any general power to enact rules on human rights or to conclude international conventions in this specific field.[7] In particular, the Court objected to the potential choice of Article 235[8] of the Treaty establishing the European Community (Maastricht) as a legal basis for accession in the absence of relevant express or implied powers. The Court argued that accession to the ECHR would entail a substantial change in the Community system for the protection of human rights, assuming a constitutional significance and would therefore go beyond the scope of Article 235, which in any case could not be used as a basis for the adoption of provisions whose effect would in substance lead to a Treaty amendment without following the procedure foreseen for that purpose.[9]

---

5   On this issue, see also the contributions of Florence Benoît-Rohmer and Jen Paul Jacqué, in this volume, at 49 and 123, respectively.

6   See Council of the European Union, Council Decision 2010/48/EC concerning the conclusion, by the European Community, of the United Nations Convention on the Rights of Persons with Disabilities, 26 November 2009, OJ L23 27.01.2010, 35.

7   Court of Justice of the European Communities, Opinion 2/94 on the Accession by the Community to the European Convention for the Protection of Human Rights and Fundamental Freedoms; and Opinion pursuant to Article 228(6) of the EC Treaty, Accession by the Communities to the Convention for the Protection of Human Rights and Fundamental Freedoms, 28 March 1996, [1996] ECR I-1759.

8   Ex Article 308 of the Treaty establishing the European Community (TEC – Amsterdam Treaty), currently Article 352 Treaty on the Functioning of the European Union (TFEU – Lisbon Treaty).

9   ECJ, Opinion 2/94, 28 March 1996 (Accession by the Community to the European

Notwithstanding the aforementioned, already in April 2004, the Council authorized[10] the Commission to join the work of the UN Ad Hoc Committee on a Comprehensive and Integral International Convention on the Protection and Promotion of the Rights and Dignity of Persons with Disabilities. The Council thus recognized that this UN Draft Convention fell within both the Community sphere of competences and that of its member states.

Regardless of the reinforcement of provisions of the EU Treaty, introduced by the Amsterdam Treaty, one should note that the general Community competence in the field of human rights did not substantially change between 1996 and 2004, nor did the Community resort to the use of Article 235 (then already renumbered to Article 308 TEC). But what makes the UNCRPD so different from the ECHR is that the former is a disability-specific convention and not a human rights treaty of a more general scope, as is the ECHR. Even if both conventions cover a range of human rights and fundamental freedoms and contain in their respective preambles references to the Universal Declaration of Human Rights, the personal scope of the UNCRPD is limited to persons with disabilities. Therefore, the question of why the participation by the EU to the UNCRPD could be envisaged is to be found in the specific and limited personal scope of this Convention.

Against this background, it is crucial to note that the Amsterdam Treaty introduced into EC primary law an explicit reference to disability. The new Article 13 of the EC Treaty enabled the Council to take appropriate action to combat discrimination based among others on the ground of disability. Furthermore, the particular characteristic of Article 13 TEC is that it constitutes an enabling provision of a general cross-cutting nature, which co-exists with other provisions of the Treaty to the extent that it does not affect their application as to limiting their effects or scope. In this context, drawing parallels between grounds contained in Article 13 and in light of ECJ case-law,[11] one could add that the principle of non-discrimination on grounds of disability can be considered as a general principle of EU law. Given the relevance of the principle of non-discrimination within the UNCRPD, Article 13 TEC opened the possibility to envisage the EC as party to the UNCRPD.

The final texts of the UNCRPD and of its Optional Protocol were adopted on 13 December 2006 by the UN General Assembly. Both treaties have been in force since 3 May 2008. The European Community, signed the UNCRPD on the day of its opening for signature, on 30 March 2007. On 26 November 2009, after relatively quick negotiations within the Working Group of the Council of the European Union on Human Rights (COHOM), the Council adopted the decision concerning the conclusion by the European Community of the UNCRPD.

Even if the deposit of instruments of formal confirmation is foreseen at a later stage, the Council Decision marks the clear commitment of the EU to become a party, for the first time, to a comprehensive human rights treaty. Furthermore, considering the previous signature of the UNCRPD and in light of the provisions

---

Convention for the Protection of Human Rights and Fundamental Freedoms), at 35.

10   Council of the European Union, Council Decision to authorize the Commission to participate in the negotiations of the draft UN Convention of the protection and promotion of the rights and dignity of the persons with disabilities, 18 May 2004, Doc. ST 9066/1/04 REV1.

11   ECJ, Case C-144/04, Mangold v. Helm, judgment of 22 November 2005, [2005] ECR I-9981, at 74.

of Article 18 (b) of the Vienna Convention on the Law of Treaties and of the corresponding rules of customary international law, the EU is presently under an obligation to refrain from acts which would defeat the object and purpose of the UNCRPD, pending its entry into force and provided that such entry into force is not unduly delayed. The provisional effects of the UNCRPD include a need for continuously screening any new draft EU legislation and policies in order to ensure consistency and conformity with the UNCRPD.

C Division of Competences between the EU and its Member States in Relation to the Subject-Matter of the UNCRPD

From the perspective of the EU, the UNCRPD is a mixed agreement: the matters it covers fall within the competences of the Union and of its member states. This refers both to exclusive and shared competences and implies that the Union and its member states are bound by the UNCRPD only to the extent of their respective competences.

The Union's competence to enter into international commitments may arise from an express attribution by the Treaty or flow implicitly from its provisions. Whenever EU law has created for the institutions of the Union powers within its internal system for the purpose of attaining a specific objective, the Union has competence to enter into international commitments necessary for the attainment of that objective, even in the absence of an express provision to that effect.[12]

Given that non-discrimination on the ground of disability brings not only negative obligations but also requires positive action, the Council derived the Community competence to negotiate the draft text of the UNCRPD both from Articles 13 and 95 TEC (the latter concerning internal market) and further pointed to four Directives[13] based on and specifying these competences.[14] In order to define the extent of its competence, the EU screened its entire legislation against the provision of the final text of the UNCRPD. The identified secondary legislation indicates an impressively large scope of human rights-based sectoral competences transferred to the Union by the member states under the Treaties.

In accordance with Article 44(1) of the Convention, the Council decided to append to its decision authorizing the EU to conclude the UNCRPD a Declaration,[15] which indicated the competences transferred to the Union by the member states under the Treaties, in the areas covered by the UNCRPD. In line with the doctrine of implied exclusive competence and given that the provisions of the

---

12 ECJ, Opinion 2/91 delivered pursuant to the second subparagraph of Article 228 (1) of the EEC Treaty in relation to Convention N° 170 of the International Labour Organization concerning safety in the use of chemicals at work, 19 March 1993, [1993] ECR I-1061, at 3.

13 Namely to Council Directives 2000/78/EC, 2001/85/EC, 1999/5/EC and 95/46/EC.

14 Council of the European Union, Annex to the Council Decision to authorize the Commission to participate in the negotiations of the draft UN Convention of the protection and promotion of the rights and dignity of the persons with disabilities, 18 May 2004, Doc. ST 9066/1/04 REV1.

15 Council of the European Union, Annex II to the Council Decision 2010/48/EC of 26 November 2009, OJ L23, 27 January 2010, 35.

UNCRPD affect legislative acts listed in this Declaration the EU derived its competence from a broad range of traditionally "first pillar areas". These extend not only to actions to combat discrimination on the ground of disability but also to the areas of compatibility of state aid with the common market, the common custom tariff, free movement of goods, persons, services and capital, agriculture, transport by rail, road, sea and air transport, taxation, internal market, equal pay for male and female workers, Trans-European network policy, statistics, a coordinated strategy for employment, quality of education, a vocational training policy economic and social cohesion, development cooperation policy and economic, financial and technical cooperation with third countries.

That explains why the original Commission's proposal[16] was based on a broader legal basis than that of Articles 13 and 95 TEC, which corresponded to the main fields covered by the UNCRPD in line with the Declaration of the Union's competence. Since the Council decided to use a more restricted substantive legal basis following the one chosen before for negotiations, the Commission put on the records its disagreement on this point making a statement for the Council minutes.

The Declaration of the Union's competence also contains the clause stating that the scope and the exercise of Union competence are, by their nature, subject to continuous development and that the EU will complete or amend this Declaration, if necessary, in accordance with Article 44 (1) of the Convention. The demarcation between the Union's competence and member states competences may change with time as a result of Treaty revisions or because of new legislative acts which may alter the current 'normative status quo'.

In the areas where the competences have been conferred to the EU by the Treaty,

"member states shall take all appropriate measures, whether general or particular, to ensure fulfilment of the obligations arising out of this Treaty or resulting from action taken by the institutions of the Community. They shall facilitate the achievement of the Community's tasks. They shall abstain from any measure which could jeopardise the attainment of the objectives of this Treaty."[17]

They should therefore exercise a "duty of close or loyal cooperation", as the Court of Justice consistently ruled in particular in relation to cases of shared competences between the EU and its member states.[18] The Court, departing from the requirement of unity of international representation, expanded the application of the obligation of sincere cooperation to the external sphere.[19]

Consequently, in particular in cases such as the UNCRPD, when the subject-matter falls partly within the competence of the Union and partly within that of the

---

16 Proposal for a Council Decision concerning the conclusion, by the European Community, of the Optional Protocol to the United Nations Convention on the Rights of Persons with Disabilities, 28 August 2008, Doc. COM (2008) 530.

17 Article 10 Treaty establishing the European Community (TEC) (now the "principle of sincere cooperation" is explicitly inscribed in Article 4.3 of the Treaty on European Union).

18 ECJ, Opinion of Advocate General Poiares Maduro in Case C-246/07, 1 October 2009, at 1.

19 ECJ, Case C-459/03, Commission of the European Communities v Ireland, judgment of 30 May 2006, [2003] ECR I-4635 at 174.

member states, the requirement of unity in the international representation of the Union indeed makes it necessary to ensure close association between the EU institutions and EU member states both in the process of negotiation and conclusion and in the fulfilment of the obligations entered into.[20] It flows from the relevant EU jurisprudence on mixed agreements that once the EU and all the member states deposit their respective instruments of formal confirmation/ratification and the UNCRPD enters into force for all of them, its implementation will entail a significant degree of close cooperation. The Council Decision of 26 November 2009 concerning the conclusion by the EU of the UNCRPD provides that the details of such close cooperation will be laid down in a code of conduct, which will elaborate on questions related to various provisions of the UNCRPD such as representation of the Union's position at meetings of the bodies and instances created by the UN Convention, as well as to monitoring, reporting and voting arrangements and to the function of the focal point. This code of conduct shall be adopted before the deposit of the instrument of formal confirmation on behalf of the Union.

However, as of May 2010, already 14 EU member states have deposited their instruments of ratification to the UNCRPD, in spite of the fact that the EU as such is not yet a party to it and the scope of the Convention falls to a certain extent under EU competence. Some EU member states are also parties to the Optional Protocol to the UNCRPD. However, as of today, there has not been the case that the EU member states that are parties to the Convention have been accused of a violation of the UNCRPD in relation to an area of exclusive or mixed competence of the EU. Nor have there been cases of recourse to the Optional Protocol. The Protocol establishes a protection mechanism providing for competence of the Committee on the Rights of Persons with Disabilities to receive and consider communications from or on behalf of individuals or groups of individuals subject to its jurisdiction who claim to be victims of a violation by that state party of the provisions of the Convention.[21] Such individual communications addressed to the Committee in relation to the conduct of an EU member state that is already party to the UNCRPD for matters related to areas of mixed or exclusive EU competence. Might raise problems and therefore the joint participation of the EU and its member states in the UNCRPD needs to be analyzed closely in light of their shared international responsibility.

D   Questions of International Responsibility

The participation by the EU in the UNCRPD represents an interesting case for the clarification of issues of international responsibility in the field of human rights in relation to the conduct of a regional integration organization. At the current stage of the development of international law, it is assumed that international

---

20   ECJ, Case 22/70, Commission v. Council ("AETR" case), judgment of 19 May 1970, [1971] ECR 263 at 6; Ruling 1/78, Ruling of 14 November 1978, [1978] ECR 2151, at 34 to 36; Opinion 2/91, at 36, Opinion 1/94, Opinion of 15 November 1994, [1994] ECR I-5267, at 108; Case 25/94, Commission v. Council ("FAO case"), judgment of 19 March 1996, [1996] ECR I-1469; and Opinion of Advocate General Poiares Maduro in Case C-246/07, Commission v. Sweden, 1 October 2009, at 37.
21   Article 1 of the Optional Protocol.

organizations, as entities that enjoy an international personality that is different from the one of their member states, can be the addressees of international obligations and may incur international responsibility. These obligations might stem from treaty law as well as from general international law. Although we do not have the possibility here to elaborate on this issue, it is worth underlining that the recent ECJ jurisprudence on the respect for human rights in the framework of the implementation of UN Security Council sanctions regime did not substantively rely on arguments of general international law.[22] In the case of treaty law, at present, the EC/EU is not yet a party to any core human rights convention, if one excludes the UNECE Convention on Access to Information, Public Participation in Decision-making and Access to Justice in Environmental Matters (the so called "Aarhus Convention"), as well as a number of agreements with third countries that either regard the protection and promotion of human rights as a prerequisite for co-operation (the so-called "human rights conditionalities") and/or as a subject of co-operation.

From the current process of codification of the responsibility of international organisation, it is not clear whether the internal norms of international organizations, or "rules of the organization", constitute norms the violation of which may be invoked by third parties. The solution to this question provided by the International Law Commission (ILC) is only indirect. The ILC seems to imply that the internal norms of the organization, meaning the constituent instruments, decisions and resolutions adopted in accordance with them, and the established practice of the organization, do not necessarily have to reflect international legal rules on division of responsibility and cannot therefore authoritatively determine the international responsibility of the organization.[23]

Yet, the case of the EU's participation to the UNCRPD demonstrates the extent to which the issue of the legal standing in the international legal system of the rules of the organization is crucial from a procedural standpoint for the apportionment of responsibility. In fact, in the present case, the demarcation of the responsibility for the implementation (and possible violation) of the norms contained in the UNCRPD relies on internal decisions of the EU. If third parties to a treaty were ready to accept that a regional organization can be a party to a treaty along with its member states, and that it can unilaterally determine with its member states the apportionment of their respective competencies, third parties should also concede that the international organization and its member states will determine who is responsible for a specific claim, subject to their internal procedures.

In practical terms, since the UNCRPD is a mixed agreement, any invocation of violation of the Convention is preceded by the attribution of a certain wrongful conduct either to the EU or to its member states. We have already underlined that the UNCRPD provides for the possibility for a regional integration organization to unilaterally determine with its member states which of the two is responsible for a specific claim invoking international legal responsibility, notably by means of a declaration laying down the distribution of subject-matter competence. In this

---

22   On this point, see Andrea Gattini, Joined Cases C-402/05P and C-415/05P, Yassin Abdullah Kadi and Al Barakaat International Foundation v. Council and Commission, judgment of the Grand Chamber of 3 September 2008, 46/1 CMLR 2009, 231.
23   See, in particular the discussion in the Second Report of the Special Rapporteur, Giorgio Gaja, presented before the 56th session of the ILC (2004), ILC Report, A/59/10, 2004, ch. V, at 10 et seq. (pp. 107 et seq.).

context, the declaration of competences serves two purposes. It helps to avoid to the maximum extent possible cases of joint and several responsibility of the EU and its member states in the implementation of the UNCRPD, as well as to prevent interpellations from both EU member states and third countries regarding the share of competences between EU member states and the EU, and therefore on the external competence and international responsibility of the EU.

Since this is the first case of the EU's participation in an international human rights treaty, there is not yet existing practice for evaluating the adequateness of the solution of the demarcation "ex ante" of competences through a declaration of competences, in relation to the specific situations of human rights norms. The specificity of these norms is that they can be hardly split into a net of synallagmatic obligations, and therefore a precise apportionment of responsibility between the EU and its member states may prove difficult.

This cannot but confirm the importance for the present case of the implementation of the principle/duty of close co-operation between the Union and its member states, which will imply, for instance, that cases of invocation of responsibility vis-à-vis the EU and/or one or more of its member states will require a coordinated reply. Therefore, taking into consideration the respective responsibilities of the Union and of its member states for matters covered by the UNCRPD, the Union and its member states shall have an obligation of mutual information and cooperation whenever EU law is at stake, directly or indirectly.

One could imagine that a third party invokes the responsibility for the violation of certain provisions by one or more EU member states. In such a situation, it is first necessary to assess whether the matter relates to any of the EU pieces of legislation listed in the declaration of competences. If that is the case, one needs to determine whether the problem lies in the identified EU provisions, which might be inconsistent with the UNCRPD, or rather in the incorrect transposition and/or application of the EU rules by member states. In the latter case, instead of the actual responsibility of a given member state for its conduct, one has to consider the international responsibility of the EU for not ensuring that its member states fulfilled their obligations under EU law. Possible cases of divergences between the EU and its member states in the apportionment of responsibility will be decided by the Court of Justice as it is foreseen in cases of internal disputes under the jurisdiction of the Court.

E   The Participation by the EU in the UNCRPD in Light of the Internal and External Dimension of EU Human Rights Policies

Since the very early stages of the process, the participation by the EU to the UNCRPD underlined the close interrelation between the EU's internal and external policies in the field of human rights. The Council took the decision to entrust COHOM with the drafting of both the decision authorizing the Commission to join the negotiation of the Convention and of the decision authorizing the Community to sign and then conclude the UNCRPD. COHOM was also requested to negotiate the aforementioned code of conduct, a process that is currently ongoing.

It is worth trying to understand the reasons that led to this focus on COHOM. On the one hand, the European Community, not having a general competence on human rights conferred by the Treaty had to draw a competence to act externally, i.e. to participate in the negotiations of multilateral conventions and to sign the UNCRPD, from its sectoral competences in the (then) 'first pillar' areas. On the other hand, this external projection of the EU was led by a working group of the Council of the European Union that is mainly competent to deal with human rights policy vis-à-vis third countries in the framework of the Common Foreign and Security Policy. In fact, the mandate of COHOM was initially established in 1987 to provide to the (then) European Political Co-operation's Political Committee expertise on the response by the EEC to violations of human rights in third countries and on the positioning in multilateral human rights forums. In February 1999, COREPER authorized COHOM to "call on experts in Community or Justice and Home Affairs matters, on an ad hoc basis" to assist it in the follow-up to the EU's declaration of commitment for actions that was delivered on the occasion of the 50th anniversary of the Universal Declaration of Human Rights, still a set of commitments that mainly related to the protection and promotion of human rights in third countries.[24] In 2003, COHOM's mandate was extended to include first pillar issues. It was specified, however, that the objective of the extension of the mandate was to allow COHOM "to have under purview all human rights aspects of the external relations of the EU."[25] This is to underline that although COHOM has indeed an institutional task to closely coordinate its actions with activities promoted under the (then) first pillar and EU internal policies, its mandate is solidly anchored within the EU external action. This is reflected also in COHOM's constituency: EU member states are represented in this Working Group by proxies from the ministries of foreign affairs and the European Commission by its Directorate-General for External Relations.

However, even if negotiations and conclusion of the international agreement fall within the external action of the EU, the content of the UNCRPD and its future implementation, which need to be taken into account while undertaking legal commitments on the international scene, mainly concern EU internal policies. These considerations, together with the fact that disability is a cross-cutting issue and given the indivisibility and interrelatedness of all human rights, explain why, in the process of consideration of the EU's participation to the UNCRPD, the work of COHOM was supported by disability experts from various national ministries and departments of the European Commission, including, for instance, those of social affairs, health and transport. It is thanks to the innovative solution of organizing extraordinary meetings back to back with the regular COHOM sessions that COHOM managed to handle this extremely complex dossier in a relative short period of time.

F   Possible Implications for the EU's Human Rights Policy in Third Countries

The norms included in the UNCRPD mainly concern the protection and promotion of the rights of persons with disabilities within the jurisdiction of each state party. Nonetheless, the UNCRPD specifically elaborates on the role of parties in protecting and promoting the rights of people with disabilities through both the

---

24   COREPER, Decision of 4 February 1999, Doc. 6252/99.
25   Council of the European Union, Decision of COREPER meeting of 18 December 2003, Doc. 16316/03.

request and delivery of development co-operation.[26] In addition to this, one can identify the following possible three key implications for the EU's policy on human rights in third countries.

A first element in this regard is of a political nature and concerns the coherence between the internal EU performance in the protection and promotion of human rights and the message of human rights and democratization that the EU imparts to its partner countries and partner organizations. Several commentators have consistently stressed in the past that the impact of such messages would be undermined in case the EU is not able to "lead by example" on human rights issues which means being able to implement internally the same human rights standards it requests from its partner countries and organizations.[27] In this sense, the participation of the EU to the UNCRPD can be considered as "an important element in the EU's efforts to ensure coherence between the internal and the external human rights policy", to paraphrase the words of a former EU Commissioner for External Relations.[28]

A second, and more significant example of implication of the EU's participation in the UNCRPD for the Union's external human rights policy, is of a legal nature. The current EU human rights policy vis-à-vis third countries relies to a large extent on political tools, such as political dialogue (including human rights dialogues and consultations), diplomatic démarches and public statements. It is not fully clear how such policy tools can be framed from the perspective of the enforcement of international human rights law. Within the work of the ILC on the responsibility of international organizations, Special Rapporteur Professor Gaja has referred to statements by the General Affairs and External Relations Council of the EU on grave violations of human rights in particular third countries in order to substantiate the emergence of a practice on the invocation by international organizations of the international responsibility of states or of other international organizations, and leading/justifying in many cases the adoption of measures, such as economic sanctions, towards these countries.[29]

Although so far limited to the scope of the norms included in the UNCRPD and more specifically to those provisions falling under the EU competence and acting in close coordination with its member states, the EU could be legitimated to invoke the responsibility of other parties for violations of norms included in the UNCRPD, and not necessarily grave violations, in light of the existence of a legal relationship between the EU as such and other parties to the UNCRPD. It is widely acknowledged that in the area of human rights law, the monitoring of the implementation of human rights conventions by each and every party vis-à-vis

---

26 See, in this respect Articles 32 and 37 of the UNCRPD.
27 See, e.g., the 1998 report "Leading by Example: A Human Rights Agenda for the European Union for the Year 2000: Agenda of the Comité des Sages and Final Project Report", reproduced in an annex to Philip Alston et al (eds.), The EU and Human Rights, Oxford 1999, 8-9. In the same volume, see for instance Philip Alston and Joseph Weiler, An Ever Closer Union' in Need of a Human Rights Policy: The European Union and Human Rights, in ibid., 3-66.
28 Cf. statement of Chris Patten at the plenary session of the European Parliament of 4 July 2001, reproduced in Andrew Williams, EU Human Rights Policies: A Study in Irony, Oxford 2004, 84.
29 See Sixth Report of the Special Rapporteur, Giorgio Gaja (60th session of the ILC (2008), ILC Report, A/63/10, 2008, ch. VII, at 9 (p. 297).

the others has been so far underdeveloped. Presumably, it is considered politically inopportune for single states to challenge, for instance in the framework of the conference of states parties to a human rights convention, another state for violations of the provisions of that convention, in particular if the violations did not amount to a certain amount of gravity or even to activate inter-state complaint procedures, this latter being a possibility that is not foreseen by the UNCRPD. The EU, which has increasingly developed strategic and institutional positions on the protection and promotion of human rights in certain countries, might consider using the invocation of *erga omnes partes* obligations of other parties to the UNCRPD as a legal device complementing the political tools of its policy for the promotion and protection of human rights worldwide.

Another related possibility for possible future EU action in this sense is protesting against reservations that are contrary to the scope and the objective of the treaty. Already in the framework of EU human rights dialogues and consultations with third countries, the EU has requested partner countries to withdraw certain reservations to core UN human rights conventions, for instance to the Convention on Elimination of All Forms of Discrimination against Women, which it considers inconsistent with the objective or the purpose of the treaty. The participation of the EU to the UNCRPD requires enhanced internal coordination of the EU with respect to the formulation of reservations and declaration of understanding to the UNCRPD by both EU member states and by third countries. This enhanced coordination in the matter of reservations and declarations of understanding could allow the EU's human rights policy to make use, as an additional tool in its political dialogue, of the legal device of formally protesting before the depositary of the Convention reservations formulated by third countries, which it considers inconsistent with the objective and the purpose of the treaty.

A third possible implication for the EU's external human rights policy is the fact that the participation of the EU to the UNCRPD requires the EU to develop a common understanding of the future work of the UN Committee on the Rights of Persons with Disabilities on matters such as the role of the Committee in interpreting the Convention (and, therefore, the position of the EU vis-à-vis future general comments of the Committee) or the possible 'severability' of reservations. In light of the increasing co-operation and coordination between UN treaty bodies, it is likely that such an EU common understanding of the work of the Committee on the Rights of Persons with Disabilities will impact the EU's position in the framework of the future process of review of the UN human rights treaty bodies' regime and more generally the co-operation between EU member states and between the EU and UN human rights treaty bodies. It cannot be excluded that since, for the first time, the EU will be submitting a report before a UN human rights treaty body, the Committee on the Rights of Persons with Disabilities will request the EU to anticipate the submission of the report about the implementation of the UNCRPD in the areas of EU competences by the submission of a "core document" with a view to providing general information on EU human rights policies, as recommended by the Harmonized Guidelines elaborated by the UN's Inter-Committee Meeting of the human rights treaty bodies.[30]

---

30   Contained in UN document HRI/MC/2006/3, issued on 10 May 2006.

G   Conclusions

The considerations above bring us to the general conclusion that the EU's participation in the UNCRPD will imply an intense degree of strategic coordination of EU member states with EU institutions, as well as internally within the EU institutions in the field of the rights of persons with disabilities and, potentially, in general in the field of human rights. One can identify two main strands for this coordination.

The first one relates to the structural organization of the coordination between the EU and its member states in the internal implementation of the UNCRPD as well as in relation to those actions that are undertaken by the EU externally. In this context such coordination of the UNCRPD dossier cannot but consider on the one hand the implications of the EU's participation in this Convention for both the internal and the external human rights policies and on the other hand the fact that the UNCRPD is a comprehensive international human rights treaty. In other words, the paradigm shift endorsed by the UNCRPD on the understanding of disability, away from a medically- and socially-informed view to one focusing on human rights, shall be reflected at the institutional level in the EU decision-making process. This is also in line with a recent study by the Office of the UN High Commissioner for Human Rights on the structure and role of national mechanisms for the implementation and monitoring of the UNCRPD,[31] which argued that the designation of the Ministry of Health as the government focal point foreseen in the UNCRPD should be avoided and "ministries with responsibility for justice and human rights" should be preferred.

The aforementioned issues underline the great challenge for COHOM in its current setting to adequately oversee the coordination between the internal and the external EU human rights policies. The proper follow up to the Council Decision, coordination and future deliberations regarding the implementation of the UNCRPD might need an approach that is more systematic. In this respect, one could eventually envisage the involvement of the newly created Council standing working party on Fundamental Rights, Citizen's Rights and Free Movement of Persons in the EU coordination concerning the UNCRPD, eventually tasking it with further deliberations in "co-attribution" with COHOM.[32]

A second question concerns the institutional arrangements within EU institutions that will be necessary to implement the UNCRPD. First, it is important to highlight that, pursuant to Article 216 (2) of the TFEU,[33] agreements concluded by the Union are binding upon the institutions of the Union. Finally, one needs to analyze how new legal frameworks and tools provided by the new treaties as amended by the Treaty of Lisbon impact the work of EU institutions with regard to human rights. Under the Lisbon Treaty, the European Community is replaced and succeeded by the European Union. The latter, with a single legal personality, is in a position to conclude international agreements and join international

---

31   OHCHR, Study on the Structure and Role of National Mechanisms for the Implementation and Monitoring of the CRPD, http://www2.ohchr.org/english/issues/disability/docs/A-HRC-13-29_AEV.pdf.

32   Point 17 of the European Parliament resolution of 14 January 2009 on the situation of fundamental rights in the European Union 2004-2008 (2007/2145(INI)), P6_TA-PROV(2009)0019.

33   Ex Article 300 (7) TEC (Amsterdam Treaty).

organizations. The EU is therefore able to speak and take action as a single entity. The Treaty of Lisbon also provides a clear basis for the EU's accession to the ECHR.[34]

Furthermore, in the second Commission under Commission President José Manuel Barroso, the "Barroso II Collège", the new mandate of a Vice-President/ Commissioner for Justice, Fundamental Rights and Citizenship assisted by dedicated services will focus on the protection and promotion of human rights within the EU. The EU human rights policy in third countries is likely to be led by the forthcoming European External Action Service, under the responsibility of the High Representative for Foreign Affairs and Security Policy/Vice-President of the Commission. It is clear that these two Commission Vice-Presidents will need to co-operate in order to promote the consistency of the EU internal and external human rights policies.

Under this new framework, the full implementation of the UNCRPD and the promotion of coherence in the EU's internal and external human rights policies will represent a significant challenge and opportunity for the EU in the coming years.

Achieving these objectives will require some rethinking and refining of the human rights architecture within the institutions of the Union. One could envisage for instance the establishment of an ad hoc EU internal/external human rights coordination mechanism, based on the experience of the former Group of EU Commissioners on Fundamental Rights. The orientations and instructions elaborated in this mechanism would need to be prepared and followed up at the service level. This could imply the development of a standing mechanism to support the co-operation between the future human rights service of the EEAS and the Directorates of the European Commission assisting the mandate of the EU Commissioner for Justice, Fundamental Rights and Citizenship (i.e. the relevant services in the Directorates-General (DGs) responsible for Employment, Social Affairs and Equal Opportunities, for Justice, Liberty and Security and for Health and Consumers). This coordination mechanism could also look at and build on the experience of a number of EU member states, which have established inter-ministerial committees on human rights exactly with the objective of overseeing the drafting of reports to be presented before UN human rights treaty bodies. Representatives of Ministries of Foreign Affairs, the Interior and ministries charged with ensuring equal opportunities for all citizens are traditionally the most active collaborators within those committees.

To conclude, in the EU system, just as in member states, the conclusion of human rights treaties has a welcomed by-product: an enhanced coordination of services responsible for human rights issues and a better coherence between internal and external human rights policies.

---

34   Article 6 (2) TEU (Lisbon Treaty).

Theodor RATHGEBER

Ambiguity as a Main Feature: The UN Human Rights Council in 2009

Table of Contents

Keywords

Human Rights Council, country mandates, special procedures, human rights, non-governmental organizations, EU

A   Introduction

The regular sessions of the UN Human Rights Council (HRC) in the year 2009 comprised the 10th session (2-27 March), the 11th session (1-18 June), and the 12th session (14 September-2 October). As a cycle of HRC sessions ends on 18 June each year, the Council's composition in 2009 was slightly different before that date[1]

---

1   The HRC Bureau until 18 June 2009 was formed by Nigeria as President, the Philippines, Argentina, Canada and Azerbaijan as Vice-Presidents. The 47 member states until 18 June 2010 were: Angola (membership runs until 2010); Argentina (2011); Azerbaijan (2009); Bahrain (2011); Bangladesh (2009); Bolivia (2010); Bosnia and Herzegovina (2010); Brazil (2011); Burkina Faso (2011); Cameroon (2009); Canada (2009); Chile (2011); China (2009); Cuba (2009); Djibouti (2009); Egypt (2010); France (2011); Gabon (2011); Germany (2009); Ghana (2011); India (2010); Indonesia (2010); Italy (2010); Japan (2011); Jordan (2009); Madagascar (2010); Malaysia (2009); Mauritius (2009); Mexico (2009); Netherlands (2010); Nicaragua (2010); Nigeria (2009); Pakistan (2011); Philippines (2010); Qatar (2010); Republic of Korea (2011); Russian Federation (2009); Saudi Arabia (2009); Senegal (2009); Slovakia

and afterwards.[2] In addition to the three regular sessions, the HRC held four Special Sessions in 2009: The Grave Violations of Human Rights in the Occupied Palestinian Territory including the recent aggression in the occupied Gaza Strip conducted in January; The Impact of the Global Economic and Financial Crises on the Universal Realization and Effective Enjoyment of Human Rights in February; The human rights situation in Sri Lanka in May, and The human rights situation in the Occupied Palestinian Territory and East Jerusalem in October 2009. Despite this frequency of sessions, the outcome when viewed from the perspective of victims of human rights violations left mixed impressions about the HRC's performance. The trend of weak resolutions on country-specific situations continued, while the rift between the African member states of the HRC has grown further and the membership of the USA has brought a new dynamic. Nevertheless, the HRC still has a long way to go if it wishes to become a body that can effectively improve human rights on the ground.

In the following, I will focus on the main dynamics inside the HRC with special reference to country mandates (section B), thematic issues (C), panel discussions (D), the role of the mandate holders of the Special Procedures (E), the specific contribution the European Union made to the Council this year (F) and the role of non-governmental organizations (NGOs) (G). In section H, I will offer some conclusions. I do not touch upon the performance of the existing subgroups of the HRC, such as the Advisory Committee, the Social Forum, the Forum on Minority Issues and the Expert Mechanism on the Rights of Indigenous Peoples. They all are too new for allowing for even preliminary analysis. My selection of topics may reveal why I chose "ambiguity" as a main characteristic for the HRC's performance in 2009: while there were negative developments, the Council continues to prove that is has potential.[3]

B   Country Mandates

The HRC was unable to establish a strong monitoring mechanism in order to address the humanitarian and human rights crises in the Democratic Republic of Congo during its 10th session in March 2009. Despite the alarming report of

---

(2011); Slovenia (2010); South Africa (2010); Switzerland (2009); Ukraine (2011); United Kingdom (2011); Uruguay (2009); Zambia (2011).

2   From 19 June 2009 to 18 June 2010 Belgium holds the HRC Presidency. The Vice-Presidents are Egypt, Slovenia, Indonesia, Chile. The Council's 47 member states until 18 June 2010 are: Angola (2010); Argentine (2011); Bahrain (2011); Bangladesh (2012); Belgium (2012); Bolivia (2010); Bosnia and Herzegovina (2010); Brazil (2011); Burkina Faso (2011); Cameroon (2012); Chile (2011); China (2012); Cuba (2012); Djibouti (2012); Egypt (2010); France (2011); Gabon (2011); Ghana (2011); Hungary (2012); India (2010); Indonesia (2010); Italy (2010); Japan (2011); Jordan (2012); Kyrgyzstan (2012); Madagascar (2010); Mauritius (2012); Mexico (2012); Netherlands (2010); Nicaragua (2010); Nigeria (2012); Norway (2012); Pakistan (2011); Philippines (2010); Qatar (2010); Republic of Korea (2011); Russian Federation (2012); Zambia (2011); Saudi Arabia (2012); Senegal (2012); Slovakia (2011); Slovenia (2010); South Africa (2010); Ukraine (2011); United Kingdom (2011); USA (2012); Uruguay (2012).

3   See also Theodor Rathgeber, Patterns of work and co-operation in the UN Human Rights Council. Conference Report, FES Geneva, December 2009.

seven thematic Special Procedure mandate holders,[4] presented by the Representative of the UN Secretary-General on Internally Displaced Persons, Mr. Walter Kälin, the African Group and its speaker, Egypt, opposed the mandate on the country situation as proposed by the European Union.[5] The mandate suggested by the EU aimed to assess the human rights situation and to provide assistance to the government of the DR Congo in a number of areas including drafting human rights policies and legislation. Particularly, the EU text would have condemned acts of sexual violence and child recruitment, called on the expert group to coordinate their work, and to establish benchmarks in order to identify progress on human rights. Instead, Egypt introduced a draft resolution on behalf of the African Group[6] which even applauded the government of DR Congo for its cooperation. The final text[7] contains a simple monitoring function for the HRC determining that the body would reconsider the situation of DR Congo in March 2010.

Despite a challenging appeal by Chile, the EU text was defeated by a narrow majority of 21 votes against and 18 in favour. The Ambassador of Chile argued that for the HRC it would be difficult not to condemn repeated violations of human rights and breaches of international humanitarian law. He related also to a speech by Desmond Tutu who at a former opportunity had expressed his concern particularly in relation to the human rights of African people. Desmond Tutu insisted on the need to urgently protect African people. Chile reminded the HRC to think about its responsibility as the main UN body on human rights with regard to what was happening, and its ability to condemn and support situations in such a case. Though the final vote did not correspond to this appeal, it may have contributed to the abstention of five African member countries (out of eight): Burkina Faso, Ghana, Mauritius, Senegal, and Zambia. In terms of strategic thinking, this suggests that there will be a chance to swing the human rights-insensitive majority towards a more human rights orientated position at some point.

The HRC also failed to fulfil its mandate during the March session as it did not respond at all to the current humanitarian and human rights crisis in Sri Lanka. The NGO Human Rights Watch stated that, amidst abuses by both government forces and the Tamil Tigers, about 150,000 civilians remained trapped in a small area of the northern Vanni region and more than 3,000 civilians had died since January 2009. Despite the urgency of the situation and the limited humanitarian assistance reaching the beleaguered population, no initiative was taken to mobilize the HRC in order to take action on Sri Lanka. Several NGOs requested in vain that the HRC should immediately convene a Special Session to examine the situation. Only in May, when the war was over, did a Special Session take place; it ended as a farce. The resolution text was drafted by the government of Sri Lanka itself.

At least, the human rights situation in Sri Lanka has been continuously addressed in the June and September session of the HRC by NGOs and some governments particularly from Western countries. In response, the governmental representatives of Sri Lanka lowered the tone, especially in the September ses-

---

4   UN Doc. A/HRC/10/59.
5   UN Doc. A/HRC/10/L.1.
6   UN Doc. A/HRC/10/L.3.
7   UN Doc. A/HRC/RES/10/33.

sion, while having previously taken an aggressive position. The Vice-Ambassador of Sri Lanka even invited his colleagues to keep articulating their concerns as it would be welcome. He promised to return most of the Internally Displaced Persons up to the end of the year 2009, while the Minister for Human Rights and Disaster Management continued to justify the situation as a consequence of the huge humanitarian challenges after the war.

As in the years before and during the time of the Commission on Human Rights (until 2006), the HRC did not take action to the situation in Afghanistan, Iran, Iraq, Yemen, Zimbabwe, China or on secret detention centers in Middle and East Europe; to name but a few. Like the former Commission, the HRC took action on Myanmar[8] and the Democratic People's Republic of Korea[9] by extending the mandates of both Special Rapporteurs for one year each during its March session. The HRC expressed serious concerns on the ongoing grave, widespread and systematic human rights violations in both countries.

The resolution on Myanmar was adopted without a vote. The same happened in September with special reference to Daw Aung San Suu Kyi and "other political prisoners" although several Asian countries voiced severe criticism and reservations.[10] The HRC expressed grave concern about the recent conviction and sentencing of Daw Aung San Suu Kyi and called for her immediate and unconditional release. The resolution also calls upon the government of Myanmar to release all political prisoners immediately and unconditionally, thus, enabling them to fully participate in the 2010 elections.

The resolution on the DPRK in March was adopted by a majority of 26 votes in favour; significantly more than in the past years when this resolution won only by a narrow majority of 22 to 23 votes. It seems that the re-established active engagement of the USA with the HRC may have contributed to that larger majority while the six votes against the mandate (China, Cuba, Egypt, Indonesia, Nigeria, and Russian Federation) are still six votes too much: six votes that support a government which starves its population.

The HRC also extended the mandate of the Independent Expert on the situation of human rights in Somalia,[11] but only for six months, which runs against the HRC's own rule of one-year extensions for country- specific mandates. This intention to undermine the country mandates by shorter terms was overcome to a certain extent in September 2009, when the Independent Expert's mandate on assistance to Somalia in the field of human rights[12] was extended for one year. Without a vote, the HRC also renewed the mandate of the Special Rapporteur on advisory services and technical assistance in Cambodia[13] for one more year.

Some remarkable shifts happened in relation to Palestine and Israel. The resolution on Israeli settlements in the Occupied Palestinian Territory[14] found a large majority (46 Yes votes, with only Canada voting No), as the EU recognized that settlements in an occupied country are illegal everywhere. The draft text for the resolution on human rights violations emanating from the Israeli military at-

---

8   UN Doc. A/HRC/RES/10/27.
9   UN Doc. A/HRC/RES/10/16.
10   UN Doc. A/HRC/RES/12/20.
11   UN Doc. A/HRC/RES/10/32.
12   UN Doc. A/HRC/RES/12/26.
13   UN Doc. A/HRC/RES/12/25.
14   UN Doc. A/HRC/RES/10/18.

tacks and operations in the Occupied Palestinian Territory[15] was orally amended in operational paragraph 2 in order to also condemn the firing of rockets on Israeli civilians. Even a new OP 9 bis was introduced urging all parties concerned to respect the rules of international human rights and humanitarian law and to refrain from violence against civilian population. Up to that moment, it was unthinkable that this kind of recognition of the responsibility of Palestinian groups would be officially stated. Despite these amendments, the resolution was adopted by a vote with 35 Yes, 4 votes against and 8 abstentions, mostly by European countries. Half a year later, in September 2009, the window of opportunity for overcoming longstanding frontiers, had been closed again as the Western countries did their utmost to prevent the HRC from adopting a resolution on the report of the Fact-Finding Mission on the Gaza Conflict led by Justice Richard Goldstone.[16] Consequently, the group of African member states together with others requested a Special Session in October which then officially adopted the Goldstone report and requested the countries concerned to deliver their response to the Commission's conclusion that war crimes had taken place within six months.[17]

The next change of political strategy took place in September during the 12th session when a country resolution under Item 4 was adopted without a vote. The resolution on Honduras[18] referred to the human rights violations in the course of the coup d'état of 28 June 2009. It was the first time in the history of HRC sessions that the members of Latin American and Caribbean Countries including Cuba presented a resolution without the consensus of the country concerned. In former times, particularly Brazil had objected to any political decision by the HRC amounting to criticizing or condemning a government of the region.

Country situations are generally brought to a vote and frequently it is Cuba, Pakistan, Egypt or the Western countries which will ask for a vote. China does not submit many resolutions in general on its own but promotes very actively non-action resolutions on country situations.

Therefore, the HRC made another positive and rather unexpected step when adopting the resolution to continue with the international monitoring on Sudan. A narrow majority (20:18) succeeded voting into existence an Independent Expert who shall implement the mandates of the former resolutions of the 6th, 7th and the 9th regular sessions[19]. Out of 13 member states of the African Group, seven did not follow Egypt's 'leadership' with regard to voting 'No', with Zambia even voting in favour of the Resolution. Surprisingly, Uganda publicly stated its disagreement with Egypt's draft presented in the name of the African Group as not being agreed at all among the African Group. The final resolution on the situation of human rights in Sudan[20] calls on the government of National Unity to continue and to intensify its efforts for the promotion and protection of human rights and created the mandate of the Independent Expert for a period of one year. Unfortunately, the resolution also praises the government for small procedural steps, while it has failed completely to improve the human rights situation on the ground.

---

15   UN Doc. A/HRC/RES/10/19.
16   UN Doc. A/HRC/12/48.
17   UN Doc. A/HRC/RES/S-12/1.
18   UN Doc. A/HRC/RES/12/14.
19   UN Doc. A/HRC/RES/6/34, A/HRC/RES/6/35, A/HRC/RES/7/16 and A/HRC/RES/9/ 17.
20   UN Doc. A/HRC/RES/11/10.

During 2009, the HRC routinely adopted the outcome of the Working Group on the Universal Periodic Review and sometimes the interactive dialogue turned into filibustering or praise. Only in June, there were substantial discussions on the UPR outcome on Israel.[21] Egypt, among others, insisted that Israel should comment on every recommendation made during the UPR while the Israeli representative simply "took note" of some of them; just as on previous occasions countries such as South Africa had done. It is also a frequent experience that nearly every government gives only minimal answers to critical recommendations. A rather strange while not unexpected phenomenon started in February 2009: attempts to manipulate the list of speakers. In June, hardly a Western country succeeded to be among the first ten in order to take the floor during the debate on the outcome. For independent NGOs it was a tough fight to get three or four among the first ten when the outcome on Cuba and China was discussed. The rest of the NGOs on the speaker's list were dominated by the very governments under review; so called governmental orientated non-governmental organizations, or GONGOs.

While the phenomenon of GONGOs is not new (they already made their appearance at the former UN Commission on Human Rights), their presence and role grew with the introduction of the UPR. During regular HRC sessions, GONGOs would read statements allocating fault for the Kashmir conflict either from the perspective of (mostly) Pakistan or India. Iran's current government is also constantly praised for its solidarity with issues of the Global South, although the number of such statements remains relatively low. The use of GONGOs during UPR discussions is obviously approached more strategically by governments from states such as Cuba, China, Tunisia and others. Cuba and China did their utmost to mobilize even participants of the General Assembly of the International Labour Organization (ILO) – which took place at the same time as the Council's review of China's UPR report did – in order have them add their names as NGOs on agenda item 6: "Considerations on UPR Reports".

C   Thematic Issues

Throughout the year 2009, the HRC adopted resolutions on the realization of economic, social and cultural rights in all countries, human rights in the administration of justice, human rights and climate change, arbitrary detention, enforced or involuntary disappearances, the right to food, cultural rights and respect for cultural diversity, protection of human rights while countering terrorism, and the follow-up to HRC resolution on human rights violations emanating from Israeli military attacks;[22] among others. Without a vote, the HRC established a new open ended working group in order to start after June 2010 the review process on the Council and its functioning.[23] Notably, the draft had found co-sponsors from all regional groups. According to UN General Assembly Resolution 60/251 establishing the HRC, the Council should be reviewed five years after its establishment, i.e. in June 2011. Joint initiatives and cross-regional efforts existed on

---

21   UN Doc. A/HRC/REC/10/108.
22   UN Doc. A/HRC/RES/S-9/1.
23   UN Doc. A/HRC/RES/12/1.

climate change, business and human rights, extreme poverty, human rights education and training as well as trafficking.

The resolutions on torture[24] and on discrimination based on religion or belief[25] were both adopted by a vote. The resolution on discrimination based on religion or belief did not achieve a majority in terms of absolute votes (22 in favour) and had to face 24 abstentions. Previously, the resolution on torture and other cruel, inhuman or degrading treatment or punishment had enjoyed broad support and had been regularly adopted by consensus. This year, Egypt and others had been reluctant to "take note" of the report of the Special Rapporteur, as the mandate holder, Manfred Nowak, widely discussed the matter of death penalty in terms of cruel, inhuman or degrading treatment or punishment. In the end, 13 states abstained.[26]

Also by a vote, the resolution on defamation of religions[27] was adopted. The resolution strongly deplores all acts of psychological and physical violence and assaults, and incitements thereto, against persons on the basis of their religion or belief, and such acts directed against their businesses, properties, cultural centres and places of worship, as well as the targeting of holy sites, religious symbols and venerated personalities of all religions. The HRC notes with concern the intensification of the overall campaign of defamation of religions and incitement to religious hatred in general. What seems to be a reasonable concern is used as a means to protect the religion as such and as a leverage to undermine the individual right of each one to choosing his or her religion or belief. The highly controversial resolution on freedom of opinion and expression in 2008 was adopted in 2009 without a vote[28] as the main aspect of controversy – to introduce the respect for a religion as a reason to restrict the freedom of expression – had been re-formulated by the main sponsors Egypt and USA; a surprising constellation too.

A controversial discussion took place with regard to the resolution on promoting human rights and fundamental freedoms through a better understanding of traditional values of humankind in conformity with international human rights law[29] which was adopted by a vote (26 in favour, 15 against, 6 abstentions). In the resolution, the HRC requests the Office of the High Commissioner for Human Rights to convene in 2010 a workshop for an exchange of views on a better understanding of traditional values of humankind underpinning international human rights norms and standards and how this can contribute to the promotion and protection of human rights and fundamental freedoms. Further thematic issues which did not find consensus in 2009 were racism, the financial crisis and the financial debt and its impacts, migration, development, counter-terrorism strategies as well as human rights aspects of sexual orientation. Currently, the HRC adopts approximately two thirds of its resolutions by consensus.

---

24   UN Doc. A/HRC/RES/10/24.
25   UN Doc. A/HRC/RES/10/25.
26   Bahrain, Bangladesh, China, Djibouti, Egypt, Ghana, India, Jordan, Malaysia, Pakistan, Qatar, Saudi Arabia, Senegal.
27   UN Doc. A/HRC/RES/10/22.
28   UN Doc. A/HRC/RES/12/16.
29   UN Doc. A/HRC/RES/12/21.

D   Special Procedures

The 11th session of the HRC experienced strong verbal attacks against mandate holders of the Special Procedures and threats even against UN human rights treaty bodies in order to make them more 'state oriented'. Leading countries in this respect have been Egypt, Cuba and China. Particularly attacked were the Special Rapporteur on Freedom of Opinion and Expression (Frank La Rue), the Special Rapporteur on Extralegal Executions (Philip Alston) and the Special Rapporteur on the Independence of Judges and Lawyers (Leandro Despouy). Cuba and Egypt initiated a resolution to add the Code of Conduct for mandate holders a more restrictive interpretation which finally was not tabled. The representative of China stipulated the idea to draft a Code of Conduct for UN treaty bodies, too. Similarly, there is a tendency at the HRC to treat the Office of the High Commissioner for Human Rights (OHCHR) as its administrative body and overloading it with workshops. It is unclear whether this is due to the need for further expertise or intended to paralyze the OHCHR. Countries like Pakistan, Egypt or Cuba are not known of being human rights-sensitive; therefore, the assumption tends to the latter.

By way of a resolution (adopted without a vote), the HRC established a new Special Procedures mandate: an Independent Expert in the field of cultural rights for a period of three years.[30] The mandate should foster the adoption of measures aimed at the promotion and protection of cultural rights through concrete proposals enhancing sub-regional, regional and international cooperation in this regard. The mandate should also identify existing gaps in the promotion and protection of cultural rights and submit proposals and/or recommendations to the HRC on possible actions to fill such gaps. The mandate holder shall also identify best practices in the protection and promotion of cultural rights at the local, national, regional and international level. The mandate further asks to identify possible obstacles to the protection and promotion of cultural rights, and to work in close coordination with intergovernmental and non-governmental organizations. The first report of the independent expert should be presented to the HRC in 2010. The EU hesitated to support this new mandate arguing that there is no compelling evidence for that mandate, since overlapping and duplicity seem to be real dangers. The EU also stressed that no one may invoke cultural diversity in order to infringe upon human rights, but finally the EU joined the consensus.

E   Panel Discussions

A new element of the methodology of the HRC was further developed in 2009: panel discussions taking place during half-day or full-day meetings organized in form of an interactive dialogue with experts. In March the HRC discussed the rights of the child and the implementation of the Convention on the Rights of the Child. In June followed a panel on human rights and climate change. The Deputy High Commissioner for Human Rights linked the issue of climate change to poverty, discrimination and unfair development. Experts on the panel conveyed the idea to establish a mandate under the Special Procedures and invited existing

---

30   UN Doc. A/HRC/RES/10/23.

mandate holders to draw attention to this subject. The Special Rapporteur on adequate housing as a component of the right to an adequate standard of living had already decided to start with and to present a report in 2010 on the potential impact of climate change on the right to adequate housing. Also in June, a high-level panel discussion on the situation of civilians in armed conflicts and on the protection of human rights defenders, journalists and vulnerable groups took place. In September, a full day panel was dedicated to women's rights particularly considering their equality before law. The discussion focused on non-discrimination in law, with a view to identifying concrete steps to foster women's equality.

The panel discussion on the issue of migrants allowed the UN High Commissioner for Human Rights to particularly warn against legal mechanisms that made children and migrants under 18 criminals. The UN Working Group on Arbitrary Detention expressed its concern that migration is frequently dealt with as a risk for the security of the state.[31] NGOs condemned detention of migrants as socially and culturally corrosive of the society. The governments of the European Union obviously tried to defend their restrictive position on migration stressing the rights of migrants in terms of substance and procedure as well as the transparency of the procedures in case of detention. While Arabic countries condemned the restrictions on migration imposed by industrialized and Western countries, their arguments were not free from hypocrisy as nothing was said about the inhuman conditions for migrants in certain countries in that region. Generally, these panel discussions are organized with the help and active participation of the Office of the UN High Commissioner for Human Rights and include experts also from the non-governmental sector.

F   European Union

Beyond the restrictive position on migration, the European Union played an active role – as in the years before – in addressing human rights violations in different parts of the world under Item 4 "Human rights situations that require the Council's attention." Compared to the oral interventions during the Commission on Human Rights addressing approximately 20 to 30 countries, the EU now concentrates on four to five countries in its general statement in each session. In 2009, the EU referred mainly to Myanmar, the Democratic People's Republic of Korea, China, Sri Lanka, Sudan, Zimbabwe, Cuba and the situation of women in Afghanistan. The general statements of the EU were followed by statements of EU members who predominantly elaborated the same subjects, adding from time to time remarks on the Democratic Republic of Congo, Fiji, Kenya and Iran while the potential of the EU to influence the direction of the discourse in the HRC towards considering severe human rights violations by its mere number has not been realized yet. Together with some countries of the Latin America and Caribbean Group (GRULAC), the EU was among the few who addressed sensitive issues such as sexual orientation.

As in the years before, cross-regional initiatives led by the EU are rather an exception. Beyond the joint resolution of the Philippines and Germany on human trafficking, there are hardly any bilateral initiatives. The resolution on water and

---

31   For more on the problem of criminalizing migration, see the contribution by Hammarberg, in this volume, at 21.

sanitation, mainly sponsored by Spain and Germany, stresses a subject vital for many countries in the Global South and yet at the beginning there was no main sponsorship sought from among countries of the South. The joint initiatives and cross regional efforts on climate change (led by the most affected countries), business and human rights (sponsored by all regional groups), extreme poverty (nine countries as sponsors from all regional groups), human rights education and training (seven countries from all regional groups) might be a step forward though doubts remain as there is still the widely shared perception that a counter-part from a different regional group per se will be a risk for the subject.

As mentioned before, not every statement and political position of the EU is an automatic embodiment of a human rights sensitive approach. The EU's unwillingness to consider some sensitive human rights issues led to an impression of selectivity which damaged the reputation of the EU and made finding new majorities difficult. One of the main obstacles in 2009 has been the attempt by the Western countries led by the USA to avoid a political assessment on the Goldstone report during the 12th regular session.

A new field for joint activities has been opened by the UN General Assembly's obligation under its Resolution 60/251 to review the HRC's performance after the first five years, i.e. in 2011. The membership of the USA in the HRC since June 2009 and the rift within the African group just opened the door for a new dynamic towards a better political assessment at least of the most severe and systematic human rights violations. In relation to a critical review, an informal meeting circle has already been established by Mexico and France in order to evaluate the gaps and to elaborate on the necessary reform, beyond the officially established working group by the HRC.[32] GRULAC and the EU are currently each other's most important allies in defending and extending the protection and promotion of human rights. Although we should not entertain the illusion that there is no hidden political agenda.

G   Non-governmental Organizations

Within the structure of HRC, it has been rather public pressure from NGOs and the work of Special Procedures or of OHCHR together with media, which produced public impact and made governments change their positions. An additional potential lies in the panel discussion scheme, which could be better used in future, e.g. in order to bring together ambassadors on the panel for cross-regional cooperation. Nevertheless, it has been NGOs which launched discourses and pushed for a victim-oriented interpretation of established rules and principles. It has been the initiative of NGOs in the last 20 years to bring victims and their testimony to Geneva in order to draw attention to protection gaps, and to provide drafts for new standards, as on enforced disappearance or on persons with disabilities.

In the last two years, NGOs also organized workshops and seminars dealing with the pattern of work by the HRC and seeking a better human rights performance of this institution. At the same time, NGO information and statements is still a matter of concern for certain governments and is sometimes dealt with as a

---

32   UN Doc. A/HRC/RES/12/1.

disturbance of the state-centered "spirit of cooperation". In relation to truly worrying human rights situations, the majority of HRC member states continue to rely on appeasement and containment. A rather prominent role is played by NGOs in the context of side events. Some of the neglected areas mentioned in previous paragraphs are dealt in these events; including the situations in West-Papua, Zimbabwe, Kazakhstan, Tibet and the fate of the Uyghur people, Chechnya, South Asia, secret detention centers in Europe or the role of parliamentarians within the UPR procedure.

With regard to the oral contribution of NGOs during HRC sessions, it is obvious that pointing to the reality on the ground is uncomfortable for governments. Thus, NGOs are often interrupted in their oral statements by points of order. This frequently happened, for instance, when the human rights situation in Tibet was addressed. From time to time, NGOs are threatened with a Code of Conduct, similar to what already exists in relation to the Special Procedures, while at the same time, in the speeches of ministers and secretaries of state during the High Level Segment, NGOs are identified as a core element of the UN human rights system; ambiguity yet again. In general, this pattern persists in the performance of the HRC: in contrast to the wording, the concrete actions tend to be very supportive of the governments in order to encourage progress in terms of human rights. This does not, however, guarantee that any such progress will take place.

H   Conclusion

Political considerations often take precedence over the objective evaluation in country evaluations and the agenda setting in general. The Western countries neglect unpleasant issues and so do other regional groups, too. But what do we expect from a 'well performing' Human Rights Council? Which priorities do we want it to take: Should the HRC address more country situations or rather proceed to faster and more objective decision-making on preventive or urgent situations including thematic issues?[33] Obviously, the HRC lacks credibility and efficiency, and a majority of states still shows low interest to discuss controversial issues. A misplaced notion of solidarity of the Global South impedes a comprehensive and serious human rights monitoring. The HRC is a political body while its construction is atypical for a political body: it combines fact finding, assessment and negotiations. Diplomats, the main actors at HRC, are normally skilled at negotiations. As the structure of HRC will not be changed within the near future, the diplomatic body requires professionals for its fact finding missions and will need to accord a more prominent role to Special Procedures and the OHCHR and will have to find procedures to better profit from the expertise of NGOs. Ambiguity will remain as a major pattern related to actions by the states while the non-state actors are challenged to make the unpleasant issues as prominent as possible and, therefore, to make their negation as costly for the reputation of each of the governments and regional groups involved. Only this will make governments change their policy.

---

33   For facts and figures to support answering these and similar questions, see German Institute of Human Rights/Elias Steinhilper, Three Years Human Rights Council: An Assessment, Berlin 2009.

III

Council of Europe

Philip CZECH

Widening the Scope of Application? The European Court of Human Rights' Case-Law on Jurisdiction in 2009

Table of Contents

Keywords

European Court of Human Rights, ECHR, territorial jurisdiction, personal jurisdiction, temporal jurisdiction, extraterritorial application

A   Introductory Remarks

In face of the number of judgments and decisions delivered by the European Court of Human Rights (ECtHR) in 2009 and the wide range of subjects concerned it is an arduous task to select particular topics for discussion. The present contribution aims at highlighting some of the Court's observations regarding general issues. In keeping with the thrust of the most important decisions delivered in 2009, the focus lies on the Court's development of the reach of its *jurisdiction* in 2009. When analyzing jurisdiction, an important distinction must be made between the concept of state jurisdiction as mentioned in Article 1 of the European Convention on Human Rights (ECHR) and jurisdiction of the Court itself, the latter being circumscribed as compatibility of an application with the Convention *ratione materiae*, *ratione personae* and *ratione loci*. While these concepts should not be confused there is a connection inasmuch as an application will be incompatible with the Convention (and the Court will therefore lack jurisdiction) if the applicants did not fall under the jurisdiction of the respondent state. In the following, the contribution will analyze the developments with regard to the territorial application of the ECHR (B) and the jurisdiction of the Court *ratione personae* (C) and *ratione temporis* (D) before drawing conclusions (E).

B   Territorial Application of the ECHR

According to Article 1 of the Convention states have to secure the rights and freedoms guaranteed to everyone "within their jurisdiction". While the notion of jurisdiction *ratione loci* may easily be affirmed in the vast majority of cases, it may give rise to difficult matters of delimitation especially when a convention state acts outside its territory.[1] The Court has already accepted the possible extraterritorial reach of the Convention where a member state exercises effective overall control over the territory, or part of it, of another state or where its agents act outside of its territory.[2] To establish jurisdiction, the victim must then be under the effective control of the state party, a state that may be considered as given especially when an arrest is made.[3]

Whether the Court is competent to rule on acts of British occupying forces in Iraq was the issue of the recent case of *Al-Saadoon and Mufdhi*.[4] The two applicants were former senior officials of the Ba'ath Party arrested by British forces in Iraq following the 2003 invasion and detained in facilities run by the British army. As they were suspected of having murdered two British soldiers the case was referred to the Iraqi criminal courts which issued an arrest warrant and asked the British forces to keep them detained in their premises as the Iraqi authorities did not have adequate detention facilities at their disposal. After the Iraqi High Tribunal had accepted its jurisdiction it requested the British authorities to transfer the applicants into its custody. The judicial review proceedings in England challenging the transfer to the Iraqi authorities did not have the desired result for the applicants.[5] Despite an interim measure indicated by the ECtHR under Article 39 of its Rules of Court they were transferred to Iraqi custody on 31 December 2008. The British government justified the transfer as being based on an international legal obligation, since the UN mandate expired that day and the Iraqi government gained full authority over its territory.[6] In Strasbourg, the applicants claimed that their transfer to the Iraqi authorities gave rise to breaches of Article 2, Article 3 and Article 6 of the Convention and of Article 1 of Protocol No. 13 as there was a real risk of being tortured in Rusafa prison and, following this, being sentenced to death and executed.

The main issue to be answered by the Court was whether the applicants fell under the jurisdiction of the United Kingdom for the purposes of Article 1. It reiterated the essentially territorial notion of jurisdiction which could be overridden in exceptional circumstances only. The Court held that the applicants were de-

---

1   Cf. Antoine Buyse, A Legal Minefield – The Territorial Scope of the European Convention, Inter-American and European Human Rights Journal 2008, 269-296.

2   ECtHR, Cyprus v. Turkey, judgment of 10 May 2001 (GC), no. 25781/94, RJD 2001-IV, at para. 77; Issa and Others v. Turkey, judgment of 16 November 2004, no. 31821/96, at para. 71. Unless otherwise noted, all cases cited hereinafter are from the ECtHR.

3   Öcalan v. Turkey, judgment of 12 May 2005 (GC), no. 46221/99, RJD 2005-IV, at para. 90.

4   Al-Saadoon and Mufdhi v. the United Kingdom, decision of 30 June 2009, no. 61498/08, EHRLR 2009, 711.

5   Cf. Matthew E. Cross/Sarah Williams, Between the Devil and the Deep Blue Sea: Conflicting Thinking in the *Al-Saadoon* Affair, ICLQ 2009, 689-702.

6   UNSC Res. 1790, 18 December 2007.

tained in British-run detention facilities established on Iraqi territory through the exercise of military force. Therefore, the United Kingdom initially exercised control and authority over them as a result of the use or threat of force. This de facto control over the premises was subsequently reflected in law as all premises of the occupying forces were declared inviolable and subject to exclusive control of the Multi-National Force until 31 December 2008.[7] Given the "total and exclusive *de facto*, and subsequently also *de jure*, control exercised by the United Kingdom authorities over the premises in question", the Court considered that all individuals detained there, including the applicants, fell within the United Kingdom's jurisdiction.[8] As to the conflict between the United Kingdom's responsibility under the Convention and its obligation under international law to transfer the applicants to the Iraqi authorities once their mandate in Iraq had come to an end, the Court held that this issue was not material to the preliminary question of jurisdiction, but had to be considered in relation to the merits of the complaints. It is to be seen whether the Strasbourg judges will deal with this conflict of norms in a more comprehensive manner than they did in the *Behrami and Saramati* decision.[9]

The Court thus laid the focus on the control exercised over the applicants because of the inviolability of the detention facilities run by the British forces and did not go into the argument forwarded by the respondent government that it lacked jurisdiction as Iraq was a sovereign state and the applicants were held only at the request of the Iraqi authorities. The effective control over the territory of Iraq or parts of it was not relevant for the Court. The decisive factor was rather seen in the exclusive control over the military premises where the applicants were detained. Thus there was no reason to assess the element of "exercise of all or some of the public powers normally to be exercised by Government" introduced in *Banković*.[10] The Court seems to take an intermediary position between *Banković* and the Northern Cyprus cases[11], where jurisdiction depended on territorial control, on the one hand, and the cases of *Issa* and *Öcalan*, on the other, taking into account personal control over the applicants. In putting emphasis on the exclusive control over the military premises, the Court still relies on a territorial element. However, this is not a case of effective control of an area but rather comparable to the exceptions exemplified by embassies, consulates, vessels and aircrafts.[12] *Al-Saadoon and Mufdhi* also confirms that the legal space argument (*espace juridique*) developed in *Banković* is not a constitutive requirement for the extraterritorial application of the ECHR.[13]

---

7   Coalition Provisional Authority Order no. 17 (revised), 27 June 2004,
      http://www.cpa-iraq.org/regulations/#Orders.
8   Al-Saadoon and Mufdhi (2009), at para. 88.
9   Behrami and Behrami v. France and Saramati v. France, Germany and Norway,
      decision of 2 May 2007 (GC), no. 71412/01 and no. 78166/01; Marko Milanović/
      Tatjana Papić, As bad as it gets: The European Court of Human Rights's (sic) *Behrami
      and Saramati* Decision and General International Law, ICLQ 2009, 267-296.
10   Banković and Others v. Belgium and 16 other Contracting States, decision of 12
      December 2001 (GC), no. 52207/99, RJD 2001-XII, at para. 71.
11   Cf. Cyprus v. Turkey (2001); Loizidou v. Turkey (Preliminary Objections) (GC),
      judgment of 23 March 1995, no. 15318/89, A/310.
12   Banković (2001), at para. 73.
13   Cf. Michael Gondek, Extraterritorial Application of the European Convention on
      Human Rights: Territorial Focus in the Age of Globalization?, NILR 2005, 349-387,
      at 376 (with further references).

In *Banković* the "gradual interpretation of jurisdiction" advocated by the applicants demanding that the responsibility under the Convention for acts set outside of the member state's borders should correspond to its factual ability to secure the rights guaranteed to the applicant had been rejected by the Court.[14] The approach taken in *Al-Saadoon and Mufdhi* seems to be consistent with this "gradual interpretation" and clarification may be expected by the Court's judgment on the merits. The crucial question to be answered is whether a member state is responsible to guarantee the full range of Convention rights once its extraterritorial jurisdiction has been established or whether its obligations are limited by the degree of control it exercises.[15] Further applications regarding the exercise of jurisdiction by British forces in Iraq are currently pending.[16] Given the fundamental legal questions involved as well as the potential consequences of extending the Convention's application to acts of armed forces of a member state wherever on the globe they are set, the outcome of these cases is eagerly awaited not only in the United Kingdom.

C   Jurisdiction *Ratione Personae*

In 2009 the Court had to decide several applications concerning the alleged unfairness of proceedings before international tribunals. The crucial issue to be determined in these cases is whether or not the proceedings before tribunals established by international organizations and their decisions are subject to the scrutiny of the Court.

The Court has so far applied two different approaches to deal with applications directed against decisions of international organizations. On the one hand applications are held to be incompatible with the Convention *ratione personae* if there is no direct involvement of the respondent state because the acts and omissions of international organizations are in principle not imputable to its member states.[17] On the other hand, states remain responsible for acts set by their own authorities in order to comply with obligations emanating from their membership to an international organization. In these cases the Court affirms its jurisdiction *ratione personae* but rejects the applications as manifestly ill-founded provided that a system of human rights protection is in place within the organization which qualifies as equivalent to the Convention system.[18] This approach was

14   Cf. Rick Lawson, Life after Bankovic: On the Extraterritorial Application of the European Convention on Human Rights, in: Fons Coomans/Menno T. Kamminga (eds.), Extraterritorial Application of Human Rights Treaties, Antwerp/Oxford 2004, 83-123, at 120.
15   Cf. Hugh King, The Extraterritorial Human Rights Obligations of States, HRLR 2009, 521-556.
16   Al-Jedda v. the United Kingdom, no. 27021/08; Al-Skeini and Others v. the United Kingdom, no. 55721/07; cf. Michael Gondek, The Reach of Human Rights in a Globalising World: Extraterritorial Application of Human Rights Treaties, Antwerp/Oxford/Portland 2009, 266-277; Francesco Messineo, The House of Lords in *Al-Jedda* and Public International Law: Attribution of Conduct to UN-authorized Forces and the Power of the Security Council to Displace Human Rights, NILR 2009, 35-62.
17   Behrami and Saramati (2007), at paras. 151-152.
18   Bosphorus Hava Yolları Turizm ve Ticaret Anonim Şirketi v. Ireland, judgment of 30 June 2005 (GC), no. 45036/98, RJD 2005-VI.

developed by the European Commission of Human Rights in the case of *M. & Co. v. Germany* clearly influenced by the German Constitutional Court's so-called "Solange II" decision.[19] The *Solange* doctrine can be summarized as follows: a transferral of powers by a contracting state to an international organization is not incompatible with the Convention so long as ("solange") fundamental rights receive an equivalent protection within the organization. In 2009 the Court has applied this *Solange* approach also in cases regarding acts of international organizations where the respondent state was involved in some form going beyond mere membership.

The first approach was applied in a case concerning the alleged unfairness of proceedings before the ICTY claimed by two Serbian war criminals convicted for their involvement in the military campaign against the Bosnian civilian population.[20] Referring to its decision in *Behrami* and *Saramati* the Court first examined whether the acts or omissions of the ICTY complained of could be attributed to the UN. Considering the manner of the ICTY's creation under chapter VII of the Charter of the UN, it held that the Tribunal was a subsidiary organ of the Security Council just as UNMIK.[21] As its acts and omissions were attributable to the UN, the Court declined its jurisdiction *ratione personae*. Regarding a possible responsibility of the Netherlands, as the state where the ICTY has its seat, the Court held that the acceptance of an international criminal tribunal pursuant to a resolution of the Security Council in a state's territory or the entering into a Headquarter Agreement could not establish the liability of that state under the Convention. Relying on *Behrami* and *Saramati* as well as on *Berić*,[22] the Court held that acts following resolutions of the Security Council aimed at the restoration and maintenance of peace could not be subjected to the scrutiny of the Court. This reasoning, developed in regard of the contribution of troops to UN security missions in Kosovo and later on extended to the acceptance of an international civil administration in its territory by a respondent state thus in the present case was applied to the creation of the ICTY, an operation regarded as "fundamental for the mission of the UN" by the Court.[23] The applications were rejected as incompatible with the Convention *ratione personae*.

The same conclusion was reached in the case of *Lopez Cifuentes* concerning proceedings before the International Olive Council (IOC), an international organization with its seat in Spain.[24] The applicant had been dismissed from his position as employee of the organization following disciplinary proceedings. He com-

---

19   ECommHR, M. & Co. v. Germany, decision of 9 February 1990, no. 13258/87; German Constitutional Court, decision of 22 October 1986, 2 BvR 197/83, BVerfG 73, 339 = EuGRZ 1987, 10; cf. Giorgio Gaja, The Review by the European Court of Human Rights of Member States' Acts Implementing European Union law: "Solange" Yet Again?, in: Pierre-Marie Dupuy/Bardo Fassbender/Malcom M. Shaw/Karl-Peter Sommermann (eds.), Common Values in International Law. Essays in Honour of Christian Tomuschat, Kehl/Strasbourg/Arlington 2006, 517-526, at 522.

20   Stanislav Galić v. the Netherlands, decision of 9 June 2009, no. 22617/07; Vidoje Blagojević v. the Netherlands, decision of 9 June 2009, no. 49032/07.

21   Cf. Behrami and Saramati (2007), at paras. 142-143.

22   Berić and Others v. Bosnia and Herzegovina, decision of 16 October 2007, no. 36357/04.

23   Galić (2009), at para. 39; Blagojević (2009), at para. 39.

24   Lopez Cifuentes v. Spain, decision of 7 July 2009, no. 18754/06.

plained to the Court claiming Spain's responsibility as "host country" of the IOC for the alleged breaches of Article 6 in the disciplinary proceedings. The Court reiterated that the contracting states could not be held liable under the Convention for acts of international organizations they were members of,[25] and held that these findings could be transposed to a state which had agreed to the presence of an international organization on its territory. As the alleged violations of the Convention occurred in the context of a labour dispute that fell within the exclusive competence of the IOC, and as Spain had in no way intervened in this dispute, they could not be attributed to her.

A labour conflict also gave rise to the case of *Beygo v. 46 member States of the Council of Europe*.[26] The applicant had been removed from his post as employee of the Council of Europe by the Secretary General. The Administrative Tribunal of the Council of Europe had upheld the dismissal upon appeal. Before the Court the applicant complained about the alleged lack of independence and impartiality of the Tribunal's members. Again the Court stressed that none of the respondent states had ever intervened in the dispute. As the application did only concern acts of organs of the Council of Europe, the Court held that the alleged violations could not be imputed to the respondent states and declared the application incompatible with the Convention *ratione personae*.

The doctrine of equivalent protection had been developed by the Court in cases regarding the relationship between the European Community and the Convention.[27] This relationship was also the subject of the case of *Cooperatieve Producentenorganisatie van the Nederlandse Kokkelvisserij U.A.*[28] The Netherlands Council of State had asked the ECJ for a preliminary ruling under Article 234 of the EC Treaty in proceedings concerning a licence entitling the applicant society's members to harvest a certain quota of cockle meat from the Wadden Sea. Before the ECtHR the applicant society claimed that its rights under Article 6 had been disregarded by the ECJ as the Court had rejected its request to respond to the Advocate General's opinion. The ECtHR did not engage in assessing whether Article 6 was applicable to proceedings under Article 234 of the EC Treaty and to what extent an interested third party, such as the applicant society in this case, could rely on its guarantees. As far as the application was directed against the European Community, the Court had no difficulties in rejecting it as incompatible *ratione personae* as the European Community is not a Party to the Convention.[29] The more interesting question to be answered was whether a

---

25 Boivin v. France, Belgium and 32 other Member States of the Council of Europe, decision of 9 September 2008, no. 73250/01; Wolfram Karl/Philip Czech, The European Court of Human Rights: Some Aspects of its Jurisprudence and Practice in 2008, in: Wolfgang Benedek/Wolfram Karl/Anja Mihr/Manfred Nowak (eds.), European Yearbook on Human Rights 2009, Vienna 2009, 176.

26 Beygo v. 46 member States of the Council of Europe, decision of 16 June 2009, no. 36099/06.

27 ECommHR, M. & Co. (1990).

28 Cooperatieve Producentenorganisatie van the Nederlandse Kokkelvisserij U.A. v. the Netherlands, decision of 20 January 2009, no. 13645/05, EHRLR 2009, 434-437.

29 Protocol No. 14 and the Lisbon Treaty provide for an accession of the European Union to the Convention. After the Russian Duma agreed to the ratification of the Protocol in January 2010, Protocol No. 14 entered into force on 1 June 2010 opening the possibility of a future direct applicability of the Convention to acts of European Union organs.

violation of Article 6 could be imputed to the Netherlands. The Court held that it could consider the case against the Netherlands as the domestic courts had actively sought the intervention of the ECJ. In contrast to the case of *Boivin*, it could therefore not be found that the facts were not subject to the jurisdiction of the respondent state.[30] In the leading judgment on the relation between the European Community and ECHR, the Court had held that there was a presumption that a member state had not departed from its obligations under the Convention where it had taken action to comply with its legal obligations flowing from its membership in international organizations as long as that organization provided for a protection of human rights equivalent to that of the Convention.[31] The Court in the same case had held that such an equivalent level of protection had to be presumed in regard of the European Community. The present application differed from that one inasmuch as it was not directed against acts of member states set to comply with international legal obligations, but against acts of an organ of the European Community itself. The Court applied this presumption to the proceedings before the ECJ and held that it was rebutted only if the protection of Convention rights was *manifestly deficient* and declined to find this to be the case in the pertinent proceedings before the ECJ. The level of protection afforded therefore seems to be reduced where the Convention is not directly applicable but where the protection afforded has to be only "equivalent", as the presumption of compliance with the Convention is only rebutted if the protection is "manifestly deficient".

This reduced level of scrutiny was confirmed by the Court expressly in regard of proceedings before the NATO Appeals Board.[32] The applicant, employed at the organization's headquarters in Brussels, had appealed to the Board in a dispute about his contributions to the pension scheme. At Strasbourg, he complained that these proceedings had not met the requirements of Article 6 as no public hearing had been held and as the Board's members lacked impartiality. The Court did not bother to review the application's compatibility with the Convention *ratione personae*, but applied the approach of equivalent protection developed in the *Bosphorus* judgment. It held that the protection afforded to the applicant by the provisions governing the procedure before the NATO Appeals Board was not "manifestly deficient". Therefore the respondent states when approving the NATO Civilian Personnel Regulations had rightly considered that the procedure laid down by these regulations met the requirements of fairness. As the presumption of compliance with the Convention was not rebutted and Italy and Belgium therefore could not be blamed for endorsing a system that was in breach of the Convention, the application was rejected as manifestly ill-founded.

An equivalent standard of protection was also assumed regarding the European Patent Organization. The Court could have rejected the application claiming breaches of the Convention in proceedings before the European Patent Office as incompatible *ratione personae*, as the respondent state had neither intervened in these proceedings nor set any measures of implementation. Nevertheless, the Court assumed its competence and stated that the protection of fundamental rights provided for in the European Patent Organization was in general

---

30   Cf. Boivin (2008).
31   Bosphorus (2005).
32   Gasparini v. Belgium and Italy, decision of 12 May 2009, no. 10750/03.

equivalent to the Convention standard. Therefore the application was rejected as manifestly ill-founded.[33]

The concurrent application of these two different approaches therefore was prolonged in the Court's jurisprudence in 2009, the exact delimitation being left open. While it is clear that the states cannot free themselves from their obligations under the Convention by transferring parts of their authority to international organizations and the Court therefore holds them liable if they do not ensure that the organizations' rules of procedure provide for an equivalent level of protection, some doubts remain about the Court's denial of jurisdiction in cases where the states "did not intervene" in a dispute between the applicant and an international organization. To avoid gaps in human rights protection it would be more appropriate to accept jurisdiction *ratione personae* – derived from the transferral of powers by the respondent state to the international organization – and assess whether its internal regulations provide for an equivalent level of fundamental rights protection. To hold member states liable if they join intergovernmental organizations without ensuring adequate internal proceedings conforming to the Convention would not overstretch their obligations accepted with the ratification and could therefore not be held as impairing international cooperation.

D   Jurisdiction *Ratione Temporis*

The reach of the Court's jurisdiction *ratione temporis* has been specified in 2009 by the Grand Chamber in two judgments concerning the states' procedural obligations arising from Article 2.

In the case of *Šilih* the Grand Chamber exercised its authority to put an end to the different approaches of several Chambers regarding their competence to deal with procedural obligations under Article 2 derived from killings which had taken place before the ratification of the Convention by the respondent state.[34] According to this latest verdict, the duty to investigate cases of death and to call to account those responsible can be separated from the substantive obligations under Article 2. The procedural obligations are therefore capable of binding the state even when the death occurred before the Convention's entry into force. This extension of the Court's jurisdiction *ratione temporis* is restricted by two conditions: First, it extends only to procedural acts or omissions that have been or ought to have been carried out after the critical date. Second, there must be "a genuine connection" between the death and the entry into force of the Convention.[35] This somehow cryptic passage can only be understood as restricting the Court's jurisdiction to cases where a limited amount of time has passed by since the event triggering the procedural obligations. The Strasbourg judges refrained from setting a certain time limit but made clear that a period of one year (as relevant in the present case) did not exceed the limit. The exact amount of time that has to pass by before a case of death can no longer be accepted as triggering procedural obligations under the Convention will have to be specified in further decisions. This is problematic regarding legal certainty as states cannot anticipate exactly under which conditions cases of death that have occurred before

33   Rambus Inc. v. Germany, decision of 16 June 2009, no. 40382/04.
34   Šilih v. Slovenia, judgment of 9 April 2009 (GC), no. 71463/01.
35   Šilih (2009), at para. 163.

their ratification of the Convention may give rise to obligations under the procedural prong of Article 2. If domestic proceedings took place after the critical date it is quite clear that the Court has jurisdiction to assess whether they complied with Article 2.[36] But if no procedural steps have been taken at all it remains unclear what period of time may pass by between the case of death and the Convention's entry into force before this jurisdiction comes to an end.

This approach has been confirmed in the case of *Varnava and Others v. Turkey* concerning the fate of nine Greek Cypriots missing since the armed conflict of 1974.[37] As Turkey ratified the Convention in 1954 but accepted the right to individual application only in 1987 (limited to events occurring after that date), it contested the Court's competence to decide whether the authorities had complied with their obligation to investigate the fate of the applicants' relatives. Referring to *Šilih*, the Grand Chamber reiterated that the procedural obligations under Article 2 operate independently. Other than in cases of killings or suspicious deaths where the Court demands proximity of the initial events to the Convention's entry into force, the procedural obligation to investigate the fate of missing persons may persist for a long period of time unless the matter is settled. The reason for this lies in the situation of ongoing uncertainty and unaccountability created by disappearances. The obligation to account for the fate of missing persons emanates also from this special situation causing pain and distress to the relatives. It may therefore, as was the case in *Varnava and Others*, still persist even after a lapse of over 34 years without any news of the missing persons. Although there may be a strong presumption of death after such a long time, the obligation to account for their faith is still owed to the relatives.

The key element distinguishing the constellations mentioned from the leading judgment, *Blečić*, where the Court stated that its jurisdiction was determined by the act constituting the interference and not by the refusal to remedy it in international proceedings,[38] is the nature of the rights violated. As the Court expressly held in *Šilih* and *Varnava*, the procedural obligations arising from Article 2 (and Article 3 as well) are separate and independent from the substantive aspect of these fundamental guarantees. The lack of an investigation into suspicious deaths or disappearances therefore does not concern a failure to remedy a violation of the substantive aspects of Article 2 or Article 3 but amounts in itself to a violation of the procedural obligations. To trace the fate of missing persons or to investigate suspicious deaths does not aim at remedying substantive violations of Article 2 but is an independent duty under this provision. The approach taken by the Grand Chamber regarding procedural obligations is therefore perfectly in line with its standing case-law as started by *Blečić*.

---

36   Cf. also Dvořáček and Dvořáčková v. Slovakia, judgment of 28 July 2009, no. 30754/04; Agache and Others v. Romania, judgment of 20 October 2009, no. 2712/02; Velcea and Mazăre v. Romania, judgment of 1 December 2009, no. 64301/01.

37   Varnava and Others v. Turkey, judgment of 18 September 2009 (GC), no. 16064/90; cf. Karl/Czech, The European Court of Human Rights (2009), 179.

38   Blečić v. Croatia, judgment of 8 March 2006 (GC), no. 59532/00, RJD 2006-III.

E   Conclusion

2009 brought a certain widening of the Convention's scope of application *ratione loci* and *ratione temporis*. Especially the extraterritorial application regarding acts of member states' armed forces in foreign countries seems appropriate to close some black holes in the protection of fundamental rights. While subjecting acts of armed forces (at least as far as deprivations of liberty are concerned) to the scrutiny of the Court may give rise to delicate questions of international law, it is highly welcome that states are held to their human rights obligations irrespective of the places on earth where their troops or agents get involved. The real impact of this widening of application highly depends on whether the Court obliges member states to guarantee the full range of Convention rights when acting outside of their territory, an issue yet to be decided.

The extension of the temporal jurisdiction to assess investigations of cases of death that occurred before the Convention's entry into force will affect some applications already pending. But for temporal reasons it is not to be expected that new applications concerning this issue will be raised in high numbers.

In both cases the approach taken shows that the judges resist the temptation of limiting the scope of the Court's jurisdiction in the face of the overwhelming number of pending applications.

Brigitte OHMS

The Coming into Force of Protocol No. 14 and the Short but Very Successful Life of Protocol No. 14bis to the European Convention on Human Rights

Table of Contents

Keywords

European human rights protection mechanism, right of individual application, principle of subsidiarity, filtering of applications, Protocol 14, Protocol 14bis, EU accession to the ECHR

A   The European Court of Human Rights: Hard Times for the "Corner Stone" of Human Rights Protection

The substantive rights enshrined in the Convention for the Protection of Human Rights and Fundamental Freedoms (hereinafter: "ECHR" or "Convention") are a well-known part of all European legal systems. Due to the European Court of

Human Rights (hereinafter: "ECtHR" or "Court") even fully developed bills of rights were significantly enriched, e.g. in the area of protection against discrimination. As the Court wrote in its 2009 report,

"[t]he application of the European Convention on Human Rights and its review by the Court have made an indisputable contribution to improving human rights in Europe, in particular by raising the standards of protection required and gradually harmonising legislation and practice."[1]

The degree of popularity of the legal protection system provided for by the Convention since its coming into force in 1953 for cases that have exhausted all domestic remedies is remarkable. The right of individual application serves as a safety anchor when national legal protection fails. The "road to Strasbourg" after all domestic remedies have been exhausted has to a growing degree been taken as given. This is why the number of individual applications registered by the ECtHR is increasing each year.[2]

It is, however, a rare exception that international courts are open to persons, non-governmental organizations or groups of individuals.[3] It was only since the coming into force of Protocol No. 11 to the Convention in 1998 which made the right of individual application available without any restriction. The judicial character of the Convention's control system and the principle that any person claiming to be a victim of a breach of the rights and freedoms protected by the Convention may refer the matter to the Court are unique. It is this particular *procedural* right that renders possible the effective implementation of the substantive rights. However, neither the procedural nor the organizational aspects of the Convention are known to the general public. People perceive the "functioning" of the ECtHR only to the extent they have to wait for a decision of the ECtHR and are not aware that these aspects are crucial.

For decades, organizational aspects of the Strasbourg human rights protection mechanism were not a major issue. In the face of the growing numbers of applications, the ECtHR adjusted its rules from time to time. However, the multistage and rather sedate structures stipulated in 1950 were not modified.[4]

---

1   Council of Europe Annual Report 2009 of the European Court of Human Rights (provisional edition), Foreword by Jean Paul Costa, President of the European Court of Human Rights, citing his speech on the occasion of the celebration of the Court's 50th anniversary, http://www.echr.coe.int/NR/rdonlyres/C25277F5-BCAE-4401-BC9 B-F58D015E4D54/0/Annual_Report_2009_versionProv.pdf, at 5.

2   According to the Annual Report 2009, by the end of the year 2009, over 57,000 new applications had been allocated to a judicial formation, an increase of 15% against the 2008 figure. Although the Court has increased its disposition of applications (over 35,000 applications, 11% more than 2008), the backlog has continued to grow. At the end of 2009, there were almost 120,000 applications pending, 22,000 more than at 2008. See ibid. The number of applications lodged against Austria is, in relation to the number of the Austrian inhabitants, one of the highest of the 47 contracting states of the Convention. Austria lies far ahead of Belgium, Denmark, France, Germany, Ireland, the Netherlands, Spain, Sweden and the United Kingdom See Annual Report 2009, 149 et seq.

3   See Article 34 of the Convention.

4   Cf., concerning the former parallel existence of Commission and Court as well as the role of the Committee of Ministers in detail, Franz Matscher, Das Verfahren vor den Organen der EMRK, EuGRZ 1982, 489-503, 517-528; for a summary, see Annual

But the issue of the operational capability of the Convention's protection mechanism was raised time and again by the Council of Europe (the "Council") since the 1960s. The topic became urgent in the mid-80s. When the number of signatories of the Convention ballooned in consequence of the Velvet Revolution, "perestroika" and "glasnost" during the early 90s,[5] the debate to which extent the Convention protection mechanism could cope with that strain and still claim authority vis-à-vis national courts and national public administrations started again. Also today this question is vitally important for the rule of law and pivotal for a democratic society.

In the following, I will give a short overview of the strategies of the Council of Europe, of the signatories and of the ECtHR to protect the continued existence of the Court and to guarantee the right of individual application in the future. I shall start with a summary of the amendments to the Court's organizational provisions until Protocol No. 11 (section B.1.), then I discuss the main substance of Protocol No 14 and the activities following its opening for signature (B.2.). I shall continue with a description of the straightforward search for interim solutions since the autumn of 2008 (C.1.) which led to Protocol No. 14bis and to an agreement for the provisional application of the two core provisions of Protocol No. 14 (C.2. and D). Next, I shall address the most recent events, i.e. the ratification of Protocol No. 14 by the Russian Federation and the Interlaken Action Plan of February 2010; the latter does not only commit the ECtHR but also the Committee of Ministers and the signatories (E). Finally, in the last chapter (D) I shall turn to the future fate of the protection mechanism of the ECtHR and discuss inter alia the Court's effectiveness.

B   Strategies to Reorganize the Court

1   Past Strategies, Including Protocol No. 11

In reaction to the increasing number of signatories due to the enlargement process and the coinciding continuously and considerably increasing number of applications and potential applicants, the control mechanism established by the Convention was for the first time radically reformed in 1994 with the adoption of Protocol No. 11[6] which entered into force on 1 November 1998.[7] Until then only small details had been adjusted gently and gradually.[8]

Report 2009, 9 et seq.; see further Brigitte Ohms, in: Karl Korinek/Michael Holoubek (eds.), Österreichisches Bundesverfassungsrecht, Article 28-31 EMRK with further references; Christoph Grabenwarter, Europäische Menschenrechtskonvention, 4th ed., Munich etc. 2009, 41 et seq.

5   Until 1990, 22 states were parties to the Convention, today there are 47 parties. See the official Council of Europe's list at www.conventions.coe.int. The Convention therefore applies to all states on the European continent.

6   Open for signature from 11 May 1994.

7   See in detail Explanatory Report http://conventions.coe.int/Treaty/EN/Reports/Html/194.htm.

8   Protocol No. 3 abolished the "Sub-Commissions" of the Commission for Human Rights consisting of seven members and charged with carrying out certain tasks. Protocol No. 5 governed the terms of office of the members as well of the Commis-

Protocol No. 11 introduced the present procedure, i.e. the ECtHR being the only instance for the examination of the admissibility and the merits of cases. Thus, the ECtHR is no longer preceded by a filtering procedure of a separate Convention body. Protocol No. 11 intended above all to simplify the system and to strengthen its judicial character. The signatories were confident to have established a sound and slim solution that enabled the ECtHR to adjudicate upon all cases within a reasonable period of time.

Already in 2000, however, the ECtHR had to realize that the backlog of pending cases was increasing each year. At the European Ministerial Conference on Human Rights in Rome in November 2000 on the occasion of the 50th anniversary of the signing of the Convention, the ECtHR signalled that urgent measures should be taken to ensure the effectiveness of the Court. Even the very existence of the Court was challenged.[9]

2   Current Strategies: Protocol No. 14

In 2001, due to the Court's distress call, the Council of Europe established expert groups to discuss possible actions to increase the efficiency of the working methods of the ECtHR in detail. These endeavours to reorganize the ECtHR led to Protocol No. 14, which was opened for signature and ratification in Mai 2004.[10] During the negotiations of the main contents of the new protocol it became evident that some states were ready to challenge the right of the individual application or, in eventu, some of its specific characteristics in view of a caseload that seemed prone to paralyze the ECtHR in the long run.[11]

It took lengthy discussions to achieve a compromise about an additional admissibility criterion which met on the one hand the ECtHR's need for relief and did not impair the applicant's position improperly on the other hand. The Protocol does not radically alter the control system set up by the Convention. Rather, the changes concern the functioning of the system; it has an impact on the ECtHR as well as on the Committee of Ministers, allows the Court more flexibility and ensures swifter execution of its judgments.[12]

---

sion as of the ECtHR; Protocol No. 8 made it possible to set up chambers and committees of the Commission; Protocol No. 10 (which never entered into force) intended to reduce the quora to make it easier to come to a decision.

9   Cf., concerning the development of the discussion, Ingrid Siess-Scherz, Bestandsaufnahme: Der EGMR nach der Erweiterung des Europarates, EuGRZ 2003, 100-107; Jeroen Schokkenbroek, Überblick über die Arbeit des Europarates betreffend die Reform des Gerichtshofes, EuGRZ 2003, 134-138; Brigitte Ohms, Bewertung des Diskussionstandes über die Entlastung des Europäischen Gerichtshofes für Menschenrechte, EuGRZ 2003, 141-148.

10   Council of Europe Treaty Series, No. 194.

11   See Report of the Evaluation Group, HRLJ 2001, 308 et seq., and Council of Europe (ed.), Reforming the European Convention on Human Rights, Strasbourg 2009, 563-607; on the Swiss-German proposal, see Klaus Stoltenberg, Neuere Vorschläge zur Reform des EGMR aus dem Kreis der Mitgliedstaaten, EuGRZ 2003, 139-141; see further Interim Report of the Steering Committee for Human Rights (CDDH), Guaranteeing the long-term effectiveness of the European Court of Human Rights, CDDH (2002)016 Addendum, §§ 44 et seq.

12   See the Final activity report of the CDDH, Guaranteeing the long-term effectiveness of the European Court of Human Rights, CM (2004) 65, § 17, in: Council of Europe

In this context I would like to highlight three elements of the Protocol: First, the introduction of a new admissibility criterion concerning cases in which the applicant has not suffered a significant disadvantage; second, the reduction of the number of judges dealing with certain categories of straightforward cases in order to improve the effectiveness of filtering and of subsequent processing of applications by the ECtHR. Thus, a single judge is empowered to reject clearly inadmissible applications (until now, this was done by a three-judge Committee). Furthermore, the Protocol entitles a three-judge Committee to declare applications admissible and give judgment on the merits, in cases where the underlying issues are the subject of well-established case law by the Court. Before, only Chambers consisting of seven judges or the Grand Chamber formation consisting of seventeen judges were empowered to declare cases admissible and to render judgments; third, the Committee of Ministers may bring proceedings before the Grand Chamber when a signatory refuses to implement a ECtHR's judgment which is directly addressed to it.

Protocol No. 14 to the Convention was adopted on 13 May 2004. During the opening for signature the signatories informally agreed to "ratify the protocol as speedily as possible, so to ensure its entry into force within two years of its opening for signature" in order to achieve the ECtHR's relief as soon as possible.[13] Thereupon 46 of the 47 signatories ratified the Protocol till October 2006. Only the Russian Federation was not in a position to do so on account of the Duma's persistent resistance, despite frequent requests of all the other signatories.

The signatories and the ECtHR, however, did not stay inactive during this interim period. The ECtHR improved its internal workflow by the comprehensive use of information and communication technologies and continuously expanded its scope of information for the general public. It made its publicly available database HUDOC, more user-friendly and improved its information policy regarding potential applicants, e.g. by issuing practice directions and application forms. Particularly useful is the information about its most important judgments and decisions in the ECtHR's annual reports because it has become more and more difficult to keep track of the ECtHR's jurisprudence in consequence of the steadily increasing number of judgments.[14]

Further to its wide range of information the ECtHR was quite creative in modifying its general procedure for the purpose of procedural economy.[15] Since 2001, in anticipation of the joint procedure stipulated in Protocol No. 14, most of the

---

(ed.), Reforming (2009), 664-668, 667; Explanatory Report to Protocol No. 14 to the Convention for the Protection of Human Rights and Fundamental Freedoms amending the control system of the Convention, in: Council of Europe (ed.), Reforming (2009), 693-711; Paul Lemmens/Wouter Vendenhole (eds.), Protocol No. 14 and the Reform of the European Court of Human Rights, Antwerp/Oxford 2005; Wolfram Karl/Philip Czech (eds.), Der Europäische Gerichtshof für Menschenrechte vor neuen Herausforderungen. Aktuelle Entwicklungen in Verfahren und Rechtsprechung, Salzburg 2007; Philip Leach, Taking a case to the European Court of Human Rights, 2nd ed., Oxford 2005, 8 et seq.

13   See Declaration "Ensuring the effectiveness of the European Court on Human Rights at national and European levels", adopted by the Committee of Ministers at the 114th ministerial session in May 2004, in: Council of Europe (ed.), Reforming the European Convention on Human Rights, 2009, 669-670, 670.

14   According to the Annual Report 2009 the Court issued 1625 judgments in 2009.

15   See the survey by Martina Keller, 50 Jahre danach: Rechtsschutzeffektivität trotz Beschwerdeflut? Wie sich der EGMR neuen Herausforderungen stellt, EuGRZ 2008, 359-369.

applications are communicated to the respondent states with the request to submit joint observations on admissibility and merits which contravenes the two step procedure according to Article 29 (3) of the Convention.[16] In autumn 2009 the ECtHR even took things one step further and no longer asks the respondent government to submit observations (while leaving open the possibility for them to do if they so wish) in cases where the Court is of the opinion that the underlying question of an application is already the subject of well-established case-law indicating a violation of the Convention ("manifestly well-founded cases").[17]

In addition the ECtHR achieves remarkable effects with so-called pilot judgments and pilot judgment procedures, which can be applied to repetitive cases revealing *systemic* human rights violations; these procedures are, however, not very transparent for the applicants and third persons. They result in a national solution developed by the respondent state to remedy effectively the underlying structural problem; if and when the ECtHR has approved the solution found, it strikes the cases out of its list. These forms of action, however, are still in development and call for clear and predictable standards.[18]

The enlargement of the organisation of the Council of Europe and the number of the contracting parties to the ECtHR, however, has still a deep impact on the control system of the Convention.[19] Even though it is not yet clear what effects the accession of the European Union to the Convention[20] might have on the

---

16 See Article 54A of the Rules of Procedure and Article 29 (1) and (2) of the Convention as amended by Protocol No. 14.
17 Article 28 (1) b of the Convention as amended by Protocol No. 14. On 8 October 2009 the Registrar of the Court sent a Circular letter to Government Agents informing them inter alia that the Court has determined to adopt its practice following the entry into force of Protocol No. 14bis and the provisional application of the relevant provisions under the Agreement between the High Contracting Parties "in respect of all applications ... even if they are decided by a Chamber under the present terms of the Convention".
18 On the evolution and application of the pilot judgment procedure, see the contribution by Agnieszka Szklanna, in this volume, at 223. See further Philip Leach, in: Krajowa Szkoła Administracji Publicznej (ed.), Pilot Judgment Procedure in the European Court of Human Rights and the Future Development of Human Rights' Standards and Procedures. Third Informal Seminar for Government Agents and other Institutions, Warsaw 2009; Marten Breuer, Das Recht auf Individualbeschwerde zum EGMR im Spannungsfeld zwischen Subsidiarität und Einzelfallgerechtigkeit, EuGRZ 2008, 121-126; Stefanie Schmahl, Piloturteile des EGMR als Mittel der Verfahrensbeschleunigung, EuGRZ 2008, 369-380. The request for rules concerning these procedures is echoed in the Interlaken action plan: see infra section E.2.
19 At the end of 2009, 10 signatories accounted for more than 75% of all pending cases (cf. Annual Report 2009, 137). This statistic illustrates the ECtHR's significant role in establishing and strengthening the rule of law in several states. It might also indicate that the ECtHR's jurisprudence cannot cope with all problems resulting from the enlargement process, which rather requires combined efforts by the signatories concerned and the Committee of Ministers acting in its capacity according to Article 46 of the Convention. In a nutshell: the entire Convention's protection mechanism is challenged. For the role of the Committee of Ministers in implementing Court decisions, see the contribution by Andrew Drzemczewski and James Gaughan, in this volume, at 233.
20 See Article 6 (2) of the Treaty on European Union as amended by the Treaty of Lisbon and Article 59 (2) of the ECHR as amended by Article 17 of Protocol No. 14.

Convention mechanism (in particular as regards the numbers of applications), it is nevertheless an additional reason to reorganize the ECtHR accordingly.

C   Protocol 14bis: An Emergency Solution

1   Genesis

The continuing non-entry into force of Protocol No. 14 worsened the situation faced by the Court as the number of new applications and the backlog of cases both kept growing. The President of the Court signaled the increasing urgency of reform on several occasions and pointed out that the effectiveness of the system and thus, the credibility and authority of the Court were seriously endangered. After years of urging the Russian Federation to ratify Protocol No. 14, the experts of the Council of Europe Committee of Minister's Steering Committee for Human Rights (CDDH) started, in autumn 2007, to discuss several options of action to reinforce the efficiency of the Court. Of course, the entry into force of Protocol No. 14 remained the first priority.[21]

Finally, on the occasion of a meeting of the Committee of Ministers in October 2008, the President of the Court drew attention to the extremely serious situation of the Court. He put the question up for discussion, whether it would be possible to implement the merely procedural provisions of Protocol No. 14 as a provisional interim measure (particularly the single judge procedure and the three-judge committee for repetitive cases). This measure could increase the efficiency of the Court by 20-25%.[22] At the same time the Registry of the Court indicated that there would be no technical obstacles to implementing "certain procedures" laid down in Protocol No. 14.[23]

This request appeared reasonable because the two procedures referred to by the President were intended for the handling of those cases the underlying questions of which were the subject of well-established case-law; therefore the respective decisions would not call for elaborate reasons. According to the ECtHR's statistical data during the last years approximately 95% of all applications could be attributed to these types of cases.

The next steps happened in quick succession: Already on 19 November 2008 the Committee of Ministers

"requested the Steering Committee for Human Rights (CDDH) to give, before 1 December 2008, a preliminary opinion on the advisability and modalities of inviting the Court to put into practice certain procedures which are already envisaged to increase the Court's case-processing capacity, in

---

On the question of accession, see the contributions by Florence Benoît-Rohmer and Jean Paul Jacqué, in this volume, at 49 and 123, respectively.

21   See the profound analysis by the Reflection Group parallel and in reaction to the work of the Wise Persons in 2005 and 2006: Report of the Group of Wise Persons to the Committee of Ministers, in Council of Europe (ed.), Reforming (2009), 609-628; and Report of CDDH (Reflection Group) transmitted to the Committee of Ministers in April 2009 (CDDH(2009)007, Addendum I). The Committee, however, did not discuss the CDDH report in detail.

22   CM(2009)56 addendum, § 8.

23   CDDH(2008)014, § 10.

particular the new single-judge and committee procedures, and a final opinion on the same matter by 31 March 2009; [and]

requested the Committee of legal Advisers on Public International Law (CAHDI) to give, by 21 March 2009, an opinion on the public international law aspects of this matter and to inform the CDDH of this opinion ...".

And indeed, during its next plenary meeting at the end of November 2008, the CDDH, after lively und serious discussions, adopted a preliminary opinion. The crucial question that had to be answered was whether there exists any legal basis which would allow the Court to put into practice the single-judge procedure and the new committee procedure for manifestly well-founded cases contained in Protocol No. 14. Against the background of the urgency of the Court's situation, the CDDH came to the conclusion, that there might hypothetically be several options to achieve the aim proposed by the Court, although it was quite obvious that most of them were highly unlikely:

- provisional application of Protocol No. 14;
- action by the Committee of Ministers under the Statute of the Council of Europe;
- unilateral declarations by state parties;
- interpretation of the Convention in the light of its object and purpose as well of the current situation of the Court and adoption of Protocol No. 14 by the Committee of Ministers and its ratification by 46 of the 47 States parties to the Convention;
- a new Protocol including some or all of the provisions of Protocol 14 but not requiring ratification by all States parties to the Convention for entry into force;
- and finally a combination of these options.

To be in a position to scrutinize each of these options, the CDDH addressed detailed questions to CAHDI on Article 25 of the Vienna Convention on the Law of Treaties (VCLT) (on provisional application)[24] and on public international law in general. Due to the experience with Protocol No. 14, the experts were anxious to avoid a delayed entry into force. Therefore CAHDI was requested to comment on the question of necessary quora for a new Protocol to the Convention.

Already in March 2009 CAHDI produced its opinion.[25] It came to the conclusion that several "options" raised by the CDDH had to be clearly rejected. There were no respective established principles of public international law to apply certain provisions of Protocol No. 14 provisionally by merely interpreting the Convention dynamically on the basis of its object and purpose. The same was true for amending the rules of the Court. The rules could not serve the purpose of amending the Convention. Neither could the measures envisaged in Protocol No. 14 be reduced to "matters relating to the internal organisation and arrangements of the Council of Europe" which according to Article 16 of the Statute of the Council of Europe would then fall within the ambit of decision-making powers of the Committee of Ministers. Also[,] unilateral declarations by States would raise serious questions of compatibility with public international law?

---

[24] Article 25 of the VCLT, a rule codifying existing customary law, provides that "a treaty or a part of a treaty [may be] applied provisionally pending its entry into force if the negotiating States have in some manner so agreed."

[25] CM(2009)56 Addendum.

Therefore amendments to the Convention should follow the traditional treaty-making procedures set out in Article 15 of the Statute. CAHDI came to the conclusion that a "temporary alternative to Protocol No. 14 will require a decision from the Committee of Ministers acting as a Council of Europe organ, in accordance with its existing rules of procedure. These rules of procedure do not require unanimity."[26]

The other solution envisaged by the CDDH, i.e. a unilateral declaration by each state consenting to the provisional application[27] of certain provision of Protocol No. 14 could only be reached via an agreement among the parties to the ECtHR as Protocol No. 14 did not contain any provision of that kind. This avenue was predetermined by Article 25 (1) lit. b of the VCLT.

Already in its March session, CDDH furnished its final opinion in line with the conclusions of CAHDI. Within only few weeks the Committee of Ministers' Rapporteur Group on Human Rights examined the issue on the basis of the CDDH and CAHDI opinions' and elaborated the draft text of Protocol No. 14bis in close cooperation with the national experts of CDDH. On 16 April 2009 the ministers' deputies sent a working draft text of the protocol to the Parliamentary Assembly for opinion. This opinion was subsequently adopted on 30 April 2009. Already on 6 May 2009, the ministers' deputies approved the text of draft Protocol No. 14bis and agreed to transmit it, accompanied by an Explanatory Report, for adoption to the 119th Ministerial Session of the Committee of Ministers (Madrid, 12 May 2009). There, the protocol was formally adopted and opened for signature on 27 May 2009.

2 Contents

The name of the new Protocol "14bis" should reflect its contents and function. It was created for the limited purpose to act as a makeshift until the entry into force of Protocol No. 14. To avoid any risk delaying its adoption, Protocol No. 14bis was limited to the introduction of the two procedural elements taken from Protocol No. 14 that would have the greatest and most immediate effect on the Court's case-processing capacity: the introduction of the single-judge formation and the extended competence of three-judge committees.

To ensure the expeditious implementation of the measures introduced by Protocol No. 14 it was prescribed that it "shall enter into force [after] three High Contracting Parties to the Convention have expressed their consent to be bound by the Protocol" (Article 6).[28] Protocol 14bis also enables the contracting states to

---

26 See Article 20 of the Statute of the Council of Europe.

27 Not an anticipated entry into force though, since Protocol No. 14 was not yet legally binding.

28 The small number of necessary ratifications was the outcome of thorough consideration. With only one exception, the entry into force of the latest protocols to the Convention required ratification by all signatories. The Explanatory Report of Protocol No. 8 noted in § 46 "that given the nature of the Protocol, it will not enter into force until all Parties to the European Convention on Human Rights have expressed their consent to be bound by it." Also the Explanatory Report of Protocol No. 11 indicates that the "fundamental character of the reform of the control mechanism necessitates approval by all States Parties to the Convention". With regard to Article 19 of Protocol No. 14 there is only the following explanation: "This article is one of the usual final clauses included in treaties within the Council of Europe" (§ 104). Protocol No. 9

declare "at any moment [...] that the provisions of this Protocol shall apply to it on a provisional basis" (Article 7). According to Article 9, Protocol 14bis "shall cease to be in force or applied on a provisional basis from the date of entry into force of Protocol No. 14 to the Convention", with other words: after the ratification of Protocol No. 14 by the Russian Federation.

Protocol No. 14bis entered into force on 1 October 2009.[29]

D   Agreement following Article 25 of the Vienna Convention on the Law of Treaties

An agreement following Article 25 of the VCLT had been identified as a solution for those states which no longer needed an involvement of their Parliament due to the ratification of Protocol No. 14. This was meant to provide them with an opportunity to rapidly agree to a provisional application of the respective provisions of Protocol No. 14 to applications pending against them.

Since some of the member states would need to engage new national procedures to seek approval of the provisional application of certain provisions of Protocol No. 14, in accordance with their constitutions, it was necessary to find a solution which would allow the adoption of such an agreement as soon as possible. According to CAHDI's opinion already mentioned above, there should be introduced an additional mechanism of acceptance, only following which the agreement would have full effect for the respective state. This two step procedure would make it possible for states to accept the provisional application according to their respective domestic law and the implementation would not have to wait for the most slow-acting state.

To secure that the rule of law is strictly applied CAHDI sketched the modalities of such an agreement in its opinion. It noted that several member states of the Council of Europe were not strictly speaking "negotiating states" of Protocol No. 14. There would be nothing, however, to prevent them from participating in the eventual provisional application process.

Furthermore, the Committee of Ministers would not be the correct organ to adopt such an agreement, as it was an organ of the Council of Europe and therefore not legitimated to adopt an agreement of this kind. Since Article 25 of the VCLT did not order a specific procedure for the adoption of an agreement, a decision by consensus and absence of disagreement by any negotiating state would be a legally sound basis for an agreement on provisional application.

Accordingly, the contracting states agreed by consensus in the margins of the 119th Ministerial Session of the Committee of Ministers, held in Madrid on 12 May 2009,

---

merely ordered that the protocol would enter into force after ten states had expressed their will to be bound by it. This was simply commented upon by referring to "model final clauses approved by the Committee of Ministers". The decisive reason in favour of an amending protocol was therefore obviously rather of practical than of legal nature.

29   Due to ratification by Denmark, Ireland and Norway; see Council of Europe Treaty Series, No. 204. These states were followed by Iceland, Monaco, Slovenia, Georgia, San Marino and Sweden. 13 further states have signed the protocol.

"that the provisions regarding the new single-judge formation and the new competence of the committees of three judges contained in Protocol No. 14 to the European Convention on Human Rights are to be applied on a provisional basis with respect to those States that express their consent, according to the modalities set out in document CM(2009)71 rev2."[30]

Some signatories availed themselves immediately of this possibility.[31]

E   Assessing Recent Developments

1   Experiences with the Implementation of the Two Procedures

A consolidated view of the increasing number of signatories implementing the single-judge procedure and the procedure for manifestly well-founded cases, be it via provisional application of Protocol. No. 14, be it via Protocol No. 14bis, indicates the success of the parallel approach: Since 1 July 2009 the two of the

---

30   Detailed modalities for the provisional application of certain provisions of Protocol No. 14 to the European Convention on Human Rights (under a possible future agreement between the High Contracting Parties to the Convention):
       "If agreement were to be reached by consensus between the High Contracting Parties, the provisional application in accordance with Article 25 of the Vienna Convention on the Law of Treaties of certain provisions of Protocol No. 14 to the Convention would take place in the following manner:
       a. *the relevant parts of Protocol No. 14 are Article 4 (the second paragraph added to Article 24 of the Convention), Article 6 (in so far as it relates to the single-judge formation), Article 7 (provisions on the competence of single judges) and Article 8 (provisions on the competence of committees), to be applied jointly;*
       b. *any of the High Contracting Parties may at any time declare by means of a notification addressed to the Secretary General of the Council of Europe that it accepts, in its respect, the provisional application of the above-mentioned parts of Protocol No. 14. Such declaration of acceptance will take effect on the first day of the month following the date of its receipt by the Secretary General of the Council of Europe; the above-mentioned parts of Protocol No. 14 will not be applied in respect of Parties that have not made such a declaration of acceptance;*
       c. *from the date on which the declaration of acceptance takes effect in respect of a High Contracting Party, the above-mentioned parts of Protocol No. 14 will apply in respect of individual applications brought against it, including those pending before the Court at that date. They will not apply in respect of any individual application brought against two or more High Contracting Parties unless a declaration of acceptance is in effect or Protocol No. 14 bis, if adopted and opened for signature, is in force or applied on a provisional basis in respect of all of them;*
       d. *the Secretary General of the Council of Europe will notify the High Contracting Parties and the European Court of Human Rights of any declaration of acceptance received pursuant to the agreement. Such a declaration will cease to be effective upon the entry into force of Protocol No. 14 bis to the Convention in respect of the High Contracting Party concerned;*
       e. *the provisional application of the above-mentioned provisions of Protocol No. 14 will terminate upon entry into force of Protocol No. 14 or if the High Contracting Parties in some other manner so agree."*
31   Switzerland, Germany, Luxembourg, the Netherlands, the United Kingdom, Estonia, Belgium, Liechtenstein, Albania and Spain.

reforms contained in Protocol No. 14 have been provisionally applied by the Court in respect of 18 countries. According to the Court's Annual Report 2009 the single-judge formation has, in relation to those states that have accepted it, taken over the function previously exercised by Committees. The President of the Court decides on the number of judges to be appointed as single judges, the duration of the appointment and the signatory in relation to which they will operate. As of 1 April 2010, 20 members of the Court have been appointed to this function. They continue to carry out their normal duties within their sections. Each single judge is assisted by a non-judicial rapporteur. These were appointed by the President of the Court from among experienced registry lawyers.

At the end of 2009, the results of these new procedures were extremely promising. The Court has adopted over 2,200 decisions under the single-judge procedure and the first judgments of the three-member Committees were adopted on 1 December 2009.[32]

2   The February 2010 Interlaken Conference

Parallel to the preparation for Protocol No. 14bis and the agreement under Article 25 of the Vienna Treaty Convention, the Swiss Government in co-operation with the Council of Europe, taking up a suggestion by the President of the ECtHR,[33] started to develop strategies to further increase the long-term effectiveness of the Court.

The reform of the ECtHR was one of the priorities of the Swiss chairmanship of the Committee of Ministers of the Council of Europe between November 2009 and May 2010. In early summer of 2009, Switzerland sent out invitations to a High-Level-Conference on the Future of the European Court of Human Rights, which took place on 18 and 19 February 2010 in Interlaken.

In preparation for this conference, the major stakeholders circulated position papers to put up for discussion their ideas of possible and preferable reform measures. The President of the ECtHR gave the go-ahead by issuing his memorandum of 3 July 2009, followed by the Steering Committee for Human Rights, then came the memorandum of the Commissioner for Human Rights, the joint appeal by NGOs, the contribution of the Secretary General of the Council of Europe in December 2009 and the conclusions of the Parliamentary Assembly in January 2010.[34] While the President raised the question whether "the right of

---

32   ECtHR, Kressin v. Germany, judgment of 22 December 2009, no. 21061/06, and Jesse v. Germany, no. 10053/08, both concerning the excessive length of proceedings; see also the press release http://cmiskp.echr.coe.int/tkp197/view.asp?item= 4&portal=hbkm&action=html&highlight=21061/06&sessionid=49968812&skin=hudoc -pr-en.

33   "I called for the organisation of a major political conference, which would reflect a new commitment by States and would be the best way of giving the Court a reaffirmed legitimacy and a clarified mandate" (Speech on the occasion of the celebration of the Court's 50th anniversary, cited in Annual Report 2009 (provisional edition), foreword).

34   For these documents, see Conference on the Future of the European Court of Human Rights, Interlaken (Switzerland), 18-19 February 2010, http://www.coe.int/t/dc/ files/events/2010_interlaken_conf/default_EN.asp; Council of Europe, Preparatory contributions (2010).

individual petition should be maintained in its current form or whether certain modalities should be attached to its exercise", the other stakeholders agreed that the right of individual application as contained in Article 34 of the Convention is not in dispute or somehow challenged. All statements have in common that they look at the Convention's system on the protection of human rights at large. Accordingly, they emphasized the primary responsibility of the signatories which is (only) completed by the ECtHR's observance according to Article 19 of the Convention and the supervision of the correct and complete execution of the Court's judgments by the Committee of Ministers.

After lengthy and in-depth negotiations a consensus was reached on the expert level on a joint declaration briefly before on the verge of the the the beginning of the Conference. On 19 February 2010, the participating ministers issued by consensus a joint political declaration to secure the long-term future of the ECtHR.

To achieve a balance between the incoming cases and the settled ones and to reduce the backlog of the Court of approximately 120,000 cases, the Declaration comprises an action plan. Based on the principle of subsidiarity inherent in the Convention which implies a shared responsibility between the signatories and the Court, the action plan does not only address the signatories but also the Court and the Committee of Ministers.

The most important aspects can be summarized as follows:[35] During the next few years the implementation of the Convention and the Court's judgments should be improved at the national level, if necessary by introducing new legal remedies. The states were called upon to

"ensure, if necessary by improving the transparency and quality of the selection procedure at both national and European levels, full satisfaction of the Convention's criteria for office as a judge of the Court, including knowledge of public international law and of the national legal systems as well as proficiency in at least one official language".

The Court should put in place, in the short term, a mechanism within the existing bench to ensure effective filtering. In addition, it was recommended to the Committee of Ministers "to examine the setting up of a filtering mechanism within the Court going beyond the single judge procedure". The Committee of Ministers should also "examine the possibility of introducing by means of an amending Protocol a simplified procedure for any future amendment of certain provisions of the Convention relating to organisational issues" (for example a Statute for the Court). With respect to the so called pilot judgment procedure the need was stressed "to develop clear and predictable standards as regards selection of applications, the procedure to be followed and the treatment of adjourned cases". And last but not least the Committee of Ministers should guarantee an effective and transparent supervision of the implementation process.

The addressees were given a rigid time-table for the implementation of these measures: By June 2011, i.e. within only 15 months, the measures that do not require an amendment of the ECtHR should be implemented. The Committee of Ministers is invited to issue within little more than two years, i.e. by June 2012, a detailed mandate for preparing measures that would require an amendment of

---

35   Interlaken Declaration, 19 February 2010, http://www.eda.admin.ch/etc/medialib/ downloads/edazen/topics/europa/euroc.Par.0133.File.tmp/final_en.pdf.

the protocol, such as the filtering mechanism. At the same time there should already exist an idea how a simplified procedure for any further amendment of the Convention could be achieved. From 2012, the measures taken up to then will be evaluated with the objective of eventual further measures on which the Committee of Ministers should decide in 2015. Before the end of 2019, the Committee of Ministers should decide on whether the measures adopted have proven to be sufficient to assure sustainable functioning of the control mechanism of the Convention or whether more profound changes are necessary.

What generally seems to be of upmost importance for the human rights protection, however, is that the Conference reaffirmed "the fundamental importance of the right of individual petition as a cornerstone of the Convention system which guarantees that alleged violations that have not been effectively dealt with by national authorities can be brought before the Court".

3 Entry into Force of Protocol No. 14

Against the background of serious and manifold efforts of the signatories to support the ECtHR and to bring fresh wind into the protection mechanism in its entirety, the Russian Federation apparently felt urged to carry on the ratification of Protocol No. 14. After some positive signals in September 2009,[36] the Russian Minister of Justice finally deposited the ratification instrument just before the opening of the Interlaken Conference in the presence of the Secretary General of the Council of Europe. Protocol No. 14 will therefore enter into force on 1 June 2010 – about four years later than planned.

F Future Prospects

From the view of human rights' protection, it has to be emphasized that the EU accession will further strengthen the protection of human rights in Europe by closing a gap and submitting the Union's legal system to the control of the Strasbourg Court, even though the interpretation of Union law will certainly remain the monopoly of the Luxembourg Court. Thus, the accession will answer the question of jurisdiction of the Court raised time and again on the occasion of cases underlying Union law since the 1980s.[37]

The exact modalities of the EU accession some of which may require a further protocol to the ECtHR or an accession treaty will have to be agreed upon by all Council of Europe member states, as well as the EU and its member states. At the beginning of 2010, preparations were starting. They are expected to be very intensive and challenging because there are fundamental issues to be clari-

---

36 Starting with a statement in the course of an interview by President Medwedjew during his visit in Switzerland on 18 September 2009. Source?
37 Cf. Commission, decision of 9 February 1990, M. & Co. v. Germany, no. 13258/87; Commission, decision of 10 July 1990, CFDT v. the European Communities and their Member States, no. 8030/77; ECtHR, decision of 30 June 2005, Bosphorus Hava Yollaru Turizm ve Ticaret anonym Şirketi v. Ireland, no. 4536/98; ECtHR, decison of 10 March 2004, SENATOR LINES GmbH v. Austria, Belgium, Denmark, Finland, France, Germany, Greece, Ireland, Italy, Luxembourg, the Netherlands, Portugal, Spain, Sweden and the United Kingdom, no. 56672/00.

fied as well on the side of the Council of Europe as on the Union's side. That renders the EU accession one of the most momentous projects of the coming months if not years.[38]

Of course the implementation of the Interlaken action plan has to be tackled as soon as possible. The action plan indicates very clearly that the securing of the existing protection mechanism will take centre stage in the next few years. Considering its comprehensive approach the action plan will occupy the Council of Europe's expert committees for years. Therefore, for the time being, additional rights and freedoms are not on the agenda. Since the ECtHR, however, is interpreting the existing rights and freedoms according to the present day conditions and regarding the Convention as a living instrument, it can be taken for granted that the judicial development of the Convention will continue.

The genesis of Protocol No. 14bis and the Interlaken Conference demonstrate that the signatories are not only aware of their shared responsibility, but also ready to put into practice the leading idea of the Convention, namely the *collective* enforcement of human rights. In unrelenting and persisting efforts they secured the entry into force of Protocol No. 14. There is also a firm agreement to provide security for the unique European human rights protection mechanism in the future. In this connexion the states did not in the least ignore "the fundamental role which national authorities, i.e. Governments, courts and parliaments, must play in guaranteeing and protecting human rights at the national level."[39]

For the present the continuance of the right of individual application according to the Convention seems secured. Notwithstanding the subsidiary nature of this and the ongoing democratization throughout Europe, this right has remained indispensable. Given the current situation of increasing regulation of almost every sphere of life, of global fight against crime and terrorism, of economic crisis and political debates in some countries this right is perhaps even more important than ever.

An observation not entirely new: As Thomas Hobbes wrote,

"[t]he safety of the people, requireth further, [...] that justice be equally administered to all degrees of people; that is, that as well the rich, and mighty, as poor and obscure persons, may be righted of the injuries done them; so as the great, may have no greater hope of impunity, when they do violence, dishonour, or any injury to the meaner sort, than when one of these, does the like to one of them [...]."[40]

---

38   Again, see the contributions of Jacqué and Benoît-Rohmer, in this volume, at 123 and 49, respectively. See further, a study of technical and legal issues of a possible EC/EU accession to the European Convention on Human Rights by the Council of Europe's Steering Committee for Human Rights, CDDH(2002)010 Addendum 2; Hans Christian Krüger/Jörg Polakiewicz, Vorschläge für ein kohärentes System des Menschenrechtsschutzes in Europa, EuGRZ 2001, 92-105.

39   Interlaken Declaration, preambular paragraph 6.

40   Thomas Hobbes, Leviathan, Part 2, Cap. 30, 15 (John C. A. Gaskin ed.), Oxford 1996.

Agnieszka SZKLANNA[*]

The Impact of the Pilot Judgment Procedure of the European Court of Human Rights on the Execution of Its Judgments

Table of Contents

Keywords

European Court of Human Rights, ECHR, pilot judgment procedure, implementation, systemic problems, general measures, dialogue, Committee of Ministers.

A   Introduction

The recent practice of the European Court of Human Rights (ECtHR) of using the 'pilot judgment procedure', although raising several questions regarding its conformity with the Convention, is undoubtedly very useful, since it aims at alleviating its workload. For the efficiency of the Convention system, it is crucial to allow the ECtHR to focus on cases concerning systemic problems and not to have it overloaded with too many repetitive cases. However, some questions arise in relation to how this new procedure may improve in practice the execution of the European Court's judgments by the respondent states. Therefore, this contribution will reflect on how the pilot judgment procedure supports the work of

---

[*]   The paper reflects the author's personal opinions and does not engage the responsibility of the Council of Europe.

223

the Committee of Ministers, which supervises the execution of ECtHR judgments pursuant to Article 46 § 2 of the European Convention on Human Rights (ECHR).

This article will first address terminological issues (section B) and then examine the general obligation to implement ECtHR judgments, which results from Article 46 § 1 of the ECHR (C.1.). Subsequently, it will try to answer the question whether the passing of a judgment in the framework of the pilot judgment procedure may accelerate its execution under the supervision of the Committee of Ministers (C.2.). Subsequently, a detailed analysis of several judgments will follow to show what kind of guidelines on execution measures the European Court gives to the defendant states and the Committee of Ministers and how both bodies identify such measures and the existence of structural problems in the states (C.3.). Special attention will be drawn to the issue of legislative reforms to be implemented following ECtHR's judgments delivered in the framework of pilot judgment procedures (C.4.). Conclusions will reiterate the main points of the analysis undertaken (D).[1]

B   Terminology

The use of the term 'pilot judgment' is confusing, since there is no legal definition. For the purpose of this paper, 'pilot judgment' will mean a judgment, in the operative part of which the ECtHR held that the violations found originated in a systemic (or structural) problem and called upon the respondent state to take all necessary steps to solve it. Examples for pilot judgments include *Broniowski v. Poland*[2], *Hutten-Czapska v. Poland*[3], *Burdov No 2 v. Russia*[4], *Lukenda v. Slovenia*[5] and *Xenides Arestis v. Turkey*[6]). The term 'quasi pilot judgment' will be used for judgments in which the ECtHR found a systemic (or structural) problem and referred to Article 46, calling upon the respondent state to take all necessary general measures to solve the systemic problem at issue (for instance *Urbarska Obec Trencianske Biskupice v. Slovakia*[7]). There are also judgments in which the ECtHR does not find the existence of a structural problem, but nevertheless

---

1   Any reference to Article 46 of ECHR made in this paper refers to its wording before the entry into force of Additional Protocol No. 14, which was eventually ratified by the Duma of the Russian Federation on 15 and 27 January 2010 and will enter into force on 1 June 2010. This Protocol amends Article 46 ECHR by granting additional powers to the Committee of Ministers in case of a state's refusal to execute an ECtHR's judgment (new §§ 3-5 in this provision). The Committee of Ministers will be entitled to refer to the ECtHR, which will have to decide whether its judgment has been properly executed. If this is not the case, the European Court will find a violation of Article 46 § 1 of the ECHR and will refer the case back to the Committee of Ministers for consideration of measures to be taken.

2   ECtHR, Broniowski v. Poland, judgment of 22 June 2004, no. 31443/96. Unless otherwise noted all cases cited hereinafter are from the ECtHR.

3   Hutten-Czapska v. Poland, judgment of 19 June 2006, no. 35014/97.

4   Burdov No. 2 v. Russia, judgment of 15 January 2009, no. 33509/04.

5   Lukenda v. Slovenia, judgment of 6/10/2005, no. 23032/02.

6   Xenides Arestis v. Turkey, judgment of 22 December 2005, no. 46347/99.

7   Urbarska Obec Trencianske Biskupice v. Slovakia, judgment of 27/11/2007, no. 74258/01.

calls upon the respondent state to take the necessary general measures and/or individual measures (for instance *Sürmeli v. Germany*[8] and *Dybeku v. Albania*[9]); these cases will be called 'Article 46 judgments'. 'Pilot judgment procedure' will be used to refer to any procedure, in which the ECtHR refers to Article 46 of the Convention, finding a violation of the latter.

C   Implementation of European Court of Human Rights Judgments Delivered in the Framework of the Pilot Judgements Procedure

1   States' Obligation to Execute Judgments: Article 46 § 1 and the Pilot Judgment Procedure

Firstly, it is worth underlining that the execution of a final judgment of the ECtHR entails for the respondent state the obligation to take certain measures: individual measures (including payment of just satisfaction), which are to erase the consequences of the violation and its negative consequences for the applicants, and/or general measures, which aim at preventing similar violations in the future. Although in a few cases, the ECtHR has also referred to Article 46 in order to motivate the States to take individual measures[10], its conclusions concerning general measures made under this article are of much greater importance for the efficiency of the Convention system, because they are meant to preempt the emergence of similar human rights violations.

From the perspective of the Committee of Ministers, a judgment delivered in the framework of pilot judgment procedure has to be executed like any other judgment of the ECtHR. Article 46 § 1 of the ECHR makes no distinction between a 'pilot judgment', a 'quasi pilot judgment', a 'judgment under Article 46' and a 'non-pilot judgment' (i.e. a judgment in which the European Court makes no specific reference to this provision of the ECHR), which the respondent state is obliged to enforce by taking individual and general measures. As regards determining general measures, in case a violation has been found by the ECtHR, the Committee of Ministers first analyses the source of the violations and then asks the respondent State to take the appropriate measures. It should be noted that comprehensive general measures may be required in case where the ECtHR delivers a judgment, without referring to Article 46 of the Convention. So far many States have had to undertake very complex reforms of their judiciary and administration system without the guidelines given by the ECtHR in the framework of the 'pilot judgment procedure'. This is true, for example, for cases concerning conditions of incarceration (e.g. *Dougoz v. Greece* and *Peers v. Greece*[11], *Kalashnikov v. Russia*[12]) and cases concerning the length of proceed-

---

8   Sürmeli v. Germany, judgment of 8 June 2006, no. 75529/01, §§ 136-139.
9   See Broniowski v. Poland (2004).
10   See, for instance, Görgülü v. Germany, judgment of 26 February 2004, no. 74969/01, § 64; Dybeku v. Albania, judgment of 18 December 2007, no. 41153/06, § 64.
11   Annotated Agenda of the 1059th DH meeting of the Committee of Ministers, CM/Del/OJ/DH(2009)1059, Section 6.1 PUBLIC.
12   Ibid., Section 4.2.

ings in Italy[13]). Many important legislative reforms have also been put in practice because of ECtHR judgments (e.g. *Hakkar c. France*[14] and *Goktepe v. Belgium*[15] which provide for the possibility of reopening a criminal case after a judgment of the ECtHR; cases concerning court martials in the United Kingdom[16]; and the reforms of Polish Criminal Procedure Code in the late 1990s[17]). Hence, from the legal point of view, the Committee of Ministers, in supervising the implementation of the Court's decisions, has no grounds to make a distinction between a judgment delivered in a pilot judgment procedure and any other judgments. However, from the procedural point of view, the Committee of Ministers may have recourse to different means in order to give a greater visibility to certain judgments, including those delivered following a pilot judgment procedure. It may, for instance, examine the execution of such judgments with debate at its 'DH' (Human Rights) meetings, and, consequently, adopt decisions with immediate effect.[18] It may also adopt interim resolutions to encourage the respondent State to adopt rapidly the necessary general measures.[19]

The Committee of Ministers always checks itself whether or not a judgment entails the adoption of general measures. However, it is noteworthy that a 'pilot judgment' or a 'quasi pilot judgment' gives a clear indication of the existence of a systemic problem, which is not always obvious for the Committee of Ministers. The Committee of Ministers deals only with the judgments finding a violation of the Convention and cannot *ex officio* have an overview of the scope of problems at national level. The ECtHR is better placed to give such directions on the basis of the number and nature of the applications it receives from applicants. The Committee of Ministers does not have this knowledge and, when assessing the systemic or non-systemic character of the problem, it needs to refer to the ECtHR and/or the national authorities. If the ECtHR indicates the existence of a systemic problem in its judgment, it may facilitate its execution. In case of a 'pilot judgment', the finding of the ECtHR in this respect is more convincing and unambiguous, since it is included in the operative part of the judgment.

2 Impact of the 'Freezing' of Repetitive Cases on Determining Systemic Problems and the Implementation of Pilot Judgments

Another important question arises in cases in which the ECtHR delivers a single pilot judgment and 'freezes' the examination of other similar pending cases, like in the cases *Broniowski v. Poland* and *Hutten-Czapska v. Poland*. In such circumstances, the Committee of Ministers has to base its assessment fully on the

---

13   Annotated Agenda of the 1051st DH meeting of the Committee of Ministers, CM/Del/OJ/DH(2009)1051, Section 4.3 PUBLIC.
14   Final Resolution of the Committee of Ministers, ResDH(2001)4 of 14 February 2001.
15   Final Resolution of the Committee of Ministers, CM/ResDH(2009)65 of 19 June 2009.
16   For instance, Findlay v. UK, Final Resolution of the Committee of Ministers ResDH (1998)11 of 18 February 1998.
17   For instance, Niedbala v. Poland, Resolution of the Committee of Ministers, ResDH(2002)124 of 21 October 2002.
18   For instance Hutten-Czapska v. Poland.
19   For instance, Broniowski v. Poland, Interim Resolution of the Committee of Ministers ResDH(2005)58 of 5 July 2009.

ECtHR's directions. Such an assessment is based on a single case and does not always reflect the whole range of different aspects that may appear in a similar context. It is based only on the legal and factual circumstances concerning one applicant and does not take into account the problems which may be related to the situation of other applicants whose applications are pending before the ECtHR. For instance, in cases against Poland the ECtHR found recently a number of violations of Article 3 (*Wenerski v. Poland*[20], *Musiał v. Poland*[21], *Kaprykowski v. Poland*[22]) and one violation of Article 2 (*Dzieciak v. Poland*[23]) due to the lack of appropriate medical healthcare in detention facilities. Two of these cases concerned lack of adequate healthcare for applicants suffering from mental disorders (*Musiał v. Poland*, *Kaprykowski v. Poland*), but two others concerned other health problems. Moreover, in the case of *Musiał v. Poland*, which had been chosen for a 'quasi pilot judgment', the ECtHR found the violation was also due to the overcrowding and resulting inadequate living and sanitary conditions in Polish detention facilities[24]. This judgment relates to two problems – lack of adequate medical care for detained persons suffering from mental disorders and overcrowding of prison facilities. However, the other judgments, which concern different factual circumstances, allow the Committee of Ministers a broader view of the scope of this systemic problem.

3   Dialogue Between the ECtHR and the Committee of Ministers on General Measures

The ECtHR may also pursue a useful dialogue with the Committee of Ministers on the issue of systemic problems. For instance, in the cases against Poland concerning excessive length of detention on remand, between 2000 and 2007 the ECtHR delivered numerous judgments (44 mentioned in the Interim Resolution) finding violations of Article 5 § 3 of the Convention. No pilot judgment procedure was used in relation to this provision.

Subsequently, the Committee of Ministers, worried about the number of these judgments and the number of similar applications pending before the ECtHR, adopted an interim resolution calling upon the Polish authorities "[...] to continue to examine and adopt further measures to reduce the length of detention on remand, including possible legislative measures and the change of courts' practice in this respect, to be in line with the requirements set out in the Convention and the ECtHR's case-law [...]."[25] In this resolution, the Committee of Ministers stated that the issue of excessive length of detention on remand in Poland was of a structural character. Almost two years later, the ECtHR referred to this resolution in its 'quasi pilot judgment' *Kauczor v. Poland*[26] and, agreeing with the Committee of Ministers' opinion on this issue, found that "[...] for many years, at least recently as in 2007, numerous cases have demonstrated that the excessive

---

20   Wenerski v. Poland, judgment of 20 January 2009, no. 44369/02.
21   Slawomir Musiał v. Poland, judgment of 20 January 2009, no. 28300/06.
22   Kaprykowski v. Poland, judgment of 3 February 2009, no. 23052/05.
23   Dzieciak v. Poland, judgment of 9 December 2008, no. 77766/01.
24   Slawomir Musiał v. Poland, §§ 95-97.
25   Interim Resolution of the Committee of Ministers ResDH(2007)75 of 6 June 2007.
26   Kauczor v. Poland, judgment of 3 February 2009, no. 45219/06.

length of pre-trial detention in Poland reveals a structural problem consisting of 'a practice that is incompatible with the Convention' [...]."[27] The ECtHR reached a similar conclusion in the case of Hilgartner v. Poland[28]. These cases show that the Committee of Ministers and the ECtHR may influence each other as regards the assessment of the structural character of the problems at stake and that a close cooperation between these two bodies is essential for the efficiency of the enforcement of the Court's judgments.

The pilot judgment procedure may sometimes be used 'too late' for the Committee of Ministers. In 2008, the ECtHR delivered two pilot judgments in the cases of Driza v. Albania[29] and Ramadhi and 5 others v. Albania[30], concerning mainly non-enforcement of domestic decisions concerning restitution of nationalized properties under the Communist regime or compensation for them. It found violations of Article 6, Article 1 of Protocol No. 1 and Article 13, in conjunction respectively with Article 1 of Protocol No. 1 and Article 6 § 1. In the case of Ramadhi and 5 others v. Albania the ECtHR found that the violations of Article 6 and Article 1 of Protocol No. 1, "[...] originated in a widespread problem affecting large numbers of people, namely the unjustified hindrance of their right to the peaceful enjoyment of their property, stemming from the non-enforcement of Commission decisions that awarded them compensation under the Property Act."[31] In the case of Driza v. Albania, under Article 46, the ECtHR noted that the violations in this case arose from shortcomings in the Albanian legal order, as a consequence of which an entire category of individuals had been and still is being deprived of the right to the peaceful enjoyment of their possessions due to the failure to enforce court judgments awarding compensation under the relevant Albanian law. There are currently dozens of similar cases pending.[32] However, a similar problem had already been found earlier in the case of Beshiri and others v. Albania[33] in 2006 and the Committee of Ministers had already asked the authorities about the general measures envisaged or taken to solve this problem.[34] Moreover, although in a different context, the Committee of Ministers had 'suspected' the existence of systemic problem of non-enforcement of domestic final decisions/judgments even earlier, in 2004, following the first judgment against Albania finding a violation[35].

It should be recalled that the obligation resulting from Article 46 § 1 of the Convention is an 'obligation of result', which means that the respondent state

---

27   Ibid., § 60.
28   Hilgartner v. Poland, judgment of 3 March 2009, no. 37976/06. §§ 46-47.
29   Driza v. Albania, judgment of 13 November 2007, no. 33771/02.
30   Ramadhi and 5 others v. Albania, judgment of 13 November 2007, no. 38222/02.
31   Ibid., § 90.
32   See Driza v. Albania, § 122.
33   Beshiri and others v. Albania, judgment of 22 August 2006, no. 7352/03 (finding violations of Article 6 § 1 and 1 of Protocol 1).
34   See Annotated Agenda of the 1059th DH meeting of the Committee of Ministers, CM/Del/OJ/DH(2009)1059.
35   Qufaj Co. Sh. P.K. v. Albania, judgment of 18 November 2004, no. 54268/00, finding a violation of Article 6 § 1 due to the non-enforcement of a final domestic judgment delivered in favour of the applicant company and ordering the municipality to pay compensation; see Annotated Agenda of the 1059th DH meeting of the Committee of Ministers, CM/Del/OJ/DH(2009)1059.

has the freedom of choice of the means it intends to put in place following the finding of a violation by the ECtHR. Thus, on one hand, the ECtHR's findings under Article 46 narrow to a certain extent the State's freedom in choosing the appropriate means to execute the judgment. On the other hand, there are cases in which this freedom has never been brought into question, since the character of the measures to be taken was rather obvious. For instance, in the cases of *Broniowski v. Poland* and *Hutten-Czapska v. Poland* the necessity of changing legislation and even adopting new legislation has never been contested. Nevertheless, the ECtHR's guidelines concerning the measures to be taken raise the very delicate issue of state competence in choosing the appropriate legal means in view of executing a judgment. In this context, it would have been better if the ECtHR had been explicitly empowered by the states to indicate the necessary measures.

The usefulness and the scope of the ECtHR's guidelines given in a pilot judgment procedure concerning the general measures to be taken by the respondent State may also raise other questions. On the one hand, they should not be too 'specific', so as not to affect the state's own competence in choosing the appropriate means of execution. On the other hand, if they are formulated in a very general way, they are neither helpful to the Committee of Ministers nor the respondent state. It appears that so far the ECtHR has managed to find a proper balance in this respect. In most of the cases, it calls upon the respondent state to adopt "appropriate legal measures and administrative practices"[36], "appropriate legal and/or other measures"[37] or "necessary legislative and administrative measures"[38]. Then it indicates for which purpose they should be intended: to "secure implementation of the property right in question in respect of the remaining Bug River claimants or provide them with equivalent redress in lieu [...]"[39]; to "secure in its domestic legal order a mechanism maintaining a fair balance between the interests of landlords and the general interest of the community, in accordance with the standards of protection of property rights under the Convention"[40]; "in order to secure appropriate conditions of detention on detained persons, in particular, adequate conditions and medical treatment for prisoners [...]".[41] In the case of *Kauczor v. Poland*, the ECtHR remained even vaguer. While it took note of the measures taken as of that time to remedy the structural problems related to pre-trial detention and welcomed them, it also emphasized that "[...] consistent and long-term efforts, such as the adoption of further measures, must continue in order to achieve compliance with Article 5 § 3 of the Convention."[42] The ECtHR also expressly refers to the state's discretion as to the manner of execution.[43]

---

36   Broniowski v. Poland, section 3 of the operative part.
37   Hutten-Czapska, section 4 of the operative part.
38   Slawomir Musiał v. Poland, § 107.
39   Broniowski v. Poland, section 4 of the operative part.
40   Hutten-Czapska v. Poland, section 4 of the operative part.
41   See § 107 of the judgment Slawomir Musiał v. Poland; similarly, Dybeku v. Albania, § 64.
42   Kauczor v. Poland, § 62.
43   Slawomir Musiał v. Poland, § 107.

However, sometimes the ECtHR is more specific. In the Albanian cases concerning lack of compensation/restitution for former property owners,[44] it stated that the respondent state should remove all obstacles to the award of compensation under the Property Act by ensuring the appropriate statutory, administrative and budgetary measures. In addition to this general statement, the ECtHR specified further that these measures should include the adoption of the property valuation maps in respect of those applicants entitled to receive compensation in kind and the designation of an adequate fund in respect of those applicants who are entitled to receive compensation in monies. All claimants who had won successful judgments awarding them compensation under the Property Act should be able to speedily obtain the sums or the land due. However, the ECtHR was fully aware of the fact that it was not competent to determine what might be appropriate measures to be taken to comply with Article 46 of the Convention.[45] It is nevertheless interesting that the Court called for the above measures, because of its concern "[...] to facilitate the rapid and effective suppression of a malfunctioning found in the national system of human rights protection"[46].

Another issue may be raised in this context: What are the limits of the execution of 'quasi pilot judgments' concerning Article 3 in cases of poor conditions in detention centres? Is the ECtHR attempting to have the Committee of Ministers take over the monitoring tasks of the European Committee for the Prevention of Torture and Inhuman or Degrading Treatment or Punishment (CPT)? The 'quasi-pilot judgments' delivered in the cases of *Dybeku v. Albania* and *Musiał v. Poland* raise these questions[47] but the Committee of Ministers has already found a *modus vivendi* in other cases.[48] It is, however, interesting to note that the execution of such judgments requires a synergy not only between the ECtHR and the Committee of Ministers, but also between these two bodies and the CPT[49].

The pilot judgment procedure may be very useful to the Committee of Ministers, if the ECtHR fixes a deadline for the adoption of general measures. Initially, this was not the case, although in some cases the ECtHR stated that the measures should be taken "rapidly"[50]. The fixing of the deadline for the Turkish authorities in the judgment of *Xenides Arestis v. Turkey* appears to have been useful, despite the doubts remaining as to the efficiency of the measures taken.[51] Even though, because of the non-entry into force of Protocol 14 to the Convention, the Committee of Ministers still cannot use any special sanction in case of non-observance of such time limit, the introduction of the latter may prompt the

---

44 Driza v. Albania and Ramadhi and 5 others v. Albania.
45 Ibid., § 125.
46 Ibid., see also Ramadhi and 5 others v. Albania, § 93.
47 See Slawomir Musiał v. Poland, § 107.
48 See Riviere v. France, Final Resolution of the Committee of Ministers CM/Res/DH(2009)2 of 9 January 2009.
49 Thus it should be pointed out that in the case of Dybeku v. Albania, the ECtHR clearly took note of the CPT's findings included in its reports on Albania of 2005-2006 (§§ 19-20), while, unfortunately, in the case of Musiał v. Poland, it did not mention the CPT's findings included in its report of 2004, even though it referred to the Committee of Ministers' recommendations concerning healthcare in prisons (R(98)7 and Rec(2006)2).
50 Driza v. Albania, § 126.
51 See Annotated Agenda of the Committee of Ministers' 1059th DH meeting.

State to adopt an action plan for the execution of the judgment and start taking the general measures without delay. In this context, it would be particularly interesting to follow the states' and Committee of Ministers practice following the *Burdov v. Russia No 2* judgment, in which the ECtHR clearly introduced deadlines for the Russian Federation, including them in the operative part of the judgment.

4   Pilot Judgment Procedure and Legislative Reforms

The use of the pilot judgment procedure shows that in the majority of cases the ECtHR is able to indicate the necessity of adopting new legislation or changing the existing legislation. The supervision of the execution of this kind of general measure is the most time-consuming, since the Committee of Ministers may keep a case on its agenda for several years, awaiting the legislative changes. The Committee of Ministers, which in practice is composed of civil servants, has very limited powers to motivate the national authorities to speed up the execution of judgments in such cases. Hence, a close cooperation between the national parliaments and the authorities responsible for the execution of the ECtHR's judgments at the national level would be welcome.

The case of *Broniowski v. Poland* shows the necessity of such collaboration. In this case the Committee of Ministers 'helped' the Polish authorities adopt the general measures required (namely the Law of 8 July 2005 on the realization of the right to compensation for property left beyond the present borders of the Polish State) by adopting, on 5 July 2005, Interim Resolution (2005)58 urging the Polish authorities to pass the draft law before the parliamentary elections of October 2005.[52] Without this resolution the Polish Parliament would possibly not have given enough attention to the bill and the whole legislative process would have been stopped and then would have had to be resumed from the very beginning after the elections. Thus, the Committee of Ministers, acting as an external and international factor, accelerated the execution of the *Broniowski* judgment, while the authorities responsible for execution at the domestic level (forming a part of the executive power) had difficulties in obtaining a rapid reaction from the legislative power in response to the first ECtHR's pilot judgment.

The role of the Parliamentary Assembly of the Council of Europe in this context should also be reconsidered and strengthened, even though, according to the Convention, the Committee of Ministers is the body responsible for supervising the execution of the ECtHR's judgments. A better cooperation between these two bodies of the Council of Europe could be advantageous for a better execution of judgments of the ECtHR, since the members of the Parliamentary Assembly, being also members of their national parliaments, can make national parliaments more aware of the obligations stemming from the Convention and the ECtHR's case-law.

---

52   See Interim Resolution (2005)58. In this resolution the Committee of Ministers called upon the Polish authorities to "[...] finalize the legislative reform and create the conditions necessary for its effective implementation."

D   Conclusions

To conclude, pilot judgments have been most of all a very useful tool for the ECtHR itself, allowing it to adjourn the examination of pending repetitive applications in certain cases. The Committee of Ministers supervises the execution of ECtHR judgments irrespective of whether or not the ECtHR has made a clear reference to Article 46 of the Convention. However, some of the statements, in particular those concerning the nature and the source of the structural problem at stake, included in the judgments delivered following a pilot judgment procedure or with a reference to Article 46 are very useful to the Committee of Ministers. The use of deadlines for the adoption of certain measures may also speed up the execution process at the national level and tighten the cooperation between the ECtHR and the Committee of Ministers. Moreover, the progress in the execution of judgments finding structural problems can also be enhanced by a better involvement of the national parliaments through the Parliamentary Assembly and its collaboration with the Committee of Ministers and the ECtHR.

Andrew DRZEMCZEWSKI and James GAUGHAN[*]

Implementing Strasbourg Court Judgments: the Parliamentary Dimension

Table of Contents

Keywords

Parliamentary Assembly, Committee of Ministers, European Court of Human Rights, parliament, scrutiny, supervision, execution, implementation, judgment

A   Introduction

"[It is necessary] to draw attention to the critical importance of the imple-mentation of the Court's judgments. If the Court's long-term viability is to be ensured, it is essential that Member States take appropriate measures to implement the Court's judgments and prevent repeat violations."[1]

The European Convention on Human Rights (hereinafter: "the Convention") has been heralded as the most effective system in the world for judicial protection of human rights.[2] Despite the achievements of the Convention, the inundation of applications received by the European Court of Human Rights (hereinafter: "the Court") has raised concerns as to the viability of the current system.[3] While deliberations as to how to ensure the long-term effectiveness of the Convention have primarily focused on the critical case-load of the Court, there has been a tendency

---

[*]   James Gaughan would like to thank the Clark Foundation for Legal Education for the assistance provided.

[1]   Lord Woolf, Review of the Working Methods of the European Court of Human Rights, December 2005, 66.

[2]   Alec Stone Sweet and Helen Keller, The Reception of the ECHR in National Legal Orders, in: Alec Stone Sweet and Helen Keller (eds.), A Europe of Rights: The Impact of the ECHR on National Legal Systems, Oxford 2008, 1.

[3]   Lord Woolf (2005), 7.

to overlook an equally worrying and inter-related problem, namely the failure and/or substantial delay of member states in executing judgments of the Court.

All state parties to the Convention have undertaken to abide by the final judgment of the Court in any case to which they are a party.[4] This obligation is a principal pillar on which the Convention functions, and exemplifies the subsidiary nature of the Strasbourg system, dictating that ultimate responsibility for ensuring the protection of the rights and freedoms enshrined in the Convention rests with member states.[5] There has been an unrelenting increase in the number of judgments pending examination before the Committee of Ministers, which exercises primary responsibility for supervising the implementation of Strasbourg judgments:[6] at the end of 2006 there were 5,636 judgments pending examination before the Committee of Ministers, while the equivalent figure for 2009 was 8,614.[7] Failure or substantial delay in executing judgments undermines the Strasbourg system and simultaneously erodes the credibility of the Court. Not only is individual justice denied, but the failure to implement effective general measures results in the recurrence of similar infringements, producing repetitive applications and distracting the Court from its essential function: "interpretation and application of the Convention and the protocols thereto".[8]

The effective functioning of the Convention system "rests on the assumption that there are strong and effective protection systems in place at national level",[9] including procedures for the implementation of Strasbourg Court judgments. The increasing volume of cases pending supervision before the Committee of Ministers and the protracted execution of judgments illustrates that this fundamental precondition has not always been realized. The problem of implementation is aggravated by the limited power exercised by the Committee of Ministers, which can do little when confronted with persistent failure to execute judgments.[10]

---

4   Article 46 § 1 of the Convention: "The High Contracting Parties undertake to abide by the final judgment of the Court in any case to which they are parties."

5   "The Court points out that the machinery of protection established by the Convention is subsidiary to the national systems safeguarding human rights." European Court of Human Rights (ECtHR), Handyside v. the United Kingdom, judgment of 7 December 1976, Series A no. 24, § 48. Unless otherwise noted all cases cited hereinafter are from the ECtHR.

6   Article 46 § 2 of the Convention: "The final judgment of the Court shall be transmitted to the Committee of Ministers, which shall supervise its execution."

7   Committee of Ministers, Supervision of the execution of judgments of the European Court of Human Rights: Second Annual Report (2008), Table 1.b of Appendix 1: Statistical data, April 2009, 33, available at http://www.coe.int/t/DGHL/Monitoring/Exe-cution/Source/Publications/CM_annreport2008_en.pdf and Herta Däubler-Gmelin, The Future of the Strasbourg Court and Enforcement of ECHR Standards: Reflections on the Interlaken Process, Document AS/Jur (2010)06, § 8. All documents of the Committee on Legal Affairs and Human Rights of the Parliamentary Assembly referred to in this text can be consulted on the Committee's website: http://assembly.coe.int/Main.asp?link=/Committee/JUR/role_E.htm.

8   Article 32 § 1 of the Convention; Committee of Ministers, Report of the Group of Wise Persons to the Committee of Ministers, 15 November 2006 (CM(2006)203), § 35.

9   Costas Paraskeva, Returning the protection of human rights to where they belong, at home, International Journal of Human Rights, 12 (2008) 3, 438.

10   As Steven Greer writes,
     "[The execution of Court judgments] is the Achilles heel of the entire Convention system because there is very little the Council of Europe can do with a state persis-

While reform of the Convention so as to increase the efficiency and transparency of the Committee of Ministers would be welcomed, the principle of subsidiarity necessitates that if the implementation process is to function effectively, domestic mechanisms ensuring the execution of Court judgments must be strengthened.

While the Committee of Ministers is attributed primary responsibility for supervising the execution of Strasbourg judgments under Article 46 § 2 of the Convention, this has not prevented the Parliamentary Assembly of the Council of Europe (hereinafter: "the Assembly") from often exercising an instrumental role in the implementation of judgments.[11] In his most recent working document, Christos Pourgourides, the Assembly's rapporteur on the implementation of Strasbourg judgments, highlighted the need to reinforce domestic mechanisms for the execution of European Court judgments.[12] The rapporteur, acknowledging the unique position of the Assembly being composed of national parliamentarians, focused on the need to strengthen the role of parliaments in the implementation of Strasbourg judgments. By emphasizing this aspect in his report, the rapporteur has not only highlighted the essential function of national parliaments in the implementation process, but provided an indication as to the future role which the Assembly may adopt in supervising the execution of judgments.

B The Evolving Role of the Parliamentary Assembly in Supervising the Implementation of Strasbourg Judgments

The Parliamentary Assembly, like the Committee of Ministers, is responsible for protecting the values of the Council of Europe and ensuring that member states honour their commitments under the Convention.[13] Yet the Assembly was never intended to be a body for monitoring the implementation of the Court's judgments. Indeed, the subject was a relatively secondary aspect of the Assembly's work until the unanimous adoption by the Legal Affairs and Human Rights Committee (hereinafter: "the LAHR Committee"), on 27 June 2000, of the first report on the

---

tently in violation, short of suspending its voting rights on the Committee of Ministers or expelling it from the Council altogether, each of which is likely in all but the most extreme circumstances to prove counterproductive."
(Steven Greer, The European Convention on Human Rights: Achievements, Problems and Prospects, Cambridge 2006, 155-156). The United Kingdom's Joint Committee on Human Rights has expressed "concerns about the speed, effectiveness and transparency of the Committee of Ministers process." (Sixteenth Report of Session 2006-2007, Monitoring the Government's response to court judgments finding breaches of human rights, (HL Paper 128, HC 728), 28 June 2007, § 6).

11   Christos Pourgourides, Implementation of Judgments of the European Court of Human Rights: Introductory Memorandum, Document AS/Jur (2008) 24, 26 May 2008 (declassified by the Committee on 2 June 2008), § 2.

12   Christos Pourgourides, Implementation of Judgments of the European Court of Human Rights: Progress Report, Document AS/Jur (2009) 36, of 31 August 2009 (declassified by the Committee on 11 September 2009), §§ 22-25.

13   Council of Europe, Parliamentary Assembly – Practice and Procedure, 10th ed., Strasbourg 2008; Bruno Haller/Hans Christian Krüger/Herbert Petzold (eds.), Law in Greater Europe: Towards a Common Legal Area, Studies in Honour of Heinrich Klebes, The Hague 2000.

matter by Erik Jurgens.[14] On the basis of the report, the Assembly adopted Resolution 1226 (2000), highlighting the importance of effective synergy between the Court, the Committee of Ministers and national authorities, and undertaking to play a greater role itself in supervising the execution of judgments.[15] Thereafter, under Resolution 1268 (2002), the LAHR Committee was assigned open-ended terms of reference and instructed "to continue to update the record of the execution of judgments and to report to [the Assembly] when it considers appropriate".[16] To this extent, the LAHR Committee, in supervising the execution of Court judgments, is not bound by Rule 25 § 3 of the Assembly's Rules of Procedure, which provides that references to committees lapse after two years. This is a key exemption which underlines the importance of the subject and enables the current rapporteur to supervise the implementation of Strasbourg Court judgments on an open-ended basis, facilitating a sustained dialogue with member states.

Since 2000, the Assembly has adopted six reports,[17] six resolutions[18] and five

---

14   Erik Jurgens, Execution of Judgments of the European Court of Human Rights, Committee on Legal Affairs and Human Rights, Assembly Doc. 8808, of 12 July 2000 (prepared on the basis of a motion for a resolution presented by Georges Clerfayt and others, Execution of judgments of the Court and the monitoring of the case-law of the European Court and Commission of Human Rights, Assembly Doc. 7777, 13 March 1997). Prior to the adoption of this report, the Assembly, exercising its general powers, had taken an interest in the subject, instructing the Committee on Legal Affairs in 1993 to report to the Assembly "when problems arise on the situation of human rights in member states, including their compliance with judgments by the European Court of Human Rights" (Order no. 485 (1993) on the general policy of the Council of Europe, 29 June 1993, § 2). The Assembly's supervision was stepped up with the introduction of the new monitoring procedure in 1993, which was extended to the honouring of obligations and commitments by all Council of Europe member states in April 1995 (Order no. 488 (1993) on the honouring of commitments entered into by new member states, 29 June 1993, § 3, extended to all member states by Order no. 508 (1995) on the honouring of obligations and commitments by member states of the Council of Europe, 26 April 1995, § 6).

15   Resolution 1226 (2000), Execution of Judgments of the European Court of Human Rights, adopted by the Assembly on 28 September 2000; see also Recommendation 1477 (2000), Execution of Judgments of the European Court of Human Rights, adopted by the Assembly on 28 September 2000, and the reply from the Committee of Ministers, adopted at the 779th meeting of the Ministers' Deputies, 9 January 2002, Doc. 9311.

16   Resolution 1268 (2002), Implementation of Decisions of the European Court of Human Rights, adopted by the Assembly on 22 January 2002, § 12.

17   Reports on the execution/implementation of Judgments of the European Court of Human Rights: PACE Doc 8808, Execution of Judgments of the European Court of Human Rights, LAHR Committee, Erik Jurgens, 12 July 2000; PACE Doc 9307, Implementation of Decisions of the European Court of Human Rights, LAHR Committee, Erik Jurgens, 21 December, 2001; PACE Doc. 9537, Implementation of Decisions of the European Court of Human Rights by Turkey, LAHR Committee, Erik Jurgens, 5 September 2002; PACE Doc. 10192, Implementation of Decisions of the European Court of Human Rights by Turkey, LAHR Committee, Erik Jurgens, 1 June 2004; PACE Doc. 10351, Implementation of Decisions of the European Court of Human Rights, LAHR Committee, Erik Jurgens, 21 October 2004; PACE Doc 11020, Implementation of Judgments of the European Court of Human Rights, LAHR Committee, Erik Jurgens, 18 September 2006.

recommendations[19] on the implementation of the Court's judgments, addressing particularly problematic instances of non-execution. The texts adopted by the Assembly aim to apply pressure on member states to take effective measures with a view to implementing the judgments identified, and to provide greater political transparency with regard to the failure or substantial delay by a significant number of member states in executing judgments of the Court. In performing his mandate, Erik Jurgens adopted several pro-active working methods. The effectiveness of two practices in particular has compelled the current rapporteur, Christos Pourgourides, to continue his predecessor's approach: first, conducting a state-by-state assessment, applying set criteria for identifying judgments, so as to ensure a non-discriminatory approach,[20] and second, conducting a pro-active dialogue with the state parties concerned, including – since 2005 – in situ visits to member states with particularly problematic instances of non-implementation.[21]

In a recent working document, Christos Pourgourides revealed that the failure of member states to fully and expeditiously implement judgments of the Court is far graver, and more widespread, than previous reports had disclosed. Applying the same objective criteria employed for the identification of judgments addressed in the sixth report, the rapporteur illustrated the significant increase in the number of judgments pending examination before the Committee of Ministers which can be considered as particularly problematic instances of non-execution.[22] The rapporteur acknowledged that, aside from being outwith the capacity of a single rapporteur, to address all the judgments falling within the criteria would result in unnecessary duplication of the work of the Committee of Ministers.[23]

Identifying the extent to which member states are failing to execute judgments of the Court, highlights the urgent need to reinforce domestic mechanisms for the

---

18 Resolutions on the execution/implementation of judgments of the European Court of Human Rights: PACE Resolution 1226 (2000); PACE Resolution 1268 (2002); PACE Resolution 1297 (2002); PACE Resolution 1381 (2004); PACE Resolution 1411 (2004); PACE Resolution 1516 (2006).

19 Recommendations on the execution/implementation of judgments of the European Court of Human Rights: PACE Recommendation 1477 (2000); PACE Recommendation 1546 (2002); PACE Recommendation 1576 (2002); PACE Recommendation 1684 (2004); PACE Recommendation 1764 (2006).

20 In preparing his sixth report, which was presented in September 2006, Erik Jurgens decided to alter the criteria applied for identifying judgments to be addressed, focusing on "judgments [...] which have not been fully implemented more than five years after their delivery [and] other judgments [...] raising important implementation issues, whether individual or general, as highlighted notably in the Committee of Ministers' Interim Resolutions or other documents." Erik Jurgens, Implementation of judgments of the European Court of Human Rights: Introductory Memorandum, Assembly Doc. 11020, 18 September 2006, § 6.

21 For the sixth report on the implementation of Strasbourg Court judgments Erik Jurgens visited five states: Italy, Russia, Turkey, Ukraine, and the United Kingdom; for the seventh report on the implementation of Strasbourg Court judgments, Christos Pourgourides has to date visited five states, namely Bulgaria, Greece, Italy, the Russian Federation and Ukraine, and is to visit another three (Moldova, Romania and Turkey) before he presents his report in 2010

22 Pourgourides (2009), § 5 and AS/Jur (2009) 36 Addendum, 31 August 2009 (declassified by the Committee on 11 September 2009).

23 Pourgourides (2009), § 8.

implementation of Strasbourg judgments. Parliamentary involvement and oversight is an important aspect in ensuring the prompt and effective execution of the Court's judgments. National parliaments may be able in specific instances, more effectively than the Committee of Ministers, to identify the social or political problems underlying a violation and understand the measures required to prevent the recurrence of similar infringements. Nevertheless, parliaments in very few member states are actively involved in the implementation of judgments of the Court (but see section C). Hence the need to reinforce dialogue with national authorities, and in particular national parliaments, on strengthening the involvement of the legislative branch of state authority in the implementation of Court judgments. The initiative for pursuing this approach appears to be based on four principal convictions. Firstly, prompt and full execution of the Court's judgments is necessary for the effective functioning of the Convention system. Secondly, the principle of subsidiarity dictates that for the Strasbourg system to function effectively, member states must ensure that the rights and freedoms enshrined in the Convention are primarily protected at a domestic level. Thirdly, national parliaments have a crucial role in supervising and contributing to the execution of the Court's judgments. Finally, the Assembly, being composed of national parliamentarians, is uniquely placed in seeking to strengthen the role of national parliaments in the implementation of Strasbourg Court judgments.[24]

The Assembly's Legal Affairs and Human Rights Committee has identified for itself a valuable role in supervising the execution of Strasbourg Court judgments. Monitoring the implementation of specific judgments according to established criteria has become increasingly difficult given the volume of cases which now fall within the mandate of the rapporteur: particularly problematic instances of non-execution.[25] This is not to imply that the Assembly's previous contributions were not of value. The efforts of Erik Jurgens were instrumental in furthering the implementation of certain judgments and providing greater visibility to protracted and negligent execution of judgments.[26] Nevertheless, it has become increasingly apparent that measures have to be implemented 'upstream', domestically, to ensure the effective implementation of Strasbourg judgments and prevent repetitive violations before the Court. Utilizing the Assembly's relationship with national parliaments provides a unique opportunity to strengthen the principle of subsidiarity: the fundamental requirement in guaranteeing the long-term effectiveness of the Convention system.

---

24   A key point to be noted is the composition of each member state's parliamentary delegation: national delegations are always composed in such a way as to ensure fair representation of the political parties or groups in their respective parliaments.

25   Pourgourides (2009), § 7.

26   According to Philip Leach, "[t]he work carried out by PACE in recent years has ensured, to a certain extent, a stronger public and democratic aspect to the [implementation] process." (Philip Leach, The Effectiveness of the Committee of Ministers in Supervising the Enforcement of Judgments of the European Court of Human Rights, Public Law (2006) 443, 455). See also Philip Leach, Opinion. On Reform of the European Court of Human Rights, European Human Rights Law Review 2009, 725, 735.

C   The Role of National Parliaments in the Implementation of Strasbourg Judgments

The obligation arising under Article 46 § 1 of the Convention is a collective responsibility for all state organs, including national parliaments.[27] A recent comparative report disclosed that state parties with strong implementation records are regularly characterized by active involvement of parliamentary actors in the execution process.[28] Organs of the Council of Europe have acknowledged that the implementation of Strasbourg judgments greatly benefits from enhanced involvement of national parliaments.[29] Despite such observations, an analysis presented by the Assembly's LAHR Committee in May 2008, revealed that "parliaments in very few states exercise regular control over the effective implementation of Strasbourg Court judgments."[30]

Being composed of democratically elected representatives, parliament exercises an essential constitutional responsibility in holding the government to account. Its power of maintaining the government, which must regularly come before parliament in order to obtain support for policies, combined with its representative function, dictates that parliament subjects executive practice to substantial scrutiny.[31] There are three principal means by which a parliament holds the government to account: debate, parliamentary questions, and committees.[32] Through such channels "Parliament, more effectively than the Committee of Ministers, can scrutinise the Government's response to ensure that it acts swiftly to fulfil the [obligation under Article 46 § 1 of the Convention], and that it does so adequately."[33]

---

27   "It is thus at national level that the most effective and direct protection of the rights and freedoms guaranteed in the Convention should be ensured. This requirement concerns all state authorities, in particular the courts, the administration and the legislature." (Appendix to Recommendation Rec(2004)5 of the Committee of Ministers to member states on the verification of the compatibility of draft laws, existing laws and administrative practice with the standards laid down in the European Convention on Human Rights, § 2).

28   JURISTRAS Project, Why do states implement differently the European Court of Human Rights judgments? The case law on civil liberties and the rights of minorities, April 2009, 23, available at http://www.juristras.eliamep.gr/wp-content/uploads/2009/05/why-do-states-implement-differently-the-european-court-of-human.pdf.

29   Ministers' Deputies, Implementation of judgments of the European Court of Human Rights, Parliamentary Assembly Recommendation 1764 (2006), Doc. CM/AS(2007) Rec1764 final 30 March 2007, Reply adopted by the Committee of Ministers on 28 March 2007 at the 991st meeting of the Ministers' Deputies, § 1; Resolution 1516 (2006), Implementation of Judgments of the European Court of Human Rights, adopted by the Assembly on 2 October 2006, § 2.

30   Secretariat of the LAHR Committee, The role of national parliaments in verifying state obligations to comply with the European Convention on Human Rights, including Strasbourg Court judgments: an overview, 23 May 2008, in: LAHR Committee, Stockholm Colloquy: "Towards stronger implementation of the European Convention on Human Rights at national level", 9-10 June 2008, Doc. AS/Jur (2008) 32 rev., of 23 June 2008, § 11.

31   Adam Tomkins, Public Law, Oxford 2003, 92.

32   Ibid., 160.

33   Joint Committee on Human Rights, Monitoring the Government's response to Court judgments finding breaches of human rights, Sixteenth Report of Session 2006-2007

Scrutiny of the government's response to an adverse judgment of the Court takes two broad forms. First, parliament should exercise oversight in ensuring that the competent authorities promptly adopt adequate measures to execute a judgment of the European Court. Parliament, in exercising a supervisory function, places an expectation upon the Government to uphold their commitments under the Convention and increases the political transparency of the implementation process. To this extent the Assembly has invited "all national parliaments to introduce specific mechanisms and procedures for effective parliamentary oversight of the implementation of the Court's judgments."[34] In the United Kingdom, the parliamentary Joint Committee on Human Rights (hereinafter: "the Joint Committee") produces an annual report monitoring the Government's response to adverse judgments of the European Court and declarations of incompatibility by domestic courts.[35] In a recent monitoring report, the Joint Committee identified obstacles to effective implementation in certain cases and judgments in respect of which execution has been particularly protracted. Recognising such problems not only highlights the urgent need to implement effective general measures in respect of such cases, but indicates deficiencies in the existing domestic mechanism for the execution of Strasbourg Court judgments. In respect of the latter, the Assembly has called upon member states to "set up, either through legislation or otherwise, domestic mechanisms for the rapid implementation of the Court's judgments."[36] To enable parliament to effectively supervise the government's response to an adverse decision of the Court, there must exist a procedure through which parliament is promptly and systematically informed of such judgments and the measures implemented in the execution thereof. Despite the practical importance of such a mechanism, an assessment conducted by the LAHR Committee revealed that such a procedure existed in a surprisingly small number of member states.[37] In his recent working document, Christos

(HL Paper 128, HC 728), 28 June 2007, § 7; "Parliament has an important role to play in scrutinising, at national level, the Government's performance of the obligations which arise following a judgment in which the ECtHR has found the UK to be in breach of the ECHR" (ibid.).

34 Resolution 1516 (2006), Implementation of judgments of the European Court of Human Rights, adopted by the Assembly on 2 October 2006, § 22.1.

35 Joint Committee on Human Rights, Enhancing Parliament's role in relation to [Strasbourg Court] human rights judgments, Fifteenth Report of Session 2009-10 (HL Paper 85, HC 455), 26 March 2010, http://www.publications.parliament.uk/pa/jt200910/jtselect/jtrights/85/85.pdf (see, in particular, §§ 1 to 17 & 195-196, and Annex: Guidance for Departments on Responding to Court Judgments on Human Rights, at pp. 69-76); Joint Committee on Human Rights, Monitoring the Government's response to human rights judgments: Annual report 2008, Thirty-first Report of Session 2007-08 (HL Paper 173, HC 1078), 31 October 2008; Joint Committee on Human Rights, Monitoring the Government's response to Court judgments finding breaches of human rights, Sixteenth Report of Session 2006-07 (HL Paper 128, HC 728), 28 June 2007; Joint Committee on Human Rights, Implementation of Strasbourg judgments: First progress report, Thirteenth Report of Session 2005-06 (HL Paper 133, HC 954), 8 March 2006.

36 Resolution 1516 (2006), Implementation of Judgments of the European Court of Human Rights, adopted by the Assembly on 2 October 2006, § 22.2.

37 Secretariat of the LAHR Committee (2008), § 10.

Pourgourides identified the Netherlands as providing a model mechanism in this respect.[38]

The second form of scrutiny to which parliament should subject the government's response, concerns the actual content of the measures proposed to execute a judgment of the Court. Scrutiny in this respect is most evident in parliament's verification of the compliance of draft legislation with Convention standards. The Committee of Ministers has recommended that member states "ensure that there are appropriate and effective mechanisms for systematically verifying the compatibility of draft laws with the Convention in the light of the case-law of the Court."[39] Therefore, 'Strasbourg vetting' of draft legislation is necessary, irrelevant of whether the bill has been introduced in response to an adverse judgment of the Court. Verification of draft legislation is a principal preventative measure in seeking to avoid unjustified infringement of the Convention guarantees.

The importance of this preventative measure is particularly evident in the context of legislation drafted in response to an adverse finding of the Court, where the adoption of new, Convention-compliant, legislation, is necessary to prevent similar future infringements. Again, despite the importance of 'Strasbourg vetting' of draft legislation, an assessment conducted by the Secretariat of the LAHR Committee revealed that "very few parliamentary mechanisms exist with a specific mandate to verify compliance [of draft legislation] with ECHR requirements."[40] Parliamentary scrutiny of legislation is not restricted to that drafted in response to a judgment of the Court. The Committee of Ministers has recommended that member states "ensure that there are such mechanisms for verifying, *whenever necessary*, the compatibility of existing laws and administrative practice" (emphasis added).[41] The delivery of a final judgment of the Court finding a violation of the Convention, would constitute the *necessary* circumstances in which parliament should examine the relevant law and practice to determine whether amendments are required to execute the judgment.

---

38   The Minister of Foreign Affairs, also on behalf of the Minister of Justice, presents an annual report to Parliament concerning Strasbourg judgments delivered against the Netherlands. In 2006, the Senate requested that the annual report also contain an overview of the implementation of judgments emanating from Strasbourg. Consequently, the report now contains information concerning the measures adopted to implement adverse Court judgments against the Netherlands; Pourgourides (2009), §§ 28-29. See also, in this connection, minutes from a hearing the LAHR held on Parliamentary Scrutiny of ECHR Standards in Paris, on 16 November 2009, Document AS/Jur (2010) 7 (available on the Committee's website) and Martin Kuijer, De betekenis van het Europees verdrag voor de rechten van de mens voor de nationale wetgever [The significance of the ECHR for the national legislator], in H. R. Schouter (ed.), Wetgever en constitutie [The legislator and the Constitution], proceedings of symposium of the Netherlands Association on Legislation and Legislative Policy, 23 April 2009, Nijmegen 2009, 44-86.

39   Recommendation Rec(2004)5 of the Committee of Ministers to member states on the verification of the compatibility of draft laws, existing laws and administrative practice with the standards laid down in the European Convention on Human Rights, adopted by the Committee of Ministers on 12 May 2004 at its 114th Session.

40   Secretariat of the LAHR Committee (2008), § 6.

41   Recommendation Rec(2004)5, 39.

Arguably of equal value to the direct effect which parliamentary supervision and scrutiny has on the implementation of judgments, is the impact which such involvement has on human rights discourse at a domestic level. Article 46 § 1 entrusts an essentially quasi-judicial function to an inter-governmental body, and is thus dependent on the will of sovereign states.[42] The political nature of the Committee of Ministers reveals limitations of the collective enforcement mechanism.[43] The strengthening of human rights culture at national level, reinforcing the principal of subsidiarity, is essential for ensuring the long-term effectiveness of the Convention system. National parliaments have an essential function to fulfil in this respect.

"The main contribution of Parliament to the process of protecting rights and creating a culture of human rights, apart from legislation, consists of using its influence and its scrutiny powers to keep human rights standards at the forefront of the minds of ministers and departments, regulators, and other public authorities. In this way Parliament can influence and encourage (or discourage) developments [...]."[44]

Scepticism may be expressed concerning the extent to which parliament is able to facilitate human rights discourse at a domestic level, particularly in political systems where the legislative branch is dominated by the executive. Emphasis on executive government, in political systems characterised by strict party discipline, can promote a political culture hostile to human rights considerations, which are perceived as an obstruction to government policy.[45] Despite the dominant role of the executive in Westminster, the United Kingdom's parliamentary Joint Committee on Human Rights has been instrumental in facilitating a political culture of rights.[46] Producing reports primarily motivated by principle, rather than partisan deliberations, the Joint Committee has increased parliamentary awareness of human rights standards, and created an expectation that government must account for its actions and justify proposals from a Convention perspective. The composition of the Joint Committee, equally constituted from both Houses of Parliament preventing government dominance, enables an approach independent of executive influence, which is essential if its observations are to exert any credible influence on parliamentarians.[47] The work of the Joint Committee has enabled greater transparency of parliamentary deliberation on Convention issues and has facilitated a human rights discourse between the legislature and executive. Such products of parliamentary scrutiny are essential for facilitating a human rights culture at the domestic level and ensuring adherence to the principle of subsidiarity as enshrined in the Convention system.

---

42 David Harris/Michael O'Boyle/Ed Bates/Carla Buckley, Harris, O'Boyle and Warbrick, Law of the European Convention on Human Rights, 2nd ed., Oxford 2009, 885.
43 Ibid., 886.
44 David Feldman, Can and Should Parliament Protect Human Rights?, European Public Law 10 (2004) 4, 651.
45 Janet L. Hiebert, Parliament and the Human Rights Act: Can the JCHR help facilitate a Culture of Rights?, International Journal of Constitutional Law (2006) 1, 11.
46 See generally Lord Lester of Herne Hill/Lord Pannick/Javan Herberg, Human Rights Law and Practice, London 2009, 871-886.
47 Hiebert (2006), 16.

Experience also suggests that national parliaments must possess an efficient "legal service" with specific Convention competence. Without such expertise at their disposal, parliamentarians cannot carry out this important work properly.

D   Concluding Observations

"Faced with a structural situation, the Court is in effect saying to the respondent state and to the Committee of Ministers that they too must play their role and assume their responsibilities."[48]

Debate concerning reform of the Convention system, and indeed proposals in this respect, have focused on increasing the effectiveness of the Court and the efficiency of the Committee of Ministers, as both bodies seek to reduce their backlog of applications and appropriate compliance with judgments, respectively. However, as already observed, the reforms proposed in Protocol No. 14 (which will at long-last enter into force on 1 June 2010) will not in themselves be sufficient to guarantee the long-term effectiveness of the Convention system.[49] Hence, the Swiss Government's initiative to discuss, at a special ministerial conference in Interlaken, on 18 and 19 February 2010, the future of the Convention system. Whether the Interlaken Declaration, together with an eight-point Action Plan adopted by ministers in Interlaken on 19 February 2010,[50] will provide sufficient political impetus to address domestic (non-)implementation of Convention standards and find solutions to ensure prompt and full compliance with Strasbourg Court judgments is difficult to foretell. Hence, the need for closely involving both the Parliamentary Assembly and national parliaments in the follow-up to the "Interlaken process".

Importantly, while the reforms may reduce worrying statistics, they will not guarantee substantially greater protection of human rights in Europe, the *raison d'être* of the Convention. An adverse judgment of the Court against a member state does not *per se* ensure justice for the victim or the prevention of future violations. Increased productivity on behalf of the Court will not necessarily translate into an equivalent rise in the number of judgments implemented within a reasonable period of time by member states. For the Convention system to func-

---

48   Luzius Wildhaber, Consequences for the European Court of Human Rights of Protocol No. 14 and the Resolution on Judgments Revealing an Underlying Systemic Problem – Practical Steps of Implementation and Challenges, in: Council of Europe, Applying and Supervising the ECHR: Reform of the European Human Rights System (2004), 26, http://www.coe.int/t/e/human_rights/1reformeurhrsystem_e.pdf.

49   Committee of Ministers (CM(2006)203), § 32;
      "Measures required to ensure the long-term effectiveness of the control system established by the ECHR in the broad sense are not restricted to Protocol No. 14. Measures must also be taken to prevent violations at national level and to improve domestic remedies, and also to enhance and execution of the ECtHR's judgments."
      (Explanatory Report to Protocol No. 14 to the Convention for the Protection of Human Rights and Fundamental Freedoms, amending the Control System of the Convention, § 14).

50   High Level Conference on the Future of the European Court of Human Rights, Interlaken Declaration, 19 February 2010, http://www.eda.admin.ch/etc/medialib/downloads/edazen/topics/europa/euroc.Par.0133.File.tmp/final_en.pdf.

tion effectively a balance must be struck between national protection and international supervision: at present Strasbourg is bearing a disproportionate burden. The Convention's subsidiary nature necessitates that if the long-term viability of its system is to be ensured, member states must strengthen domestic mechanisms for the protection of human rights.

While the emphasis for ensuring the effectiveness of the Convention must shift on to member states in accordance with the principle of subsidiarity, the Council of Europe is not helpless in securing its own future. Acknowledging that the problem of late and non-implementation is far graver and more widespread than previous reports of the Assembly have disclosed, Christos Pourgourides has committed to strengthening national parliamentary involvement in the execution of Court judgments. To this end the rapporteur is utilizing the double-mandate of his peers, as members of both the Assembly and their respective national parliament. Reinforcing parliamentary involvement in the execution process will require time. However, the rapporteur is uniquely placed in having an open-ended mandate. Parliamentary oversight of the implementation of judgments, and scrutiny of measures proposed for this purpose, is an important aspect in any mechanism for the effective execution of Strasbourg Court judgments. This obligation derives not only from Article 46 § 1 of the Convention, but from the constitutional responsibility of parliament, being composed of democratically elected representatives, to hold the executive to account. Strengthening the role of national parliaments in the execution process, will not only enhance the implementation of individual judgments, but will reinforce human rights culture in domestic politics. This is necessary if member states are to ensure the effective domestic protection of the rights and freedoms enshrined in the Convention and its protocols.

Rory O'CONNELL

Only Partial Neglect? Developments in the Case-Law of the European Court of Human Rights on Socio-Economic Rights of Non-Nationals

Table of Contents

Keywords

Social and economic rights, immigrants, non-nationals, European Convention on Human Rights

A   Introduction

This paper examines the extent to which the European Convention on Human Rights (ECHR) protects the socio-economic rights of non-nationals. In a sense these are rights that are doubly or even triply marginalized. Non-nationals face significant discrimination and disadvantage in their own right,[1] and there is still a tendency to see socio-economic rights as being tied to citizenship. Further, the ECHR tends to sideline socio-economic rights.

Section B considers the legal background, including how the ECHR text addresses socio-economic rights (B.1), and how the ECHR deals with non-nationals and non-discrimination (B.2). Section C explores the scope for using

---

1   Article 16 ECHR contemplates discrimination against non-nationals in political matters.

the ECHR to protect specific socio-economic rights of non-nationals. Section C.1 explains how the European Court of Human Rights has come to endorse the principle of non-discrimination on grounds of nationality in social security cases. Section C.2 considers the right to work, and highlights some of the unsatisfactory reasoning on non-discrimination in the recent *Bigaeva* case, though welcoming other aspects of that judgement. Sections C.3 and C.4 examine how the case law of the European Court offers some protection for other socio-economic rights of non-nationals. The Conclusion (D) stresses the need for more interpretative developments in this field. Specifically the ECHR text can be interpreted to give more protection to socio-economic rights, while the concepts of indirect discrimination and positive obligations remain underutilized.

B   Legal Background

1   Socio-Economic Rights in the Text of the ECHR

The Universal Declaration of Human Rights 1948 (UDHR) recognizes a wide range of rights including many socio-economic ones. The International Covenant on Economic, Social and Cultural Rights of 1966 (ICESCR) gives legal effect to these rights for the states party to the Covenant.[2] The rights listed in the ICESCR include, inter alia, the rights to work (Articles 6 and 7), to unionize and strike (Article 8), to social security (Article 9), to family life and support during childbirth (Article 10), to a standard of living (food, clothing and housing) (Article 11), health (Article 12) and education (Article 13).

By contrast the ECHR protects mainly civil and political rights, though it does include – albeit in the terminology of a liberal human rights conception – the right to freedom from forced labour (Article 4), family rights and the right to marry (Articles 8 and 12) the right to form unions (Article 11), the right to property (Protocol 1, Article 1) and the right to education (Protocol 1, Article 2). The main Council of Europe treaty dealing with economic and social rights is the European Social Charter 1961 (ESC 1961), revised in 1996 (ESC 1996). This document explicitly protects a range of economic and social rights, but the level of protection offered is unsatisfactory. The ESC has received much less publicity than the ECHR. States party to the ESC have the option (within certain limits) to pick and choose which rights to protect.[3] The original ESC did not provide for any sort of complaints mechanism; today the ESC allows for certain organizations to make collective complaints, but does not allow for individual complaints.[4] Again, not all states have ratified the revised ESC or accepted the collective complaints mechanisms.

---

2   Manisuli Ssenyonjo, Economic Social and Cultural Rights in International Law, Oxford 2009.

3   ESC 1996 Part III, Article A.

4   ESC 1996, Part IV, Article D referring to the earlier Additional Protocol to the ESC.

2 Treatment of Non-Nationals and Non-Discrimination in the Treaties

The ECHR guarantees rights to everyone within the jurisdiction of a ratifying state. In this it is similar to most human rights treaties,[5] though surprisingly its sister document, the ESC, is more restrictive.[6] However, as noted above the rights in the ECHR do not include all the socio-economic rights recognized in the UDHR or ICESCR. In some treaty systems such a gap might be partly filled through the existence of a freestanding equality clause, one which guarantees equality in the enjoyment of any legal right.[7] However, the non-discrimination right in the ECHR is not a free standing one. Article 14 ECHR prohibits distinctions in the enjoyment of Convention rights, on "any ground" (and goes on to name exemplary grounds, such as sex, race, colour, national or social origin, birth or "other status"), unless the state can offer an objective and reasonable justification for the distinction.[8]

Despite the apparent limitation that the non-discrimination principle in Article 14 ECHR applies to the enjoyment of Convention rights or within the "ambit" of

---

5   ICESCR protects the rights of "everyone", without discrimination on a range of grounds including national origin or other status (Article 2 § 2). Article 2 § 3 also includes an exemption for developing countries to determine the extent to which they will recognize the economic rights of non-nationals. The ICESCR Committee has recently confirmed that the ICESCR rights should be observed without any discrimination based on nationality or any status such as being a refugee, stateless person, migrant worker, etc. CESCR, General Comment No. 20 on Non-Discrimination in Economic, Social and Cultural Rights, UN Doc. E/C.12/GC/20, para. 30. See also CERD, General Recommendation No.30: Discrimination Against Non Citizens, 1 October 2004.

6   The Appendix to the ESC 1996 provides that the rights in the Charter apply to "foreigners only in so far as they are nationals of other Parties lawfully resident or working regularly within the territory of the Party concerned". This appears to be a sweeping exclusion, but caution is necessary. The European Committee on Social Rights has said that the Charter must be interpreted as a living instrument, and any restrictions on rights must be narrowly interpreted. The Committee will decide in what circumstances the exclusion in the Appendix will apply compatibly with human rights principles: European Committee of Social Rights, International Federation for Human Rights (FIDH) v. France, 8 September 2004, no. 14/2003 (2004), at paras. 27-32. It is noteworthy however that Article 19 of the ESC 1996 has detailed provisions on the rights of migrant workers. Whilst these rights only apply to nationals of states party to the ESC, this may include countries not in the EU, most notably Iceland, Norway, FYROM and Turkey.

7   An example of this is Article 26 of the International Covenant on Civil and Political Rights (ICCPR), which has sometimes been used to promote equality in the field of socio-economic rights. See for example Human Rights Committee, Zwaan de Vries v. Netherlands, 9 April 1987, Selected Decisions under the Optional Protocol 2 (1987), 209; Human Rights Committee, Broeks v. Netherlands, 9 April 1987, Selected Decisions under the Optional Protocol 2 (1987), 196.

8   The Council of Europe has adopted a Protocol 12 to the ECHR which would introduce a free standing right to freedom from discrimination. However, as of 1 January 2010, only 17 countries have ratified Protocol 12 and the ECtHR has handed down only one judgment based on this Protocol: ECtHR, Sejdic v. Bosnia and Herzegovina, judgment (GC) of 22 December 2009, nos. 27996/06 and 34836/06. Unless otherwise noted, all cases cited hereinafter are from the ECtHR.

ECHR rights, the ECtHR has given it an expansive interpretation. Article 14 may be violated even in cases where the substantive Convention right has not been violated. For example, there is no ECHR right to free civil legal aid in Article 6 ECHR (right to a fair hearing), but if the state creates such a system it must avoid unjustified discrimination on grounds of nationality.[9]

Furthermore, Article 14 does not exhaustively enumerate the prohibited grounds for discrimination ("such as") and contains the explicit referral to "other status". This open-ended quality means that it covers discrimination on grounds of nationality (among many other grounds).

The remainder of this paper discusses how individual non-nationals may be able to protect their socio-economic rights by using the ECHR. The paper focuses on the jurisprudence of the European Court of Human Rights (ECtHR), though also drawing on some case-law from the United Kingdom where the courts have interpreted ECHR rights under the Human Rights Act 1998. Sometimes non-nationals have been able to invoke one of the ECHR's explicitly specified socio-economic rights. In other cases, the ECtHR has extended its interpretation of Convention rights to include social and economic dimensions.[10] Finally, even where a Convention right does not implicitly protect socio-economic interests, such interests may nevertheless be within the "ambit" of a Convention right, thus allowing the non-discrimination principle in Article 14 to be brought into play.

C   Social and Economic Rights

1   Right to Social Security

There are several situations where Convention rights do not expressly protect a socio-economic right, but it nevertheless comes within the ambit of a Convention right and so the non-discrimination obligation applies.

For instance, there is no right to social security in the ECHR. However, in the 1996 case of *Gaygasuz v. Austria* the ECtHR held that decisions not to pay a particular welfare payment will fall within the ambit of the right to property if the welfare payment is based on contributions, rather than merely being funded by general taxation.[11] For a number of years there were arguments as to whether it was necessary for a benefit to be contribution-based to be within the ambit of the

---

9   Anakomba Yula v. Belgium (legal aid), no. 45413/07, judgment of 10 March 2009.

10   Eva Brems, Indirect Protection of Social Rights by the ECtHR, in: Daphne Barak-Erez and Ayeal Gross (eds.) Exploring Social Rights, Oxford, 2007; Rory O'Connell, Social and Economic Rights in the European Convention of Human Rights in: Rule of Law and Fundamental Rights of Citizens: The European and American Conventions on Human Rights (Alfa Dikia II Project 2006-2008), London 2009; Luke Clements and Alan Simmons, European Court of Human Rights in: Malcolm Langford (ed.), Social Rights Jurisprudence: Emerging Trends in International and Comparative Law, Cambridge 2009; Frédéric Sudre, Exercise de jurisprudence-fiction: la protection des droits sociaux par la Cour européenne des droits de l'homme and Françoise Tulkens, Les droits sociaux dans la jurisprudence de la nouvelle Cour européenne des droits de l'homme, in: Constance Grewe/Florence Benoît-Rohmer (eds.), Les droits sociaux ou la démolition de quelques poncifs, Strasbourg 2003.

11   Gaygusuz v. Austria, EHRR 23 (1996), 364.

right to property.[12] In *Stec v. UK*, an admissibility decision in 2005, the ECtHR extended the ambit of property rights to cover any social welfare payment, even non-contributory ones, thus demanding that they respect the non-discrimination principle.[13] The later Grand Chamber judgment on the merits did not disturb this aspect of the admissibility decision.[14]

The decision that social security payments fall within the ambit of the right to property is a very important one, as the ECtHR has said that discrimination based on nationality is extremely suspect and will therefore be very difficult to justify. The *Gaygasuz* case itself concerned nationality-based discrimination.[15] Gaygasuz would have been entitled to emergency unemployment assistance but for the fact that he did not have Austrian nationality. The ECtHR briefly concluded that Austria could not demonstrate any objective and reasonable justification for the difference in treatment, brushing aside (without actually addressing) the argument that the state owed a special duty of protection to its own nationals.[16] The ECtHR was also unimpressed with the argument that Austria had no treaty with Turkey providing for reciprocity in this area: such a situation could not detract from the obligation to secure the enjoyment of Convention rights to everyone within her jurisdiction.[17]

During 2009, the ECtHR has considered different cases involving nationality-based discrimination in relation to social security.[18] The strongest guidance in this area comes from a case with an unusual background, *Andrejeva v. Latvia.*[19]

The case arose from the process by which Latvia separated itself from the Soviet Union. The applicant had moved to Latvia in 1954 at the age of 15. She worked in Latvia since 1966. For certain periods she was assigned to departments in parts of the USSR outside of Latvia, though continuing to work in Latvia itself. She worked in Latvia after it gained its independence in 1990, though now she was officially a stateless person. When she sought a pension upon retire-

---

12   See Koua Poirrez v. France, no. 40892/98, judgment of 30 September 2003, where the ECtHR ruled that a failure to pay a non-national disability benefit violated Article 14 in combination with Article 1 of Protocol 1. One judge dissented on the grounds that the benefit was not contribution-based (though he ruled there was a violation anyway as the matter fell within the ambit of Article 8).

13   Stec v. United Kingdom, Decision of 6 July 2005, no. 65900/01, EHRR 41 (2005), SE18, paras. 47-55.

14   Stec v. United Kingdom, judgment of 12 April 2006, no. 65900/01, EHRR 43 (2006), 47.

15   Gaygusuz v. Austria, EHRR 23 (1996), 364.

16   Ibid., paras. 42-52.

17   Ibid., para. 51. Koua Poirrez demonstrates this strong approach. France did not provide a disability benefit to certain adult foreigners unless their country of origin had a treaty making reciprocal provision for French citizens. Foreigners whose country of origin did have such a treaty could receive the benefit. The ECtHR ruled this was not an acceptable distinction: France was obliged to secure the rights of everyone within their jurisdiction. See.Koua Poirrez v. France, judgment of 30 September 2003, no. 40892/98. See also Luczak v. Poland, judgment of 27 November 2007, no. 77782/01.

18   Weller v. Hungary, judgment of 31 March 2009, no. 44399/05. Hungary provided maternity payments to parents of children where the mother was a Hungarian national and the father a foreigner, but not where the mother was a foreigner. This was a violation of Article 14 combined with Article 8. See also Zeibek v. Greece, judgment of 9 July 2009, no. 46368/06.

19   Andrejeva v. Latvia, judgment of 18 February 2009, no. 55707/00.

ment, she was told that, being a foreigner or stateless person, only the periods she worked in Latvia would count towards her pension – this excluded a period of some 15 years.

The majority of the Grand Chamber considered the issue as a simple one of principle. The applicant was treated differently based solely on her nationality. Latvia had refused to pay a pension in respect of work done outside of Latvia by the applicant, a resident non-citizen; if she had been a Latvian citizen the pension would have been paid. Any such nationality based discrimination would have to be justified by "very weighty reasons".[20] According to the Court there was nothing to demonstrate any objective difference between her situation and that of a national. The Court rejected the argument that there was no treaty in place to regulate the situation: states undertook to secure Convention rights to everyone within their jurisdiction; further the Court rejected the argument that the applicant could have become a naturalized Latvian citizen.[21]

The case is striking because the Court could have decided it on a much narrower basis. It could for instance have put more stress on the fact that the applicant was a stateless person and no other state could assume responsibility for her. The Court referred to this feature, but its reasoning did not turn on this.[22] Similarly the Court might have found it was not justifiable to conclude that the applicant should have been treated as working outside of Latvia, but the Court did not go down that route either.[23] One has to agree with the sole dissenting judge that the judgement sends a "strong message" that social security laws must not discriminate on grounds of nationality, residence or other status "unless some truly weighty justifications are provided."[24]

Despite this strong decision of the Grand Chamber, it is not always the case that every nationality-based distinction in any payment made by the state to individuals is a violation of the Convention. First, the ECtHR does not regard every payment made by the state to an individual as falling within social security. For instance, Germany established a system for compensating some victims of World War II, but the scheme excluded former prisoners of war. The ECtHR ruled that such a one-off payment, made in relation to events dating to before the coming into force of the Convention, did not amount to a social security-type payment and so did not fall within the scope of Article 1 of Protocol 1.[25]

Second, it is not the case that discrimination based on nationality or national origin can never be justified. The ECtHR has accepted that a state may charge a reduced fee for a residence permit where someone has a close connection with the country because of national origin (as opposed to someone with a more distant connection). This is because there are "in general persuasive social reasons for giving special treatment to those who have a special link with a country" when it comes to matters of residence.[26]

---

20   Ibid., para. 87
21   Ibid., paras. 90-91.
22   Ibid., para. 88.
23   Ibid., para. 85.
24   Para. 42 of the partly dissenting opinion of Judge Ziemele.
25   Associazione Nazionale Reduci dalla Prigionia dall'Internamento e dalla Guerra di liberazione v. Germany Application no. 45563/04, judgment of 4 September 2007.
26   Ponomaryov v. Bulgaria Application no. 5335/05, Decision of 18 September 2007. The Court decided that this part of the complaint was inadmissible.

Finally on social security, we should note that non-nationals may be able to benefit from the ECHR to vindicate their socio-economic rights not only against their host state but also against their home state. While the focus of this paper is on situations where a host state denies the socio-economic rights of non-nationals, it appears that the Convention can be invoked in certain cases where the home state denies certain benefits to nationals on the grounds that they are resident abroad. The ECtHR has recently decided a case dealing with the payment of British pensions to pension-holders residing abroad. The ECtHR concluded that the failure to index-link pensions paid to persons abroad did not violate Article 14.[27] This case has now gone to the Grand Chamber.

To conclude our discussion of the right to social security, 2009 saw the Grand Chamber firmly approve the proposition that there should be no nationality-based discrimination in social security matters, absent weighty justification.

2   Right to Work

The ECHR does not explicitly recognize the right to work. However, it is still possible for the ECHR to be brought into play in right to work-type cases. For example, the ECHR does recognize one of the minimum core requirements of the right to work, the right to be free from slavery, servitude, forced or compulsory labour (Article 4). This right, like other Convention rights can be exercized by everyone, and so non-nationals may benefit from its protection.

This is exemplified by the *Siliadin* case.[28] Siliadin was a Togolese national who arrived in France at the age of 15. A French couple seized her passport, and "lent" her to another couple to perform unpaid housework and childcare. The couple never paid her and expected her to work seven days a week, her working day lasting from 7.30 in the morning to 10.30 in the evening. The couple did nothing about her immigration status or education. This lasted for a period of about three years and ended with the police prosecuting the couple. The domestic courts subsequently ordered the couple to pay compensation to the applicant; however, for procedural reasons it was not possible to impose a criminal sanction on the couple. The ECtHR ruled that France had violated its positive obligations under Article 4. The violations of the applicant's Article 4 rights were so severe that there should be an effective criminal law remedy, as well as compensation. For our purposes this case demonstrates that non-nationals, even those who are not regularly present and working in a state, may successfully invoke Convention rights.

Apart from Article 4, Article 8's ambit also arguably extends into the field of employment. This is clear from case-law involving sweeping exclusion from certain fields of private employment in respect of people formerly associated with an undemocratic Communist regime. In several cases, the ECtHR has ruled that such measures violate Article 8 in combination with Article 14.[29] These cases suggest that the Convention may protect a right to a "private professional life".[30]

---

27   Carson v. United Kingdom, no. 42184/05, judgment of 4 November 2008.

28   Siliadin v. France, judgment of 26 July 2005, no. 73316/01, EHRR 43 (2006), 16.

29   ECtHR Sidabras v. Lithuania, judgment of 27 July 2004, no. 59330/00, EHRR 42 (2006), 6.

30   Jean-Pierre Marguénaud/Jean Mouly, Le droit de gagner sa vie par le travail devant la Cour européenne des droits de l'homme, Paris 2006, 477.

Against this though, there is some authority in the Chamber decision of *Bigaeva v. Greece* that a discriminatory exclusion from one profession would not engage Article 14 since the Convention does not guarantee the freedom to exercise a certain profession.[31] Here a Russian national had moved to Greece in 1993, learned the language and studied law at undergraduate and postgraduate levels. She was allowed to undertake an eighteen month placement as part of the process of becoming a lawyer, even though she was ineligible to qualify due to her nationality. Subsequently, she was not allowed to qualify as a lawyer. The ECtHR held that Article 8 was applicable[32] and had been violated. The position of the public authorities lacked 'coherence' according to the ECtHR.[33] They had permitted her to complete an eighteen month placement even though she did not meet the nationality requirement, and so could not deny her the benefit now.[34]

The Chamber rejected the applicant's Article 14 argument. The Chamber noted that the Convention did not guarantee a right to exercise a particular profession; further the profession of a lawyer was one closely related to the administration of justice and so there were particular limits on lawyers.[35] Accordingly, states were entitled to a large margin of appreciation; the decision to impose a nationality requirement did not by itself amount to a "discriminatory distinction" between the different categories of persons.[36]

The reasoning of the Chamber in *Bigaeva* is open to challenge. It is not entirely clear whether the Chamber believes that Article 14 is not engaged, that there is no distinction or that there is a distinction but it is justified given the wide margin of appreciation appropriate in the case. The last reason seems the most plausible explanation. It is difficult to accept that Article 8 was not engaged for the purposes of Article 14 since the Court actually found a violation of Article 8. Further the reference to the absence of a "discriminatory distinction" most likely means that there is no "unjustifiable" distinction. Even assuming that the Chamber is addressing the issue on the question of justification, the generous margin of appreciation accorded to the State in setting conditions for access to the legal profession seems out of line with the statement in other Article 14 cases that nationality discrimination is very hard to justify.[37] Further the case is disappointing in not drawing on comparative jurisprudence on nationality discrimination. There is no reference to the landmark decision of the Canadian Supreme Court in *Andrews* which found that a nationality restriction on access to the legal profession violated the right to equality in the Canadian Charter.[38]

Notwithstanding these disappointments *Bigaeva* has some positive dimensions. The applicant in *Bigaeva* was a Russian national. Neither European Community law nor the European Social Charter would have offered any straightforward redress in the situation, whereas she was able to win on the Article 8 argument in Strasbourg.

---

31   Bigaeva v. Greece, judgment of 28 May 2009, no. 26713/05.
32   Ibid., para. 24.
33   Ibid., para. 35.
34   Ibid., para. 33.
35   Ibid., para. 39.
36   Ibid., para. 40.
37   Gaygusuz v. Austria 23 EHRR (1996) 364, para. 42.
38   Supreme Court of Canada, Andrews v. Law Society of British Columbia 56 Dominion Law Reports (1989) (4th ed.), 1.

3 Right to a Certain Standard of Living, Food, Clothing and Housing, and Right to Health

The ECHR does not explicitly protect the right to an adequate standard of living or the right to health. Nevertheless it is possible that in certain cases extreme denial of these rights might violate Article 3 (freedom from torture, inhuman or degrading treatment) or Article 8 (right to respect for private and family life, and home). These rights require the provision of resources to meet basic human needs when non-nationals are being detained in centres pending their removal from the state.[39] During 2009, the ECtHR has found a breach of Article 3 because of the conditions of detention of an asylum seeker in Greece: detaining an asylum seeker for two months in a centre without the ability to leave, without access to clean sheets and blankets or sufficient hygiene products, amounted to degrading treatment.[40]

Articles 3 and 8 clearly apply when the state detains non-nationals (or anyone else). Do they have any purchase in non-detention cases? A decision of the UK House of Lords (then still sitting as the UK's highest court) demonstrates the potential of Article 3 in this area. The case, *Limbuela*, concerned UK asylum and immigration law.[41] Section 55 of the UK Nationality, Immigration and Asylum Act 2002 allows for welfare support to be denied to asylum seekers if they do not claim asylum as soon as "reasonably practicable" upon arrival. Section 55 (5) however provides that support shall still be provided if this is necessary to prevent a breach of Convention rights as protected by the UK's Human Rights Act 1998. The House of Lords ruled that reducing an asylum seeker to a state of destitution, of such a severity that one can speak of inhuman or degrading treatment, violated Article 3 ECHR.

Even if Article 3 or Article 8 is not violated, a failure to ensure an adequate standard of living may come within the ambit of a Convention right, and so the non-discrimination principle would apply. This is seen in the UK case of *Morris*. The UK Housing Act 1996 declared that, when determining housing priority, a local authority should disregard a child who is subject to immigration control. The courts found that this was unjustified discrimination on grounds of nationality and issued a declaration of incompatibility.[42]

Non-nationals' right to an adequate standard of living or right to health might be endangered by deportation or extradition to a state where these rights would not be so well observed. Individual non-nationals have no ECHR right to enter or remain within a state.[43] In certain situations the ECHR prevents the deportation or extradition of non-nationals. Typically, this is where the non-national faces a risk of torture in his or her home country; or where the non-national has estab-

---

39   Riad and Idiab v. Belgium, judgment of 24 January 2008, no. 29810/03.

40   S.D. v. Greece, judgment of 11 June 2009, no. 53541/07, para. 51.

41   House of Lords, R (Limbuela) v. Secretary of State for the Home Department, [2005] UKHL 66, Appeal Cases 1 (2006), 396.

42   Court of Appeal (Civil Division) of England and Wales, R. (Morris) v. Westminster City Council [2005] EWCA Civ 1184, judgment of 14 October 2005. See also High Court of England and Wales, R (Gabaj) v. First Secretary of State, judgment of 28 March 2006.

43   Article 3 of Protocol 4 prohibits the expulsion of nationals. Article 4 of the same Protocol prohibits the collective expulsion of non-nationals. Article 1 of Protocol 7 establishes certain procedural safeguards concerning expulsion of non-nationals.

lished such links in the host country that it would be a disproportionate violation of the right to private and family life to remove him or her.[44]

It is clear that a non-national can invoke the rights not to be killed or tortured to argue against deportation or extradition. What of the situation where a non-national's socio-economic rights will be denied in the receiving state? In one extreme situation, it has been held that a non-national cannot be deported to his country of origin, if he is seriously ill with a terminal illness and his home state has much inferior medical facilities.[45] Subsequent cases have established that this was an exceptional case.[46]

4   Other Social Rights: Family Rights, Right to Education

Despite the view that the ECHR protects mainly civil and political rights, some social rights are explicitly protected. These include the right to respect for family life (Article 8), the right to marry (Article 12) and the right to education (Article 2 of Protocol 1). Non-nationals can benefit from these rights whenever they are "within [the] jurisdiction" (Article 1) of a state party.

In extreme cases violations of family rights might violate Article 3. This was the situation in the appalling case of *Mayeka and Mitunga v. Belgium*.[47] A Congolese national, recognized as a refugee in Canada, sought to bring her five-year-old daughter to join her. Her brother brought the daughter via Brussels airport, where it was discovered that she had no travel documents. The five-year-old was detained in an adult detention centre in Belgium, separated from her mother. Her mother could only contact her by telephone. The child was then deported back to the Congo without anyone being able to meet her at the airport. The mother was only told after the event. The ECtHR found that both the treatment of the child, but also the worry inflicted on the mother, amounted to a violation of Article 3.

The UK courts have considered the right of non-nationals to get married in the *Baiai* case.[48] UK legislation required non-EU nationals to obtain the consent of the Home Secretary before they could get married (unless they were getting married according to the rites of the Church of England). This astonishing restriction was introduced to prevent marriages of convenience designed to obtain some sort of immigration advantage. In fact, the Home Secretary consented in the majority of cases (86 % of cases during a 14 month period).[49] The UK courts considered that combating marriages of convenience was a legitimate aim but this particular measure was disproportionate. The House of Lords concluded that the statute had to be read as if it required the Home Secretary to consent unless there was evidence that the proposed marriage was a sham.[50]

---

44   Ruth Rubio-Marín and Rory O'Connell, The European Convention and the Relative Rights of Resident Aliens, European Law Journal, 5 (1999) 4.
45   D. v. United Kingdom, EHRR, 24 (1997), 423.
46   N. v. United Kingdom, judgment of 27 May 2008 (GC), no. 26565/05.
47   Mayeka and Mitunga v. Belgium, judgment of 12 October 2006, no. 13178/03.
48   House of Lords, R (Baiai) v. Secretary of State for the Home Department, judgment of 30 July 2008, [2008] UKHL 53, Appeal Cases 1 (2008), 287.
49   Ibid., para. 43.
50   Ibid., para. 32.

D   Conclusions

Despite obvious shortcomings, the ECHR offers some protections for non-nationals in the area of socio-economic rights. 2009's main ECtHR decisions on this question present a mixed message. *Andrejeva* – a nearly unanimous Grand Chamber judgement – offers strong affirmation of the principle that discrimination on grounds of nationality in social security is prohibited by the ECHR. In *Bigaeva*, a Russian national won a finding that there had been an arbitrary interference with her Article 8 rights, in relation to her ambition to become a lawyer in Greece. On the other hand, the Article 14 discussion in *Bigaeva* is rather disappointing.

The mixed messages are worrying given the nature, extent and severity of discrimination against non-nationals that is revealed in the case-law. It is astonishing that a country like the United Kingdom might choose to impose special restrictions on the right to marry of certain immigrants, and even more extraordinary that the same state might deny welfare benefits to asylum seekers who did not immediately declare their status upon arrival in the UK. The ECtHR was right to criticize France in the *Siliadin* case, but that tale of servitude and mistreatment is only one story among many in Europe.[51] That Belgium might detain a five year old girl in a detention centre for adults shows a "lack of humanity";[52] that the state would deport such a child to an airport in the Congo without ensuring that a relative was there to meet her demonstrates a "total lack of humanity".[53]

Even on an optimistic reading of the case-law, there is still more that could be done to further the protection of the socio-economic rights of non-nationals under the Convention. First, the process by which socio-economic rights or interests have been protected under the ECHR needs further development. Certainly there are limits on how far the ECHR may protect such rights, but those limits have not yet been reached. Contrary to what the Court said in *Bigaeva*, there is certainly scope for the Article 8 right to protect the right to pursue a livelihood.

Second, much of the case-law has so far involved *direct* discrimination on grounds of nationality. This is welcome, but it can only be a first step. Equality cannot be assured unless indirect discrimination is also tackled. For a long time the ECtHR had a poor record on indirect discrimination but in 2007 the Grand Chamber handed down an important ruling in *DH v. Czech Republic* and found an indirect race discrimination,[54] a significant step in developing a more substantive equality jurisprudence.[55] Distinctions based for example on language or residence or the possession of a certain level of education or of professional qualifications are also indirectly based on nationality.

---

51   Parliamentary Assembly of the Council of Europe, Recommendation 1663 (2004): Domestic slavery: servitude, au pairs and "mail-order brides", http://assembly.coe.int/main.asp?Link=/documents/adoptedtext/ta04/erec1663.htm.
52   Mayeka and Mitunga, para. 58.
53   Ibid., para. 69.
54   D.H. v. Czech Republic, judgment of 13 November 2007 (GC), no. 57325/00, EHRR 47 (2008), 3.
55   Rory O'Connell, Cinderella comes to the Ball: Article 14 and the right to non-discrimination in the ECHR, Legal Studies: The Journal of the Society of Legal Scholars, 29 (2009), 211.

Third, there is scope to develop the positive obligations in this field. These might include provision of special language classes for immigrants or their children in the education system, or provision of translation services.

These are only three obvious steps that could be taken under the ECHR, if suitable cases are brought, and the ECtHR is so minded. If such steps are not taken then the achievements so far under the ECHR may seem, at best, a false promise; at worst, an ideological fig leaf that distracts from the extent and severity of discrimination against non-nationals.[56]

---

[56] See, for example, the criticism of the ECtHR's jurisprudence on race discrimination in Marie-Bénédicte Dembour, Still Silencing the Racism Suffered by Migrants ... The Limits of Current Developments Under Article 14 ECHR, European Journal of Migration and Law, 11 (2009), 221-234. Since the writing of this paper, the ECtHR has handed down three important decisions. In *Rantsev v. Cyprus and Russia*, the ECtHR identified several positive obligations on states to tackle people trafficking, including an obligation to reform immigration laws and an obligation on states to co-operate in investigations into people trafficking: Application no. 25965/04, 7 January 2010, Chamber. In *Oršuš and others v. Croatia*, the Grand Chamber recognized a positive obligation to provide language assistance for Roma students so that they can join mainstream school classes: Application no. 15766/03, 16 March 2010, GC. Finally, the Grand Chamber confirmed the Chamber decision in *Carson: Carson v. United Kingdom*, Application no. 42184/05, 16 March 2010, GC.

Joachim RENZIKOWSKI[*]

Coming to Terms with One's Past: the Strasbourg Court's Recent Case-Law on Article 7 ECHR and Retroactive Criminal Liability

Table of Contents

Keywords

Nulla poena sine lege, retroactive punishment, crimes against humanity, war crimes, European Court of Human Rights

A   Introduction

When a legal system in a state changes, the question of transitional criminal justice often poses a fundamental problem. The desire of victims of the previous, unjust system to punish their tormentors is all too comprehensible and already the International Military Tribunal, in the Nuremberg cases against selected representatives of the Nazi regime, stated that "[i]t would be unjust if his wrong were allowed to go unpunished."[1] However, the generally recognized principle of *nulla poena sine lege* requires that criminal liability must already exist at the moment when a criminal act is committed. Otherwise a sanction would not be punishment for a crime but rather revenge.[2] In its judgement on the firing order at the inner

---

[*]   The author would like to express his gratitude to Wolfram Karl, Lisa Heschl and Matthias C. Kettemann for their support in finalizing the present contribution.

[1]   International Military Tribunal, Göring et al., judgment of 1 October 1946, International Military Tribunal, vol. 1, Nuremberg 1947, at 219.

[2]   See Thomas Hobbes, Leviathan or The Matter, Forme, & Power of a Common-Wealth Ecclesiasticall and Civill, London 1651, Chap. XXVIII: "Harme inflicted for a Fact done before there was a Law that forbad it, is not Punishment, but an act of Hostility."

German border, the ECtHR recognized that the subjective foreseeability of criminal liability was the precondition for a punishment in accordance with the ECHR.[3]

If the national criminal law in force at the time the crime was committed foresees adequate penalties the principle of non-retroactivity is not affected. Still, for the authorities responsible for the former repression and their accomplices the reassessment of their acts under henceforth constitutional standards may well appear as the retroactive re-interpretation of the former law. However, the ECtHR ruled in the Grand Chamber cases *Streletz, Kessler* and *Krenz v. Germany* and *K.H.W. v. Germany,* that a legitimate expectation of the future impunity of a crime cannot be deduced from the factual temporary non-application of a law.[4] Since the Court treats positive law and legal practice as a unity,[5] the decisive point is whether the adjustment to new societal conditions – permissible as it was – could be foreseen by the person concerned.[6] The Court found this precondition to be fulfilled in the case of the firing order at the inner German border. Moreover, it stated that the firing order had even been inconsistent with the applicable law of the former German Democratic Republic (GDR). The contradicting state practice is irrelevant in the light of the Constitution of the former GDR and the International Covenant on Civil and Political Rights.[7] Thus, the punishment was foreseeable for the members of the State Council of the former GDR who implemented the unlawful system at the inner German border despite their knowledge of the breach of constitutional and international law. But not even a mere soldier can be absolved from his blind obedience to commands outrageously violating constitutional and human rights.[8] Consequently, the Court

---

3   ECtHR, Streletz, Kessler and Krentz, judgement of 22 March 2001 (GC), RJD 2001-II, paras. 50, 77-89; K.H.W., judgment of 22 March 2001 (GC), paras. 45, 68-91; see also Helmut Kreicker, Art. 7 EMRK und die Gewalttaten an der deutsch-deutschen Grenze, Berlin 2002, 46 et seq. Unless otherwise noted, all judgments are from the ECtHR.

4   Streletz, Kessler and Krentz (2001), paras. 78-79; K.H.W. (2001), para. 82; see also Glässner, decision of 28 June 2001, RJD 2001-VII, concerning a case of perversion of justice; Ireneu Cabral Baretto, La jurisprudence de la nouvelle Cour européenne des Droits de l'Homme sur l'article 7 de la Convention européenne des Droits de l'Homme, in: Andreas Donatsch (ed.), Strafrecht, Strafprozessrecht und Menschenrechte. Festschrift für Stefan Trechsel, Zurich 2002, 3, 13 et seq.

5   See Kokkinakis, judgment of 25 May 1993, Series A/260-A, paras. 40, 52; K.A. and A.D., judgment of 17 February 2005, para. 52; Jorgic, judgment of 12 July 2007, para. 101; cf. also Paul Tavernier, L'actualité du principe de non-rétroactivité dans le cadre de la Convention européenne des Droits de l'Homme, in: Jean-François/ Michéle De Salvia (eds.), La Convention européenne des droits de l'homme: développements récents et nouveaux défis; actes de la journée d'études du 30 novembre 1996 organisée à l'Institut des hautes études européennes de Strasbourg à la mémoire de Marc-André Eissen, Strasbourg 1997, 113, 131 et seq.; Joachim Renzikowski, Kommentar zu Art. 7 EMRK in: Wolfram Karl (ed.), Internationaler Kommentar zur Europäischen Menschenrechtskonvention, Cologne 2009, Art. 7, n. 53.

6   Essentially, S.W., judgment of 22 November 1995, Series A/335-B, paras. 37-47; C.R., judgment of 22 November 1995, Series A/355-C, paras. 35-44.

7   Streletz, Kessler and Krentz (2001), paras. 57-75, 90-105; K.H.W. (2001), paras. 52-67, 92-105; see also UN Commission on Human Rights, Baumgarten, decision of 31 July 2003, paras. 9.3-9.5, EuGRZ 2004, 143, 149 et seq.

8   Streletz, Kessler and Krentz (2001), paras. 78; K.H.W. (2001), paras. 75 and 81.

approved the conviction of the applicants by German courts and did not find a breach of the principle of non-retroactivity of Article 7 ECHR.[9]

If the conviction cannot be based on a domestic criminal law in force at the time the crime was committed, the legal situation changes fundamentally. In these cases, Article 7 ECHR allows resort to international law. According to Article 7 § 1 ECHR, domestic criminal law may be complemented by international law encompassing, firstly, international treaties including treaties requiring the signatory states to enact corresponding domestic criminal law and those introducing self-executing provisions on criminal offences, and secondly, criminal offences acknowledged by customary international law.[10] Article 7 § 1 leaves the decision to prosecute crimes against international law to the state parties to the Convention, while enabling them at the same time to apply corresponding domestic criminal law retroactively.[11]

§ 2, on the other hand, refers to the "general principles of law recognised by civilized nations". The main intention of this so-called "Nuremberg Clause" was to justify the allied war crime tribunals.[12] However, it also incorporates the generalizable principle that grave breaches of human rights shall not remain unpunished because the effective law at the time did not contain pertinent criminal offence. In the strict sense this provision does not imply an exception from the prohibition of *ex post facto* penal laws since the "general principles of law" must have been in force at the time when the acts were committed. Consequently, retroactive international customary law constituting crime offences is forbidden.[13] Still, the relation between § 1 and § 2 remains unclear.[14]

---

9   Cf. Kreicker (2002), 5; Wolfgang Naucke, Bürgerliche Kriminalität, Staatskriminalität und Rückwirkungsverbot, Festschrift für Stefan Trechsel (2002), 505, 507 et seq.; Christian Starck, Die Todesschüsse an der innerdeutschen Grenze, Juristenzeitung 56 (2001), 1102, 1105 et seq.; Gerhard Werle, Rückwirkungsverbot und Staatskriminalität, Neue Juristische Wochenschrift, 2001, 3001, 3007 et seq.; critically Ben Juratowitch, Retroactive Criminal Liability and International Human Rights Law, British Yearbook of International Law 75 (2004), 337, 345 et seq.; Markus Rau, Deutsche Vergangenheitsbewältigung vor dem EGMR – Hat der Rechtsstaat gesiegt?, Neue Juristische Wochenschrift 2001, 3008, 3010 et seq.; generally, Renzikowski (2009), Art. 7, n. 80 et seq.

10 For details, see David Harris/Michael O'Boyle/Colin Warbrick, Law of the European Convention on Human Rights, Oxford, 2nd ed. 2009, 336; Renzikowski (2009), Art. 7, n. 86 et seq.

11 Edwin Bleichrodt in: Pieter Van Dijk/Godefridus J. H. Van Hoof (eds.), Theory and Practice of the European Convention on Human Rights, The Hague et al., 4th ed. 2006, 661.

12 Travaux Préparatoires, vol. 3, 194, 262; Harris/O'Boyle/Warbrick (2009), 339.

13 Renzikowski (2009), Art. 7, n. 82; see also Kononov, judgment of 24 July 2008, para. 119.

14 On the one hand it is supposed, that the general principles are already part of international law under § 1 and consequently § 2 has merely a declaratory meaning, see Christoph Grabenwarter, Europäische Menschenrechtskonvention, Munich, 4th ed. 2009, § 24 n. 135; Bleichrodt, in: Van Dijk/Van Hoof (eds.) (2006), 660 et seq. On the other hand, § 2 is attributed an original content, see Antonio Cassese, Balancing the Prosecution of Crimes against Humanity and Non-Retroactivity of Criminal Law, Journal of International Criminal Justice 4 (2006), 410, 415; Harris/O'Boyle/Warbrick (2009), 338 et seq.; Juratovich (2004), 360 et seq.; Kreicker (2002), 96 et seq.; in favour there is the suggestion that Article 38 § 1 (c) of the ICJ Statute treats the "general principles of law recognised by civilized nations" as a third source of international law beside the treaty law and the customary law. These principles are

To date the ECtHR has dealt on three occasions with the compatibility of the penalization of Stalinist crimes and the prohibition of *ex post facto* penal laws. Its jurisprudence on these cases has been met with harsh criticism.[15] The pertinent decisions in relation to criminal proceedings in Estonia, Latvia and Hungary will be analyzed in the following.

B   Recent Case-law on Retroactive Criminal Liability in Eastern Europe

1   *Kolk* and *Kislyiy v. Estonia*

The applicants had participated at the organizational and bureaucratic level in the preparation and execution of the deportation of many thousands of civilians from Estonia to remote areas of the Soviet Union in March 1949. On 10 October 2003, the applicants were convicted of crimes against humanity under Article 61-1 § 1 of the Estonian *Kriminaalkoodeks* to eight years suspended imprisonment. Both complained under Article 7 ECHR that they had been punished on the basis of a retroactive application of criminal law. The relevant criminal provision was only introduced in the Estonian Criminal Code in 1994 after the restoration of independence in 1991 and was valid irrespective of the time the offence was committed, whereas the Soviet Penal Code in force in 1949 had not identified the acts in question as criminal offences.

In its decision the ECtHR referred to Article 6 (c) of the Charter of the Nuremberg Tribunal, as confirmed by Resolution 95 of the UN General Assembly, adopted on 11 December 1946. Hence, the responsibility for crimes against humanity had universal validity and could not be limited to the nationals of certain countries or to acts committed within the specific time frame of the Second World War. The conflicting Soviet law of that time was to be disregarded, especially since the Soviet Union was a member state of the United Nations.[16] The Court interpreted Article 7 § 2 ECHR to mean that all civilized nations recognized crimes against humanity indepedently of a statute of limitations.[17] The retroactive application of domestic criminal law could consequently not be used as an argument against the conviction because the acts had already been punishable under international law at the time they were committed. Therefore the application was dismissed as manifestly ill-founded.

One important question raised in this context was whether the Nuremberg Principles were inseparably linked with situations of armed conflict. According to Cassese, this link was only removed by the Convention on the Non-Applicability of Statutory Limitations to War Crimes and Crimes against Humanity of 26 No-

---

found by comparing the various domestic legal systems. Some legal writers set aside the agreement by various domestic systems and refer to the consent of the community of states about basic values. Generally, see also Renzikowski (2009), Art. 7, n. 95.

15   See Friedrich-Christian Schroeder/Herbert Küpper, Der EGMR und die Bestrafung stalinistischer Verbrechen, Jahrbuch für Ostrecht 50 (2009), 213-221.
16   Kolk and Kislyiy, decision of 17 January 2006.
17   See Naletilić, decision of 4 May 2000, RJD 2000-V; Papon, decision of 15 November 2001, RJD 2001-XII, para. 5.

vember 1968 explicitly recognizing the deportation of the civilian population as a crime against humanity irrespective of the state of war. In 1949, however, this nexus still existed.[18] Nevertheless, Cassese agreed with the Court's final ruling recognizing the nexus between the deportations from Estonia and the war. For him, the deportation of civilians in 1949 had been a direct consequence of Estonia's invasion by the Soviet Union in 1940.[19]

The limitation of the Nuremberg Principles to the prosecution of the main perpetrators of war crimes only had implications on the jurisdiction but not on the description of the criminal conduct. It was the main objective of the military tribunals consisting only of military judges to punish crimes directly linked to the Nazi regime committed before and during the war.[20] Control Council Law no. 10 already abandoned this restriction which was consequently not longer applied in the following trials against high-ranking officials of the Third Reich.[21] The Appeals Chamber in the *Tadić* case shared this interpretation with regard to Article 5 ICTY Statute also linking the prosecution of crimes committed with "armed conflict" (as opposed to Article 3 ICTR Statute). Still, it seems that the nexus with an armed conflict is again rather a question of jurisdiction than a substantive element of crimes against humanity since grave breaches of human rights may not only occur in times of war.[22]

2   *Penart v. Estonia*

The applicant was a former member of the Ministry of the Interior of the Estonian SSR who had organized the extrajudicial killing of three persons who were hiding in the woods from the repression by the Soviet occupation authorities in 1953 and 1954. On 2 September 2003, he was convicted of crimes against humanity under Article 61-1 § 1 of the *Kriminaalkoodeks* to eight years of suspended imprisonment with probation.

The Court declared the complaint of breach of Article 7 ECHR as manifestly ill-founded by referring – as already in the *Kolk and Kislyiy* case – to Article 6 (c) of the Nuremberg Principles. The Court deduced from Article 7 § 2 ECHR that a retroactive application of national criminal law merely realized the criminal liability for crimes against humanity as already acknowledged by all civilized nations at the time of the offence. Hence, from the Court's standpoint, no direct or indirect nexus to acts of war has to be shown to exist.[23]

---

18   Cassese (2006), 413 et seq.

19   Cassese (2006), 417 et seq. – of course a very loose nexus.

20   Cf. International Military Tribunal (1946), at 254. In this context it should be noted that the convictions of Streicher and von Schirach (see ibid., at 301 et seq. and at 317 et seq.) under crimes against humanity had no true relation to the war, except in relation to the time criterion. This is also pointed out by Antonio Cassese, International Criminal Law, Oxford, 2nd ed. 2003, 106.

21   For further developments, cf. M. Cherif Bassiouni, Crimes Against Humanity in International Criminal Law, Dordrecht/Boston/London 1992, 176 et seq.

22   See ICTY (Appeals Chamber), Tadić, Decision on the Defence Motion for Interlocutory Appeal on Jurisdiction of 2 October 1995, § 140; ICTY, Tadić, Appeals judgment of 15 July 1999, §§ 249, 251; cf. also House of Lords, Ex Parte Pinochet, judgment of 24 March 1999, per Lord Millet, [1999] UKHL 17.

23   Penart, decision of 24 January 2006.

3 Kononov v. Latvia

The *Kononov* case was related to crimes committed by Soviet partisans against the Latvian population during World War II. On 27 May 1944, the applicant led an attack against the village of Mazie Bati to take revenge for the previous extradition of partisans to the German Wehrmacht. Five inhabitants were killed or shot; four more were burnt in their houses, among them a pregnant woman. After an extensive trial, Kononov was sentenced for war crimes under Art. 68-3 of the Latvian *Kriminālkodekss* of 1993 to one year and eight months imprisonment. In his application *Kononov* raised the issue of retroactive criminal responsibility since, so he argued, the acts he was charged with constituted, at the time of their commission, neither an offence under domestic nor under international law.

This application to the Strasbourg Court raised several questions. Concerning the law applicable at the time the crimes were committed, the Court referred to the judgement of the Nuremberg Tribunals which had ruled that Article 6 (b) of the Charter of the Nuremberg Tribunal merely enumerated the elements of war crimes recognized as such by customary international law in 1939. Consequently, it was considered irrelevant that neither the USSR nor Latvia had signed the Hague Convention of 1907 concerning the laws and customs of war on land.[24] The following rules of the Hague Convention were important for the *Kononov* case: Under Article 1 and 2 volunteers are treated as belligerents if they carry their arms openly. Article 23 (1) prohibits the treacherous killing of individuals and the destruction of property unless justified by warfare. Moreover, Article 25 prohibits attacking undefended houses. Therefore, it is decisive, whether the killed victims are regarded as civilians in need of protection or as combatants.

First, the Court differentiated between the six male and the three female victims. With regard to the male victims, it pointed out that the German military administration provided the male inhabitants of Mazie Batie with rifles and grenades for the protection from assaults by partisans. Whereas the Supreme Court of Latvia did not want to deduce a consequential combatant status from this, the ECtHR did, additionally referring to a collaboration of the victims with the Nazis which could not be legitimated under any conceivable point of view.[25] Due to this consideration the Court even denied the killed women the status of protected civilians[26] and assessed the situation as a selective execution of armed collaborators of the Nazi enemy. Since many similar operations were conducted by the Allied Forces at the same time, the conviction had no plausible legal basis in international law.[27] In case the applicant had incurred a penalty under domestic law, the statute of limitations for the offence had run out in 1954 according to the Criminal Code of Soviet Russia. The extension of an already expired statutory limitation would also present a breach of the Convention.[28] Finally, the Court

---

24 Kononov (2008), paras. 117-122; cf. also Kai-Michael König, Die völkerrechtliche Legitimation der Strafgewalt internationaler Strafjustiz, Baden-Baden 2003, 281 et seq.

25 Kononov (2008), paras. 127-131; this aspect is also stressed by Judge Myjer in his concurring opinion, at n. 10.

26 Ibid., paras. 138-140.

27 Ibid., paras. 134 and 137.

28 Kononov (2008), paras. 141-144; cf. also Renzikowski (2009), Art. 7, n. 34.

considered a separate examination of Article 7 § 2 ECHR to be superfluous.[29]

The judgment was very contested among the judges as was reflected by the voting pattern of 4 to 3 votes. Indeed, the decision is not convincing. The assessment of the victims as belligerents is objectionable. After all, the Court accepts that the events did not happen in the context of a combat situation, that the victims were not members of the Latvian auxiliary police and did not carry arms openly. Contrary to the Court's very formal consideration, the Judges Fura-Sandström, Thór Björgvinsson and Ziemele rightly emphasized in their dissenting opinion, that the preamble of the Hague Convention (the so called "Martens-Clause") provides for a primacy of humanitarian considerations in cases of doubt. Furthermore, the Court disregarded other sources to determine the international law applicable at the time of the offence.[30] What is decisive, however, is the fact that combatants are by no means deprived of all legal protection. Even in war, there is no right to arbitrary executions by any means whatsoever. Remarkably, the Court did not make any efforts to examine the military necessity of executing the male victims, after they had been captured without resisting (cf. the wording of Article 6 (b) of the Nuremberg Principles). Nor does it seem, in retrospect, to have been a military necessity to burn the female victims alive in their houses. The reference to the selective character of the operation does not help the debate. Because of the collaboration with the Nazis, the Court denies the victims their need of protection under international humanitarian law. This line of argumentation is conceptually wrong.[31]

4   *Korbely v. Hungary*

The *Korbely* case is connected to another chapter of transitional justice, namely the national uprising in Hungary in October 1956. The applicant was captain of an instruction unit of non-commissioned officers and was ordered, on 26 October 1956, to recapture a police station occupied by insurgents. He succeeded without encountering resistance. However, in the course of events several occupants were shot, though it was controversial whether the leader T. was armed. After a long trial, *Korbely* was convicted by a military court on 8 November 2001 on the basis of Article 3 (1) of the Geneva Convention (IV) on the Protection of Civilian Persons in Time of War of 1949, for crimes against humanity and was sentenced to five years in prison. Due to an amnesty, however, he was released earlier. *Korbely* complained that he had been retroactively punished since the acts charged did not constitute an offence under Article 3 of the Geneva Convention which was not applicable to the non-international conflict under review. Furthermore, in contradiction to the findings of the domestic courts, the victims had in fact taken an active part in the hostilities.

Similarly to the *Kononov* case, the ECtHR determined for itself the effective legal position at the time of the offence, especially since the domestic courts had

---

29   Kononov (2008), para. 147; however, the foregoing relativization of the meaning of § 2, viz. the legitimation of the (retroactive) prosecution of Nazis and their collaborators (para. 115), constitutes a move backwards.

30   But see Jorgic, judgment of 12 July 2007, paras. 40-47, where the Court dealt with these sources.

31   In this direction see also the dissenting opinion of Judges Fura-Sandström, Thór Björgvinsson and Ziemele, ibid., at n. 3 and 12; Schroeder/Küpper (2009), 216, 219.

neglected this point. Once again, it referred to the Nuremberg Principles but also to the corresponding elements of the crimes under review described in the statutes of the International Criminal Tribunals for the Former Yugoslavia and Rwanda and the ICC Statute. In so doing, the Court found that murder was already acknowledged as one of the offences capable of amounting to a crime against humanity by customary international law in 1956.

In accordance with its former jurisprudence the Court found it again unnecessary to establish a nexus with warfare or armed conflict. However, the assault in question had to be a state action or part of a state policy or, alternatively, part of a widespread and systematic attack on the civilian population. In the ECtHR's opinion the domestic courts did not take this element sufficiently into consideration when ruling on the matter.[32] Furthermore, it disagreed with the perception of the domestic courts that T. had not taken part actively in the hostilities. After the non-violent recapture of the police station, T., holding a pistol in his hand, started an intensive verbal dispute with the appellant. Thus, he did not surrender in an unambiguous and clear manner.[33] Consequently, since the conviction of Korbeley was not in conformity with the international standards at that time, it constituted a breach of Article 7 ECHR.[34]

As proved by the 11-6 voting pattern for finding a violation, this decision was again controversial among the judges. In their dissenting opinions the Judges Lorenzen, Tulkens, Zagrebelsky, Fura-Sandström, Popović and Loucaides objected rightly that the Court substituted its own consideration of the evidence for the factual findings of the domestic courts.[35] The conclusion by the domestic courts that T. had only handed over his weapon was not unreasonable. Moreover, the Court had ignored in its judgement that the former conviction of the applicant was not only based on the actual shooting of T., but rather on the fact that due to the firing order unarmed persons, some of them even on the run, were killed by the continuous fire of machine guns. In the end, the domestic courts had provided enough evidence for a widespread and systematic attack on the civilian population.

C   Conclusion

It is difficult to assess whether and to what extent the reviewed decisions of the ECtHR constitute a turning away from its own well-established methodology.[36] A number of observations can be made: In the *Kononov* decision, the Court seems to claim more competence for controlling the assessment of the status of international law more closely, especially where no case-law has been established yet.[37] This approach can be well justified by the purpose of the principle *nulla poena sine lege*, precisely because the Court considers written and unwritten law and its application by judges as a unit.[38] At the same time this raises, on the one

---

32   Korbely, judgment of 19 September 2008 (GC), paras. 80-84.
33   Korbely (2008), paras. 86-91.
34   Ibid., paras. 93, 95.
35   So the allegations by Schroeder/Küpper (2009), 218 et seq.
36   See ibid., 220 et seq.
37   See Kononov (2008), para. 110.
38   For details, see Renzikowski (2009), Art. 7, n. 53.

hand, problems with regard to the foreseeability of the conviction and, on the other hand, puts the supervisory function of the Court at risk.[39] The domestic courts are generally obliged by their constitutions to apply and interpret international law. And finally, questions of a reasonable assessment of facts cannot be subsumed under Article 7 ECHR, but belong rather to the guarantees of a fair trial under Article 6 ECHR.[40] Consequently, the Strasbourg Court should be reluctant to criticize the consideration of evidence by the domestic courts as long as the trial cannot be rejected as unfair.

If the Court stretches its competence as far as it did in the cases of *Kononov* and *Korbely*, its reasoning must be absolutely convincing – otherwise it runs the risk of losing its high moral authority.

---

39   See ibid., n. 60.
40   See also Harris/O'Boyle/Warbrick (2009), 339.

Franziska KLOPFER[*]

Towards Greater Freedom of Expression and Information Online: Recent Standard-Setting Practice of the Council of Europe

Table of Contents

Keywords

Freedom of expression, Council of Europe, standard-setting, Internet Service Providers, media literacy, information literacy, access, harmful content, Internet filters, public service value of the Internet, removal of content

A   Introduction

Council of Europe (CoE) standards in the Internet field strive to promote the core values of the organization, democracy, human rights and the rule of law. Human rights do not only exist in the offline world. They fully apply to citizens moving around in the new online environment. In light of Article 10[1] of the European

---

[*]   The opinions expressed in this article are those of the author and may not necessarily reflect those of the Council of Europe

[1]   Article 10 of the ECHR, guaranteeing the freedom of expression, provides:
"(1) Everyone has the right to freedom of expression. This right shall include freedom to hold opinions and to receive and impart information and ideas without interference by public authority and regardless of frontiers. This article shall not prevent States from requiring the licensing of broadcasting, television or cinema enterprises.
(2) The exercise of these freedoms, since it carries with it duties and responsibilities, may be subject to such formalities, conditions, restrictions or penalties as are pre-

267

Convention of Human Rights (ECHR), the Committee of Ministers – the Council of Europe's main decision-making body – declared in 2005 that freedom of expression, information and communication should be respected in a digital as well as in a non-digital environment, and should not be subject to restrictions other than those provided for in Article 10 of the ECHR, simply because communication is carried in digital form.[2]

Internet services and technologies will continue to create new ways and forms of expression which will, no doubt, influence human behaviour. Our younger generations – "the digital natives"[3] – appear to adapt themselves almost seamlessly to a panoply of information and communication services and technologies. Notwithstanding our adaptability over time in this regard, there remain a number of challenges to the full exercise of our rights and freedoms: How can children be protected against harmful content without a disproportionate restriction on freedom of expression and access to information? How should tools such as filters be used? Given their key role in producing and controlling content, what responsibilities do the private sector and the individual Internet user have?

In the past five years the Council of Europe has developed a number of standards and benchmarks that address these and other issues.[4] The following article will first concentrate on CoE standards on the role of governments in ensuring real access to technology and content (section B). It will then explore the issue of media or information literacy, which the Council of Europe has supported strongly not only as a way for users to protect themselves against possible harm but also to fully realize their rights to expression and to seek information (C). Media education is particularly relevant in the context of the protection

---

scribed by law and are necessary in a democratic society, in the interests of national security, territorial integrity or public safety, for the prevention of disorder or crime, for the protection of health or morals, for the protection of the reputation or rights of others, for preventing the disclosure of information received in confidence, or for maintaining the authority and impartiality of the judiciary."

2   Declaration of the Committee of Ministers of the Council of Europe on human rights and the rule of law in the Information Society, 13 May 2005. Its text and that of all other standards and documents quoted below can be found at www.coe.int/media.

3   The term was popularized though not coined by John Palfrey/Urs Gasser, Born Digital: Understanding the First Generation of Digital Natives, New York 2008.

4   Even though the following text will concentrate on work related to Article 10 of the European Convention of Human Rights, this is not to suggest that it is the only human right that needs particular attention as regards the Internet nor is it the only area in which the CoE has set standards. By concentrating only on the organization's standard-setting work on freedom of expression and information in the Information Society, this paper can only consider part of the standards developed by the CoE for online activities. Other issues include cybercrime, data protection, children and Internet, e-democracy, accessibility for people with disabilities. The present contribution also cannot cover the case-law of the European Court of Human Rights on this issue. Nor will it go into the considerable contribution of the organization to the international multi-stakeholder dialogue on Internet Governance, which include, but are not limited to, the participation of the CoE in the Internet Governance Forum (IGF) or the organization of the European Dialogue on Internet Governance (EuroDIG). For more information on the contribution of the CoE to the development of the agenda of Internet Governace and to the IGF, specifically, see http://www.coe.int/t/information society. The CoE has also supported since its inception in 2008, the EuroDIG (www.eurodig.org), a regional forum for discussing Internet Governance issues.

268

of children from harmful content. The next section also outlines other tools or measures to ensure security but also freedoms for children (D). Section E then concentrates on the obligations of the private sector and the importance of co- and self-regulation. The last section will introduce the concept of public service of the Internet and outline how states' responsibilities need to guarantee the public's interest in an Internet that is accessible to all and functioning well and that offers them a variety of essential services (F). Finally, conclusions will be offered (G).

B   Access to Content

Ensuring freedom of expression and information in online environments means giving individuals and communities real choice in content. People need diverse and reliable information in order to discover and form opinions on political, social and cultural ideas and participate in a democratic society.

Guaranteeing choice in content includes ensuring access to the Internet; but what is the state's responsibility in ensuring this access? Access presupposes effective use of the Internet but do we all (including older users, persons with disabilities, communities and marginalized persons and groups) have the skills to readily master the services and technologies freely offered to us? This becomes all the more important as Europe embarks on a journey towards a single Euro- pean digital space where Internet access is an increasing priority. Finland and Spain recently passed laws making it a legal right for their citizens to receive high-speed Internet access, a legislative move that has created momentum in other European states.

According to a 2007 Council of Europe Recommendation,[5] access means that content and services should be free or at least affordable. Another Council of Europe instrument[6] stresses that access also has to be non-discriminatory thereby underlining that *all* people should have at least a minimum level of ac- cess irrespective of their social position or geographic location For most people it is relatively easy to access the Internet. But some might lack the financial re- sources to pay for the technical equipment or internet access or they live in a region with no Internet infrastructure. Others, for example older people, might need training first to familiarize themselves with information and computer tech- nologies. Or they might need special equipment in order to use a computer be- cause of a disability. Member states, in cooperation with the private sector and civil society should therefore ensure a functioning market where Internet access is affordable for all and give financial or other assistance for those who need.

C   Information Literacy

Access to content, however, does not automatically lead to real choice of content or to diverse and quality information which is needed by the user to exercise her

---

5   Recommendation Rec(2007)11 of the Committee of Ministers to member states on promoting freedom of expression and information in the new information and com- munications environment.

6   Recommendation Rec(2007)3 of the Committee of Ministers to member states on the remit of public service media in the information society.

right to access information and to freedom of expression. Many users consider a lot of the content they find online unreliable. They find it difficult to judge which piece of information they can trust. Many users also feel uncomfortable with certain online content which may, or may not, be illegal.[7] Offensive or violent content might be protected under Article 10, but might nonetheless be extremely harmful, especially for children.

To ensure maximum freedom of expression online, Council of Europe standards advocate that governments should ensure that users are enabled to make informed and free choices. The alternative option, blocking access or introducing "quality control" checks on information and services online, is to be avoided wherever possible.

To enable Europeans to effectively seek information and to express themselves online, the Council of Europe therefore encourages member states to enhance their national media education strategies so as to make Internet users "information literate".[8] Information literacy is defined as

> the competent use of tools providing access to information, the development of critical analysis of content and the appropriation of communication skills to foster citizenship and creativity, and training initiatives for children and their educators in order for them to use information and communication technologies and services in a positive and responsible manner.[9]

Users should have the knowledge and skills to use the Internet freely and with confidence. Media education should help users become aware of the rights of others and their correlative obligations when using and creating content online. Cyber-bullying, publishing insults, spreading rumors and disseminating personal information of others can cause real and lasting harm and can, in most cases, lead to criminal sanction or civil causes of action. Information literacy therefore also means that the user is able to respect the rights and dignity of others and is aware of inappropriate or potentially harmful behaviour.

The Council of Europe has been working on practical tools to help children increase their information literacy. For example, it has published an Internet literacy handbook for teachers and parents. The handbook is comprised of factsheets which provide the reader with technical know-how about the Internet but also highlights ethical issues that an Internet use should be aware of. Parents and teachers are also given tips on how children can constructively use the Internet, for example as part of their school work. An online game for children

---

7   There is also the fear to come across fraudulent and criminal behaviour online. The Internet has facilitated the sexual exploitation of children. Spam, trojans and Internet hoaxes are just three more examples of how Internet frauds and criminal online behaviour can target unsuspecting and innocent Internet users. An international treaty, the Council of Europe Convention on Cybercrime, sets out international standards for preventing criminal content on the Internet. The instrument also determines a duty for state parties to cooperate in its implementation, including with relevant non-state actors.

8   See, for example, Recommendation Rec(2006)12 of the Committee of Ministers to member states on empowering children in the new information and communications environment.

9   Recommendation Rec(2006)12 of the Committee of Ministers to member states on empowering children in the new information and communications environment.

allows children to discover about their rights on the Internet. Both are freely available online, in different European languages.[10]

D   Empowering Children: Confidence-building Environments, Filters, Content Removal

The issue of empowering children and young people to deal with harmful and/or illegal content was addressed by the Council of Europe in a 2009 Committee of Ministers Recommendation.[11] The Recommendation promotes public-private partnerships to create and facilitate confidence-building environments ("walled gardens") for children to safely explore the Internet, and to create a human rights-based pan-European trustmark which uses new and existing online content labelling systems.

The use of Internet filters is one possible means of protecting children against content which might be harmful or offensive to them but remains available on the Internet for others to see and consume. Internet filters can, however, be abused to stifle freedom of expression and information, including the freedom of expression of children and young people. In a Recommendation on Internet filters[12] the Council of Europe therefore underlined that children need to have access to filters which are age-appropriate and "intelligent" (that is, filters that can adapt to the child's developmental age or that can differentiate between the actual harmful content and mere references to it). Filters should be used to encourage and not discourage access to, and use of, the Internet. They should be proportionate and not lead to the over-protection of children and young people.

The power to remove content is an important means of giving users control and a degree of responsibility. Children might not always be aware that information they post about themselves online could be misused by criminals and used to trace them. Content published by children could become embarrassing and even prejudicial to them in later life, for example when a prospective employer finds compromising information when considering a job application. It is difficult to remove information from the Internet once it has been put there. At the same time, children should not be afraid to express themselves online. In early 2008, the Council of Europe adopted a Declaration on dealing with the electronic footprint of children online, including proposals to make the Internet learn how to forget.[13] The Declaration asks member states to work together to explore the feasibility of removing or deleting content created by children and traces of their

---

10   For the online game, see "Through the Wild Web Woods" http://www.wildwebwoods.org/popup_langSelection.php; for the handbook, see Council of Europe Internet Literacy Handbook http://www.coe.int/t/dghl/standardsetting/internetliteracy/hbk _EN.asp.

11   Recommendation Rec(2009)5 of the Committee of Ministers to member states on measures to protect children against harmful content and behaviour and to promote their active participation in the new information and communications environment. See also Recommendation Rec(2006)12.

12   Recommendation Rec(2008)6 of the Committee of Ministers to member states on measures to promote the respect for freedom of expression and information with regard to Internet filters.

13   Declaration of the Committee of Ministers on protecting the dignity, security and privacy of children on the Internet, 20 February 2008.

online activities within a reasonably short period of time, if such content and traces can cause them prejudice. A new Council of Europe intergovernmental committee was set up in 2009 to look more closely into the issue and to come up with concrete steps that member states together with the private sector could take to delete children's traces.[14]

E   The Responsibilities of Internet Service Providers

Even the most extensive media education will never be able to prepare users for every situation online in which human rights might be under threat. New services appear on the Internet every day. How can the users know, for example, whether it is safe to give away certain personal details about themselves in order to use a service, or what will happen if they click on a link or post material in a new online space?

The Council of Europe regularly underlines the important role of private sector and civil society actors in promoting the enjoyment of fundamental rights including freedom of expression and information. The 2007 Recommendation by the Committee of Ministers on promoting freedom of expression and information in the new information and communications environment states that the private sector, including Internet Service Providers (ISPs), should familiarize itself with its ethical roles and responsibilities, and if appropriate, set up self-regulatory mechanisms. This means also that ISPs have a responsibility to provide users with clear information about how their services function, and on how they can protect themselves if their human rights are violated by indicating, for example, where they can complain or seek redress if they feel that they have been victimized.[15]

To this end, the Council of Europe has developed human rights guidelines for ISPs and online games providers in close cooperation with the European Association of Internet Service Providers (EuroISPA), and the Interactive Software Federation in Europe (ISFE), respectively. In the guidelines for games providers, the designers and publishers of online games are encouraged to assess the possible impact a new game may have on human dignity or the sensibilities and values of gamers before publishing it. In practice this should include, for example, avoiding the portrayal of gratuitous violence in their games.[16]

F   Public Service Value of the Internet

The Internet is an integral part of the lives of over 400 million citizens in Europe and this number is still increasing. We shop, meet, communicate and do business online. In some countries, the Internet and other information and communication technologies (ICT) provide an important means to circumvent censorship

---

14   More information on the committee, the Committee of Experts on New Media (MC-NM) can be found at http://www.coe.int/t/dghl/standardsetting/media/MC-NM/default_en.asp.
15   Recommendation Rec(2007)11.
16   Human rights guidelines for Internet service providers http://www.coe.int/t/dghl/ standardsetting/media/Doc/H-Inf(2008)009_en.pdf; Human rights guidelines for online games providers http://www.coe.int/t/dghl/standardsetting/media/Doc/H-Inf(2008)008_en.pdf.

and repression. The Internet is a unique way to communicate easily with other people, to build confidence and establish relations. This is particularly the case for persons with a disability. It is in this light that the Council of Europe under-stands and underlines that the Internet offers an important public service value and is not just a commercial marketplace.

In the 2007 Recommendation by the Committee of Ministers on measures to promote the public service value of the Internet,[17] member states agreed to de-velop strategies, in cooperation with the private sector and civil society, aimed at promoting access to new ICTs which allow the general public to use public ser-vices and essential privately owned facilities.

The Recommendation also encourages states "to ensure that Internet and ICT content is contributed by all regions, countries and communities so as to ensure over time representation of all peoples, nations, cultures and languages". Because ICTs play an essential role for inclusion, social cohesion and ex-changes, their accessibility and openness need to be guaranteed. A number of specific measures are proposed in the Recommendation to allow participation, representation and exchanges of individuals and their communities. For exam-ple, to support local expression and culture, the production of digital content by national or local cultural industries should be promoted by governments. To encourage access to educational, cultural and scientific content, governments and other stakeholders are encouraged to preserve digital heritage of lasting cultural, scientific, or other values. It also stresses that the Internet needs to be available in all languages, including indigenous and minority languages, to en-sure that all people can produce their local content and also access content produced by their own and by other communities.

G   Conclusion: Looking to the Future

In the past five years the Council of Europe instruments have addressed major Internet policy issues. They have underlined the key importance of access to the Internet and defined the concept in broad terms, underlining for example the importance of affordable access. Future work of the Council of Europe might build on this principle, for example when it comes to defining access to informa-tion in the context of a possible right to broadband access.

Filtering and blocking has been and still is considered by many as an impor-tant tool for managing content on the internet, for example by governments that want to stop allegedly illegal or harmful content. The CoE Recommendation on online filters[18] was therefore an important milestone because it ensures that the use of filters does not violate human rights. This approach could be a good basis for a future policy on network management, an issue that is currently hotly de-bated and that a new CoE working group has also started to look into.[19]

The concept of public service value of the Internet will be an important guiding principle for future Internet policy in Europe. The new digital environment has to

---

17   Recommendation Rec(2007)16 of the Committee of Ministers to member states on measures to promote the public service value of the Internet.
18   Recommendation Rec(2008)6.
19   Committee of Experts on New Media (MC-NM), see supra, note 14.

be protected and shaped so as to guarantee an Internet in the public interest and as a public asset.

The CoE instruments on child protection[20] have proven to be of great value because they insist on a holistic protection and promotion of all human rights, instead of a one-sided focus on security. The child not only has a right to be protected from danger but also enjoy freedom of expression and other rights, such as the participation in social life online. These instruments underline the importance of information and media literacy and this will have to be followed up with real practical action. Ministers at a 2009 Council of Europe Conference of Ministers responsible for Media and New Communication Services therefore called on the organization to work on new ways to enhance media literacy in member states.[21]

At the same conference, the ministers also laid down the broad lines for future Council of Europe work in the field of freedom of expression with a focus on ensuring the provision of diverse quality content, the protection of content providers' freedoms and individuals' human rights online as well as the security of the network.[22] A working group on cross-border internet was set up in 2009 will explore possibilities of developing a broader legal response to the need to protect the cross-border flow of Internet traffic and the protection of critical internet resources.[23]

Another working group[24] is currently looking into new governance models for public service media that should guarantee not only public service media's independence, but also allow it to provide people with relevant and quality information. This could include in particular the use of new ICTs by public service media as a way of ensuring the provision of a diversity of quality content also in the online space.

Finally, work has also started on a new policy document reviewing the concept of media to include not only press and broadcasting but also new actors and platforms which carry out the same functions as so-called 'traditional' media.[25] Given their importance for providing content to the public, their freedom, privileges but also responsibilities might also be considered similar to those attributed to press and broadcasters.

---

20   Recommendation Rec(2006)12 , Recommendation Rec(2009)5.
21   Political Declaration and Resolutions adopted at the 1st Council of Europe Conference of Ministers responsible for Media and New Communication Services, 28 and 29 May 2009, Reykjavik, Iceland, http://www.ministerialconference.is/media/images/ MCM2009011_en_final_web.pdf. On this issue, see also the contribution by Kettemann, in this volume, at 335.
22   Ibid.
23   Ad hoc Advisory Group on Cross-border Internet (MC-S-CI), http://www.coe.int/t/ dghl/standardsetting/media/MC-S-CI/default_en.asp.
24   Ad hoc Advisory Group on Public Service Media Governance (MC-S-PG) http://www.coe.int/t/dghl/standardsetting/media/MC-S-PG/default_en.asp.
25   Committee of Experts on New Media (MC-NM), see supra, note 14.

Emma LANTSCHNER[*]

Evolution and Value of the Thematic Commentaries of the Advisory Committee of the Framework Convention for the Protection of National Minorities

Table of Contents

Keywords

Framework Convention for the Protection of National Minorities, Advisory Committee, thematic commentaries, education, participation, standard setting, soft law

A   Introduction

When the Framework Convention for the Protection of National Minorities (FCNM) entered into force in 1998,[1] it was criticized by many as a toothless tiger. One of the issues of concern was the allegedly weak monitoring mechanism,[2] consisting only of the regular review of state reports by the Committee of Ministers, assisted in this effort by an Advisory Committee (ACFC).[3] Twelve years later, with the FCNM having entered already the third monitoring cycle, it is widely acknowledged that the Advisory Committee has managed to develop working methods which focus more than those of most other monitoring bodies

*   This article has been prepared in the framework of the project "Standard-Setting through Monitoring", financed by the Oesterreichische Nationalbank (Jubiläums-fonds, project number 13530).

1   Framework Convention for the Protection of National Minorities (FCNM), Strasbourg, 1 February 1995, CETS no. 157, http://conventions.coe.int/Treaty/en/Treaties/Html/157.htm. As of 1 March 2010, the FCNM has 39 ratifications and accessions.

2   See, e.g., Gudmundur Alfredsson, A Frame with an Incomplete Painting: Comparison of the Framework Convention for the Protection of National Minorities with International Standards and Monitoring Procedures, IJMGR, 7 (2000) 4, 291-304.

3   Articles 24-26 of the FCNM.

on a constructive dialogue with all stakeholders, that it produces high quality opinions which are most of the time fully reflected in the resolutions of the Committee of Ministers and that, through its practice, it has managed to put flesh on the bones of the sometimes vague and general formulations of the FCNM provisions.[4]

While in the first years of its existence the Advisory Committee focused on state by state monitoring and producing country-specific opinions, it has more recently also turned to the adoption of thematic commentaries. The idea to produce such documents was present from the very beginning, but the ACFC "did not want to run before [it] learned to walk."[5]

Already in the First Activity Report, the ACFC agreed to establish, in line with Rule 35 of its Rules of Procedures,[6] not only country-specific, but also thematic working groups.[7] When the issue of thematic work was discussed again by the Advisory Committee in 2001, it was decided "that it was still premature to commence the work of such groups and that it would be preferable to do this only after a greater number of opinions had been adopted by the Advisory Committee."[8] In 2003, the Parliamentary Assembly of the Council of Europe recommended the Committee of Ministers to "encourage the advisory committee to consider thematic issues and to comment on them, so as to assist states and minorities in developing good practices."[9] Further support for embarking in this endeavour came from the conference with which the fifth anniversary of the FCNM was celebrated.[10] Participants stressed that such commentaries would allow for a combined interpretation of interrelated articles of the FCNM in the light of the Convention's objects and purposes (as opposed to the article-by-article approach taken in the country-specific opinions),[11] would contribute to greater

---

4   For a reflection of this, see all the reports about the monitoring process of the FCNM in the European Yearbook of Minority Issues; Annelies Verstichel et al. (eds.), The Framework Convention for the Protection of National Minorities: A Useful Pan-European Instrument? Antwerp 2008; Emma Lantschner, Soft jurisprudence im Minderheitenrecht. Standardsetzung und Konfliktbearbeitung durch Kontrollmechanismen bi- und multilateraler Instrumente, Baden-Baden 2009.

5   Rainer Hofmann, The Framework Convention at the end of the first cycle of monitoring, in: Council of Europe, Filling the Frame: Five years of monitoring the Framework Convention for the Protection of National Minorities, Proceedings of the conference held in Strasbourg, 30-31 October 2003, Strasbourg 2004, 19-25, at 22. According to Hofmann, a former president of the AC, the lack of resources was another reason for not starting the thematic work earlier.

6   Rules of Procedure of the ACFC, adopted by the ACFC on 29 October 1998, ACFC/INF(1998)002, http://www.coe.int/t/dghl/monitoring/minorities/2Monitoring/PDF_AC FC_RulesProcedure_en.pdf.

7   ACFC, First Activity Report covering the period from 1 June 1998 to 31 May 1999, 15 September 1999, ACFC/INF(1999)001, para. 14.

8   ACFC, Meeting Report, 10th meeting, 2-6 April 2001, para 12.

9   PACE, Recommendation 1623 (2003), Rights of national minorities, adopted by the Assembly on 29 September 2003 (27th sitting), para. 12(ix).

10   Filling the Frame: Five years of monitoring the Framework Convention for the Protection of National Minorities, conference held in Strasbourg, 30-31 October 2003.

11   See, e.g., Duncan Wilson, Report: A critical evaluation of the first results of the monitoring of the Framework Convention on the issue of minority rights in, to and through education (1998-2003), in: Council of Europe (2004), 163-228, at 169.

clarity and consistency in the opinions,[12] and could also offer guidance to good practice and thus be a useful tool for states during the process of implementa-tion.[13] After the conference, the ACFC decided to work on the issues of participa-tion, education and media, initially focusing on education.[14]

As a result, the Advisory Committee adopted in March 2006 its first thematic commentary on education under the FCNM (hereinafter "Commentary on Educa-tion").[15] Two years later, in February 2008, it adopted its second commentary, the one on the effective participation of persons belonging to national minorities in cultural, social and economic life and in public affairs (hereinafter "Commen-tary on Participation").[16] While other thematic work was going on simultaneously over the past years, such as on the definition of the term "minority", or the im-provement of the monitoring of the FCNM vis-à-vis the Roma, the ACFC decided in 2009 to produce the next thematic commentary on the issue of language.

This contribution is not going to analyze the content of the already adopted thematic commentaries as this has already been done elsewhere.[17] Rather, it will explore the evolution that these two commentaries have gone through in terms of form and drafting processes (B), analyze the question of their (legal) value and impact (C) and offer some conclusions (D) as to their future role.

B   Evolution in Terms of Form and Drafting Process

When the Advisory Committee started work on thematic commentaries, two different approaches to this exercise were discussed: the first was to focus on an analytical overview of the findings of the Advisory Committee during the first monitoring cycle, the second to produce more general comments or recommen-dations on the selected themes.[18] Contingent upon this choice were the ques-

---

12   Tove Skutnabb-Kangas, Commentary: The status of minority languages in the edu-cation process, in: Council of Europe (2004), 234-254, at 247.

13   Marc Weller, Conclusions – Workshop on participation; as well as Duncan Wilson, Conclusions – Workshop on education, both in: Council of Europe (2004), 257-263, at 263; and 266-270, at 270.

14   ACFC, Meeting Report, 18th meeting, 24-28 November 2003, para. 23; ACFC, Meet-ing Report, 19th meeting, 24-28 May 2004, para. 16.

15   ACFC, Commentary on Education under the Framework Convention for the Protec-tion of National Minorities, 2 March 2006, ACFC/25DOC(2006)002.

16   ACFC, Commentary on the Effective Participation of Persons Belonging to National Minorities in Cultural, Social and Economic Life and in Public Affairs, 27 February 2008, ACFC/31DOC(2008)001.

17   For an analysis of the Commentary on Education, see Antti Korkeakivi, Framework-ing: Review of the Monitoring Process of the Council of Europe Framework Conven-tion for the Protection of National Minorities, European Yearbook of Minority Issues, 5 (2005/6), 255-272, at 264-266. For an analysis of the Commentary on Participa-tion, see Joseph Marko, The Council of Europe Framework Convention on the Pro-tection of National Minorities and the Advisory Committee's Thematic Commentary on Effective Participation, in: Marc Weller and Katherine Nobbs (eds.), Political Par-ticipation of Minorities. A Commentary on International Standards and Practice, Ox-ford 2010, 222-255; Francesco Palermo, The Dual Meaning of Participation: The Advisory Committee's Commentary to Article 15 of the FCNM, European Yearbook of Minority Issues, 7 (2008a), 409-424.

18   ACFC, Meeting Report, 18th meeting, 24-28 November 2003, para. 24.

tions regarding the sources on which to draw when drafting the commentaries as well as whom to involve in the process.

The main source of both commentaries are the opinions drafted by the ACFC in their country-by-country monitoring. The aim they pursued in that is largely the same but differs in nuances which are also reflected in the format and style of the two commentaries. The Commentary on Education mentions as its first aim to "*summarize* [...] the experience of the Advisory Committee in working with and for education rights".[19] The main objective of the Commentary on Participation, on the other hand, is to "*highlight the interpretation* given by the Advisory Committee, mainly in its country-specific opinions adopted between 1999 and 2007, to provisions of the Framework Convention relating to effective participation of persons belonging to national minorities."[20] While the first commentary seems to be more a stock-taking exercise, the second is more willing to come up with normative recommendations.[21] For example, it clearly states that "[l]anguage proficiency requirements imposed on candidates for parliamentary and local elections are not compatible with Article 15 of the Framework Convention".[22] Interesting to note, however, is the fact that an earlier proposal, which would have divided the Commentary on Participation in one part containing a "prescriptive list of key findings" of the ACFC and a second part containing an explanatory report,[23] was finally dropped. This might be a reflection of the fact that the opinions within the Advisory Committee about a more or less normative approach to be taken in the thematic commentaries differed.

While the first commentary takes a more academic approach, the second is more normative in nature. To take its own opinions as the main basis for drafting its recommendations also had another purpose. The ACFC identified in both commentaries areas which will need further attention in its future monitoring, but also in the work of other stakeholders.[24]

Another difference between the two documents is their structure. Both commentaries highlight the interdependencies between various articles of the Convention in the areas of education and participation. While however the first commentary still presents itself in an article-by-article format, this approach has been completely abandoned by the Commentary on Participation.

The ACFC opinions were, however, not the only source from which the ACFC drew in the drafting of its commentaries. Both documents reflect also the information provided by the states in their regular reports submitted to the Advisory Committee and other sources. After all, one of the goals of the commentaries was also to put the work and the views of the ACFC within a broader international context. The amount and scope of the sources other than those connected to the monitoring process varies considerably between the first and the second commentary. The first commentary was mainly based on the drafts of an individual member of the ACFC, substantiated by the discussions in the plenary to which also external participants were invited. These were representatives of the Office of the OSCE High Commissioner on National Minorities (HCNM), members of the Committee

---

19 Commentary on Education, 5 (emphasis added).
20 Commentary on Participation, para. 2 (emphasis added).
21 Palermo (2008a), 422-423.
22 Commentary on Participation, para. 102.
23 ACFC, Meeting Report, 28th meeting, 20-23 February 2007.
24 Commentary on Education, 5; Commentary on Participation, paras. 3 and 150.

of Experts and the Secretariat of the European Charter for Regional or Minority Languages and of other related CoE offices. Only a few external experts took part in these consultations. For the second commentary it was however emphasized

"that the discussions could not be completed [...] in the absence of mean- ingful consultations with the various national and international players concerned (representatives of minorities, NGOs, the academic world and international oganisations)."[25]

The Advisory Committee wanted to show that it was not only preaching the participation of minorities but also practicing it. A draft of the commentary was sent out to national minority representatives and academics who could comment in writing. A revised version was then presented in a two-days round-table in October 2007 at which members of the Advisory Committee discussed the draft with representatives of minorities, international organizations and the academic community. A number of comments and suggestions made in these contexts were incorporated into the final version of the commentary.[26] The inclusion of civil society in the drafting of the commentary was widely considered as a suc- cess and the Advisory Committee plans to keep this element as a constant fea- ture of its future thematic work.[27]

Apart from the input given by civil society, the Advisory Committee tried to develop its commentaries also in light of the existing European and universal documents and experiences in the field of education and participation. In this context, the Hague and the Lund Recommendations of the OSCE High Commis- sioner on National Minorities were of special relevance and the cooperation with the High Commissioner's Office very close. The Commentary on Education drew further inspiration from the UN Convention on the Rights of the Child and other relevant UN treaties. The Advisory Committee was, however, very careful in showing that evidence of all the statements made in the commentaries could be found in the material stemming from the monitoring process (mainly state reports and opinions).

Interesting to note in terms of process is the fact that, unlike the opinions of the Advisory Committee, the thematic commentaries are not submitted to the Committee of Ministers. The pros and cons of such an involvement will be dis- cussed below under C.

C   Value and Impact of Thematic Commentaries

The fact that the thematic commentaries are adopted in a way that differs from the manner in which country-specific opinions are adopted leads to the question of the legal value and the role of these documents. Are they an authoritative interpretation of the text of the FCNM? Do they unfold any legally binding force upon member states or future members to the FCNM? What role will they play in the future monitoring of the FCNM?

---

25   ACFC, Meeting Report, 25th meeting, 27 February-3 March 2006.
26   Françoise Kempf, Review of the Monitoring Process of the Council of Europe Framework Convention for the Protection of National Minorities, European Yearbook of Minority Issues, 7 (2008), 483-495, at 487.
27   ACFC, 6th Activity Report covering the period 1 June 2006-31 May 2008, para. 65.

To answer these questions it is useful to look into the experience of UN treaty monitoring bodies that have started with the practice of developing thematic commentaries already long ago. The pioneer in this context was the Human Rights Committee (HRC), monitoring the implementation of the International Covenant on Civil and Political Rights (ICCPR). Upon its entry into force it was impossible for the HRC to adopt country-specific concluding observations due to controversies rooted in opposing Cold War ideologies. The HRC therefore started adopting General Comments on its interpretation of individual provisions of the ICCPR. The practice that has started as a substitute for country-specific findings has been maintained even after the adoption of concluding observations on individual countries had become possible.[28] By the time the HRC started its country-specific work it had already adopted 21 General Comments. While part of the thematic work of the HRC was thus carried out before it had gained experience through the examination of state reports and was considered as a "means of laying down some solid foundations for the future development of its jurisprudence",[29] the Advisory Committee started working on thematic issues only once it had gained considerable experience in the course of an entire monitoring cycle.

Considering that the General Comments of the UN treaty bodies are widely accepted, though with some outliers, such as the US, as a prominent source of interpretation of the underlying treaty obligations, it would all the more be justified to accept the same also with regard to the thematic commentaries of the ACFC as they could build already on a consolidated 'jurisprudence'. This jurisprudence was to a very large extent also supported by the Committee of Ministers in its resolutions on individual countries. That the Committee of Ministers always supported the early publication of opinions, even before it adopted its own conclusions and recommendations reflects the Committee of Ministers' confidence concerning the legal quality of the opinions.

But also bodies outside the CoE context strengthen the role of the ACFC in the interpretation of the Framework Convention. The HCNM stressed that in the context of the

"ongoing elaboration and interpretation of the legal framework by national and international bodies [...] particular attention should be paid to the contribution of the Advisory Committee on the Framework Convention for the Protection of National Minorities, which plays an important role in interpreting minority rights standards."[30]

---

28 Asbjørn Eide, The work of the Advisory Committee on the Framework Convention for the Protection of National Minorities on thematic commentaries, and the potential impact of these commentaries, presentation during the conference: Enhancing the Impact of the Framework Convention, Strasbourg, 9-10 October 2008, at 4, available at www.coe.int/minorities.

29 Philipp Alston, The Committee on Economic, Social and Cultural Rights, in: Philipp Alston (ed.), The United National and Human Rights: A Critical Appraisal, Oxford 1992, 494. While Alston refers to the CESCR, the same can be said about the HRC.

30 HCNM, Statement: Effective participation of national minorities in public life – developing and concretizing practical forms of participation drawing on the Lund Recommendations, Warsaw, 28 September 2005, 3, available at http://www.osce.org/documents/odihr/2005/09/16460_en.pdf.

Further, the European Commission refers to the opinions of the ACFC in its regular reports and scholars have no doubt about the leading role of the ACFC in construing minority rights standards.[31]

As has been rightly pointed out by Asbjørn Eide,[32] the preparation of thematic commentaries requires not only that sources are read and summarized but also considerable conceptual work. This presupposes independent thinking, which can indeed best be carried out by an independent expert body like the Advisory Committee, supported by the Secretariat and in consultation with minority representatives and experts in the field. In light of the support given by the Committee of Ministers to the opinions of the ACFC and in order to increase the acceptance of the commentaries by the FCNM state parties it might, however, be useful to consider an endorsement of the commentaries by the Committee of Ministers. Such a procedural role (albeit informal) might enhance the feeling of ownership amongst the states and thus improve the reception of and respect for the contents of the commentaries. Sceptics of such a proposal believe that this would result in an "intergovernmental negotiation that might not be best suited towards that purpose [of developing and advancing a standard]."[33] An indirect form of endorsement could take place if the Committee of Ministers referred to the Commentaries in its own work. A cursory review of documents adopted by the Committee of Ministers from 2008 till today shows, however, that it does not make reference in its documents to any of the commentaries, not even in its resolutions on the implementation of the FCNM.

In order for commentaries to be acceptable for states in terms of content, the ACFC has to be very careful on how far it pushes the just mentioned purpose of thematic commentaries: to develop and advance a standard through conceptual work. Can the Advisory Committee by means of thematic commentaries "anticipate [...] state practice" or "serve the progressive development of a rule"?[34] This question is no less important, of course, with regard to country-specific monitoring work. In both cases the ACFC may progressively interpret the provisions of the FCNM if new challenges or needs appear that could not have been anticipated. On the other hand it is of course important that the ACFC does not veer away too much from the underlying obligation contained in the Convention and the existing or emerging interpretation of it. If, for instance, a very much disputed conceptual issue is decided by the ACFC in a thematic commentary in the one or the other way, the Committee might risk a loss of authority, as in the view of some states it would go beyond the scope of the FCNM and the opposition of those opposing the approach of the ACFC might be more pronounced. This

---

31   For an example, see, Krzysztof Drzewicki, The Lund Recommendations on Effective Participation of National Minorities in Public Life – Five Years After and More Years Ahead, IJMGR, 12 (2005) 2-3, 123-131, at 130.

32   Eide (2008), 14.

33   Such doubts were raised during the conference on Enhancing the Impact of the Framework Convention, Strasbourg, 9-10 October 2008, as reported by Marc Weller in the summary of the roundtable discussion of Workshop 3, dealing with the Advisory Committee's Thematic Work, 6, http://www.coe.int/t/dghl/monitoring/minorities/ 6_Resources/IAConf_File_en.asp. Others point out that by endorsing the commentaries of the AC, the Committee of Ministers would attribute the AC an obvious standard-setting role which would not find the consensus of many states.

34   Weller (2008), 2 and 4-5.

would damage not only the acceptance of the commentary but maybe even lead to long-term reputational costs for the Advisory Committee itself. This might be a reason why the ACFC decided to continue its flexible approach to the personal scope of application of the FCNM and to leave open the question of defining the concept of "national minority".[35]

What the Advisory Committee can and should do is to be very explicit in what it considers a minimum standard under the Framework Convention. As already mentioned above, the second commentary was more inclined to use quite normative language as compared to the first commentary.

The normative substance of the second commentary is notable in two ways: on the one hand the commentary clarifies in more practical terms the content of the legal obligation under the FCNM, making the minimum standards emerging from its soft jurisprudence[36] (at least de facto) binding. In doing so it does not go beyond its findings of the country-specific opinions. The binding force of these practical minimum standards holds true particularly for new member states that, upon ratification of the FCNM, are aware of how its monitoring body interprets it.[37] On the other hand, by drawing on emerging standards or best practice in place in individual countries identified during the country-by-country monitoring, the commentary provides the states with a toolbox of options and possibilities on how to implement the respective provision of the FCNM.[38] Furthermore, the standards defined by the ACFC can become binding for individual states if they serve as a basis in national[39] or European court decisions. In this context it is particularly relevant to remember the judgment of the European Court of Human Rights in *D.H. v. the Czech Republic*, where the Court quoted entire paragraphs of the ACFC's opinion on the Czech Republic in order to substantiate the decision in favour of a violation of the ECHR.[40]

While it is quite clear that the commentaries are no source of hard law (and maybe only the minimum standards contained in them have the potential of turning into the latter), it is reasonable to conclude that the commentaries are an instrument of soft law.[41] As such they have the purpose to "give substance to the

---

35   ACFC, Meeting Report, 25th meeting, 27 February-3 March 2006, para. 5.

36   The term 'soft jurisprudence' has been coined by Rainer Hofmann in New Standards for Minority Issues in the Council of Europe and the OSCE, in: Jorgen Kühl/Marc Weller (eds.), Minority Policy in Action: The Bonn-Copenhagen Declarations in a European Context 1955-2005, Flensburg 2005, 239-277, at 243-244.

37   Palermo (2008a).

38   Similarly see Marko, Council of Europe Framework Convention (2010). On the distinction between minimum standard, emerging standard and best practice see Lantschner (2009), 26-28.

39   For an analysis of the impact of the FCNM and the AC opinions on national jurisprudence, see Francesco Palermo, Domestic Enforcement and Direct Effect of the Framework Convention for the Protection of National Minorities, in: Annelies Verstichel et al. (eds.), The Framework Convention for the Protection of National Minorities: A Useful Pan-European Instrument? Antwerp 2008, 187-214.

40   ECtHR, Appl. No. 57325/00, D.H. et al. v. Czech Republic, Judgment (Grand Chamber) of 13 November 2007.

41   Francesco Palermo, The Dual Meaning of Participation: The Advisory Committee's Commentary on Participation, presentation during the conference: Enhancing the Impact of the Framework Convention, Strasbourg, 9-10 October 2008b, at 5, available at www.coe.int/minorities.

provisions in international law and to facilitate at the national level the practical implementation of the international commitments".[42] The Commentaries can therefore be seen as a means to help all actors involved to better understand their rights and obligations under the FCNM as they further specify its provisions. As such they are complementary to the Convention.[43]

Which role will the commentaries play in the future monitoring work? A lot will depend on a successful dissemination of the commentaries amongst all stakeholders. The Commentary on Education is available in six, the one on participation in seven different languages. The Advisory Committee makes regularly reference to them in its opinions. As has already been mentioned, it does not seem that the Committee of Ministers is contributing to the dissemination by referring to the commentaries in its own documents. Considering the fact, however, that the Committee of Ministers conforms most of the times to the opinions of the Advisory Committee, which are in turn formed and informed by the considerations expressed in the commentaries, it thereby makes the commentaries indirectly normative. This effect would of course be all the more explicit and direct if the text proposed by the ACFC to the Committee of Ministers for its resolutions would contain a reference to the commentaries. It is, however, questionable whether such a proposed resolution would be accepted by the Committee of Ministers. In some of the follow-up meetings special sessions are devoted to the presentation and discussion of the contents of the commentaries. However, this does not seem to be an established practice.[44] The state reports submitted after the adoption of the commentaries do not explicitly mention them, but it seems that some shadow reports prepared by minority organization do so.

Outside the CoE context, one can point out that the Commentary on Participation has been mentioned in the background document to the recommendations on minorities and effective political participation prepared by the UN independent expert on minority issues, Gay McDougall.[45] In spite of this positive cross-referencing amongst bodies of international organizations, it appears that much more needs to be done in order to make all persons concerned, minority representatives and decision-makers alike, aware of the existence of the thematic commentaries and on the use they can make of it. Regional or national training sessions and seminars could be organized by the secretariat of the FCNM. However, the secretariat is facing limitations both in terms of human resources as well as financial possibilities. Therefore, the follow-up meetings are an important possibility for disseminating information about the commentaries. National and local NGOs, who already refer to the commentaries in their shadow reports, could engage more strongly in disseminating their knowledge of the

---

42   Asbjørn Eide, The Oslo Recommendations: An Overview, International Journal on Minority and Group Rights, 6 (1999) 3, at 325.

43   Palermo (2008b), at 5.

44   According to programmes of follow-up meetings available on the website of the FCNM, the Commentary on Education has been presented only once (in Sweden), the one on participation three times (in Sweden, Slovenia and Norway) out of the five follow-up meetings that have taken place after the adoption of this commentary.

45   Human Rights Council, Forum on Minority Issues, Second session, Geneva, 12–13 November 2009, Background document by the independent expert on minority issues, Gay McDougall, on minorities and effective political participation, 8 October 2009, A/HRC/FMI/2009/3.

commentaries to the wider society. The responsibility for the awareness raising should, however, not only be placed on the shoulders of the secretariat or the civil society but also on the state. Funds should be made available for a translation of the commentaries into the national and/or minority languages. They should be distributed to members of parliament, focusing on those working in sub-committees dealing with minority issues. The possibilities for disseminating the commentaries are manifold. The present article would like to make a contribution to the rising of the awareness within the academic community.

D   Conclusions

Over the last decade the Advisory Committee has not only learned to walk, but has now also accelerated its pace. On the basis of the jurisprudence developed in the course of its country-specific monitoring it has published two documents: a Commentary on Education and one on Participation, which can help states in the implementation of their obligations and the ACFC in carrying out its monitoring. They further outline the issues that will require further attention, indicating to states parties already the direction in which the journey will continue. Through the consultation process put in place during the drafting of the second commentary the ACFC has already successfully involved those protected by the FCNM as well as other bodies dealing with the protection of minorities, thereby putting the implementation of the FCNM into a broader international context. While the ACFC is certainly the right place for thematic work on the FCNM, some form of involvement of the Council of Ministers might be worth considering.

The commentaries are an important contribution to the standard-setting function by the Advisory Committee. The normative approach taken in the second commentary could further be strengthened in the course of adopting new commentaries. In my view there is no reason why the minimum standards identified during the country-specific monitoring should not be spelled out in straightforward language. On the other hand it is clear that the fields covered by the FCNM do not lend themselves to one-size-fits-all solutions. For what cannot be considered a minimum standard, the commentaries should thus be understood as a toolbox from which states can chose the appropriate instruments for the implementation of the FCNM in their specific context.

Finally, the commentaries can only become effective if they are known and used by those concerned, be it minority representatives, politicians or civil servants. For the time being, it seems that more could be done to disseminate the commentaries and to raise awareness about their existence. After all, people should know that the "baby" has grown up.

IV

OSCE

Bernhard KNOLL and Jens-Hagen ESCHENBÄCHER[*]

Human Rights and Security in the OSCE Region in 2009

Table of Contents

Keywords

OSCE, ODIHR, human rights, democratic elections, election observation, hate crimes, European Union, Armenia, Moldova

A   Introduction: the 2009 OSCE Athens Ministerial Council

At the OSCE Ministerial Council meeting in Athens in December 2009, the foreign ministers of the OSCE's 56 participating states reconfirmed their commitment to a "free, democratic and more integrated OSCE area" without dividing lines.[1] To achieve this goal, they formally endorsed a new process, initiated earlier in 2009 at an informal ministerial meeting on the Greek island of Corfu. This initiative, now dubbed "Corfu Process", is meant to give new impetus to revitalizing the dialogue between states and finding common ground on security issues in the region. It is also seen as providing a forum for discussing the Russian proposal for a new binding "European Security Treaty".[2]

From a "human dimension" perspective – the term used in the OSCE context for human rights and democracy as key components of a comprehensive secu-

---

[*]   This article reflects the authors' personal opinions which are not necessarily those of the OSCE or ODIHR.

[1]   OSCE Ministerial Council, Ministerial Declaration on the Corfu Process: Reconfirm-Review-Reinvigorate Security and Co-operation from Vancouver to Vladivostok, Athens, 2 December 2009, MC.DOC/1/09, para. 1.

[2]   President of the Russian Federation, European Security Treaty, 29 November 2009, http://eng.kremlin.ru/text/themes/2009/11/291600_223080.shtml.

rity concept – the Athens Ministerial was significant in that the participating states reconfirmed their adherence to the concept of comprehensive, co-operative and indivisible security, and pledged compliance with OSCE norms, principles and commitments in all three OSCE dimensions. They expressed concern that the principles of the Helsinki Final Act and OSCE commitments were not fully respected and implemented, including in the human dimension where states identified the need for achievements in the field of human rights to be "fully safeguarded and further advanced".[3]

Indeed, while it has been acknowledged that there can be no lasting stability in the OSCE region without functioning democracies that respect the human rights of their citizens, events throughout the year 2009 again sharply illustrated the need for greater respect for human rights and implementation of OSCE commitments. This article will review some of these implementation gaps and major developments in the human dimension during 2009, with a focus on activities undertaken by the OSCE's Office for Democratic Institutions and Human Rights (ODIHR) to assist participating states in improving implementation of OSCE commitments.

B   Trials Following the Post-Election Violence in Armenia in March 2008

The violent clashes that erupted in Armenia's capital Yerevan on 1-2 March 2008, in the aftermath of the 19 February presidential election, resulted in the death of at least eight people and left countless others injured. Thousands of demonstrators had been protesting against the results of the election which they saw as rigged in favour of the incumbent. The situation escalated in the early morning hours of 1 March 2008 when police in riot gear, ostensibly in search for weapons, closed in on a group of some 1000 protesters camping on Yerevan's Opera Square. The ensuing clashes turned out to be the most deadly incident of election-related violence in the OSCE region in recent years.

ODIHR had observed the election preceding the violent incidents of 1-2 March,[4] and maintained a presence in the country, in consultation with the OSCE Chairmanship and the Armenian authorities, to gather information on the human rights situation with the aim of keeping the Chairmanship informed and to advise on possible future activities. A team of human rights experts from ODIHR was in the country between 8 March and 12 April 2008. The report of the information-gathering visit, which includes a detailed account of the events of 1-2 March based on first-hand sources, was conveyed to the Armenian authorities.[5]

Following the information-gathering visit, ODIHR obtained agreement from the Armenian authorities to monitor the trials of the individuals charged in con-

---

3   Ministerial Declaration on the Corfu Process (2009), paras. 2 and 5.
4   OSCE/ODIHR, Election Observation Mission Final Report, Republic of Armenia, Presidential Election, Warsaw, 30 May 2008.
5   See also Commissioner for Human Rights of the Council of Europe, "Special Mission to Armenia, Yerevan 12-15 March", Strasbourg, 20 March 2008, http://www.coe.am/docs/special/1eng.pdf.

nection with the 1-2 March events[6]. Over 100 persons were arrested in connection with their participation in the demonstration. ODIHR was able to observe 93 criminal cases involving 109 defendants. Most defendants were convicted, often to prison terms ranging from one to nine years, although some were later released on various grounds. At the end of the trails, 58 convicted persons remained imprisoned. As a result of a general amnesty adopted by the Armenian Parliament on 19 June 2009, most individuals sentenced to imprisonment in connection with the 1-2 March events were released.[7]

The monitoring report, published in March 2010, revealed shortcomings in the adjudication of the trials and concluded that a comprehensive reform of Armenia's criminal justice sector is warranted in order to bring it closer to OSCE commitments and other international standards.[8]

The report makes recommendations in a number of areas where shortcomings were observed. For example, with regard to the right to liberty, the report says custody decisions were not reasoned properly and did not address the facts in the individual cases. It recommends changing the pattern of ordering and extending custody by default, so that pre-trial detention becomes an exception, as required by international standards, rather than the rule.[9]

The trials raised doubts whether the defendants were in fact presumed innocent until proven guilty, and the report recommends ensuring that judges understand and apply the principle of presumption of innocence, and that violations give rise to disciplinary action.[10]

Judges displayed openly hostile attitudes to the defence, and systematically denied defence motions to introduce or examine additional evidence, thus seriously undermining the principle of equality of arms and the possibility of the defence to present its cases. There was also an over-reliance on written witness testimonies and police testimonies, without giving the defence the opportunity to verify and examine such testimonies. This led the Parliamentary Assembly of the Council of Europe (PACE) to conclude that, contrary to its demands, "a significant number of prosecution cases and convictions was based solely on police testimony, without substantial corroborating evidence".[11]

Although there have been reports of torture and ill-treatment by police, these allegations were not addressed and judges relied on witness statements allegedly obtained under duress. Defence motions to exclude such evidence were ignored or denied. The report concludes that serious efforts must be made to root out abuses of power by police and investigators, and ensure respect for the prohibition of using evidence obtained through illegal means.[12]

The report's findings point to systemic shortcomings in Armenia's justice system. It thus can serve as a basis for the reforms needed to bring the country's justice system in line with international standards and OSCE commitments.

---

6   OSCE/ODIHR, Final Report of the Trial Monitoring Project in Armenia, April 2008-July 2009, Warsaw, 8 March 2010.
7   Ibid., at 12.
8   Ibid., at 6-9.
9   Ibid.
10   Ibid.
11   PACE Resolution 1643 (2009), Implementation by Armenia of Assembly Resolutions 1609 (2008) and 1620 (2008), 27 January 2009, para. 4.1.
12   OSCE/ODIHR, Final Report of the Trial Monitoring Project in Armenia (2010).

C   Hate Crimes in the OSCE Region

Hate crimes are a problem of great concern in many countries of the OSCE region. OSCE participating states have collectively recognized the dangers posed by hate crimes and manifestations of intolerance and its potential for creating political instability in the OSCE region since the 1990s. In recent years, participating states have agreed on a comprehensive set of norms which serve as a basis to address this problem,[13] and the issue has come to the forefront of the Organization's activities.

ODIHR's most recent annual report on hate crimes in the OSCE region, published in November 2009, confirms the serious threat hate crimes pose to domestic and international security, as they can undermine societal cohesion and sow the seeds of conflict and wider-scale violence.[14] The report describes numerous instances of intimidation, threats, vandalism, assault, arson and murder across the entire region. People were targeted because of their "race", ethnicity, religion or other status. However, despite the increased attention afforded to hate crimes in recent years, the report concludes that the full extent of hate crimes remains obscured by a lack of reliable data. There are significant gaps in data collection in most participating states. Some do not collect any statistics on hate crimes at all, while others do not make this data public.

Without common data collection standards, available figures cannot be used to compare countries and identify trends. For example, the fact that the United Kingdom reported nearly 40,000 cases of racially motivated hate crimes[15] – more than any other OSCE participating state – does not necessarily mean that this country is worse affected by racist violence than other states. It could simply mean that the United Kingdom has a more developed or comprehensive data collection system compared to other states. Similarly, the fact that Greece did not report a single case of racist hate crime also does not necessarily mean that this country is free of racially-motivated violence.[16]

One of the countries particularly affected by hate crimes in 2008 and 2009 was Hungary. In a series of at least 40 attacks targeting the country's Roma minority, the majority of which appeared to be ethnically motivated incidents, at least six people were killed. Civil society actors inside Hungary and international community representatives drew urgent attention to these violent incidents in late 2008 and called for vigilance in investigating these crimes and protecting Roma communities. In view of the gravity of the events and the concern they raised within the Hungarian Government and the international community, ODIHR decided to send a delegation on a field assessment visit to Hungary. The delegation, led by ODIHR's Contact Point on Roma and Sinti Issues, visited a number of locations in Hungary in June and July 2009 to assess the situation of Roma, looking specifically at factors leading or contributing to the escalation of violence and attacks against Roma, including economic disparities, housing segregation

---

13   See OSCE Ministerial Council Decisions No. 4/03, Maastricht, 2 December 2003, and No. 12/04, Sofia, 7 December 2004.
14   OSCE, Hate crimes in the OSCE region – incidents and responses. Annual Report for 2008, Warsaw, 16 November 2009, http://www.osce.org/publications/show_pub lication.php?id=41314.
15   Ibid., at 34.
16   Ibid., at 33.

and discrimination, deeply entrenched stereotypes and distrust among majority ethnic Hungarian and minority Roma communities. Particular challenges identified during the field assessment are the relative frequency of extremist anti-Roma statements in the media and public/political discourse and the weakness of legal or political mechanisms to restrict or counter such extremist rhetoric.

Other challenges include the weakness of legislation specifically addressing bias-motivated hate crimes and the limited capacity to investigate or prosecute such crimes, a challenge which is compounded by the lack of ethnically disaggregated data or the population at large and for victims of crime in particular. The delegation recommended that the authorities develop methods of disaggregated hate crime data collection to more effectively implement relevant OSCE commitments in the area of hate crimes. More broadly, Hungarian law enforcement, prosecutorial and judicial authorities will need to develop greater capacities to investigate hate crimes and bring the perpetrators of such crimes to justice.

Among the most relevant areas for priority long-term engagement are Roma education, with a long-term focus on early childhood education as well as better Roma outreach by Hungarian social service providers, greater efforts by Roma and ethnic Hungarian community leaders to encourage dialogue among their constituencies, and public information activities to overcome negative stereotypes of Roma in the media and public opinion.

D   Observation of Elections

The importance of elections for human rights and security is undisputable. If held in line with international standards, elections are vital expressions of the exercise of human rights and fundamental freedoms, they transfer legitimacy to governments and thus contribute to ensuring stability and security. The presence of international observers can serve as a deterrent against fraud, can enhance confidence in the electoral process and can point to weaknesses that have the potential to result in tensions.

The elections observed by ODIHR in 2009 were conducted generally in a peaceful manner. The only exception was *Moldova*, where peaceful protests against the outcome of the 5 April 2009 parliamentary elections turned violent on 7 April when demonstrators alleging election fraud stormed the presidential administration and parliament buildings.[17] Three persons were found dead shortly after these events; two of them allegedly died in police custody, but the circumstances of their deaths were the subject of controversy. Hundreds of people were arrested in relation to the riots, and there were numerous reports of ill-treatment in police custody.[18]

In its final report on the elections, which were won by the governing Party of Communists, ODIHR concluded that many OSCE commitments were met, but also said that improvements were required to ensure an electoral process free from undue administrative interference and to increase public confidence. The

---

17   OSCE/ODIHR, Election Observation Mission, Republic of Moldova: Parliamentary Elections, Post Election Interim Report, 6-17 April 2009.

18   Commissioner for Human Rights of the Council of Europe, Report following the visit to Moldova, 25 to 28 April 2009, 17 July 2009, CommDH(2009)27, http://www.unhcr.org/refworld/docid/4a5c75e12.html.

report added that the observation of post-election day developments revealed further shortcomings that challenged some OSCE commitments, in particular the disregard for due process in adjudicating complaints of alleged irregularities and deficiencies in the compilation of voter lists lodged by opposition political parties.[19]

After the early parliamentary elections of 29 July 2009, which were necessary due to the failure of parliament to elect a president and led to a new parliamentary majority for the former opposition, ODIHR's overall assessment was similar: many OSCE commitments were met, but there were shortcomings that needed to be addressed, in particular a campaign environment negatively affected by subtle pressure, intimidation, misuse of administrative resources and bias in media coverage.[20]

While there has been considerable speculation about wide-spread fraud in the first round, this could not be confirmed by the observers who concluded that the two elections – while leading to different results – were of similar quality (or lack thereof).

Most progress was noted in the spring 2009 elections in *Macedonia* and in *Montenegro* which "met most"[21] and "almost all"[22] OSCE commitments, respectively. Among the elections observed by ODIHR in 2009, the gap between OSCE commitments and their implementation was greatest during the 23 July presidential election in *Kyrgyzstan*. This election, ODIHR concluded in its final report, "failed to meet key OSCE commitments for democratic elections". The report said the election fell short of international standards in particular with regard to guaranteeing equal suffrage, ensuring that votes are reported honestly and that political campaigning is conducted in a fair and free atmosphere, and maintaining a clear separation between party and state.[23]

In 2009, the OSCE/ODIHR covered 15 different elections in 26 participating states – ten of them visited for the first time – and in one state that remains out of the OSCE area (Afghanistan). A number of important elections took place in *long-standing democracies*, including Germany, Greece, Iceland, Norway and Portugal, all of which were assessed by ODIHR. It found all these elections to be generally in line with OSCE commitments. They were characterized by political pluralism, respect for fundamental freedoms and rights, a free and diverse media environment and a high degree of public trust in the election administration and the integrity of the process as a whole.

However, in all cases ODIHR election experts also found shortcomings and made recommendations for improvements. In *Germany*, for example, it remains of concern that the legislation does not provide for a judicial review of decisions made by the election administration before election day, thus diminishing access

---

19   OSCE/ODIHR, Election Observation Mission Final Report, Republic of Moldova: Parliamentary Elections, Warsaw, 16 June 2009.

20   OSCE/ODIHR, Election Observation Mission Final Report, Republic of Moldova: Early Parliamentary Elections, Warsaw, 14 October 2009.

21   OSCE/ODIHR, Election Observation Mission Final Report, The Former Yugoslav Republic of Macedonia: Presidential and Municipal Elections, Warsaw, 30 June 2009.

22   OSCE/ODIHR, Election Observation Mission Final Report, Montenegro: Early Parliamentary Elections, 10 June 2009.

23   OSCE/ODIHR, Election Observation Mission Final Report, Kyrgyz Republic: Presidential Election, Warsaw, 22 October 2009.

of citizens to timely and effective remedy as prescribed by OSCE commitments and other international legal instruments.[24] In *Iceland*, ODIHR noted the structural imbalances in the weight of the vote between constituencies, most marked between the Southwest and Northwest, calling into question the principle of equality of the vote.[25] In *Norway*, the constitutional obligation of citizens to accept candidacy, and possibly election, without their consent, and the unequal weight of the vote among constituencies, diverge from international standards.[26] In *Portugal*, ODIHR found that independent candidates are not permitted to contest elections in contravention of OSCE commitments, and that members of parliament who change parties lose their mandate.[27] ODIHR also visited *Greece* – the country that led the organization in 2009 – and identified, *inter alia*, the need for introducing comprehensive and secure mechanisms allowing hospitalized and homebound voters, those with reduced mobility, and Greek citizens abroad to exercise their constitutional right to vote.[28]

The assessment of the elections to the European Parliament was undertaken with an entirely novel format that required invitations from 27 EU member states. Constituting the largest electoral event in the OSCE area, 736 members of parliament were elected by an electorate of approximately 375 million people. Given the complexities of these elections, the limited interest among much of the electorate, and the specificities of national election legislation, ODIHR concluded that some aspects of the legal and administrative frameworks both at EU and national levels need to be improved and harmonized.

In particular, the report recommended that eligibility requirements for candidates in EP elections should be harmonized. It also suggested that in order to ensure equality of the vote, the EU should adopt minimum standards on voting rights for EP elections. Such a review could include consideration of voting rights for EU residents not holding citizenship of any state.[29] Another important recommendation concerned the transparency and accountability of political parties and campaign finance. ODIHR concluded that EU member states should enact a regulatory framework for the disclosure and auditing of party financing and expenditures, to be accompanied by an enforcement mechanism.[30]

A second activity undertaken in unusually challenging circumstances was that of supporting stakeholders in the 20 August presidential and provincial council elections in *Afghanistan*.[31] These elections – the first to be Afghan-led – were

---

24   OSCE/ODIHR, Election Assessment Mission Report, Federal Republic of Germany: Elections to the Federal Parliament (Bundestag), Warsaw, 14 December 2009.

25   OSCE/ODIHR, Election Assessment Mission Report, Iceland: Parliamentary Elections, Warsaw, 28 June 2009.

26   OSCE/ODIHR, Election Assessment Mission Report, Norway: Parliamentary Elections, Warsaw, 27 November 2009.

27   OSCE/ODIHR, Election Assessment Mission Report, Portugal: Parliamentary Elections, Warsaw, 23 December 2009.

28   OSCE/ODIHR, Election Assessment Mission Report, Greece: Early Parliamentary Elections, Warsaw, 23 December 2009.

29   OSCE/ODIHR Expert Group Report, Elections to the European Parliament, Warsaw, 22 September 2009, p.19.

30   Ibid., at 26.

31   The deployment followed a decision by the OSCE's Permanent Council, which tasked ODIHR with assisting Afghanistan's government and the international community in their efforts to organize the forthcoming elections and prepare a report on

held in a volatile security environment, with a lack of effective measures to prevent irregularities, widespread fraud on Election Day, and a failure of the Afghan-formed Independent Election Commission (IEC) to respond resolutely to malpractices. These deficiencies heavily damaged public trust in the process. ODIHR recommended that parliamentary and district elections be delayed until at least the most basic conditions for democratic elections are more firmly in place.[32] In addition, it recommended that such delay must coincide with the elaboration of a clear timeline of activities designed to drive forward serious reform – both amendments of the electoral code and the completion of a full voter register. It concluded that priority should be given to restoring confidence in the IEC, whose commissioners should be replaced and appointed through a broader process of consultation among all stakeholders.[33] The transparency of its work must be increased by for instance opening its meeting to observers and party agents. Both the Electoral Complaints Commission (ECC) and domestic observation must, on the other hand, be further supported and strengthened as the final line of defense against fraud and corruption. The ECC, ODIHR concluded, should be made a permanent body; domestic observation support must include a focus on organizational capacities and strengthening observation methodology, including analytical capabilities and reporting.[34]

E   Conclusion

The end of the Cold War, sealed by the CSCE Charter of Paris in 1990,[35] ushered in an era of unprecedented change and progress towards the basic principles agreed in Paris. Two decades later, Europe is less divided and characterized more by co-operation than by confrontation. Democracy and human rights have flourished in many countries previously under one-party rule, and economies have prospered, despite the current crisis. Europe today is arguably more stable and secure than it has ever been in recent history.

The OSCE has, in its human dimension, developed commitments that are the normative baseline upon which it has built values and a sense of ownership in the region. Enshrined in the OSCE's *acquis* are some of the best-developed

---

the electoral process, with recommendations on how to improve the conduct of future elections, see PC.DEC/891, Election Support Team to Afghanistan, 2 April 2009.

32   OSCE/ODIHR, Election Support Team Final Report, Islamic Republic of Afghanistan: Presidential and Provincial Council Elections, Warsaw, 8 December 2009. Parliamentary elections were postponed to 18 September 2010 after initially being scheduled for 22 May.

33   Ibid., at 15. Recent events indicate a lack of political will to make serious efforts to improve public confidence in elections. None of the IEC members, including the chairperson, were held accountable for the massive fraud that occurred in 2009, despite being responsible for the conduct of that election. All members remain in their posts.

34   Ibid., at 18, 19 and 35, 36. Regrettably, and contrary to these recommendations, the President altered the ECC's structure which has put into question its impartiality and credibility for future elections. Discussions continue regarding how this crucial body will be constituted for the forthcoming elections.

35   Charter of Paris for a New Europe, Paris, 19-21 November 1990, http://www.osce.org/item/4047.html.

human rights and democracy standards in the world.[36] The obligation to implement them in good faith is the basis for OSCE's understanding of accountability of individual states – to their citizens and to other OSCE states as laid down in the Moscow Document of 1991.[37]

Yet as the examples discussed in this contribution show, security and human rights in the OSCE region remain significantly challenged. While the aftermath of the conflict in Georgia stuck out due to its consequences for the affected population,[38] other developments also gave rise to serious concern in 2009, in a wide range of countries located in different parts of the OSCE region.

On the normative side, the year ended with decisions on how to move the Organization's work in the human dimension forward in specific areas, including combating hate crimes, ensuring the sustainable integration of Roma and Sinti and increasing women's participation in political and public life,[39] as well as a reconfirmation of the key principles that underpin the OSCE's comprehensive security concept. At least on paper, there remains a broad consensus about the importance of human rights and democracy standards being an essential element of the OSCE's comprehensive concept of security. The "Corfu Process", launched in 2009, will show whether the idea that peace among states is intrinsically linked to the respect for human rights and democracy standards within states remains at the heart of discussions about the future of Europe's security architecture.[40]

---

36   Cf., in particular, the Document of the Copenhagen Meeting of the Conference on the Human Dimension of the CSCE ('Copenhagen Document', 1990), §§ 3, 5, 7.

37   Document of the Moscow Meeting of the Conference on the Human Dimension of the CSCE, Moscow, 3 October 1991, http://www.osce.org/item/13995.html.

38   Cf. Jens-Hagen Eschenbächer/Bernhard Knoll, The OSCE, Human Rights and Security in 2008, Wolfgang Benedek/Wolfram Karl/Manfred Nowak/Anja Mihr (eds.), European Yearbook on Human Rights Yearbook 2009, Vienna 2009, 225-232 (227-229).

39   OSCE Ministerial Council, Decision on Women's Participation in Political and Public Life (MC.DEC/7/09); Decision on Enhancing OSCE Efforts to Ensure Roma and Sinti Sustainable Integration (MC.DEC/8/09); Decision on Combating Hate Crimes (MC.DEC/9/09), 2 December 2009.

40   For the "Corfu Process" and the human dimension see the contribution of Christian Strohal, in this volume, at 297.

Christian STROHAL[*]

Alive. And Well? The Need for a Stronger Peer Engagement in the OSCE

Table of Contents

Keywords

Human rights, commitments and implementation gaps, OSCE, comprehensive security, UN, peer review, NGOs

---

[*]   The thoughts contained in this article have been presented first to the 18th Partnership for Peace International Research Seminar on the "Indivisibility of Euro-Atlantic Security" organized jointly by the NATO Defense College and the Austrian government in February 2010 in Vienna. They represent the personal views of the author.

*"An organisation can be no better than the members wish it to be [...].
Therefore [...]: a successful concept must be continued and not abandoned ."*
Dietrich Genscher[1]

"Congratulations. The OSCE is Alive and Well."
Stephan M. Minikes[2]

A   Overview

There have been quite some voices in recent years arguing that the Organization for Security and Cooperation in Europe (OSCE) is in crisis, or at least in need of substantial reform, or is no longer 'useful' for (some of) its 56 members. Numerous reasons have been put forward in support of such criticism – lack of progress on finding solutions for so-called frozen conflicts, its inability to prevent the war in Georgia 2008, the purportedly destabilizing effects of election observation missions conducted by its Office for Democratic Institutions and Human Rights (ODIHR), the repeated incapacity of Ministers to agree on a political declaration at their annual conferences, the lack of support for a summit since 1999, and others.[3] In 2009, however, a somewhat more optimistic view was taking hold, after the so-called "Corfu Process" was launched at a meeting of foreign ministers in June 2009 intended to "restore confidence and take forward dialogue on wider European security", in the words of the Chairmanship-in-Office for 2010, Kazakhstan.

This article concentrates on the question how this dialogue, and process, can strengthen trust in what many see as the key success of the OSCE and also as a litmus test for mustering the political will necessary for its continuation – that is: to effectively implement the commitments in what the organization calls its "human dimension", i.e. human rights, the rule of law, and pluralist democracy, as part of a comprehensive security concept (section B). It argues that the neces-

---

1   Former German Foreign Minister Dietrich Genscher, the first Chairman-in-Office of the OSCE, issued his warnings in Dietrich Genscher, Is the OSCE underestimated? On the Discrepancy between the Effectiveness and Importance of the OSCE and its Utilization and Treatment by the Participating States, in: IFSH (ed.), OSCE Yearbook 2001, Hamburg 2001, 21-28, at 27.

2   An article with this title was published by the then-Permanent Representative of the USA to the OSCE in a special focus section of the OSCE Yearbook 2005 on the occasion of the 30th anniversary of the Helsinki Final Act, see Stephan M. Minikes, Congratulations. The OSCE is Alive and Well, in: IFSH (ed.), OSCE Yearbook 2005, Hamburg 2005, 69-77. In the same section, a well-informed observer from Moscow, Andrei Zagorski, reminded us that a "clash between Moscow and the Human Dimension" characterized already the CSCE on its way from the Vienna Follow-up Meeting 1989 to the Copenhagen Meeting of the Conference on the Human Dimension of the CSCE; see Andrei Zagorski, The Clash between Moscow and the Human Dimension of the CSCE: From Vienna to Copenhagen (1989-1990), in ibid., 47-60.

3   Cf., as some examples for many, already Ursel Schlichting, Is the OSCE Going Through a Crisis?, in IFSH (ed.), OSCE Yearbook 2001, 13, and Victor-Yves Ghebali, The Unfreezing of Frozen Conflicts in Georgia: What Implications for the OSCE? in: Daniel Warner (ed.), OSCE Future Operations and Leadership (CIG Occasional Paper 2/2008), 7-20.

sary institutions, instruments, and processes exist, but that they need to be used more fully and systematically (C). More specifically, the peer review (D) conducted by the delegations of the member states in the Permanent Council in Vienna should be further developed in order to allow for genuine peer engagement (E). The United Nations (UN) could provide inspiration in this regard (F).

B   The "Human Dimension": Failure or Success Story?

The protection of human rights, the realization of the rule of law, and the development of pluralist democracy are essential elements of a modern and comprehensive security concept. The OSCE stands proud witness to this concept it has developed. The UN have adopted, with the World Summit Outcome Document of 2005, a similar concept.[4] But what are essential elements in turning such a security concept effectively into reality? More specifically, how can we address persistent criticism from some governments, and maintain trust and ownership by all, while building on the strong achievements of the OSCE, and also take into account those of other international frameworks?

Why does one need to raise question-marks at all? One could have thought that in the human dimension, the Euro-Atlantic world would have established the main parameters if not already in 1975 with the Helsinki Final Act, then with the Charter of Paris and the Copenhagen Document,[5] 20 years ago, once and for all, and that all that remained to be done would have been the faithful implementation of the broad and detailed range of the commitments contained in these documents. As the last OSCE summit put it, in 1999, in its Istanbul Charta for European Security:

> "Participating States are accountable to their citizens and responsible to each other for their implementation of their OSCE commitments. We regard these commitments as our common achievement and therefore consider them to be matters of immediate and legitimate concern to all participating States."[6]

Obviously, subsequent developments have not fully lived up to expectations, especially in the human dimension. Therefore, the Organization has repeatedly addressed the question how to reduce the implementation gap. Also the Corfu process is to be seen in this perspective and should be welcomed. Already a decade ago in Istanbul, heads of State and Government have set the frame clearly: "We reaffirm that respect for human rights and fundamental freedoms,

---

4   UN General Assembly resolution 60/1 of 24 October 2005, para. 9: "We acknowledge that peace and security, development and human rights are the pillars of the United Nations system and the foundations for collective security and well-being. We recognize that development, peace and security and human rights are interlinked and mutually reinforcing."

5   This article will not present a full list of sources, as all documents mentioned are readily available, especially at the various websites indicated. All quotes from CSCE and OSCE documents can be found on www.osce.org and, more specifically, in an ODIHR publication, OSCE Human Dimension Commitments, in a chronological and thematic compilation, respectively, at www.osce.org/odihr/item_11_16238.html and www.osce.org/odihr/item_11_16237.html.

6   See supra, note 5.

democracy and the rule of law is at the core of the OSCE's comprehensive concept of security".

The OSCE has rightly been proud of this comprehensive, cooperative, and indivisible security concept. Concept and reality, however, have been clashing – some would argue: increasingly so – over the last decade. Human rights and democracy standards and their effective implementation remain essential elements in any work intended to further refine this concept and fully realize it, but opinions differ among some of the OSCE governments on how to proceed.

In other words, not all agree that respect for human rights is a prerequisite for security: Since a few years, some governments[7] have been criticizing the trajectory the OSCE has taken in their view. They note a lack of 'balance', lamenting what they describe as inappropriately strong focus on human rights issues. This criticism has built up in particular after the so-called "colour revolutions" in Georgia, the Ukraine and Kyrgyzstan[8] and further intensified in the run-up to the elections in the Russian Federation in 2007 and 2008.[9] The criticism has, however, not been all that constructive in that it has deliberately not taken into account the interdependence of the three dimensions, nor has it been accompanied by efforts to re-balance it through strong proposals in the two other dimensions. And, of course, never has the case been made why less human rights would be better for long-term security. Rather, the arguments used by these countries could be, and have been, summarized as "shoot the messenger".

The critique may have a point, however, if one examines how violations of commitments in the human dimension have been dealt with by the collective structures set up by the OSCE governments, in particular the Permanent Council. This article therefore will look at ways to improve the peer review, and consequently peer engagement, in the OSCE framework.

The criticism still persists – and so do human rights violations. But over the longer time-horizon, much has been achieved. The OSCE and its institutions, as they have evolved from the CSCE, are given credit for many of these achievements. So, has the OSCE become, for some of its members, too much of a success story in advancing the protection of human rights, the rule of law and pluralist democracy?

---

7   In particular Russia, Belarus, Armenia, Uzbekistan, Turkmenistan, Tajikistan and Kazakhstan, in a number of statements and working documents to the Permanent Council and ministerial meetings. Cf. Andrei Zagorski, Election Observation in the OSCE Area: Political Challenges, in Warner (ed.), OSCE Future Operations, 134-159.

8   After seriously fraudulent elections, in 2003, 2004 and 2005, respectively, documented, like around 100 other elections since 1993, by OSCE/ODIHR election observation missions.

9   The professional and long-term election observation of the ODIHR, for many governments one of the signature successes of the OSCE as a whole, and the 'gold standard' of international election observation, has been blamed, in this criticism, as contributing to "destabilizing" certain countries and being an "instrument" of US interests, in total disregard of numerous and detailed OSCE commitments, as well as of the reality of its professionalism proven in over 100 long-term observation missions, on the basis of a public methodology emulated by other international organizations. Cf. Christian Strohal, Democratic Elections and their Monitoring: Can This OSCE Success Story be Maintained? in: Wolfgang Benedek et al. (eds.), European Yearbook on Human Rights 2009, Vienna etc. 2009, 247-264.

It is interesting that the OSCE concept, while being criticized from within, was being emulated at the same time in the global framework of the UN. Kofi Annan, in his report In Larger Freedom[10] for the summit in 2005, put it into a nutshell: "not only are development, security and human rights all imperative; they also reinforce each other".[11]

If one attempts to frame a renewed outlook on European security, there is a clear systemic duty to start by re-confirming the human dimension commitments and to proceed to identifying areas and mechanisms, wherever necessary, for their further strengthening. In this, one has to examine the processes and instruments at the disposal of governments for effective implementation control and redress. Only by maintaining, and further strengthening, the focus on human rights as a core component of comprehensive security and cooperation will it be possible for a process of *"reconfirm[ing]-review[ing]-reinvigorat[ing]"* security and co-operation, as the Corfu decision puts it rightly,[12] to succeed in practice.

C   Implementation Gaps

The central yardstick for these discussions remains the *'reconfirm'* – the reaffirmation of shared commitments by all participating States, including the commitment to implement. The OSCE has developed an impressive catalogue of them, and such a reaffirmation should come naturally as 2010 also marks the 20th anniversary of the Copenhagen Document. But ever since its adoption there were strong indications that performance by governments was uneven, in substance as well as geographically, and sometimes lacking altogether. In 2006, the ODIHR responded to an explicit request by the OSCE Ministers with a detailed appraisal of implementation gaps. The findings in its report 'Common Responsibility: Commitments and Implementation' are still highly relevant. The report concluded that states, as a matter of urgency, should address challenges particularly in the following areas:

- democratic elections;
- freedom of assembly and association;
- human rights in countering terrorism;
- human rights defenders and national human rights institutions;
- aggressive nationalism, racism, chauvinism, xenophobia and anti-semitism;
- involuntary migration; and
- freedom of expression and threats to the independence of the media.

This list has not become less relevant or less urgent. It originated, in fact, in a similar list issued already ten years earlier by the ministers themselves, in the

---

10   UN, In larger freedom: towards development, security and human rights for all, Report of the Secretary-General, UN Doc. A/59/2005.

11   Ibid., para. 16. And he continued (para. 17): "Accordingly, we will not enjoy development without security, we will not enjoy security without development, and we will not enjoy either without respect for human rights. Unless all these causes are advanced, none will succeed." See also supra note 4.

12   Ministerial Declaration on the OSCE Corfu Process: Reconfirm-Review-Reinvigorate Security and Co-operation from Vancouver to Vladivostok, MC.DOC/1/09 of 2 December 2009.

Lisbon Declaration on a Comprehensive Security Model for Europe for the Twenty-First Century. An examination to what concrete actions it has inspired OSCE governments would go far beyond the scope of this article; suffice it to point out that one cannot see systematic follow-up activities.

D   The Parameters of the Current OSCE Peer Review Process

What would be an appropriate framework in which to tackle these challenges? We would like to follow the Director of ODIHR, Janez Lenarčič,[13] in drawing attention to another document: the 2005 Report of the Panel of Eminent Persons, 'Common Purpose. Towards a more effective OSCE.' The Panel named four key ingredients to define the OSCE's approach to security:

- its comprehensive mandate and commitments;
- the political dialogue it stimulates;
- the flexible institutions it has created; and
- the broad range of instruments it has developed.

Five years after the publication of the Panel's report, it is interesting to see how these elements can be applied to today's discussions, the *'review'* foreseen for the Corfu Process:

First, let us consider the mandate and commitments. The OSCE has, in its human dimension, developed detailed commitments that have provided political obligations for the participating states, in addition to their legal obligations under international human rights law. They reflect, and foster, a sense of ownership across the whole OSCE region. There is no need to revisit, or "fix", these human dimension commitments, in particular if this were to be understood in the sense of lowering standards in order to make them conform better with the reality in some states. If anything, as the ODIHR puts it, one might see a need for some additional commitments in selected areas, such as

- transparency, accountability and public confidence especially in the field of elections;
- the separation of powers;
- the independence of the judiciary, and, possibly,
- for addressing hate crimes more effectively.[14]

So if the commitments are there, and relevant, and (supposedly) shared, what are we lacking? The answer has changed little over time: the effective implementation of the commitments, and strong and collective political support by all 56 for this obligation.

This answer benefits from some differentiation: it is helpful to distinguish between the – relatively rare – cases of a difficulty to implement fully because of incapacity, e.g. in acute conflict situations, or in the early stages of transition from a communist and totalitarian past, and those – more frequent – other ones

13   Janez Lenarčič, The Human Dimension in the European System of Security, address at the Corfu Process Meeting, Vienna, 27 October 2009, http://www.osce.org/documents/odihr/2009/10/41023_en.pdf.
14   Ibid.

arising out of a lack of sufficient political will to implement; thirdly, there are also some situations where complex phenomena in society, such as racism and anti-Semitism, might challenge the capacity of governments to find the appropriate response and prevention strategies. Finally, there are a few isolated cases where political leaders still purport their sovereign right to be different[15], and to be protected from what they term interference in internal affairs, even if numerous OSCE and other international documents have proclaimed the opposite.[16]

Overall, the obligation to implement in good faith remains the basis for the OSCE's understanding of accountability of individual States – to their citizens as well as to other OSCE states, as laid down in the Moscow Document of 1991, and reaffirmed ever since.

This leads to the second element in the report of the Panel of Eminent Persons: political dialogue to address security challenges. Political dialogue is an essential element in the concept of peer-review which is one of the key elements of the OSCE's implementation regime. It is the Permanent Council which has been put in charge by participating States, at the summit in Budapest 1994,[17] to be the key actor in this regard, and to act in response to cases of non-compliance.

This has created the common responsibility of participating states to raise concerns in the Permanent Council (PC) as they arise: this is being done, on a regular basis, in the Vienna Hofburg, by government representatives, and annually, at the Warsaw Implementation Meeting by government and NGO representatives, and, in a more practical manner, on the ground, through OSCE field activities.

But how is the PC living up to this mandate, and these expectations? Before coming to this question, let us briefly look at the third element in the Panel's report, i.e. flexible institutions.

There are excellent institutions in the human dimension: the ODIHR, the High Commissioner on National Minorities,[18] and the Representative on Freedom of

---

15   As Russian Foreign Minister Sergey Lavrov put it, somewhat less crudely than others, on 1 December 2009 in his address to the Ministerial Council of Athens: "it is important that human rights discussions take into account the fact that these rights are based on traditional human values and cultural and civilizational diversity, diversity which must of course be respected."

16   Two examples of many: First, the OSCE Moscow Document (Document of the Moscow Meeting of the Conference on the Human Dimension of the CSCE 1991):
      "The participating States emphasize that issues relating to human rights, fundamental freedoms, democracy and the rule of law are of international concern, as respect for these rights and freedoms constitutes one of the foundations of the international order. They *categorically and irrevocably declare that the commitments undertaken in the field of the human dimension of the CSCE are matters of direct and legitimate concern to all participating States and do not belong exclusively to the internal affairs of the State concerned"* (emphasis added).
      Second, the Vienna Declaration and Programme of Action of the UN World Conference for Human Rights of 1993: "[T]he promotion and protection of all human rights is a legitimate concern of the international community."

17   Budapest Document: Towards a Genuine Partnership in a New Era, especially ch. VIII, paras. 5 et seq.

18   Technically, the High Commissioner is an institution of the first, politico-military, dimension, as he is seen as an instrument of early warning on possible conflict situations. On substance, however, his activities cannot be separated from the human dimension.

the Media. In fact, some of them were there before the PC was established. They have been given strong mandates and a wealth of concrete tasks by governments. Consequently, they have developed a broad range of strong tools and instruments to facilitate engagement with governments and address concrete challenges on the ground. And they have identified and addressed new substantive issues as they emerged, all in order to assist states to improve their responses.

Finally, let us turn to the instruments. In looking at them, one must wonder if participating states have gone with the times as strongly as the institutions have. Are the so-called Vienna and Moscow mechanisms – which provide the possibility for states to request information from each other and to send ad hoc missions of experts – systematically applied? Practice shows that they are not, not even unsystematically.[19]

One does not have to share the opinion expressed recently by the current president of the Parliamentary Assembly – and I certainly do not – when he postulates that "[t]he decision-making structures in Vienna are virtually unable to reach agreement, particularly on key political issues" and "for many years now the Permanent Council has proved unable to come to a single decision that in any substantive way improves upon the existing commitments that we already have."[20] But how do we ensure, as Lenarčič reminded us, that the PC effectively enacts the obligation to implement? An obligation, in the words of the OSCE 'Strategy to Address Threats to Security and Stability in the 21st Century'[21], of states who are effectively "responsible to each other for the implementation of their OSCE commitments"?

E   Towards an Improved Framework for Peer Engagement

A possible answer to this third element of the Corfu Process, the 're-invigorate', lies in the development of an enhanced regime of peer review, and peer engagement, in order to narrow perceived tensions between the two principles of equality of members, and of implementation of their obligations by all.[22]

In order to do this, one could do worse than take inspiration from the relatively new instrument of the Universal Periodic Review (UPR) of the UN Human Rights

---

19   These are specific processes of peer engagement developed at the respective Meetings in 1989 and 1991, but used only in a handful of cases since its inception in 1991, mostly in the early 1990s. Cf. ODIHR, Human dimension mechanisms http://www.osce.org/odihr/13483.html.

20   The Portuguese parliamentarian João Soares in his speech at the Ministerial Meeting in Athens, 1 December 2009. - However, it is often the Parliamentary Assembly itself where little, if any, systematic work regarding the implementation of OSCE commitments is being undertaken, in spite of the clear responsibilities of parliaments at the national level, due to its loose structures and the weak support from its small secretariat in Copenhagen.

21   Strategy to Address Threats to Security and Stability in the 21st Century, Maastricht Ministerial Meeting 2003, para. 18.

22   Cf. Susan Stewart, Russland und die OSZE. Zum Spannungsverhältnis zwischen Gleichheit und Verpflichtung, in: Stiftung für Wissenschaft und Politik: SWP-Aktuell 66, December 2007, http://www.swp-berlin.org/common/get_document.php?asset_id=4573.

Council. Within four years, and periodically thereafter, all UN member states are reviewed with regard to the fulfillment of their human rights obligations and commitments. This review is being conducted by all states vis-à-vis each other, in a universal, structured and inter-active manner. Importantly, it does not re-place any of the numerous human rights monitoring processes and mechanisms of the UN – rather, it provides added value. The protection of human rights by every state is being examined in a process involving all other states and based on information not only from the State itself, but also from these mechanisms, i.e. monitoring bodies established by human rights treaties and the Special Proce-dures of the Human Rights Council, as well as the UN High Commissioner for Human Rights (OHCHR) and NGOs.[23]

While this process is still in its early stages (it has been started only some two years ago), key elements certainly include the following:

- engagement of all states – with each other, with institutions, and with civil society;
- a broad and systematized information-base on each State under review from institutions and civil society;
- strong features of dialogue and periodicity;
- openness and publicity – the debate is transmitted via webcast; and
- a framework for follow-up through recommendations made by Human Rights Council members in the course of the review.

It is, of course, this follow-up which will eventually determine the success of the UPR; but already today its results are being used by the OHCHR in their country activities; furthermore, they are being fed into the country activities of the broader UN system as a whole.

Without wanting to praise the UN system beyond what it deserves, one can briefly look at some of these features in the OSCE context:

- With regard to *state engagement* – where do we stand within the OSCE sys-tem? Take a recent example: there was a sizeable military conflict between two states of the OSCE region in 2008, and the organization was criticized for not being able to quell it, in spite of early – *and late* – warning. From within the OSCE system, the only publicly available information on human security aspects of the conflict came from ODIHR and its report on the human rights situation in the war-affected areas.[24] As far as is known, none of its recom-mendations were made subject to systematic deliberations and follow-up ac-tivities in the Permanent Council.
- With regard to *a systematic stream of impartial information emerging from institutions*: In the OSCE system, how systematically are governments re-sponding to information on alleged violations of human dimension commit-ments and, in particular, offering recommendations and assistance to the

---

23   The basis for this process is Res. 5/1 of 18 June 2007 of the UN Human Rights Coun-cil, in particular section I of its Annex. All documents of the review process can be found at the website of the High Commissioner for Human Rights, www.ohchr.org.

24   OSCE/ODIHR, Human Rights in the War-Affected Areas Following the Conflict in Georgia (2008), http://www.osce.org/documents/odihr/2008/12/35656_en.pdf, a "re-port on the human rights situation following the armed conflict in Georgia [...] a joint undertaking by the ODIHR and the HCM", as the ODIHR director put it in his trans-mission letter to the Chairman-in-Office.

state concerned? This question not only relates to information from the outside, especially from non-governmental organizations, but also from within, in particular OSCE institutions and field missions: while information is provided, follow-up action is only pursued in exceptional cases, and then not always, and not systematically.

- With regard to *openness and publicity*, where do we stand in the OSCE? How many sessions of the Permanent Council or other discussion fora can be followed via the Internet on live-stream? The only times when states are not meeting behind closed doors and therefore some publicity is being achieved are a few human dimension meetings scattered across the year.[25]

- With regard to *follow-up regarding the recommendations*: When was the last time we heard a substantial, and sustained, exchange of views on the election-related recommendations contained in ODIHR Final Election Reports? When have we seen concrete follow-up action to them, collectively through states, and well in time before the next elections? And how have government representatives in Vienna responded to some of their own priority documents, such as the OSCE Action Plans on Trafficking in Human Beings or on Roma and Sinti, through subsequent debate and follow-up action?[26] Can follow-up really be left to the institutions and field missions?

In all these elements, *civil society* plays a crucial role: To what extent is civil society made part of this dialogue, both at the national and the international level?[27] We mention civil society in this context especially because one reason to be optimistic on the situation in the OSCE region certainly lies in the existence of a vibrant civil society throughout, especially in transition societies, in spite of sometimes severe harassment by governments.[28] This is also where the ultimate accountability of states lies – not vis-à-vis other governments, but to their own people. International monitoring and response can only provide support in addition to monitoring and responding to human rights violations at the national and local level. The role of international organizations such as the OSCE must therefore encompass the provision of the best possible framework for the vital devel-

---

25 The annual two-week Implementation Meeting and a three-day 'Seminar' in Warsaw as well as three two-day Meetings in Vienna constitute the only institutionalized OSCE fora where NGO representatives are admitted and participate on an equal footing with government representatives; journalists, however, are normally admitted to the opening and closing sessions only.

26 On election reports, follow-up is largely left to the ODIHR itself. Regarding action plans, which have been negotiated painstakingly by PC delegations and regularly adopted and referred to in Ministerial Decisions, they contain a broad range of policy objectives and concrete measures for their implementation, but no systematic review clause.

27 This involvement can provide the necessary complement of a bottom-up review to any peer review. Cf. Christian Strohal, The Quest for Protection: The Role of International Organizations and NGOs, in Roland Minnerath et al. (eds.), Catholic Social Doctrine and Human Rights, The Pontifical Academy of Social Sciences Acta 15 (Vatican City 2010), 541-558. In addition to their role at the national level, NGOs provide international fora with concrete information but face, all too often, reprisals in some countries – just see the annual ODIHR reports on Human Rights Defenders.

28 Thus, the situation of civil society is also a clear indicator on systemic shortcomings. Cf. ibid.

opment of the NGO landscape in all participating states, and ensure feed-back, in both directions.

This last point also applies to the media and their protection, also increasingly under threat in a number of OSCE participating states.[29] Active civil society and free and independent media constitute two essential elements to ensure and strengthen two key pillars of democracy – accountability and transparency.

F   The Way Forward

Today, the questions just raised are hard to answer with much optimism. But the instruments, structures and procedures to realize all this certainly exist. The 56 OSCE states must assure their best use. To this end it may be time for the OSCE to learn from the experiences of the UN regarding peer review. This would seem only natural as the UN have taken the three-dimensional security concept of the OSCE on board, as mentioned at the outset.

In such a strengthened peer review, one must not only build on the 'acquis' of the UN, but adapt it in order to maximize the impact of specific OSCE achievements, in particular the interplay of its institutions. Peer reviews quickly reach limits if they do not allow outside information, feedback, and follow-up. The OSCE institutions, and field missions, provide exactly that. Therefore, they should not only be made a core element in such a peer review, they should be put to good use in a more systematic manner. So should national human rights institutions and civil society. All of them should not only provide information, but also be involved with the government in preparing for the review, and, most importantly, in following up on the review's findings.

The advantage of such a peer review system is that it does not focus primarily on the lowest common denominator or on those states which fail most persistently to meet their commitments, but actively engages all states also in the search for model solutions and good practices. Peer review systems can strengthen the sense of ownership of governments and strengthen the crucial move of human rights instruments from foreign policy concerns to political, legislative and practical priorities at the national level.

This means that not only the handful of governments who have been critical about the OSCE's activities in the human dimension would feel affected, but all 56, and necessarily so, as two examples would demonstrate:

– The fight against terrorism has brought questions about fundamental rights back into the public debate in countries where even a simple debate about restricting rights would have been impossible. A strong international framework is a necessary safeguard for all states in this regard.
– The ODIHR's more recent election assessment activities have come up with substantial recommendations directed not only at countries in transition but

---

29   Cf. the annual reports of the OSCE Representative on Freedom of the Media, and his overall warning, in OSCE/ODIHR (ed.), Yearbook of the OSCE Representative on Freedom of the Media 10 (2008), Warsaw 2009, that
"(a)fter a decade of operation, we are encountering an emerging trend that I find more worrying than all our everyday challenges: the questioning of the universality of the OSCE's commitments. It signals what I would like to call a certain meltdown of these commitments [...]."

also at long-established democracies, showing that scrutiny can be beneficial to all states.

Moreover, with such a systematic peer review one would ensure that states, individually and collectively, would find it increasingly impossible to shut their eyes to serious and consistent non-compliance. One also would make sure that every government has not only an opportunity to engage, but indeed an obligation. And finally, most importantly, one would create a factual basis for mutual accountability, difficult to assail, to engage systematically in addressing shortcomings and challenges in order to close the implementation gap.

Without real accountability, at the national as well as at the international level, there can be no lasting security.

Understood in this way, the Corfu Process can be the right way to build and consolidate understanding around the importance of the human dimension in the wider security architecture through realizing a stronger and more systematic peer review. This can be achieved by building on the unique achievements of the OSCE, while also drawing inspiration from developments in other international organizations, such as the UN. This means: systematic and genuine engagement, as well as opening up the process, including to civil society, and following through on the obligations, individually and collectively.

Only then will we be able to continue to align with the optimism of Minikes rather than with the warnings of Genscher.

Ženet MUJIĆ

The OSCE Representative on Freedom of the Media – an Intergovernmental Watchdog: an Oxymoron?

Table of Contents

Keywords

Media freedom, human rights, freedom of expression, Organization for Security and Co-operation in Europe, Representative on Freedom of the Media, Helsinki Final Act, monitoring and early warning

A   Introduction

Civil society and international media freedom advocates reacted with scepticism when, in 1996, Freimut Duve proposed to the Organization for Security and Co-operation in Europe (OSCE) the establishment of an office to observe and protect the professional freedom of journalism. Duve, a former journalist and German parliamentarian, was the chair of the Human Rights Commission of the OSCE's Parliamentary Assembly. He later became the OSCE's first Representative on Freedom of the Media (RFoM). The rationale behind placing such an office within the framework of an intergovernmental *security* organization was not only that press freedom was a cornerstone of human rights and that independent media were vital for building and sustaining democracy. Rather, the consequences of synchronized or controlled media in Europe's recent history had shown that press freedom, independent and pluralistic mass media, and freedom of expression are supporting pillars of a lasting security structure for every state.

However, the question remained: Wasn't governmental non-intervention the prerequisite for a truly independent office tasked with defending press freedom? How sincere would an effort by an intergovernmental body, by nation states be to draw up a firm and credible mandate for an institution that was to defend the

{off}

states' fourth estate and especially given that all major media freedom advocacy bodies were non-governmental in nature for a good reason?

Twelve years after the creation of the post, in spring 2010, the term of the second Representative on Freedom of the Media, Miklós Haraszti, comes to an end. With over one decade of institutional history and after two Representatives, it is time to take stock of the results.

Section B. outlines the history of the institution and its mandate. It presents the instruments with which the OSCE member states equipped the incumbent and also introduces the specifics of the nomination process leading to the appointment of the RFoM. Section C. focuses on the fields of activity, the achievements reached over the last decade and the challenges the media face today. The fourth and final part (section D.) discusses future prospects.

B   The Mandate

The way leading to the realization of an Office of Media Freedom was difficult and lengthy. The negotiations within the OSCE did not prove easy. They were dominated by the concern of duplicating already existing intergovernmental institutions, namely respective offices within the UN and the Council of Europe. During the Lisbon Summit of Heads of OSCE states in 1996, however, the member states unanimously declared that

> [f]reedom of the press and media are among the basic prerequisites for truly democratic and civil societies. In the Helsinki Final Act, we have pledged ourselves to respect this principle. There is a need to strengthen the implementation of OSCE commitments in the field of the media, taking into account, as appropriate, the work of other international organizations. We therefore task the Permanent Council to consider ways to increase the focus on implementation of OSCE commitments in the field of the media, as well as to elaborate a mandate for the appointment of an OSCE representative on freedom of the media to be submitted not later than to the 1997 Ministerial Council.[1]

During the preliminary stages of drafting the mandate for the envisaged Representative on Freedom of the Media, the OSCE sought the assistance of non-governmental press freedom organizations. Initial scepticism stemmed from the disappointment regarding the unmet expectation of civil society with regard to the UN Commission on Human Rights' Special Rapporteur on Freedom of Expression and Opinion, who was considered to mediate rather than to advocate. The final text of the mandate of the OSCE's Representative on Freedom of the Media, adopted on 5 November 1997 by the OSCE Permanent Council, however, proved to be incomparable to its UN counterpart and pioneering for an intergovernmental structure dating back to 1975. The first RFoM was appointed by the OSCE's foreign ministers during the Copenhagen Ministerial Council meeting and took office on 1 January 1998.[2]

---

1   OSCE Lisbon Document 1996, Lisbon Summit Declaration, OSCE DOC.S/1/96, 3 December 1996, http://www.osce.org/documents/mcs/1996/12/4049_en.pdf.
2   OSCE Ministerial Committee, Decision on the Appointment of the OSCE Representative on Freedom of the Media, 18-19 December 1997, OSCE MC(6).DEC/1, http://www.osce.org/documents/mcs/1997/12/4167_en.pdf.

The mandate and responsibilities of the post, the status of the incumbent and the range of activities demonstrate the political far-sightedness of the OSCE's members and their understanding of the comprehensive post-Cold War security concept: "freedom of expression is a fundamental and internationally recognized human right and a basic component of a democratic society and [...] free, independent and pluralistic media are essential to a free and open society and accountable systems of government."[3]

The principal objective for the establishment of a media freedom office was to "strengthen the implementation of relevant OSCE principles and commitments as well as to improve the effectiveness of concerted action by the participating States based on their common values."[4] Furthermore, the member states confirmed, "that they will co-operate fully with the OSCE Representative on Freedom of the Media. He or she will assist the participating States, in a spirit of co operation, in their continuing commitment to the furthering of free, independent and pluralistic media."[5] Though couched in highly diplomatic language, this formulation recalls statutes of self-regulatory bodies within the media field. Indeed, one could argue that the OSCE members sought to foster politically binding media freedom commitments by institutionalizing them in this office and establishing an authority mandated to monitor adherence: an approach akin to national media accountability systems.

The then 54 OSCE foreign minsters consensually agreed to mandate a rapporteur on media freedom – independent of the OSCE's Secretariat and individual states and directly accountable to the organization's decision-making body, the Permanent Council – to monitor their countries adherence to media freedom obligations, to "observe relevant media developments in all participating States, [...] advocate and promote full compliance with OSCE principles and commitments regarding freedom of expression and free media."[6]

The main tasks of the RFoM are, firstly monitoring, early warning and rapid response in cases of serious breach of freedom of expression standards and "identified obstruction of media activities and unfavourable working conditions for journalists."[7] Secondly, assistance to participating states complements the core mission and is provided in the form of recommendations, legal assessments of media relevant (draft) legislation and projects aimed at developing an environment conducive to media freedom.

It was agreed that the office would be funded by the member states through the overall OSCE budget, thus ensuring financial independence.

1   Instruments of the RFoM

The mandate holder's own international esteem and level of reputation coupled with the option to go public about possible threats to media freedom represent

---

3   Mandate of the OSCE Representation on Freedom of the Media, OSCE PC.DEC No. 193, 5 November 1997, PC Journal No. 137, http://www.osce.org/documents/pc/1997/11/4124_en.pdf.
4   Ibid.
5   Ibid.
6   Ibid.
7   Ibid.

the foremost instruments at the RFoM's disposal.[8]

All mechanisms – a) the possibility and in fact requirement to address questions, recommendations or warnings regarding media freedom to OSCE states; b) the prescribed cooperation with state and non-governmental actors; c) the possibility to "collect and receive information on the situation of the media from all bona fide sources"[9] (including media themselves); and d) the authorization to receive suggestions for fostering compliance with relevant OSCE commitments from civil society – all these instruments would have a much lower impact had the OSCE not agreed that the RFoM was to "be an eminent international personality with long-standing relevant experience from whom an impartial performance of the function would be expected [and who is] guided by his or her independent and objective assessment regarding the specific paragraphs composing this mandate."[10]

It is this obligation to independently assess not only any given media situation or possible violation of human rights but also to define the most appropriate ways of addressing media freedom issues and of suggesting remedies – irrespective of any preferences by OSCE member states – that empowers the office of the RFoM. The RFoM is thus not confined to a simple data collection function, providing information services for the OSCE's participating states. Within the structure of the organization, it represents an autonomous institution with inherent powers and authority to not only assess and enquire, but also to remind participating states and follow up on its recommendations.

Unlike the OSCE High Commissioner on National Minorities, whose approach and indeed strength is silent diplomacy, the RFoM has the authority and in fact the duty to go public in order to warn of serious instances of non-compliance with the commitments.

One venue of the RFoM's public arena is the theatre of international community, that is, the audience of diplomats. Regular reports, usually impatiently and sometimes anxiously awaited by the participating states, are presented to the Permanent Council and made publicly available. They include an account on the watchdog's communication exchange with OSCE participating states and the office's projects and activities. They also point out the state of affairs of media freedom concerning any particular media freedom dimension (defamation, media regulation, public service broadcasting, violence against journalists, etc.)[11]. More visibly and not less importantly, the RFoM has also the power to issue – at its own discretion – public statements and press releases on media freedom viola-

---

8   The first RFoM, Freimut Duve, held the post from 1997 until 2003. He is a well known publisher-journalist and parliamentarian who focused on the defence of human rights. Duve received the Hannah Arendt Award for Political Thinking in 1997. Miklós Haraszti, in office from 2004 until 2010, is a Hungarian writer, journalist and human rights advocate who co-founded the Hungarian Democratic Opposition Movement. In 1980, he became editor of the samizdat publication Beszélő. After the collapse of the Iron Curtain, he took part in the roundtable on free elections and became member of the Hungarian parliament.

9   Mandate of the OSCE Representation on Freedom of the Media, OSCE PC.DEC No. 193, 5 November 1997.

10   Ibid.

11   See RFoM's regular reports to the OSCE Permanent Council, http://www.osce.org/fom/documents.html?lsi=true&limit=10&grp=296.

tions as they occur. While the main addressees of the regular reports are clearly the fifty-six OSCE participating states, the public statements are meant for and reach a much wider audience, which includes civil society and media themselves in the respective states and beyond. Compared to the regular reports, public statements have a different impact and objective: the aim of the former is to inform governments and to recommend certain action to them, whereas the latter's is to fulfil the early-warning function fundamental to the post by making the issue a topic of the state's political process and raising the awareness of its civil society.[12]

So-called "assessment visits" paid to any given OSCE participating state by the RFoM combine both of these approaches. They are well-prepared series of meetings with major stakeholders: government officials, representatives of civil society, and media professionals. Assessment visits are generally concluded with press conferences and followed by a comprehensive written report, which is then presented to the OSCE Permanent Council and also made publicly available.[13]

Only by being mandated to revert to the public via both, the government and the civil society, can the RFoM comply with the mandate's specific request to "concentrate [...] on rapid response to serious non-compliance with OSCE principles and commitments."[14]

2 Independent Intergovernmental Function

The intergovernmentally agreed independent nature of the RFoM's post and mandate relies on three main elements: the nomination process of the office-holder, the above-mentioned option to go public, and the autonomous character of the institution.

Although they are not laid out in detail, the nomination, selection and appointment processes of the RFoM are rather simple. Due to the OSCE's consensus principle,[15] inherent in all decision-making procedures, the appointment procedure is, however, lengthy and characterized by intense behind-closed-doors negotiations – not uncommon for international organizations. The appointing authority is nominally the Ministerial Council that follows the recommendation of the country holding the Chairmanship. It is also the Chairman-in-Office who formally initiates the nomination and selection procedure, ensures consensus and recommends a candidate.

Reaching political consensus on a candidate – someone who meets the criteria of being an *eminent international personality* with extensive experience in the field of media or human rights advocacy and at the same time is acceptable to all fifty-six member states – is comparable in difficulty to the political negotiations involved in drafting the mandate. Indeed, the transition from Freimut Duve to Miklós Haraszti was anything but smooth. For months, the OSCE participating states could not agree on a candidate leaving the office in a limbo, without a

12   See RFoM's press releases, http://www.osce.org/fom.
13   See RFoM's country reports, http://www.osce.org/fom/documents.html?lsi=true& limlt=10&grp=295.
14   Ibid.
15   Consensus is not defined as unanimity, but as the absence of any significance disagreement.

voice and thus toothless for several weeks. With Haraszti leaving the post in mid-March 2010 and a successor having been recommended for appointment only at the beginning of March[16], there was concern that this scenario might reoccur. Such a situation would have inevitably weakened an otherwise strong and well-respected institution.

Having said this, a candidate on whom political consensus eventually could be reached profits from a robust mandate that is protected by the same consensus requirement. Any decision made by consensus has the advantage of having had all OSCE members agree to it. Contrary to (qualified) majority voting, no participating state can claim to have been in opposition. In the case of the RFoM, the incumbent is thus able to perform the tasks independent of any outside influence or obstruction.

As indicated above, the RFoM's option to issue public statements lies at the core of the post's political independence and is its mightiest tool. The defence of media freedom and the protection of the right to freedom of expression by definition need to be placed in the public sphere. Public, pluralistic debate cannot develop behind closed doors and by means of silent diplomacy. The RFoM also depends on the public as a channel through which to exert influence. The incumbent is free to publicly and prominently pin-point shortcomings of a country's media freedom situation and to urge government's and law-enforcement agencies to change their course of action. The RFoM's tasks also include calling on politicians to respect the right to freedom of expression and to refrain from exercizing influence on public media, and reminding public officials that they have to tolerate a higher degree of criticism by the media. The RFoM shares this privilege only with the OSCE Office for Democratic Institutions and Human Rights (ODIHR) located in Warsaw.

Neither the Permanent Council, due to the consensus principle, nor the OSCE Secretariat, due to its rather supportive and neutral role, nor the OSCE field missions, due to the fact that they generally operate based on an invitation by the host country, have the possibility to function with such transparency in reaching out to the wider public: the media's audience and readership.

Only in very grave circumstances is it imaginable that the Permanent Council would reach consensus to jointly issue a public statement of concern. As a rule, it is the country holding the Chairmanship and setting the overall political agenda that has the right and the duty to be in the public spotlight. The OSCE field missions, unless placed under an UN mandate as is the case with the OSCE field missions in Kosovo and in Bosnia and Herzegovina, depend on the agreement of their host country. Over-critical and unfavourable public statements bear the risk

---

16   On 4 March 2010, the OSCE Permanent Council adopted a decision recommending to the OSCE Ministerial Council the appointment of the next Representative of Freedom of the Media. This decision was made adopted through a so-called silence procedure which ended on 10 March 2010, Haraszti's last day in office: Rather than having actively to agree to the appointment of the next RFoM, the recommended candidate was to be considered appointed if no participating state disagreed within the set period. On 11 March 2010, the Chairperson of the Permanent Council announced that Ms Dunja Mijatović was appointed the new and third Representative. See Permanent Council Decision No. 928 of 4 March 2010, www.osce.org/pc/documents.html?lsi=true&limit=10&grp=336, and OSCE Ministerial Council Decision MC.DEC/1/10 of 10 March 2010.

of deteriorating or freezing political relationships and stalling democratization and security reforms.

The consensus principle in the OSCE also means that every participating state has de-facto a veto right – making it technically almost impossible to reach an agreement on criticizing a situation in any country without the consensus of that particular country.[17]

What distinguishes the RFoM from non-governmental media freedom advocates is his/her ability to operate in the public arena beyond the confines of behind-the-scene negotiations (its most powerful instrument). The participating states let the media freedom watchdog decide when, how and to what extent to intervene, while they simultaneously oblige themselves to cooperate. Also, the RFoM is free to decide whom to address: the governments, individual politicians or the public at large. The range of addressees of the message, the level of criticism, the directness of the recommendation – all of these elements are adjustable and can be 'customized' depending on the intended aim and recipient.[18]

Furthermore, by being able to reach out to both politicians and the public, by being obliged by the mandate to closely work with both governments and the civil society, the RFoM constitutes the juncture in a triangular-structure where civil society, media and governments are brought together on disputed or controversial issues. Each conference, each seminar organized by the RFoM forces public officials and media professionals to constructively and jointly analyze their mutual relationship, media policies and practice, media legislation, etc. A boycott by one or the other side is highly unlikely since it would damage their credibility.

The third pillar of the institution's independence is represented by the autonomous character of the office of the RFoM. While being bound to the gen-

---

17   At the 1992 CSCE Council Meeting in Prague, the Ministers decided to adopt the "consensus-minus-one" principle. Article IV, para. 16, allows that "appropriate action may be taken by the Council or the Committee of Senior Officials, if necessary in the absence of the consent of the State concerned, in cases of clear, gross and uncorrected violations of relevant CSCE commitments" (OSCE Prague Document on Further Development of CSCE Institutions and Structures, Prague Meeting of the CSCE Council, 30-31 January 1992, p. 17, http://www.osce.org/documents/mcs/1992/01/4142_en.pdf). This "consensus-minus-one" mechanism was used only once in the history of the CSCE/OSCE against a participating state: on 8 July 1992, Yugoslavia was suspended form the OSCE for its involvement in the conflict in Bosnia and Herzegovina.

18   RFoM's press release of 8 February 2010 on Kazakhstan "misuse of libel laws to muzzle the press" illustrates an example of the effectiveness of the office's intergovernmental character: on 1 February, the Almaty district court had ordered the seizure of the print runs of five independent newspapers. All papers had published letters by an exiled government minister who accused Timur Kulibaev, the President's son-in-law, of corruption. The court also banned any reports "damaging the honor and integrity" of Kulibaev. Only hours after the RFoM voiced criticism in a press release of 8 February 2010, the same court not only reversed the ruling but also dismissed Kulibaev's defamation lawsuit against the five independent papers. See OSCE media freedom representative criticizes 'misuse' of libel laws to muzzle the press in Kazakhstan, Tajikistan, and Hungary, OSCE RFoM Press Release, 8 February 2010, http://www.osce.org/fom/item_1_42678.html. See also Kazakh Court Overturns Media-Criticism Ban, Radio Free Europe/Radio Liberty, 9 February 2010, http://www.rferl.org/content/Kazakh_Court_Overturns_Media_Criticism_Ban/195279.html.

eral OSCE rules and regulations, covering financial and administrative areas, the office is financed by the overall OSCE budget: the consensus budget is composed of contributions from all participating states, and is approved as a whole and not along individual budget lines. The RFoM is free to propose the size of the budget, to set the office's multi-year policy as well as the annual strategy and to prioritize activities or areas of involvement anytime at its own discretion. OSCE member states may and do suggest projects or fields of activities; however, the final decision as to the 'if and how' remains the sole responsibility of the RFoM.

C   Fields of Activity, Achievements and Challenges

The office of the RFoM operates both vertically and horizontally: vertically, by observing each OSCE country's security situation for journalists, its media framework and media structures regardless of the medium (print, radio-television, new media); horizontally, by analyzing thematic pillars of free media across the OSCE, including the state of public service broadcasting, access to information regimes, defamation provisions, and the free flow of information on the Internet.[19]

The RFoM refrains from comparing the situation in one country with the situation in another country or establishing ranking systems, but rather measures development and progress against universal standards and OSCE commitments.

During its mere twelve years of existence, the office, through its two Representatives, managed to help the participating states to cover a significant distance on their road towards implementing and fulfilling today's media freedom standards.

At first, Freimut Duve's biggest success was, however, the respect he and the new institution gained amongst civil society and international media advocates. It was Duve's personal dedication with which he shaped and interpreted the office's mission and his steadfastness with which he pursued the defence of media freedom and freedom of expression that made his tenure so effective.[20] Within a few years he managed to establish friendly, professional, and moreover durable relationships with all major media advocacy bodies, turning the office into an established and esteemed partner regardless of its intergovernmental character and the initial scepticism it was confronted with.

It was also under Duve that the first declaration of the three international rapporteurs on freedom of expression was issued, establishing a new international mechanism. For the first time, in November 1999, the UN Special Rapporteur on Freedom of Opinion and Expression, the OSCE RFoM and the Special Rapporteur on Freedom of Expression of the Organization of the American States got together to issue a joint declaration recalling freedom of expression as a fundamental and internationally recognized human right and stressing the indispensability of independent and pluralistic media for a free society and accountable governments.[21]

---

19 For more information on the RFoM's activities see the web site: http://www.osce.org/fom.
20 See also Christiane Hardy/Rebecca Law (eds.), Letter to a Man of Letters. A Tribute to Freimut Duve, Essays in Honour of Freimut Duve on the Occasion of the End of his Tenure as the first Representative for Freedom of the Media, Vienna 2003.
21 International Mechanisms for Promoting Freedom of Expression: Joint Declaration by the UN Special Rapporteur on Freedom of Opinion and Expression, the OSCE

Every winter since then, the three rapporteurs would meet again to issue a declaration focusing on particular threats to freedom of the media. In December 2006, the group was extended to include the new Special Rapporteur on Freedom of Expression of the African Commission on Human and Peoples' Rights and, in February 2010, after having warned of numerous threats to media freedom and having suggested remedies to existing shortcomings, the four international watchdogs issued their latest declaration commemorating the tenth anniversary and identifying ten key challenges to freedom of expression in the next decade.[22]

What had started successfully under Duve's tenure was continued and extended during Haraszti's term. This is valid also for the assistance provided to those participating states that, after the fall of the Iron Curtain, found themselves in a changed socio-political system and were slowly moving from state media structures to a system of pluralistic, independent and critical media. Particularly between 1999 and 2003, the office was essential in supporting the countries of Southeast Europe in the transition from state to public broadcasting. While many countries have completed this transition, some other states have yet to fully complete the public service broadcasting reform and, moreover, to identify appropriate mechanism of independent financing.[23]

The completion of the transition process from state to public service broadcasting could be described as moving eastwards. However, it was the former socialist countries that assumed the leading role in decriminalizing defamation. Under Haraszti's tenure, the office embarked on a long-term lobbying project aimed at removing criminal libel provisions in the OSCE area, on one hand, and strengthening voluntary self-regulation systems, on the other. Bosnia and Herzegovina, Estonia and Georgia, followed by Croatia, the former Yugoslav Republic of Macedonia and Serbia, were the first new democracies to reform their libel provisions and decriminalize and 'deprisonize' defamation – with most of the established democracies in the OSCE area keeping these obsolete provisions on the statute books. It was also thanks to Haraszti's persistence over the years that in 2009, the parliaments of Ireland, Romania and the United Kingdom decided to follow suit and removed libel as a criminal offence, thus strengthening the right to freedom of expression and freeing the media from chilling effects.

Representative on Freedom of the Media and the OAS Special Rapporteur on Freedom of Expression, 26 November 1999, http://www.osce.org/documents/rfm/1999/11/198_en.pdf.

22 International Mechanisms for Promoting Freedom of Expression: Joint Declaration by the UN Special Rapporteur on Freedom of Opinion and Expression, the OSCE Representative on Freedom of the Media, the OAS Special Rapporteur on Freedom of Expression, and the African Commission on Human and Peoples' Rights Special Rapporteur on Freedom of Expression and Access to Information, 2 February 2010, http://www.osce.org/documents/rfm/2010/02/42638_en.pdf.

23 The new EU member states and some EU candidate countries have successfully completed the transition to public service broadcasters. Sustainable financing mechanisms have to be implemented for the public broadcasters in Albania, the former Yugoslav Republic of Macedonia and Kosovo. The reform and unification of the public broadcasting system in Bosnia and Herzegovina has stalled and it remains fragmented along ethnic lines.

Despite these remarkable achievements, the media situation in the OSCE area has seen some worrying developments over the last few years. More, not fewer, journalists have lost their lives in the course of their duty. Violence against journalists is increasing in Southeast Europe and parts of Central Asia.[24] In some of the countries of the European Union, politicians and public officials are trying to silence critical journalists and media outlets by demanding exorbitant financial damages in civil defamation lawsuits, thus ignoring the core function of media as a fourth critical pillar of any democratic state. Across the OSCE, countries, in an attempt to enforce national security or copyright legislation, are restricting the free flow of information and freedom of expression on the Internet. Commercial pressure on media and journalists is also a challenge which can be observed in many if not all OSCE participating states.

D   Outlook

The above mentioned ten key challenges to freedom of expression, jointly out-lined by the four rapporteurs on freedom of expression in their tenth anniversary declaration of early 2010, distil the most serious challenges, all affecting areas indispensable for a politically and financially independent, free, and safe media environment.[25] The prospects are not encouraging.

The universality of international human rights standards, also in the context of the OSCE and its media freedom commitments, is being questioned. During its 2009 Chairmanship, Greece – in an attempt to further OSCE media freedom commitments and develop stronger tools for the RFoM – proposed to adopt a decision on "fostering freedom of the media and enhancing pluralism" at the 2009 Ministerial Council Meeting. After lengthy discussions, many objections and several revised and (in the course of negotiations) softened draft versions, two Central Asian member states could not agree on adopting the following main points: guaranteeing free flow of information on the Internet, preventing media concentration and state ownership of broadcast media, combating of violence against journalists, and the encouraging of media to establish self-regulatory mechanisms. By objecting to subscribe to these four pillars of a free media framework, the countries in fact questioned the very structure and basic prereq-uisite of a true democracy.

Politicization of media and attempts by politicians and governments to manage or control freedom of expression and the free flow of information always have and will continue to represent the foremost threat to free media, particularly pub-lic service media. Existing governmental or political ownership of media, stalled privatization processes of media, or attempts by politicians to exercise influence

---

24   See also the annual press freedom indices of Freedom House, http://www.freedom house.org/template.cfm?page=251&year=2009, and Reporters without Borders, http://www.rsf.org/en-classement1003-2009.html.

25   International Mechanisms for Promoting Freedom of Expression: Joint Declaration by the UN Special Rapporteur on Freedom of Opinion and Expression, the OSCE Representative on Freedom of the Media, the OAS Special Rapporteur on Freedom of Expression, and the African Commission on Human and Peoples' Rights Special Rapporteur on Freedom of Expression and Access to Information, 2 February 2010, http://www.osce.org/documents/rfm/2010/02/42638_en.pdf.

over editorial content, financing, advertising, or regulatory aspects are cases in point.

Related to the politicization of media are efforts to legislate or enforce (by law, fear or violence) "neutral" speech irrespective of the public interest, by banning speech which disrespects the reputation of public officials or the state, statement of opinions, and articles that criticize ideologies, religions or schools of thought.

The attempt to monopolize media does, however, not come from governments alone. The increasing commercial pressure to which media are exposed, the battle for advertisers, readers and audience shares, as well as the industry's evolving fight over the Internet supremacy, have led to a rising media concentration. With the development of multi-media and new media platforms, concentration is no longer the simple merger or grouping of media outlets. Media concentration in the information society also means the combination of information, telecommunication, software, and web technologies under one roof – it means the controlling of communication channels, the collection, storage, evaluation, and selling of data of media consumers for either commercial or political purposes.

While traditional and independent print and broadcast media are the fourth estate of a democratic society, monopolized and commercially instrumentalized online media and the Internet might fall victim to the same industry that helped develop and foster it.

It remains to be seen whether some governments' attempts to control, guide, filter, or silence debate and criticism, and to restrict freedom of expression, will be a political feature only or whether and to what degree information and software corporations will follow suit.

V

Civil Society, NGOs and Cross-Cutting Issues

Sihem BENSEDRINE

Les valeurs démocratiques européennes à l'épreuve de la realpolitik: les accords d'association Tunisie-UE – modèle ou caricature

Table de matières

Mots-clés

Accords d'association Tunisie-UE, valeurs démocratiques, liberté de l'expression, libertés académiques, processus de Barcelone, Union européenne, WSIS

A   Introduction

C'est par sa face démocratique que l'Europe se présente au monde et son image est portée par ces valeurs; le cahier de charges que les candidats à l'Union européenne (UE) sont appelés à remplir pour accéder au statut d'Européens se résume pour les trois quarts à des conditions liées au respect des valeurs démocratiques et de droits l'homme; de même les accords d'associations que l'UE noue avec ses partenaires de l'Europe de l'Est ou de Méditerranée sont basés sur ces principes. On peut dire sans risque d'exagération que l'identité européenne est construite sur ces valeurs de droits humains.[1]

---

1   Voyez, sur ce point, aussi les contributions de Jean Paul Jacqué et Florence Benoît-Rohmer, dans ce livre.

C'est en vertu de ce référentiel, déclaré et affiché, qu'ont été prises des sanctions à l'encontre de gouvernements jugés malmenant les valeurs démocratiques; tel fut le cas avec la Biélorussie où des sanctions ont été décrétées par l'UE suite aux violations de l'Etat de droit lors des élections de 2006; comme pour le Zimbabwe contre lequel l'UE a pris des sanctions en 2002 à la suite des élections présidentielles frauduleuses et reconduites en février 2010.

La mobilisation de l'UE en vue de faire reconnaître la vérité des urnes en Ukraine, lors des élections controversées de décembre 2004, a été décisive. Pourtant, dans d'autres situations, les décideurs qui veillent aux destinées de l'Europe se pressent d'oublier ce référentiel et parfois de lui tourner le dos. L'application de ces valeurs semble parfois à géométrie variable. L'exemple de la Tunisie illustre à souhait ce paradoxe entre les principes affichés et les pratiques politiques qui les bafouent.

B   Un processus détourné de ses objectifs premiers

1   Un partenaire actif

La Tunisie a été le premier pays à signer les accords d'association avec l'UE en 1995, entrés en vigueur le 1er mars 1998. Ce rôle de précurseur lui a valu le statut de «modèle» brandi pour inciter d'autres partenaires méditerranéens à signer à leur tour ces accords. Les politiques européens n'hésitent pas à le rappeler chaque fois qu'il est question d'adresser une ébauche de critique au gouvernement tunisien: « La Tunisie est le premier pays de la région euro-méditerranéenne à avoir signé un accord d'association,» C'est un partenaire actif dans la politique de voisinage de l'Union européenne,» déclarait récemment Louis Michel, ancien Commissaire européen au développement et à l'aide humanitaire lors du débat en plénière sur la Tunisie tenu le 21 janvier 2010 à Strasbourg, comme pour excuser son déficit démocratique.[2]

Il est un fait que la Tunisie n'a jamais rechigné à approuver les réformes institutionnelles exigées par Bruxelles et s'est presque toujours acquittée de son rôle sur le plan formel. Seulement formel; car dans la réalité, il en allait tout autrement. Maitrisant remarquablement la rhétorique alignée sur les dogmes du libéralisme, le régime tunisien, dirigé par le général Ben Ali depuis 23 ans, a compris qu'il ne coûtait presque rien de signer des «papiers», pourvu qu'il soit préservé de tout mécanisme contraignant. Dans la pratique, un dirigisme économique demeure en vigueur, camouflé derrière une profusion de mesures de nature libérale; tandis que sur le plan politique, une dictature *soft* se profile derrière une façade institutionnelle démocratique.

La supercherie n'a jamais échappé aux responsables européens qui savaient faire preuve d'une toute autre fermeté sous d'autres latitudes; mais le jeu leur convenait pour des raisons géostratégiques se rapportant à la lutte contre l'immigartion clandestine et la lutte anti terroriste. C'est ainsi que Salvatore Lacolino,

---

2   Parlement européen, procès-verbal du 21 janvier 2010, 2. Relations UE/Tunisie (débat), http://www.europarl.europa.eu/sides/getDoc.do?pubRef=-//EP//TEXT+CRE +20100121+ITEM-002+DOC+XML+V0//FR.

député PPE déclarait au cours de ce même débat en plénière du 21 janvier 2010 :

> « La Tunisie comme toute la région du Maghreb constitue une zone stratégique avec un potentiel de croissance très important et attire donc de nombreux intérêts pas seulement économiques mais entre autres et aussi beaucoup les intérêts européens. Des programmes ont été mis en place de coopérations transfrontalières avec l'UE. Et donc, il faut renforcer effectivement nos relations avec les pays frontalier de l'Afrique y compris la Tunisie, »

évoquant de façon pudique la lutte contre l'immigration clandestine. Le partenaire tunisien de son côté, a su tirer le meilleur profit de cette situation, en s'appliquant à demeurer «présentable» en sauvant les apparences Le résultat a été que le processus de Barcelone, censé impulser une démocratisation, a été réduit à une plateforme d'appui aux régimes autoritaires.

2   Processus de Barcelone : mythe ou réalité ?

Lorsque la déclaration de Barcelone[3] avait été adoptée en novembre 1995, elle avait soulevé bien des espoirs. Aujourd'hui encore, quinze ans après son entrée en vigueur, autant pour ses partisans que pour ses détracteurs, elle constitue le cadre de référence privilégié pour interroger, évaluer, projeter un avenir commun des pays Méditerranéens avec l'Europe.

Mais l'échec patent de ses performances est devenu un lieu commun évoqué tant par les officiels que les sociétés civiles des pays partenaires.

Faudrait-il pour autant éliminer ce cadre pour mieux avancer, comme tentent de le faire les promoteurs de l'Union pour la Méditerranée (UPM), une structure perçue par beaucoup comme un relais de l'influence française dans la région? « Les soucis actuels que rencontre l' UPM pour trouver son organisation fonctionnelle, sont-ils juste des péripéties éphémères ou des indices d'un échec annoncé? Relais de l'influence française dans une région traditionnellement privilégiée ? »[4] s'interrogeait le professeur d'histoire à Reims, Yohann Chanoir.

Une chose est sûre, en contournant les principes fondateurs de l'Europe et en axant l'Union sur des projets économiques, l'UPM a grevé son avenir et s'embourbe actuellement dans les enjeux de pouvoir qui la minent. Sa débâcle plaide encore davantage pour le processus de Barcelone que le président français a vite fait d'enterrer.

En dépit de ses aléas et de ses revers, le processus de Barcelone demeure encore un cadre qui, par ses objectifs et sa démarche politique, conserve toute sa validité. Grâce à lui de nombreux réseaux ont été créés dans divers domaines tissant un vaste maillage favorisant un échange culturel et social pertinent. Il demeure le seul cadre qui permette de maîtriser la communauté de destin dans laquelle la région est historiquement embarquée.

---

3   Créé en 1995, le processus de Barcelone encadre les relations politiques économiques et culturelles entre les 27 pays de l'Union européenne et 11 pays de la rive sud de la Méditerranée (Algérie, Autorité palestinienne, Egypte, Israël, Jordanie, Liban, Maroc, Mauritanie, Syrie, Tunisie, Turquie).

4   Yohann Chanoir, UPM, nouvel acronyme pour dire mare nostrum ?, Mediapart, 12 janvier 2010, http://www.mediapart.fr/club/edition/mediterranee/article/120110/upm-nouvel-acronyme-pour-dire-mare-nostrum-0.

Nul n'a mis en doute ses principes fondateurs ou sa démarche; tous les reproches que l'on adresse à ce processus se concentrent sur sa mise en œuvre et les pratiques politiques de l'Union qui ont abouti à une forme de détournement de ce processus de ses visées premières. Force est de constater que les signaux envoyés par l'UE aux sociétés de la rive sud ont souvent été à contresens des objectifs affichés du partenariat (politique parcimonieuse d'octroi des visas, politiques d'immigration frileuses, racisme antimusulman etc.)

Le Partenariat établi entre l'UE et ses partenaires de la rive sud repose sur trois volets: un volet politique et de sécurité, un volet économique et financier et enfin un volet social et culturel.

Au moment de son lancement, le processus de Barcelone ambitionnait de développer la prospérité, favoriser le rapprochement des peuples et garantir le respect des droits humains. Il était censé enclencher un cercle vertueux de démocratisation des sociétés partenaires, par le biais d'une libéralisation économique.

Inutile de préciser qu'aujourd'hui, rares sont ceux qui continuent de croire à la dynamique vertueuse d'une libéralisation économique qui déboucherait spontanément sur la démocratie.

3   Maigre bilan pour un projet ambitieux

Le bilan économique du partenariat Euromed a été clairement résumé par Joseph Borrell, l'ancien président du Parlement européen, lors de la célébration de son 10e anniversaire à l'ouverture du sommet de Barcelone:

> «Au cours de la dernière décennie, le PNB par habitant de l'UE des Quinze est passé de 20.000 à plus de 30.000 dollars et celui des nouveaux États membres de 6.000 à quelque 15.000 dollars. Dans le même temps, dans le sud de la Méditerranée, le revenu par habitant a stagné, passant d'un peu moins de 5.000 dollars à un peu plus de 5.000. L'évolution du commerce n'a guère été favorable aux pays du sud puisque leur déficit commercial vis-à-vis de l'UE a doublé au cours des dix dernières années[,] »[5]

une analyse confirmée par Ph. de Fontaine Vive, vice-président de la banque européenne d'investissement qui soulignait, le 2 novembre 2007, lors d'une conférence de presse à Tunis:

> « Le mode d'intégration euro-méditerranéen actuel n'a permis aux pays de la rive sud de gagner qu'un seul point de croissance avec des taux variant entre 4 et 5% par pays au lieu des 7% requis pour réduire le taux de chômage. »[6]

Sur les acquis économiques du partenariat, il n'est pas besoin d'être expert pour mesurer son impact sur le citoyen ordinaire qui vérifie chaque jour à ses dépends la baisse régulière de son niveau de vie en même temps qu'il est sub-

---

5   Parlement européen, Le Président Borrell souhaite un second souffle au partenariat euroméditerranéen, 28 novembre 2005, Communiqué de presse 20051128IPR029 39, http://www.europarl.eu.int/news/expert/infopress_page/030-2940-332-11-48-903-20051128IPR02939-28-11-2005-2005--false/default_fr.htm.

6   Mustapha Sehimi, Tunis mise sur le partenariat, Maroc Hebdo, http://www.maroc-hebdo.press.ma/MHinternet/Archives_766/html_766/tunis.html.

mergé de produits de consommation venant d'Europe qu'il est tenté d'acquérir par un endettement de plus en plus grand encouragé par l'Etat qui a grand ouvert les vannes des crédits à la consommation.

C'est ainsi que l'économiste tunisien dénonce

« une aggravation des déficits commerciaux: un système productif figé, une structure des exportations inchangée, une polarisation géographique des exportations accrue et limitée à un nombre réduit de produits traditionnels subissant une forte concurrence (le textile, le tourisme). Ces facteurs n'ont pas manqué ensemble d'aggraver le déficit commercial avec l'UE pour la quasi-majorité des pays du Sud non pétroliers. Cette situation se trouve encore aggravée par la détérioration des termes de l'échange et la perte continue de la valeur des monnaies locales des pays du Sud. »[7]

Par ailleurs, la libéralisation commerciale n'a pas eu l'effet de levier espéré. Cette libéralisation a de plus été pervertie par le climat opaque des affaires, les privilèges des lobbies, le coût des services, les prestations administratives et un certain nombre d'usages contraires à la bonne gouvernance, particulièrement la corruption.

4 Quand le sécuritaire est au top de l'agenda

Quant au volet politique, il a été vidé de sa substance pour se résumer à la question sécuritaire.

« L'Europe, qui parle pourtant à l'envi de partage et d'échanges humains, s'est progressivement édifiée en une forteresse (par les accords de Schengen) qui cherche à se protéger des «envahisseurs du Sud» par des politiques extrêmement sévères en matière de migration et de droit d'asile et en délégant aux régimes autoritaires du Sud le soin de mener des politiques internes répressives pour contenir ces flux humains. »[8]

L'Europe qui brandit avec fierté ses valeurs démocratiques se retrouve à fricoter avec l'un des régimes les plus archaïques et les plus dictatorial de la région comme la Libye; il est vrai que la ceinture de sécurité (dispositif FRONTEX) mis en place par l'UE pour contrôler les flux migratoires hors de ses frontières fonctionne pour l'essentiel avec ce pays.

« Il faudrait que nous acceptions de n'être qu'une frontière pour une Europe qui veut être sécurisée » ironisait le secrétaire général de l'Union du Maghreb arabe, Habib Boulares lors d'une conférence préparatoire au Sommet 5+5. En effet Bruxelles a produit ces dernières années des directives très sévères se rattachant à la circulation des personnes dans l'espace Schengen.

La plus célèbre est la controversée Directive 2008/115/CE du Parlement européen et du Conseil de l'Europe du 16 décembre 2008 relative aux normes et procédures communes applicables dans les États membres au retour des ressortissants de pays tiers en séjour irrégulier, qualifiée de directive de la honte par de nombreuses ONG qui lui reprochent de « renier les valeurs fondamenta-

---

7   Abdeljelil Bedoui, Dix ans de partenariat: quel résultat? Forum social Euromed, Tunis Décembre 2005.

8   Sihem Bensedrine/Omar Mestiri, L'Europe et ses despotes, Paris 2004, p. 21.

les de l'Europe ». Au cours d'une conférence de presse tenue le 9 février 2010 à Bruxelles, le Commissaire aux droits de l'homme du Conseil de l'Europe, Thomas Hammarberg stigmatisait de son côté en ces termes ces mesures lors de la présentation d'un document thématique sur ce sujet:

> « La criminalisation de l'entrée et de la présence irrégulières des migrants en Europe porte atteinte aux principes établis du droit international. Elle est aussi à l'origine de nombreuses tragédies humaines sans pour autant atteindre sa finalité, qui est de maîtriser réellement l'immigration. »[9]

Ainsi, c'est une autre politique qui s'est progressivement substituée au généreux projet initial de Barcelone, celle du rejet, des frustrations et de la montée des autoritarismes.

Il est utile de rappeler ici que le Processus de Barcelone est un processus intergouvernemental. Et le refus des pays non démocratiques du Sud, à associer les diverses composantes de la société civile, a dès le départ hypothéqué ce partenariat. Par ailleurs, la hantise du développement de l'Islamisme, fut-il modéré, reste l'un des fondamentaux de la politique européenne, même s'il en coûte l'appui à des régimes corrompus et autoritaires et le blocage des alternatives démocratiques.

5   Le statut avancé, prime à la dictature

La sincérité des élections est l'un des critères essentiels d'un régime démocratique. Mais là encore, l'UE donne le sentiment d'appliquer ce principe selon un double standard.

Le 25 octobre 2009, en Tunisie, Ben Ali s'octroyait 89,60% des suffrages pour un nouveau mandat de 5 ans, au terme d'une farce électorale où il était à la fois joueur et arbitre; bien entendu l'UE n'avait pas envisagé d'observer ces élections comme elle l'avait fait pour d'autres pays de la région, pour ne pas gêner un régime apprécié pour sa stabilité et son étroite collaboration dans le domaine sécuritaire!

L'unique observation crédible qui avait eu lieu concernait les performances des médias durant la campagne électorale; et les résultats de ce monitoring effectué par cinq ONG indépendantes de la société civile tunisienne sont édifiants: 97,14% de l'espace de la presse écrite avait été monopolisé par le président sortant durant la campagne, contre 0,22% pour le candidat de l'opposition réelle Ben Brahim, indique le rapport.[10]

9   Thomas Hammarberg, Commissaire aux droits de l'homme, « Il est injuste de sanctionner pénalement les migrations », 29 septembre 2008, http://www.coe.int/t/commissioner/viewpoints/080929_FR.asp?. Voyez aussi « La criminalisation des migrations en Europe : quelles incidences pour les droits de l'homme? », Document thématique commandé et publié par Thomas Hammarberg, Commissaire aux droits de l'homme du Conseil de l'Europe, Strasbourg, 4 février 2010, CommDH/IssuePaper(2010)1 et son contribution dans cette volume, p. 21.
10   Observatory of Freedom of Press, Publishing and Creation, Observation de la Couverture des élections législatives et Présidentielles, 28 février 2010, http://www.olpec-marsed.org/fr/News-file-article-sid-23.html.

6   Les voix démocratiques embastillées

Plus grave encore, cette campagne avait été accompagnée d'une vague de répression sans précédent touchant les journalistes et les défenseurs de droits humains; La veille du scrutin, Ben Ali prononçait un discours menaçant contre ceux qui

« n'ont pas respecté le caractère sacro-saint de la patrie ni son intégrité et ont poussé l'audace jusqu'au recours aux allégations mensongères et à l'incitation à une campagne désespérée auprès de certains journalistes étrangers, pour mettre en doute les résultats des élections avant même le dépouillement du scrutin. »[11]

Cinq jours plus tard, le journaliste Taoufik Ben Brik, qui avait publié des articles critiques dans la presse étrangère durant cette campagne était arrêté et condamné à 6 mois de prison à l'issue d'un procès inéquitable.

Auparavant, le 20 octobre, Zouhayr Makhlouf, le correspondant de Assabil Online (un site web basé à l'étranger) était arrêté et condamné à 3 mois de prison ferme et une amende de 6000 dinars le premier décembre pour avoir effectué un reportage vidéo sur la pollution à Nabeul.

Subissant ainsi le même sort que Radio Kalima auparavant,[12] la police a effectué un raid le 22 octobre 2009 sur Radio6,[13] une web radio indépendante, et a confisqué tous les équipements; l'équipe de la radio était en sit-in depuis le 17 octobre 2009 pour exiger son droit à une licence de diffusion sur les ondes, qui jusque-là, n'avait été accordée à aucune radio indépendante.

Durant toute la période électorale, des journalistes indépendants (Slim Bagga, Sihem Bensedrine) ont fait l'objet d'une campagne de diffamation et d'atteinte à leur honneur par les journaux aux ordres. Cette campagne de diffamation s'est poursuivie plusieurs mois après les élections allant jusqu'aux menaces de mort.[14] Les défenseurs sont accusés de trahison, de mauvaises mœurs et d'intelligence avec les services secrets israéliens.

7   Les libertés académiques logées à la même enseigne que les libertés publiques

Du 22 au 26 janvier 2010, Martin Scheinin, le Rapporteur Spécial des Nations Unies pour la promotion et la protection des droits de l'homme et des libertés fondamentales dans la lutte antiterroriste, a effectué une mission d'enquête en Tunisie. Au terme de sa mission il a rendu public un rapport où il a souligné l'écart entre la loi et la réalité déclarant notamment:

---

11   Info Tunisie, Allocution du Président Ben Ali à l'occasion des élections présidentielle et législatives, 24 octobre 2009, http://www.infotunisie.com/?p=23986.

12   Radio Kalima Tunisie, Note juridique sur l'illégalité de la fermeture des locaux de radio Kalima, proposé par la rédaction le 30 janvier 2010, http://www.kalimatunisie.com/fr/News-sid-Note-juridique-sur-l-illegalite-de-la-fermeture-des-locaux-de-radio-Kalima-143.html.

13   Radio 6 Tunis, http://www.radio6tunis.net.

14   Réseau euro-méditerranéen des droits de l'homme, Grave developments in Tunisia threaten the lives of human rights defenders, http://en.euromedrights.org/index.php/news/member_releases/4077.html.

« Ces carences du cadre juridique peuvent ériger un bouclier d'impunité pour les auteurs de torture ou de mauvais traitements. L'expérience la plus troublante que j'ai faite pendant ma mission était de constater de graves incohérences entre la loi et ce qui se passait dans la réalité, selon les informations que j'ai reçues. J'ai décidé d'exprimer quelques-unes de mes principales préoccupations :

- Il semblerait, et les autorités l'ont admis, que la date d'arrestation peut être postdatée, ce qui revient à contourner les règles relatives à la durée permissible d'une garde à vue, constituant ainsi la détention au secret et la disparition de la personne ;

- Le recours fréquent aux aveux comme élément de preuve devant les tribunaux, en absence d'enquête appropriée sur les allégations de torture ou d'autres mauvais traitements. »[15]

La police politique ne cible pas seulement les libertés publiques traditionnelles, mais également les libertés académiques.

« Censure, surveillance et inquisition sont le lot quotidien des universitaires. Surveillance et censure d'Internet, appauvrissement des bibliothèques qui subissent des restrictions budgétaires régulières. Surveillance des travaux et des enseignements, surveillance des participations aux rencontres internationales à l'étranger par l'obligation faite aux universitaires tunisiens, par voie de circulaire, de demander l'autorisation et de remettre le texte ou le thème de leur communication avant leur départ à l'étranger [,] »

dénonce l'universitaire Monia Ben Jemia dans une communication publiée sur le journal Attariq al Jadid.[16]

Plus récemment les enseignements délivrés par l'Université Libre de Tunis (l'ULT) ont été suspendus et sa licence retirée[17] en janvier 2010 à cause d'un conflit politique avec son directeur qui avait refusé d'inscrire une personne proche de Ben Ali qui n'avait pas le niveau requis. C'est dire jusqu'où vont les violations des libertés dans ce pays qui a ratifié tous les instruments onusiens qui protègent toutes les libertés.

8   Des députés exigent un débat en plénière sur la Tunisie

Face à cette situation le Parlement européen organisait le 21 janvier 2010 à Strasbourg un débat en plénière avec le Conseil et la Commission sur les relations UE-Tunisie, à la demande de plusieurs députés qui s'alarmaient de la dégradation de la situation des droits humains en Tunisie et s'inquiétaient de voir l'UE répondre favorablement à la demande de statut avancé formulée par la Tunisie. Alors que rien dans les performances du gouvernement tunisien ne le justifiait, le principe de faire bénéficier la Tunisie d'un statut dans le cadre des

---

15   Haut-commissariat des Nations Unies aux droits de l'homme, L'expert des Nations Unies sur les droits de l'homme dans la lutte anti-terroriste termine sa visite en Tunisie, 26 janvier 2010, http://www.ohchr.org/FR/NewsEvents/Pages/DisplayNews.aspx?NewsID=9772&LangID=F.

16   Monia Ben Jemia, Les libertés académiques, http://ettajdid.org/spip.php?article14.

17   Voyez Letters on Tunisia, 18 février 2010, http://www.mesa.arizona.edu/caf/letters_tunisia.html#tunisia100218.

accords d'association avec l'UE était décidé complaisamment par la présidence française en décembre 2008; perçu par les défenseurs de droits humains en Tunisie comme une prime à la dictature, ce statut encore en négociation, permet un traitement communautaire privilégié.

Les parlementaires étaient divisés sur la réponse à donner à la demande tunisienne;[18] Il y a eu ceux pour qui les acquis de la Tunisie justifient de ne pas être trop regardants sur les violations de droits humains comme le commissaire Louis Michel qui affirmait: « La Tunisie a réalisé des progrès substantiels, qui se sont traduits par un très bon niveau de développement avec des résultats socio-économiques reconnus par les institutions internationales. » Ou encore Charles Tannock:

« La Tunisie a besoin de notre soutien d'encouragement et de dialogue, n'a pas besoin d'invectives incessantes et c'est ironique aussi de consta-ter que la Gauche, qui était tellement favorable au droit de la femme a at-taqué la Tunisie malgré le fait que ce pays offre aux femmes, les libertés jamais vues précédemment dans le monde arabe. »

A cela, le député autrichien Andreas Mölzer répliquait:

« On pourrait penser, que tout va pour le mieux au monde, mais l'aide de l'UE est aussi rattachée à la protection des droits de l'homme. D'où la con-tradiction que nous constatons à savoir que l'argent donné par l'UE contri-bue à maintenir en place une dictature et tout un appareil dictatorial. C'est un problème que nous rencontrons très souvent dans nos accords d'association. Et c'est là qu'il faut agir parce qu'il n'est pas possible que l'UE contribue ne serait-ce qu'indirectement à la violation des droits de l'homme ni en Tunisie, ni dans le Congo et naturellement pas non plus dans le pays de candidat d'adhésion de la Turquie. »

Et la députée Marie Christine Vergiat regrette que:

« ce débat n'ait pas été accompagné du vote d'une résolution. Les paroles passent, seuls les écrits restent. Plus ancien partenaire de l'Union, la Tu-nisie reçoit les aides les plus importantes, par tête d'habitant, parmi les pays du Sud. Les accords de partenariat de l'Union comportent désormais des clauses relatives à la démocratie et aux droits de l'homme. Celles-ci doivent être examinées avec la même vigilance que les clauses économi-ques. Or, le rapport de la Commission, sur la mise en œuvre de la politi-que de voisinage, ne peut pas être satisfaisant en la matière. Il y a un vrai deux poids, deux mesures. ».

Malheureusement, malgré les dénonciations répétées de certains députés minoritaires qui tirent la sonnette d'alarme, l'Etat de non-droit en Tunisie ne ren-contre aucun dispositif dissuasif de la part de ses partenaires européens, de nature à freiner sa dérive autoritaire.

---

18   Voyez Parlement européen, procès-verbal du 21 janvier 2010, 2. Relations UE/Tunisie (débat), http://www.europarl.europa.eu/sides/getDoc.do?pubRef=-//EP// TEXT+CRE+20100121+ITEM-002+DOC+XML+V0//FR.

9   Les accords à l'épreuve du WSIS

De fait, aucune résolution n'a suivi ce débat, comme ce fut le cas pour tous les débats sur la Tunisie et notamment celui qui devait évaluer le WSIS (World summit on the Information Society) tenu à Tunis le 16 novembre 2005.

Les partenaires européens n'ont pas pu comprendre que cette gestion totalitaire, réservée d'habitude aux autochtones, s'étende à eux.

Le cadre international et extraterritorial du Sommet tenu sous l'égide de l'ONU n'a pas été respecté. La censure a été largement pratiquée dans l'enceinte du site ; Un rapport d'Amnesty International a été censuré et interdit de distribution. Des sites Internet à contenu critique continuaient à être bloqués. Les participants n'ont pas bénéficié de l'immunité que leur confère ce cadre.

Un workshop organisé par le Parlement européen et la Commission est saboté et les représentants officiels européens subissent à leur tour les méthodes musclées de la police de Ben Ali.

Mais l'épisode le plus grave qui a marqué ce sommet a été l'agression à l'arme blanche dont avait été victime à cinq jours de l'ouverture du sommet le journaliste de Libération, Christophe Boltanski, qui dénonce « le sentiment d'impunité »[19] des autorités tunisiennes.

Le 13 décembre 2005, le Parlement européen consacre une séance à l'évaluation du WSIS, où le Conseil et la Commission s'expriment publiquement sur les droits de l'homme et la liberté de la presse en Tunisie. La colère des partenaires européens éclate publiquement.

Le Conseil, par la voix de son président Geoff Hoon,[20] a déclaré :

« Le Conseil partage les inquiétudes des députés de cette Assemblée concernant la situation des droits de l'homme en Tunisie et il a pleinement conscience des lacunes qui existent dans ce pays, en particulier en ce qui concerne les actes d'intimidation et de harcèlement commis par les autorités à l'encontre de la société civile [...] Il est à présent temps que nous insistions sur la mise en œuvre par les autorités tunisiennes des engagements pris par le président Ben Ali en matière de démocratie, de bonne gouvernance et de droits de l'homme fixés dans le plan d'action de la politique européenne de voisinage. »

Alain Hutchinson, vice-président du PE (PSE) déclare dans cette historique séance du 13 décembre :

« s'il y a une chose dont il faut se réjouir au lendemain du sommet, c'est qu'il a eu pour effet positif de montrer à la face du monde ce que trop de gens ne voulaient pas voir [...] à savoir que la démocratie est bafouée chaque jour en Tunisie [...] j'ai effectivement été étonné, après avoir interrogé la Commission et le Conseil au retour d'une mission là-bas, de la timidité de leurs réactions face à ce que l'on peut qualifier de véritable violation de l'accord de partenariat entre l'UE et la Tunisie. J'ose croire que cette timidité

<del>19 Christophe Boltanski, « Les autorités tunisiennes ont un sentiment d'impunité », chat sur liberation.fr, 15 novembre 2005, http://www.tunezine.com/forum/read.php?f=1& i =178897&t=178897&PHPSESSID=334dd246cfb028da5d5560b4774d304c#reply_178897.</del>
19 Christophe Boltanski, « Les autorités tunisiennes ont un sentiment d'impunité », chat sur liberation.fr, 15 novembre 2005, http://www.tunezine.com/forum/read.php?f=1& i =178897&t=178897&PHPSESSID=334dd246cfb028da5d5560b4774d304c#reply_178897.
20 Parlement européen, procès-verbal du 13 décembre 2005, Droits de l'homme et liberté de la presse en Tunisie et évaluation du Sommet mondial de la Société de l'Information de Tunis.

n'est pas directement liée à d'autres perspectives, notamment l'organisation par les pays du Maghreb, comme certains le souhaitent, d'une sorte de police de nos frontières, afin de limiter l'immigration clandestine. »

10 Après la colère : L'amnésie

On ne peut être plus explicite et plus unanime dans le jugement porté sur un partenaire. Quelles sont les mesures qui ont suivi cette démarche collective des institutions européennes ? Et que s'est-il passé depuis? Rien, absolument rien ; Après le coup de gueule, l'amnésie !

L'eau a coulé sous les ponts depuis et les relations ont repris à leur niveau habituel; Souvenons-nous de ce que disait la commissaire Viviane Reding ce fameux 13 décembre 2005 : « Au début de l'année, nous réévaluerons la situation avec les États membres et nous déciderons, en l'absence de progrès, si des mesures supplémentaires doivent être prises.» Quatre années plus tard, alors que la situation générale a empiré, pas même une résolution, ni aucune mesure incitant les autorités tunisiennes à respecter leurs engagements n'a été prise au niveau de l'UE.

Dans une interview à la chaîne européenne Euronews, diffusée le 19 novembre 2005[21], le chef de la délégation de l'UE à Tunis, Marc Pierini, sortait de sa réserve, fustigeant «des méthodes habituellement utilisées en Tunisie, mais qui frappaient pour la première fois des étrangers ». Il y dresse aussi le bilan d'une gouvernance zéro:

« Nous avons échoué à mettre en œuvre un programme en faveur de la société civile, qui était pourtant inscrit d'un commun accord dans notre programmation. Nous avons mis en œuvre avec beaucoup de difficultés un programme de formation des journalistes. Et nous travaillons depuis 4 ans à mettre en place un très grand programme de modernisation de la justice, jusqu'à ce jour sans succès. Par ailleurs, les financements accordés aux associations de défense des droits de l'homme ou aux ONG de santé ou autres, sont très fréquemment bloqués. »

Marc Pierrini a été déclaré persona non grata par Tunis qui avait fini par obtenir son départ du poste d'ambassadeur représentant la Délégation européenne à Tunis. Il a été remplacé par une personne plus accommodante et les subventions destinées à la société civile qu'il avait bloquée sont allées alimenter les caisses des organisations satellites du parti au pouvoir.

11 Un soutien indéfectible

Ainsi, pour 2010, la Commission européenne a prévu un programme d'appui à « l'amélioration de la gestion des ressources en eau (57 [millions] €), ainsi qu'un complément d'aide budgétaire pour aider le gouvernement à sortir de la crise économique (20 [millions] €) ».[22] La Banque européenne d'investissement a,

---

21 Euronews, interview avec Marc Pierini, 19 novembre 2005, rtsp://stream1.euro news.net:554/europeans/europeans-t36-fr.rm?cloakport=8080%2c554%2c7070.

22 Délégation de l'Union européenne en Tunisie, Document de stratégie pour la Tunisie et Programme Indicatif National, http://ec.europa.eu/delegations/tunisia/eu_tunisia/ tech_financial_ cooperation/stra_pin/index_fr.htm.

quant à elle, octroyé, sur cette même période, un montant total de prêts de plus d'un milliard € (principalement pour des opérations industrielles, assainissement et transport).

A ce jour, le total cumulé des opérations financées par l'UE en 2007, 2008 et 2009 s'élève donc à 1243 millions €, hors programmes régionaux. Le Programme Indicatif National de l'UE en Tunisie, pour la période 2011-2013 a été approuvé par les États membres de l'Union européenne en décembre 2009 pour un montant de 240 millions € sur 3 ans. Comme on le voit, le soutien financier communautaire continue de couler à flot pour consolider une dictature.

Premier du genre, l'accord d'association avec la Tunisie se voulait un modèle. Il est en passe de devenir une véritable caricature. Ce serait là une catastrophe pour les Tunisiens comme pour les Européens.

C   Conclusion

Le développement de la Tunisie ne peut pas faire l'économie de l'État de droit et des libertés fondamentales parce qu'il ne peut y avoir de véritable développement sans démocratie. La corruption, le népotisme, l'arbitraire, nous le rappellent tous les jours. La libération politique est actuellement l'objectif prioritaire qui conditionne tous les autres. Toute approche de développement qui sera limitée au domaine économique en occultant les aspirations légitimes des populations vers le développement politique et la démocratie sera inévitablement vouée à l'échec.

Les dirigeants de l'Union européenne devraient s'engager avec plus de détermination pour que l'article 2 de l'accord d'association entre la Tunisie et l'Union européenne qui fonde cette relation privilégiée sur le respect des droits de l'Homme et des droits fondamentaux, soit pleinement respecté.

Le soutien apporté par les pays occidentaux à des dictatures comme celle du Président Ben Ali discrédite le modèle démocratique, crée un sentiment de frustration et représente une menace pour l'avenir du partenariat euro-méditerranéen.

Matthias C. KETTEMANN

Internet Governance and Human Rights in Europe: Towards a Synthetic Approach

Table of Contents

Keywords

European Union, Council of Europe, Internet Governance, Affirmation of Commitments, human rights, multi-stakeholder participation, policies, standards

A   Introduction

2009 was a exciting, if not completely successful year for European Internet Governance initiatives. The standards and policies developed and promulgated, if not actively promoted, by the European Union and the Council of Europe exerted only limited influence on the normative evolution of the playground of the digital natives. The most important overhaul in the Internet's core architecture, the dismissal from US governmental control of the Internet Corporation for Assigned Names and Numbers (ICANN) and the new accountability regime that supplanted it, seemed to have unrolled without much European input. Was 2009, we have to ask, a lost year for the European Union and the Council of Europe with regard to their attempts to export European conceptions of the normative framework best suited to respond to the challenges Internet Governance will face in the years to come?

I will answer this question with a qualified yes and propose a theory that can be formulated in the following terms: The EU suffers from proposing policies without standards and the Council of Europe from developing standards without policies.

I will elaborate on and test this theory using two overarching themes: the central role of human rights in the development of Internet Governance and the import of multi-stakeholder participation as a means to enhance the legitimacy of governance-related decisions in Information Society.

Before outlining my argumentative structure, "policies" and "standards", the two terms central to understanding my approach, need to be briefly defined. I will understand "policies" to denote broader concepts based on certain societal goals that shape normative instruments. "Standards" are one example of these normative instruments and share many structural characteristics with rules, including their usually definite, non-hortatory language, but are – unlike the latter – not authoritatively set. They thus exert persuasive power and do not oblige qua the threat of enforcement.

Naturally, my theory which is formulated in simplistic terms mainly in order to highlight what I perceive as differences in the two organizations approach to Internet Governance is in need of substantial qualification. I should like to note parenthetically that I expect critical voices to point out that opposing "policies without standards" and "standards without policies" runs the serious danger of ignoring the multifaceted nature of the European organization's normative output. This, I do not deny. I find, however, that the advantages of using these opposing concepts as conceptual lenses through which a clearer picture of the underlying policy choices may be discernible outweighs, for the purposes of this contribution, their disadvantages. I note, however, that they serve merely as characterizing signets that help focus my analysis and may stimulate debate on what I feel is a topic in dire need of increased scholarly attention.

Further, the last year has seen an important move by the Council of Europe towards policy. In May 2009, the 1st Council of Europe Conference of Ministers Responsible for Media and New Communication Services in Reykjavik (Iceland) passed a political declaration and resolutions on a "new notion of media".[1]

Due to the separation of competences between member states and the EU, the latter is simply not able to develop substantive human rights standards with regard to Internet Governance. I accept this, but consider it possible to still criticize the status quo, by implicitly arguing that member states should give the EU the necessary competence to follow through on its policy propositions.

Summing up, I stand by my characterization of "policies without standards" and "standards without polices" as a structurally useful tool to sharpen the ensuing analysis.

It will take the following form: After first addressing why ensuring human rights and providing for multi-stakeholder participation are valid concerns both to policy-makers and standard-setters (section B.1.), I will briefly outline the changes to the Internet's core architecture through the Affirmation of Commitment (B.2.), which will provide the foil for my subsequent critical analysis of European policies and standards.

---

1   See infra, D.1.

As part of my appraisal of selected EU and Council of Europe Internet Governance policies of 2009 I have framed, as sketched briefly above, the debate in terms which for me identify the major thrust of the organizations' respective approaches and serve, by their contradictory nature, to highlight the differences between them. Critiquing "policies without standards", I first address the European Union's grand policy schemes and how little impact they have had on the evolution of Internet Governance (C). Subsequently, I will contrast the EU's approach to the Council of Europe's micro-management of the Internet Governance debate under the heading of "standards without policies" and identify the problems that this approach inheres (D).

Having captured the benefits and drawbacks in both, the EU's policy-focused approach and the Council of Europe's standards-oriented conception of Internet Governance, the conclusions (E) will contain a call for a synthetic European approach. The EU, it will be argued, should invest more in setting standards to form and inform its policies while the Council of Europe should take a step back from its standard-setting activities and refocus them with the help of a broader policy vision.

The call for a synthetic European approach would not be complete without mentioning (though without considering in depth), the role of the Organization of Security and Cooperation in Europe.[2] Some OSCE participating states have started to rely on a more belligerent approach to security risks on the Internet, including cyberwarfare and cyberattacks.[3] Covering an area from "Vancouver to Vladivostok"[4], the OSCE has the potential to emerge as an important forum for coordination of European and international Internet Governance policies and standards. The means of cooperation will still need to be refined, but a 1 September 2009 meeting, upon the invitation of the Swedish EU presidency, between the EU's working party on human rights (COHOM), the UN Special Rapporteur on Freedom of the Media and the OSCE Representative on Freedom of the Media shows the potential of coordinating efforts.[5]

---

2   With regard to the activities of the OSCE Representative on Freedom of the Media, see the contribution of Ženet Mujić, in this volume, at 309.

3   With European organizations having remained largely inactive, it is American authors and policy-makers that dominate the debate on the dangers of cyberattacks and their influence on the development on the international law on the use of force. See Michael Schmitt, Computer Network Attack and the Use of Force in International Law: Thoughts on a Normative Framework, Columbia Journal of Transnational Law 37 (1999), 885-937, and Duncan B. Hollis, New Tools, New Rules: International Law and Information Operations, G. David/T. McKeldin (eds.), Ideas as Weapons: Influence and Perception in Modern Warfare, Washington 2009, 59-72. On the US approach, see National Academy of Sciences (William A. Owens/Kenneth W. Dam/Herbert S. Lin (eds.)), Technology, Policy, Law, and Ethics Regarding U.S. Acquisition and Use of Cyberattack Capabilities, http://www.anagram.com/berson/nrcoiw.pdf. For a critical view of current US policies, see Jack Goldsmith, Can we stop the global cyber arms race?, Washington Post, 1 February 2010, http://bit.ly/8YMWJr.

4   OSCE Ministerial Council, Ministerial Declaration on the Corfu Process: Reconfirm-Review-Reinvigorate Security and Co-operation from Vancouver to Vladivostok, Athens, 2 December 2009, MC.DOC/1/09, www.osce.org/item/41848.html.

5   OSCE Representative on Freedom of the Media, Regular Report to the Permanent Council, 29 October 2009, in ibid., Yearbook 11 (2009), 166.

A synthetic approach will allow for a stronger European impact on Internet Governance and ensure that the professed European values in Internet Governance, including human rights protection and multi-stakeholder participation, regain purchase. This can only happen in the framework of current policy developments. Two of these will now be considered.

B   The Debate Situated

There is no useful way to engage in an analysis of European Internet Governance policies and standards in 2009 without grounding them in an international context. Substantively, the concentration on human rights and multi-stakeholder participation as a yardstick for Internet Governance policies needs to be justified (B.1.). Gaining, further, a passing understanding of the substantive and procedural implications of the adoption of ICANN's new regulatory framework, the Affirmation of Commitment, is necessary as it will provide the foil for the arguments to follow in subsequent sections (B.2.).

1   Human Rights and Internet Governance

International policy debates on Internet Governance[6] cannot be meaningfully led without recourse to the overarching principles that delineate the impact of information and communication technologies (ICTs) on traditional regulatory frameworks and inform the application of the latter to the former. In the Tunis Commitment of 2005, a document that was adopted at the conclusion of the agenda-setting second phase of the World Summit on the Information Society, these overarching principles were understood to encompass "the purposes and principles of the Charter of the United Nations, international law and multilateralism, [and] the Universal Declaration of Human Rights."[7] This substantial commitment to a human rights-based development of a "people-centred, inclusive and development-oriented Information Society"[8] was enriched by a procedural one to multi-stakeholderism.[9]

International organizations play a central role as actors, facilitators and translators of this commitment. In Tunis, states highlighted the importance of improving the "coordination of the activities of international and intergovernmental or-

---

6   For the purposes of this contribution, Internet Governance is understood as "the development and application by Governments, the private sector and civil society, in their respective roles, of shared principles, norms, rules, decision-making procedures, and programmes that shape the evolution and use of the Internet" (World Summit on the Information Society, Second Phase, Tunis Agenda for the Information Society, WSIS-05/TUNIS/DOC/6(Rev.1) (2005), para. 34).

7   World Summit on the Information Society, Second Phase, Tunis Commitment, WSIS-05/TUNIS/DOC/7 (2005), para. 2.

8   Ibid. Generally, on the role and import of human rights in the development of Internet Governance, see Wolfgang Benedek, Internet Governance and Human Rights, in Wolfgang Benedek/Veronika Bauer/Matthias C. Kettemann (eds.), Internet Governance and the Information Society: Global Perspectives and European Dimensions, Utrecht 2008, 29-47 (29).

9   Tunis Agenda for the Information Society (2005), para. 35.

ganizations" and explicitly held that "[a] multi-stakeholder approach should be adopted, as far as possible, at all levels."[10] Insofar as the EU and the Council of Europe (hereinafter "the European organizations") were involved in the process of outlining this commitment, they were actors. They were facilitators by enabling other actors in the multi-stakeholder process to engage in discussions on Internet Governance on the regional level and thereby simultaneously translate the commitment into concrete normative or para-normative outputs. The European Dialogue on Internet Governance, of which I will speak more below, is an important example of an exercise in facilitating discourse and translating commitments to multi-stakeholderism by European organizations into concrete action.[11]

It is these two elements then that can be used to gauge new structural and substantial developments in Internet Governance: Do they respect the international community's commitment to human rights and are they based on, or work towards ensuring, multi-stakeholder participation? An international Internet Governance agreement that is not multi-stakeholder-based will be met with a higher level of scrutiny, especially with regard to its impact on human rights, than a regulatory scheme in the elaboration of which non-state actors, and especially civil society organizations, were intensely involved.

This proposition can be used to evaluate the important changes the Internet's regulatory architecture underwent in 2009 when the Affirmation of Commitments (AoC)[12] replaced the Memorandum of Understanding/Joint Project Agreement (MoU/JPA)[13] between the U.S. Department of Commerce (DOC) and the ICANN. The process leading up to the conclusion of the AoC also saw the development, by the European Union, of alternative suggestions for the evolution of a more democratic and sustainable Internet Governance. Their dismissal by the AoC – and the consequences that I suggest European organizations should draw – will inform the following sections. Therefore, a brief overview of the new institutional framework of Internet Governance is necessary.[14]

---

10 Ibid., para. 37.

11 The stakeholders participating in the open-ended, yearly European Dialogue on Internet Governance include civil society representatives, business sector, representatives from the technical and academic communities, members of European governments and representatives of European organizations, including the EU Presidency, the European Commission, the European Parliament, the Council of Europe and the European Broadcasting Union. See European Dialogue on Internet Governance, http://www.eurodig.org.

12 Affirmation of Commitments by the United States Department of Commerce and the Internet Corporation for Assigned Names and Numbers, 30 September 2009, http://www.icann.org/en/announcements/announcement-30sep09-en.htm#announcement.

13 Memorandum of Understanding (MoU) Between ICANN and U.S. Department of Commerce, 25 November 1998, http://www.icann.org/en/general/icann-mou-25nov98.htm, as amended by the Joint Project Agreement (JPA) of 29 September 2006, http://www.icann.org/general/JPA-29 sep06.pdf.

14 For a more thorough overview, see e.g. Matthias C. Kettemann, Reform statt Revolution: ICANNs neues Accountability-Regime im Lichte europäischer Kritik, jusIT (2009) 6, 215-220, which this sub-section partly draws from. For an analysis of the underlying policy issues, see also Matthias C. Kettemann, ICANN und Internet Governance: Aktuelles zur Suche nach Patentrezepten gegen Legitimationsdefizite, jusIT (2008) 5, 165-168.

2   The New Institutional Framework of Internet Governance

On 30 September 2009, the Affirmation of Commitments replaced the MoU/JPA as one of the central legal arrangements that bear on Internet Governance.[15] The AoC is revolutionary in the sense that it ends the monopoly of control regarding the Internet Protocol address space and the Top Level Domains (TLDs) that the US government had enjoyed since the emergence of the modern Internet. Further, the AoC introduces what could one day develop into a meaningful international accountability regime for ICANN. What are the Affirmation of Commitment's main characteristics and why are they relevant for the assessment of the Internet Governance policies of European organizations?

With the AoC, ICANN is now successfully privatized, a "multi-stakeholder, private sector led" "not for profit corporation" with its headquarters in the US, but not under the "control by any one entity".[16] The role of US government as guarantor of the organization's accountability should now be assumed by the "community" and the Governmental Advisory Council, a committee of government representatives that has up to now given largely effective, if sometimes controversial, policy recommendations to the ICANN Board.

Among the key commitments by the US Department of Commerce we find one to "a multi-stakeholder, private sector led, bottom-up policy development model for [Domain Name System] technical coordination that acts for the benefit of global Internet users."[17] The most important innovation contained in the Affirmation of Commitments is the introduction of review teams in order to assess the performance of ICANN with regard to four policy areas:

- "accountability, transparency and the interests of global Internet users"; including performance reviews of the ICANN Board, assessment of the role and effectiveness of the Governmental Advisory Council; ICANN procedures for receiving public input, including, importantly "adequate explanation of decisions taken and the rationale thereof"; and the level to which ICANN decisions are "embraced, supported and accepted by the public and the Internet community";
- preserving security, stability and resiliency of the Domain Name System;
- promoting competition, consumer trust, and consumer choice with regard to, essentially, top-level domain space; and
- ICANN policy relating to WHOIS, a protocol used to identify registrants of assignees of Internet resources, such as domain names or IP addresses.[18]

The review for each of these policy fields will be conducted by "volunteer community members", which include the Chair of the Governmental Advisory Council, the Chair of the Board of ICANN, the Assistant Secretary for Communications and Information of the DOC (only with regard to the accountability review), representatives of the relevant ICANN Advisory Committees and Support-

---

15   For the role of ICANN in the institutional framework of Internet Governance, see Erich Schweighofer, Role and Perspectives of ICANN, in Benedek/Bauer/Kettemann (eds.), Internet Governance and the Information Society (2008), 79-92.

16   Affirmation of Commitments, para. 8 (b), (c).

17   Ibid., para. 4.

18   Ibid., para. 9.

ing Organizations and independent experts.[19] The reviews will result in recommendations which will then be provided to the Board of ICANN and posted for public comment. The Board "will take action within six months",[20] presumably with a view to implementing the recommendations. What concrete action should be taken is not specified; nor is there a control system if the Board fails to act upon the recommendations.

With its explicit reference to the importance of a multi-stakeholder approach to Internet Governance and the reflection of this approach in the constitution of the review teams the AoC appears to be a step into the right direction. Before a meaningful evaluation of its practical implications can be made, however, a number of questions need to be answered. They include exactly how multi-stakeholder-based the review teams will be, what procedural and substantive role the different stakeholders will have, what purchase the recommendations will find and what the standard of review for the teams will be. One hopes that the human rights standards enunciated by the Tunis Commitment will play a larger role in the assessment of ICANN's accountability in the AoC age than in times of the JPA/MoU, where they were barely, if ever, used to guide ICANN decisions.

Providing answers to these questions lies beyond the purview of this contribution. What is essential, though, is to understand the basic outline of ICANN's new regulatory framework, which will provide the foil for the subsequent analysis of the contributions of the EU and the Council of Europe to the development of Internet Governance in 2009.

C   The European Union: Policies without Standards

The European Commission has described the EU as having been an "early mover" with regard to Internet Governance.[21] In an economic context, it is empirically sound to argue that early movers enjoy substantial advantages when new markets are created.[22] With regard to the 'market' of Internet Governance regulation, however, the EU could not translate this advantage into influence for its normative agenda. In the following, I will analyze this phenomenon in light of two sweeping EU proposals to overhaul Internet Governance (C.1.) and will suggest that the lack of a cohesive system of standards developed in their implementation (or foreshadowing them) is one of the reasons why the policies failed to attract support by multiple stakeholders (C.2.).

---

19   Ibid., paras. 9.1-9.3.
20   Ibid.
21   Communication from the Commission to the European Parliament and the Council, Internet governance: the next steps, COM(2009) 277 final, 18 June 2009 (hereinafter "Commission Communication (2009)").
22   Cf. Govert E. Bijwaard/Maarten C. W. Janssen/Emiel Maasland, Early mover advantages: An empirical analysis of European mobile phone markets, Telecommunications Policy 32 (2008) 3-4, 246-261 (pointing out that the mobile phone penetration rate and the concentrated industry made entry easier for early entrants). Similarly, an emerging legal field can be more easily regulated by early normative movers than by normative latecomers.

1   EU Internet Governance Policies in 2009

In its normative reaction to the challenges of Information Society, the European Union has followed what could be termed a "visionary approach", setting policies without implementing them through concrete standards. I would like to refine this argument with the help of the EU's two most important proposals on Internet Governance reform of 2009. First, the Communication from the Commission to the European Parliament and the Council on "Internet governance: the next steps" of 18 June 2009,[23] and then, earlier in time but further reaching in content, the proposals by Viviane Reding, the EU commissioner responsible for Information Society.[24]

Already in February 2009, Commissioner Reding had called upon states to develop measures towards an "improved, more effective and inclusive Internet".[25] In May 2009, she opened a debate on Internet Governance with the ominous questions:

"Have you ever asked yourself who actually is in charge of ensuring that millions of computers can connect to each other 24 hours a day? And who decides on new top level domains [...]? [...] Who, in the last instance, guarantees the stability and openness of the internet for users in the whole world?"[26]

She criticized that, while the US Department of Commerce had hitherto exercised its oversight function over ICANN in a "reasonable manner", such a special role for a government department of any single country was "not defendable".[27] It was in light of her proposals that the Commission adopted, in June 2009, a communication outlining the "next steps" to be taken with regard to Internet Governance. Its most important elements will now be discussed. Note, however, the general character of the proposal, which clearly is a policy-type and not a standard-setting-type document, even though the call to "take steps" might indicate an approach progressing from standard to standard.

The Commission Communication first highlights that "governance of the Internet continues to be a crucial public policy priority."[28] The Communication then highlights the role of states: "Users will also inevitably turn to their governments if there is any major national disruption to their Internet service".[29] Governments are "increasingly require[d] [...] to be more actively involved in the key decision making that underlies the Internet's development."[30] Self-critically, the EU points

23   Commission Communication (2009).
24   Viviane Reding, Weekly Videomessage, Theme: The Future of Internet Governance: Towards an Accountable ICANN, 4 May 2009, http://ec.europa.eu/commission_barroso/reding/video/index_en.htm (video); http://ec.europa.eu/commission_barroso/reding/video/text/message_20090504.pdf (text) (hereinafter "Reding, Future of Internet Governance (2009)").
25   Viviane Reding, Speech: Internet of the future: Europe must be a key player, Brussels, 2 February 2009, at 2, http://ec.europa.eu/commission_barroso/reding/docs/speeches/2009/brussels-20090202.pdf.
26   Ibid., p. 2.
27   Ibid., at 3.
28   Commission Communication (2009), para. 1.
29   Ibid., para. 2.
30   Ibid., para. 3.

out that some of the objectives it had set itself with regard to domain name regulation had not been fully achieved. These include, inter alia, an increased oversight of ICANN activities and the transfer of control over the root server system from the Department of Commerce to ICANN "under appropriate international supervision by public authorities".[31]

After referring, importantly, to the "digital divide" that exists between the digital haves and the have-nots, the Communication goes on to outline "Internet Governance Principles", which merit quotation in full:

> "The Commission believes in maintaining the EU's strong emphasis on the need for security and stability of the global Internet, the respect for human rights, freedom of expression, privacy, protection of personal data and the promotion of cultural and linguistic diversity."[32]

This triad of security, human rights and diversity is supplemented by five "key principles":

− the open, interoperable and user-focused core architecture of the Internet;
− the private sector leadership of "day-to-day Internet management" with governments focusing on "principle issues of public policy";
− the development of Internet Governance in a multi-stakeholder process;
− the full interaction of governments with these multi-stakeholder processes, coupled with the acceptance by non-governmental stakeholders "that it is governments alone who are ultimately responsible for the definition and implementation of public policies"; and
− the improved integration of developing countries in Internet Governance decision-making fora.[33]

Turning to the role of ICANN (the Communication was published when the discussion on the future development of ICANN was still ongoing) the Commission identified a dual accountability deficit. Internally, the accountability and transparency of ICANN decision-making needed to be enhanced. More interestingly, however, ICANN also needed to be held "accountable externally to the global Internet community", which the Communication understands, slightly incongruously, to mean "in the first instance (partly by virtue of the absence of alternatives in many countries) [...] being accountable externally to the governments of the various countries of the world."[34] Instead of unilateral control through the US government, as foreseen until 30 September 2009 by the MoU/JPA, the Commission thus proposed a multilateral state-centred accountability regime.

The vague language the Commission Communication resorted to suggest that Commissioner Reding's policy proposals, to which we will now turn, met with criticism within the Commission and had to be watered down considerably in the discussions leading to the adoption of the document. This seems a reasonable conviction to hold, as the Commissioners propositions were hardly popular. The US establishment saw them as too internationalist; the Global South considered them to be too Euro-centric and reflective of entrenched power structures in

---

31   Ibid., para. 5.
32   Ibid., para. 7.
33   Ibid., para. 7.
34   Ibid., para 8.6.

international relations and EU policy-makers judged the proposal to be largely illusory. To a degree all three critiques are on point.

Commissioner Reding first warned in her proposal that a reduction of US oversight over ICANN needed to be met with an increase in internal accountability. Secondly, a "full judicial review" of ICANN decisions should be available to all those affected by a "small, independent, international tribunal" outside of California (where ICANN is based).[35] While the first suggestion repeats a known EU position and the second develops on a rather uncontroversial theme, Reding's third suggestion goes further. While its foundations – that day-to-day management of the Internet should be left to ICANN and a multilateral (and not, notably, a multi-stakeholder) forum should be "available for governments to discuss general internet governance policy issues" – met assent, her conclusions were controversial. In light of the need of "swift[ ] and efficient[ ]" decision-making (which, in Reding's analysis excluded the United Nations), Reding called for a new international forum: a "G-12 for Internet Governance". The forum would meet twice a year, be geographically balanced and make recommendations to ICANN.[36]

2   Evaluation

The policy proposals by the Commission and Commissioner Reding exerted no discernible influence on the Affirmation of Commitments and had only a limited impact on the international debate on Internet Governance. I will argue that this political stillbirth can be explained, inter alia, by the EU's focus on developing ambitious policies without confirming it by and basing it on a coherent body of Internet Governance standards. While I will not posit that this is the only explanation for the lack of success of the EU policy suggestions,[37] the following two examples provide some weight for my argument.

First, increasing the internal and external accountability of ICANN is a central component of both the EU proposals and the Affirmation of Commitment. The AoC did not take up, however, the suggestion of Commissioner Reding to foresee an "independent international tribunal" in cases of violations of rights. If the EU had developed substantive human rights standards regarding online violations, the policy suggestions would have been more credible.

Second, the Commission Communication refers to human rights as part of the triad of principles informing Internet Governance policies. The Affirmation of Commitments does not mention human rights at all, and only refers to "rights" in the context of the protection of Intellectual Property Rights regarding domain names.[38] I posit that the reason why the EU's laudable focus on human rights could not exert commanding influence was that it lacked a substantive anchor through standards developed in EU law and applied by EU and member states authorities. This is problematic because the Affirmation of Commitments remains silent as to the standards to be applied by the review teams: Californian law, US

---

35   Reding, Future of Internet Governance (2009), at 4.
36   Ibid., at 4.-5.
37   Internal US politics undoubtedly played a role, as did the dynamics of international relations in the aftermath of the financial crisis when even the G20 was faced with serious doubts as to the legitimacy of its decisions in light of the limited representativeness of its membership structure.
38   Affirmation of Commitments, para. 9.3.

law, international law? If the EU had developed human rights-based Internet Governance standards on which its policies could comfortably rest and applied them in the European context, a strong case for using them in the review could have been made.

That the EU has barely tapped its potential of developing substantive human rights standards regarding ICT-related aspects of EU law can be inferred from the focus on the work of the EU Agency for Fundamental Rights (FRA). While the Council has made "information society and, in particular, respect for private life and protection of personal data"[39] one of the thematic areas of the FRA, human rights issues relevant to Internet Governance policy do not figure prominently in the FRA's Mission and Strategic Objectives 2007-2012. The Internet is mentioned, in passing, as a locus for possible human rights violations in substantive sections on racism, xenophobia, anti-Semitism and related intolerance[40] and on discrimination.[41] In the section elaborating on the thematic area, the FRA commits itself, inter alia, to undertaking a number analysis regarding citizens' access to personal data; mechanisms of protection of personal data; measures to avoid the use of personal data to avoid ethnic profiling; "measures and practices having an impact on freedom of expression and information in the world wide web"; measures "to include vulnerable groups in the information society"; and "measures and practices aiming to improve access to internet information" and the consequences of "lack of information".[42] By early 2010, however, the only available document focusing on human rights issues on the Internet appears to be a report of 2002 by the FRA's institutional predecessor on "Racism, Football and the Internet" of 2002 – hardly a standard-setting exercise that a coherent policy scheme would warrant.[43]

In this brief evaluation we have seen that the EU's conceptual overreach with regard to policies is increased by the lack of applicable standards that could inform and influence the policy. These contradictions are endemic to the European Union's approach to Internet Governance. They are, however, also explainable by the limited nature of EU competences. Much of the legislation necessary to comprehensively follow through on the policy commitments would necessitate the transfer of competences previously held by member states. As the protracted EU reform process has shown, this is not likely to happen in the near future. Until member states decide to allow the EU to pass substantial legislation with regard to the protection human rights and multistakeholder participation in Internet Governance, any critique has to be understood to contain the caveat of limited competence.

---

39 Council of the European Union Decision (2008/203/EC) of 28 February 2008 implementing Regulation (EC) No 168/2007 as regards the adoption of a Multi-annual Framework for the European Union Agency for Fundamental Rights for 2007-2012, OJ L 63/15 of 7 March 2008, Article 2 (h).

40 See European Union Agency for Fundamental Rights, Mission and Strategic Objectives 2007-2012, http://fra.europa.eu/fraWebsite/attachments/FRA-mission-strategic-objectives_en.pdf, 2 (obliging the FRA to address hate speech in all its forms, "including when featuring on the internet").

41 Ibid., at 2.

42 Ibid., at 3-4.

43 European Monitoring Centre on Racism and Xenophobia, Racism, Football and the Internet (2002), http://fra.europa.eu/fraWebsite/attachments/Football.pdf.

What the EU can do, however, is to make use of the competences it has. These include, in the field of human rights and information and communication technologies, monitoring the processing of personal data by Community institutions and bodies. Already in 1995, the Council of the European Union passed the Data Protection Directive 95/46/EC,[44] the "central piece of legislation on the protection of personal data in Europe".[45] Regulation (EC) No 45/2001[46] went on to establish the European Data Protection Supervisor, as an independent supervisory authority. The role of the Supervisor is to advise, inter alia, on proposals for new legislation with data protection impact. His practice shows that the EU, when it is provided with the necessary competences, can set standards that confirm and implement its policies in relation to information and communication technologies.

Other EU institutions, such as the European Parliament, have also shown an interest in the protection of human rights on the Internet, as a call for a study that was published in 2009, proved. These activities are important to increase overall human rights sensibility with regard to Internet Governance among EU institutions.

In light of the current relationship between member states and the Union, the conclusions seems obvious, however, that EU's grand Internet Governance policy scheme was just that: too grand. Abandoning it, however, is no solution either, as a comparative analysis of the standard-setting endeavors of the Council of Europe in 2009 will show, to which this contribution now turns.

D   Council of Europe: Standards Without Policies

This section will address critically the tendency of the Council of Europe to develop multiple standards without grounding them sufficiently in an overarching policy framework. While the Council presents its legal activities in terms of "standard-setting", "conventions" and "cooperation", a policy dimension seems largely absent.[47] In the following, I will first review selected normative developments of 2009 that bear on Internet Governance (D.1.). Thereafter, I will discuss why the lack of policy can undermine the effectivity of these standards (D.2.).

---

44   Directive 95/46/EC of 24 October 1995 on the protection of individuals with regard to the processing of personal data and on the free movement of such data, OJ L 281, 23 November 1995, 31.

45   European Data Protection Supervisor, Legislation, http://www.edps.europa.eu.

46   Regulation (EC) No 45/2001 of 18 December 2000 on the protection of individuals with regard to the processing of personal data by the Community institutions and bodies and on the free movement of such data, OJ L 8, 12 January 2001, 1. See also Decision No 1247/2002/EC of 1 July 2002 on the regulations and general conditions governing the performance of the European Data protection Supervisor's duties, OJ L 183, 12 July 2002, 1.

47   See Council of Europe, Media and Information Society, http://www.coe.int/t/dghl/standardsetting/media. It is interesting to note that the URL itself contains as a subdomain the word "standardsetting" – clear evidence of the depth of the Council of Europe's commitment to this normative approach.

1 Council of Europe Internet (Governance)-Related Standards of 2009

In 2009, the Council of Europe saw a growth in the committees discussing and preparing standards set to influence the development of the Information Society. These now include a Steering Committee on the Media and New Communication Services, a Committee on Experts on New Media, an Ad hoc Advisory Group on Public Service Media Governance, an Ad hoc Advisory Group on Cross-border Internet and an Ad hoc Advisory Group on the Protection of Neighbouring Rights of Broadcasting Organisations.[48]

While space does not allow for even a cursory discussion of the standards adopted in the last years,[49] even a brief analysis reveals the Council of Europe's focus on the freedom of expression in the context of new information and communication technologies.[50] Both the Council of Europe Committee of Ministers' 2009 Recommendation on measures to protect children online[51] and the earlier 2008 Recommendation on Internet filters and freedom of expression and information[52] are firmly anchored in Article 10 of the European Convention on Human Rights. This apparent focus on media standards is reinforced by the Committee of Minister's Declaration of February 2009 recognizing the social value of community media.[53]

In 2008, the Council in Europe also developed important guidelines on human rights standards with regard to Internet Service Providers and online games providers.[54] These standards confirm the Council's approach to multi-stakeholderism in standard-setting, as they were both drafted in cooperation with industry representatives. This guarantees a sense of 'ownership' of the standards by the industry, and is likely to enhance compliance levels.

Even the briefest review of normative activities by the Council of Europe in 2009 would not be complete without a reference to the 1st Council of Europe Conference of Ministers responsible for media and new communication services

---

48 Ibid.

49 See the contribution by Franziska Klopfer, in this volume, at 267.

50 See, however, the Declaration of the Committee of Ministers of the Council of Europe on human rights and the rule of law in the Information Society, 13 May 2005, CM(2005)56 final (providing for a much broader approach to the human rights challenges posed by ICTs).

51 Rec(2009)5 of the Committee of Ministers to member states against harmful content and behaviour and to promote their active participation in the new information and communications environment, 8 July 2009.

52 Recommendation CM/Rec(2008)6 of the Committee of Ministers to member states on measures to promote the respect for freedom of expression and information with regard to Internet filters, 26 March 2008.

53 Declaration of the Committee of Ministers on the role of community media in promoting social cohesion and intercultural dialogue, 11 February 2009.

54 Council of Europe, Human rights guidelines for Internet service providers, developed by the Council of Europe in co-operation with the European Internet Services Providers Association (EuroISPA), Doc. H/Inf (2008) 9, http://www.coe.int/t/dghl/stan dardsetting/ media/Doc/H-Inf%282008%29009_en.pdf; Council fo Europe, Human rights guidelines for online games providers, developed by the Council of Europe in co-operation with the Interactive Software Federation of Europe, Doc. H/Inf (2008) 8, http://www.coe.int/ t/dghl/standardsetting/media/Doc/H-Inf%282008%29008_en.pdf.

that was held in Reykjavik in late May 2009.[55] This meeting was groundbreaking and promising insofar as it proved the potential of a comprehensive policy approach to Internet Governance of a European organization, but fell short of its potential as it focused, again, rather closely on the media- and freedom of expression-related challenges of Internet Governance and ignored the broader issues connected with the reform of ICANN's structure.[56] Only in the last two resolutions adopted in Reykjavik did the Ministers address policy questions in the broader sense.[57] I will focus on the first, as it shows the potential of the Council of Europe for developing clear policy frameworks.

First, the Council highlights the role of fundamental rights "and Council of Europe standards and values" that apply to both the online and the offline world.[58] In a language similar to that used by the European Union Commission Communication, the Council points to the "legitimate expectation [of people] that Internet services should be accessible and affordable, secure, reliable and ongoing." While not expressly suggesting, as did the EU, that this expectation needs to be met by governments, the Council of Europe's reference to the "particular[ ] relevance" of the "notion of positive obligations developed in the case law of the European Court of Human Rights [...] in this context" is language to the same effect.[59] The Council goes on to point out the accountability deficit of ICANN and the inspirational sources for the member states' "standard-setting work": the Tunis Agenda for the information society and the United Nations-led Internet Governance Forum (IGF).[60] In conclusion, Ministers committed themselves to supporting pan-European efforts to enhance "co-operation on Internet governance, "having due regard to the Council of Europe's values and standards on human rights, democracy and the rule of law, and the need for a multi-stakeholder approach to it".[61] The last subparagraph of the Resolution contains an interesting if rather vague commitment to

---

55   1st Council of Europe Conference of Ministers Responsible for Media and New Communication Services, 28 and 29 May 2009, Reykjavik (Iceland), A new notion of media? Political declaration and resolutions, MCM(2009)011, 29 May 2009 (hereinafter "Reykjavik Document (2009)").

56   This focus may lead to a dangerous tunnel vision of digital rights advocates. The human rights community's digital natives have to take care not to lead a meta-debate on online human rights protection, especially in online human rights protection fora. The case of the "Hub", an online forum for human rights advocacy, lends itself as an example. On the "Hub" freedom of opinion and expression was the "most mentioned issue" in the last two years (see Priscila Néri, Looking Back at 2 Years of the Hub - Top 10 Most Mentioned Issues, 22 December 2009, http://hub.witness.org/en/HUB2Years-MostMentionedIssues). Any comprehensive human rights policy with regard to Internet Governance needs to transcend this concentration.

57   Council of Europe Conference of Ministers Responsible for Media and New Communication Services, Resolution on Internet governance and critical Internet resources, Reykjavik Document (2009), at 9; Resolution on Developments in anti-terrorism legislation in Council of Europe member states and their impact on freedom of expression and information, ibid., at 11.

58   Resolution on Internet governance and critical Internet resources (2009), para.1.

59   Ibid., para. 4.

60   Ibid., paras. 6, 9.

61   Ibid., para. 11, subpara. 1.

"explor[ing] further the relevance of Council of Europe values and, if necessary, ways in which to provide advice to the various corporations, agencies and entities that manage critical Internet resources [...] in order for decisions to take full account of international law including international human rights law and, if appropriate, to promote international supervision and accountability of the management of those resources."[62]

2   Evaluation

Through its standards that answer to important aspects of the regulatory demand of the Information Society, the Council of Europe is on the verge of developing a coherent body of what could be termed "soft law of the Internet". Through the, partly worldwide, application and implementation of its largely expertly drafted standards (and conventions, e.g. the Convention on Cybercrime), time will contribute to crystallizing this soft law. Though the focus of the recommendations on substantive issues related to freedom of expression could be criticized as overly monothematic, the real problems lie elsewhere.

What the Council of Europe lacks is a clear commitment to overarching Internet Governance policies to a policy framework to provide the red lines along which standards can develop. While multi-stakeholder-based approaches to furthering pan-European discussion on Internet policy and politics, such as the European Dialogue on Internet Governance, are important events, one looks without avail to the normative output of 2009 when searching for a clear statement of guiding policies.

The Resolution on "Internet governance and critical Internet resources" contained in the Reykjavik document can be seen as a tentative step towards policy-making, loosely aligned with the foundational 2005 Declaration of the Committee of Ministers on human rights and the rule of law in the Information Society.[63] While both documents give weight to the assertion that the Council of Europe is a more important actor with regard to the protection of human rights online than the EU – mainly through the documents' reference to the applicability of human rights standards to the normative development of Internet Governance –, not even a very benevolent observer would call them visionary. It does not suffice as a policy approach to commit to enhancing pan-European cooperation efforts on Internet Governance "having *due regard* to the Council of Europe's values and standards on human rights, democracy and the rule of law", as the Resolution puts it (my emphasis). The Council of Europe needs, rather, to develop a value-based policy framework, a grand scheme that is informed and formed by its standards and that, conversely, gives life and meaning to them and ensures the coherence and cohesiveness of future standard-setting activities. The Council of Europe values can be of central importance for the development of Internet Governance policies. That the revolution of the Internet architecture through the adoption of ICANN's new normative arrangement with the US Department of Commerce took place before these values could be framed in policy terms, amounts to a missed chance.

---

62   Ibid., para. 11, subpara. 6.
63   Declaration of the Committee of Ministers of the Council of Europe on human rights and the rule of law in the Information Society, 13 May 2005, CM(2005)56 final.

Now that essential questions regarding the concrete application of the open-ended language in the Affirmation of Commitments loom, a policy-based standard-setting Council of Europe can make an important European contribution to international, human rights-anchored, multi-stakeholder-based Internet Governance policy.

The Council will also be able to increase the policy dimension of its Internet Governance approach by providing enhanced organizational support and thematic input to the European Dialogue on Internet Governance (EuroDIG).[64]

In this perspective, the Council of Europe's submission to the 2009 Internet Governance Forum in Sharm-el-Sheikh (Egypt) points into the right direction. It clearly focuses on policy issues, including access, the plurality of Internet content, and the assurance of multi-stakeholder, rights-based approach to internet governance, and highlights those parts of the Reykjavik Resolution on Internet Governance that are relevant to implementing Council of Europe values and standards.[65] Unfortunately, the submission repeated, sometimes verbatim, formulations from the Resolution instead of developing – in this most important of all multi-stakeholder-based international forum on Internet Governance – the Council of Europe's policies. The inclusion, as an appendix, of the Reykjavik Action Plan somewhat remedies this shortfall, as we find here, first, still tentative buds from which may grow a strong Council of Europe policy framework on Internet Governance.

E   Conclusions

The previous chapters have shown that during the last year the influence of European normative proposals towards a more multi-stakeholder-oriented human right-based Internet Governance was limited. I have identified shortcomings in, and taken issue with, both the European Union's policy-focused approach (mainly its failure to allow it to form and inform substantive standards) and the Council of Europe's standards-oriented conception of Internet Governance (chiefly its lack of vision to inform and form them). Based on the conviction that standards without policies are dogmatically flat and policies without standards conceptually empty, the call for a synthetic approach gains contours and importance. But how can this synthetic approach be achieved? I propose three steps, the first two of which are procedural, while the last relates to more substantive issues.

---

64   Council of Europe, 2009 EuroDIG stakeholders support the protection of human rights and universal access as key priorities for Internet governance, 23 September 2009, http://www.coe.int/t/dghl/standardsetting/media/News/EuroDIG_2009_en.asp ("EuroDIG supported that the Council of Europe [...] provides the secretariat to ensure the sustainability of EuroDIG, which should continue to be organised in cooperation with other organisations and stakeholders, including the European Parliament (EP)").

65   Council of Europe (Media and Information Society Division/Directorate General of Human Rights and Legal Affairs), Contribution for the 2009 Internet Governance Forum, DG-HL(2009)18, http://www.coe.int/t/informationsociety/documents/Contribution_COE_IGF2009_en.pdf.

First, the two European organizations need to cooperate more closely with regard to the protection of human rights in the Information Society and the use of multi-stakeholder-based decision-making structures. With regard to the former, the road to be taken is clear. Under the terms of Protocol No. 14 to the European Convention on Human Rights and the Treaty of Lisbon, the European Union will soon join, as a party, the European Convention system.[66] While important aspects of the human rights protection framework, including the relationship of the Strasbourg-based European Court of Human Rights and the Luxembourg-based European Court of Justice, will still need to be worked out, this cooperation points into the right direction.

Second, due to the overlap in membership between the Council of Europe and the European Union an informal thematic coalition of like-minded European states can work together, influencing the institutional structures of both organizations to align their human rights-based policies and standards.

Third, a synthetic approach acknowledges that the contribution of Europe to Internet Governance policies and standards is historically located within a specific matrix of normative traditions of the different organizations. The EU has traditionally focused on ambitious policy goals, while sometimes failing to meet them (the European Constitution being a sad example). The Council of Europe however, has traditionally been a rather traditional, but no less powerful normative actor, exerting influence less through visionary policy proposals than through substantively convincing normative standards. While I do not argue that the two organizations should change their approaches fundamentally (a development from which they are precluded by their founding treaties), they could benefit from intra-European normative cross-fertilization.

Without unnecessarily duplicating the Council of Europe's approach, the EU should thus allow is policies to form and inform concrete standards that bear on human rights in the Information Society and actively promote them as normative exports in the international debate on the future of Internet Governance, including in the development of standards for assessing the internal and external accountability of ICANN. Conversely, the Council of Europe needs to develop a policy vision that frames its standards and allows them to merge into, and be understood as forming, a more cohesive and comprehensive whole.

This call for a synthetic approach to European Internet Governance policies and standards should not be misconceived as a call for either the European Union to start setting standards in areas covered by the Council of Europe or for the latter to start investing intellectual capital in the development of grand policy schemes that stay ineffective. Rather, a synthetic approach, combining policy and standards, should influence and permeate the pan-European approach to Internet Governance at a time where new institutional structures are untested and new challenges emerge. Apart from its intrinsic advantages, the synthetic approach also lends legitimation to the transformation of normative instruments necessary to answer to the challenges of information and communication technologies. It will provide the groundwork for a stronger European impact on Internet Governance and ensure that the professed European values in Internet Governance, including human rights protection and multi-stakeholder participation, regain purchase.

---

66   See the contribution by Jean Paul Jacqué, in this volume, at 123.

The call for synthesis is especially important in a time when the US government seems ready to reassert some of the control lost through granting independence to ICANN in the Affirmation of Commitment. On 24 February 2010, Assistant Secretary of Commerce for Communications and Information, Lawrence E. Strickling, called for an end to the traditional US policy of "leaving the Internet alone" and proposed a new "Internet policy 3.0" which was essentially based on the conviction that stronger government involvement in Internet policymaking was necessary to reestablish trust of all actors on the Internet.[67] European organizations must be ready to press for European values in Internet Governance in the framework of collaborative international governance efforts that Strickling imagines to be made "among government agencies, foreign governments when appropriate, and key Internet constituencies – commercial, academia, civil society."[68] European organizations need to make sure that they are included in these processes by making themselves relevant through the development of mutually enforcing policies and standards that form a cohesive normative whole. A positive step in this direction is the EU's Granada Ministerial Declaration on the European Digital Agenda of 19 April 2010 in which EU ministers agreed to coordinate more effectively in order to strengthen the role of the EU in furthering the "international dimension of the Digital Agenda" and to ensure that the principles established in the Tunis Agenda continue to guide the evolution of Internet Governance.[69]

To end on a more general note, it should be pointed out that Internet Governance is the fulcrum on which the future development of human rights will turn. I have attempted to show how European organizations can increase their influence on the direction and speed of the movement. This, in essence, is what the proposed synthetic approach militates for. Internet Governance needs to be discovered as one of the few normative arenas where the battle between a human being-oriented international order and a state-centred perception of international relations will be openly fought. The outcome, far from fixed, will impact the very processes through which new normative instruments are created and the role of different stakeholders in their creation. While states may argue that new normative imperatives legitimate a transformation of the underlying values, Information Society is by no means a society in a permanent Schmittian-Agambian state of exception.[70] The challenges posed by information and communication technologies are not qualitatively different, they are just new and the norms must change in light of their underlying principles. By adding standards to its policies (EU) and enriching its policies with standards (Council of Europe), European organizations can contribute to creating a norm-oriented governance sphere, a sphere where human rights protection is norm-based and thus – normal.

---

67 The Internet: Evolving Responsibility for Preserving a First Amendment Miracle, Remarks of Lawrence E. Strickling, Assistant Secretary of Commerce for Communications and Information, The Media Institute, 24 February 2010, http://www.ntia.doc.gov/presentations/2010/MediaInstitute_02242010.html.
68 Ibid.
69 Granada Ministerial Declaration on the European Digital Agenda, 19 April 2010, http://www.eu2010.es/export/sites/presidencia/comun/descargas/Ministerios/en_declaracion_granada.pdf, paras. 26-27.
70 Giorgio Agamben, State of Exception, Chicago 2005 (Kevin Attell, transl.), 40.

Biographies

Wolfgang BENEDEK

Wolfgang Benedek holds a PhD in international law and a Master in economics (University of Graz). Since 1990, he is professor at the Institute of International Law and International Relations, University of Graz. He is also director of the European Training and Research Centre for Human Rights and Democracy (ETC), Graz and chair of World University Service (WUS) Austria, and a regular lecturer at the Vienna Diplomatic Academy and the European Master Programmes on Human Rights and Democracy in Venice and Sarajevo. His main research interests include human rights and human security, on both of which he has published substantially; wolfgang.benedek@uni-graz.at.

Florence BENOÎT-ROHMER

A former president of the Université Robert Schuman (URS), Strasbourg, Florence Benoît-Rohmer is Professor at its Law Faculty. She is currently Secretary General of the European Interuniversity Center of Human Rights and Democratisation (EIUC), Venice, human rights expert for the Council of Europe and EU, and president of the Scientific Committee of the Fundamental Rights Agency of the EU. She is also member of the scientific committees of several international journals specializing in human right; florence.benoit-rohmer@eiuc.org.

Sihem BENSEDRINE

A graduate from the philosophy department of the University of Toulouse (France), Sihem Bensedrine is a Tunisian journalist and writer and currently editor-in-chief of the online magazine Kalima and Radio Kalima which is broadcast on the web and via satellite. She is an active human rights defender and General Secretary of the Observation for the Defence of Press, Publishing and Creation Freedom (OLPEC, an IFEX network member) and spokeswoman of the National Council for Civil Liberties in Tunisia (CNLT); sbensedrine9@gmail.com.

Philip CZECH

Philip Czech holds a Mag.iur. and a Dr.phil. degree from the University of Salzburg. He is researcher at the Austrian Institute for Human Rights and editor of "Newsletter Menschenrechte", a periodical which reports on the current case-law of the European Court of Human Rights; philip.czech@menschenrech te.ac.at.

Andrew DRZEMCZEWSKI

Andrew Drzemczewski is a qualified barrister, holds an LLB and PhD in international law (LSE, London), and a Master in Law (University of California, Berkeley). He has worked in the Council of Europe, in Strasbourg, since 1985 and is presently Head of the Parliamentary Assembly's Legal Affairs and Human Rights Department. He also teaches at the University of Strasbourg, France. He has published widely in the field of human rights and, since 1986, writes Human Rights Law Reports for "The Times" newspaper in London; andrew.drzemczewski@coe.int.

Jens-Hagen ESCHENBÄCHER

Jens-Hagen Eschenbächer holds a MA Phil (University of Saarbrücken) and is the spokesman of the OSCE Office for Democratic Institutions and Human Rights (ODIHR) in Warsaw; jens.eschenbaecher@odihr.pl.

James GAUGHAN

James Gaughan holds an LLB (University of Glasgow) and a Diploma in Legal Practice (Glasgow Graduate School of Law). He is a Legal Officer at the Council of Europe's Department for the Execution of ECtHR judgments; james.gaughan@coe.int.

Thomas HAMMARBERG

Thomas Hammarberg has held the post of Council of Europe Commissioner for Human Rights since April 2006. Previously, he was Secretary General of Amnesty International, the Swedish NGO Save the Children and the Olof Palme International Center. As ambassador he advised the Swedish government on human rights issues. He has also served as the Special Representative of the UN Secretary General for Human Rights in Cambodia. Being a former journalist and teacher he has published widely on various human rights issues; commissioner@coe.int.

Jean Paul JACQUÉ

Jean Paul Jacqué was professor at the University of Strasbourg and director fo the legal service of the Council of the European Union. He teaches at the Collège d'Europe in Bruges and the Collège européen in Parma as well as in the framework of the European Master in Human Rights and Democratization in Venice. The author of numerous books on human rights, constitutional rights and European rights, he recently published Droit constitutionnel et institutions politiques (Dalloz 2010) and Droit institutionnel de l'Union européenne (Dalloz 2010); jeanpauljacque@mac.com.

Matthias C. KETTEMANN

Matthias C. Kettemann holds a Magister iuris degree from the University of Graz (2006) and a Certificat de Droit Transnational from the University of Geneva (2005). He is currently, as a Fulbright and Boas Scholar, pursuing a LL.M. degree at Harvard Law School, and a doctoral degree at the University of Graz, where he also worked as a research and teaching fellow at the Institute of International Law and International Relations. His research interests include human rights, evolving security paradigms and information and communication technologies; matthias.kettemann@uni-graz.at.

Franziska KLOPFER

Franziska Klopfer holds a BA in Media Studies from the University of East Anglia and an MA in Human Rights (University College London). She works as a programme adviser in the Media and Information Society Division, Directorate of Standard Setting, Directorate General for Human Rights and Legal Affairs Currently, she is acting as Secretary to the Council of Europe Committee of Experts on New Media (MC-NM), a Committee reporting to the Council of Europe's Steering Committee on Media and New Communication Services (CDMC); franziska.klopfer@coe.int.

Bernhard KNOLL

Bernhard Knoll holds Mag. iur. (University of Vienna), MA (SAIS/JHU) and PhD (European University Institute) degrees. He is advisor to the Director of the OSCE Office for Democratic Institutions and Human Rights (ODIHR) in Warsaw; bernhard.knoll@eui.eu.

Emma LANTSCHER

Emma Lantschner holds a PhD in law from the University of Graz. She is a Senior Researcher at the Institute for Minority Rights at the European Academy Bolzano/Bozen (Italy) and the Centre for Southeast European Studies at the University of Graz. She has worked as an expert of the Council of Europe on the implementation of the Framework Convention for the Protection of National Minorities in Kosovo. Her current research focuses on the practice of minority protection in Central Europe; emma.lantscher@uni-graz.at.

Markus MÖSTL

Markus Möstl holds a Magister iuris degree from the University of Graz, is doctoral student and researcher at the Institute of International Law and International Relations at the University of Graz and researcher at the European Training and Research Centre for Human Rights and Democracy in Graz, Austria. His research interests focus on the Common Security and Defence Policy, human security and Council of Europe human rights monitoring bodies; markus.moestl@uni-graz.at.

Anna MÜLLER-FUNK

Anna Müller-Funk graduated from Aston University (UK) and the Centre for the Study of Global Ethics at the University of Birmingham (UK) and is now a PhD student at the University of Vienna. She works as Assistant of Professor Hannes Tretter and is researcher at the Ludwig Boltzmann Institute of Human Rights, Vienna; anna.mueller-funk@univie.ac.at.

Ženet MUJIĆ

Ženet Mujić holds a M.A. in Media Studies (Constance) and an M.A. in International Relations (Budapest). She is currently a Senior Adviser to the OSCE Representative on Freedom of the Media. She is a member of the Steering Committee of the Oxford-based International Media Lawyers Association; zenet.mujic@osce.org.

Manfred NOWAK

Manfred Nowak, Dr. iur. (University of Vienna), LL.M. (Columbia University), is, since 1992, the director of the Ludwig Boltzmann Institute of Human Rights (Vienna). Since 2007, he is professor for international human rights at the University of Vienna where he heads the interdisciplinary research platform "Human Rights in the European Context". Since 2008, he is visiting professor holding the Swiss Chair on Human Rights at HEI, Geneva. From 2002-2006, Manfred Nowak was member of the EU Network of Independent Experts in Fundamental Rights. Since 2004, he is also the UN Special Rapporteur on Torture; manfred.nowak@univie.ac.at.

Rory O'CONNELL

Rory O'Connell has a Bachelor of Civil Law (European Legal Studies), an LL.M. degree from University College Dublin and a PhD from the EUI, Florence. He lectured in Comparative Law at Lancaster University Law School from 1997 to 2001, when he took up a post at Queen's University of Belfast. In Belfast he teaches Human Rights, Constitutional Law and Equality. In 2008 he was appointed a Senior Lecturer at Queens. His current research interests focus on equality and non discrimination, socio-economic rights and democratic participation in human rights and comparative constitutional law; r.oconnell@qub.ac.uk.

Brigitte OHMS

Brigitte Ohms is the Deputy Government Agent of Austria at the European Court of Human Rights and the Austrian National Liaison Officer to the European Union Agency for Fundamental Rights. Since 1997, she is a member of the staff of the Constitutional and Legal Service of the Federal Chancellery, and, since 1999 she is the deputy head of the Division for International Affairs and General Administrative Affairs in the Federal Chancellery. She has published and lectured widely on constitutional and human rights law; brigitte.ohms@bka.gv.at.

Theodor RATHGEBER

Theodor Rathgeber, PhD, is a political scientist and has dealt with human and minority rights since 1983 as a freelance consultant on human rights, international law and development policies. He is lecturer at the University of Kassel (Germany), Department on Social Sciences. Since 2003, he is official observer to the UN Commission on Human Rights, and, since 2006, to the UN Human Rights Council assigned by the German NGO network "Forum Human Rights" (Forum Menschenrechte); TRathgeber@gmx.net.

Michael REITERER

Michael Reiterer, studied law at the University of Innsbruck (Dr. iur.) and holds diplomas in international relations from the Johns Hopkins University (Bologna Center) and the HEI, Geneva. In 2005 he became adjunct professor (Dozent) for international politics at the University of Innsbruck. As an official of the European Union he is presently EU Ambassador to Switzerland having served before as Deputy Head of Mission in Japan; michael.reiterer@uibk.ac.at.

Joachim RENZIKOWSKI

Joachim Renzikowski is Professor of Criminal Law and Legal Philosophy/Theory of Law at Martin-Luther-Universität Halle-Wittenberg. His main fields of research are the theory of norms, crimes against sexual autonomy and the European Convention on Human Rights; renzikowski@jura.uni-halle.de

Gerald STABEROCK

Gerald Staberock studied at the Rheinische Friedrich-Wilhelms-Universität Bonn and at Geneva University and holds an LLM (highest honors) in International and Comparative Law from George Washington University, Washington, DC. He is qualified as a lawyer in Germany. He is Director of the Global Security and Rule of Law Initiative of the International Commission of Jurists. Recently, he was secretary to the most comprehensive global study on counter-terrorism and human rights undertaken so far by an independent panel of high level jurists. Before joining the ICJ, he was a Rule of Law Officer for the OSCE Office for Democratic Institutions and Human Rights; gerald.staberock@icj.org.

Christian STROHAL

Christian Strohal, Dr. iur. (University of Vienna), studied law, economics and international relations in Vienna, London and Geneva. He is a Austrian diplomat with long-standing involvement in human rights issues, including in the 1993 World Conference of Human Rights. From 2003-2008 he was director of the OSCE Office for Democratic Institutions and Human Rights (ODIHR). Currently, he is Ambassador and Austrian Permanent Representative to the UN and other international organizations in Geneva; christian.strohal@bmeia.gv.at.

Agnieszka SZKLANNA

Agnieszka Szklanna holds a Magister (MA) in applied linguistics and in legal sciences from Warsaw University, an MA in European Studies from the College of Europe, Natolin, and a PhD in International Law from Warsaw University. She is Co-Secretary in the Secretariat of the Committee on Legal Affairs and Human Rights, Parliamentary Assembly of the Council of Europe. Qualified as an adwokat at the Warsaw bar, her research interests include human rights protection systems in Europe, the legal situation of aliens and the law of international organizations; agnieszka.szklanna@coe.int.

Hannes TRETTER

Hannes Tretter holds a PhD in Law and is Professor for Fundamental Rights and Human Rights Law at the University of Vienna. He is also Director of the Ludwig Boltzmann Institute of Human Rights (BIM) in Vienna, and Vice-chair of the Management Board of the European Union Agency for Fundamental Rights (FRA). Further, he is a Member of the Austrian League for Human Rights and Member of the Interdisciplinary Research Plattform "Human Rights in the European Context" at the University of Vienna. His main research interests include fundamental and human rights in Europe, European and international Law, data protection and data retention as well as anti-discrimination Policy, all of which he has published on substantially; hannes.tretter@univie.ac.at.

Davide ZARU

Davide Zaru studied human rights law and politics in Padova and Geneva. Since 2007, he is International relations officer at the Human Rights Unit of the European Commission, Directorate-General External Relations (RELEX), dealing in particular with the EU human rights policy towards the UN. He is currently undertaking PhD research at the University of Padova on "The Impact of Human Rights Law on the Constitutionalisation of International Law"; davide.zaru@unipd.it.

Maria ZUBER

Maria Zuber studied international relations and law in Warsaw, Madrid and Lille. Since 2007, she is a legal officer at the Integration of People with Disabilities Unit of the European Commission, Directorate-General for Employment, Social Affairs and Equal Opportunities, dealing in particular with the process of the EU's conclusion of the UNCRPD; maria.zuber@ec.europa.eu.